MW00574767

The Title to the Poem

Published with the assistance of a grant from the Ingram Merrill Foundation, awarded in honor of the late David Kalstone and in recognition of the learned and passionate attention he brought to the study of poetry.

The Title to the Poem

ANNE FERRY

Stanford University Press
Stanford, California

Stanford University Press

Stanford, California

© 1996 by the Board of Trustees of the
Leland Stanford Junior University

Printed in the United States of America

CIP data are at the end of the book

A portion of Chapter 3 appeared as "The Naming
of 'Crusoe'" in *Eighteenth-Century Life* 16
(November 1992). Frank Bidart's "Self-Portrait,
1969" from *In the Western Night: Collected
Poems 1965–90* is reprinted by permission of
Farrar, Straus and Giroux, Inc. © 1990 by Frank
Bidart. Alan Shapiro's "What Makes You Think
It's Fear" is reprinted by permission of the poet.
Stevie Smith's "Intimation of Immortality" from
Collected Poems is reprinted by permission of
New Directions Publishing Corp. © 1972 by Stevie
Smith. John Ashbery's "Out over the Bay the
Rattle of Firecrackers" from *As We Know* is used
by permission of Viking Penguin, a division of
Penguin Books USA Inc. © 1979 by John Ashbery.

For David
of course

Acknowledgments

V IRTUALLY everyone I know has helped in the making of this book by responding to my questions and supplying me with fresh ones of their own. For many specific scholarly and critical contributions I am specially indebted to Rodney Dennis, Elizabeth Ferry, Stephen Ferry, Dayton Haskin, William Moran, Christopher Ricks, Dennis Taylor. John Hollander, who read the book in manuscript, made many suggestions that have been gratefully absorbed into the final version, leaving unmistakable marks of his finely tuned readings and prodigious learning. The staff of the Houghton Library, Harvard University made the enterprise possible by generous help given with extraordinary patience and good humor. To all these aiders in the endeavor I give my thanks.

David Ferry's gifts as poet, critic, and ideal reader have enriched this book in its every dimension.

A.F.

Contents

Clearing the Title

Because the wind has changed, because I guess
My poem (what to call it though?) is finished,

—James Merrill

The claims of the title

T HE FIRST definition given for the noun *title* (from the Latin *titulus*) in the earliest dictionaries of English makes it synonymous with *inscription*, written words, and it will be thought of in that association here. In the discussions to follow, what will be meant by the title of a poem will be wording inscribed above the text of the poem in the space it has traditionally occupied at least since the early stages of printing. No very clear and distinct lines, either historical or theoretical, can be drawn between titles and the names poems were known by, what they were called, before they appeared on the page above the poem. Still, some practical distinctions can be drawn for purposes of discussion.

The distinctions here will make it possible to talk about titles of poems from two different perspectives that are actually inseparable in our experience as readers. They will allow analysis of historical tendencies that have shaped the making of titles in the changing cultural situations of poetry, and discussion of some of their particular expressive possibilities that shape the responses of readers to them. These possibilities accumulate as we experience a title in widening concentric contexts. First we read it as an autonomous grammatical unit, usually sealed off from the grammar of what follows; then we reexperience it in its association with the text of the poem, as it works in the volume it appears in, and in its wider relations to titles of earlier and contemporaneous poems by the same or other poets.

The expectation of wording in the space above a poem is largely a development of printing. In the earliest European manuscripts, where poems were copied onto scrolls, longer ones were identified by some sort of name or label, usually given after the poem as a practical signal to the reader that the scroll had been unwound as far as the end of the poem. If any wording appeared before the poem, it most often consisted of *incipit*, "here beginneth," followed by the opening phrase. The habit of identifying the work at its close was carried over, when it was no longer a physical necessity, to manuscripts in page form, and then even to some early printed books (often made to resemble manuscripts as closely as possible). At the same time titles, even for shorter poems, began to be placed more regularly above the text, although not with reliable consistency (except in some volumes prepared with special attention) until late in the seventeenth century. This shift in typography was at once cause and effect of profound changes in cultural attitudes toward the making and presenting of poems and corresponding changes in the responses of readers to them.

Wording above the poem is visually set apart from the text by shape, spacing, and, in print, often by a variety of typographical features (as were marginal glosses, which earlier performed some of the interpretive functions of a title). Even so, what occupies the title space claims association with what follows it. It presents the text of the poem visually, acting as a kind of frame, and in a more important way temporally, because the title is placed in an introductory position, to be read before the text. This placing gives the title authority because it tells someone who presumably has not yet read the poem something about it. The presence of a title above the text implies that whoever has conferred it has the right to present the poem. This claim is predicated on the presumption that the titler is either the author or someone else familiar with the poem by virtue of having read it before the reader it is presented to. Sometimes the maker of the presentation, even if someone other than the poet, is also privy to information the poem itself omits, or to secrets it hides or merely hints at. In either situation, the titler is assumed to know more about the poem than the reader it is presented to, knowledge that the title itself may choose to offer or may in varying degrees withhold in another exercise of authority.

By its very nature, then, a title has certain inescapable attributes that bring into play some fundamental assumptions. To begin with, because it is situated to be read first, the title's presence presupposes a reader: if only the author were to see the poem, it would be a redundant gesture for the poet to put wording above it telling something about it not yet known. This means that a title inevitably involves the poem in a kind of public interchange, a presentation of it by the titler to an actual or hypothetical reader. Because the title purports to say something *about* the poem, it is not taken to be wording *of* the poem; and because it says something in brief, there must be other things that might be told about the poem that the title does not say. Either it is selective or it is secretive about what it leaves out in favor of what it includes, choices powerfully expressive of its interpretive authority. Since this is so, the title would usually (but with exceptions to be discussed) be presumed to be made after the text of the poem. For the poem would need to exist—either in the poet's mind, at least potentially, if the poet is also the titler, or on the page, if someone else is the maker of the presentation—before the titler could choose what to say about the poem.

Titles seeming to ignore these attributes or to challenge the assumptions they bring into play come to mind. One simple example would be the category of poems written for or about a specific occasion. Their titles could easily precede every aspect of the poem except the poet's decision to write it: Edmund Spenser could have chosen the title "Epithalamion," Andrew Marvell could have thought of "An Horatian Ode upon Cromwell's Return from Ireland" without more knowledge of the intended poem than its occasion and formal kind. This is a genuine exception to the general premise that the title is, or is assumed to be, written after the poem.

There are other categories that seem to evade what I have called the inescapable attributes of titles but that actually confirm their existence. One such would include poems of the twentieth century with the title space filled by a grammatical fragment that is then completed by the text of the poem. Part of the design of such phrases in the title space must be to work against the assumptions that the title is determined after the completed poem as a frame imposing a perspective on it, and that it is not an integral part of the process of making it. Recent titles that seem extravagantly unrelated to the poem make a more violent assault on the kinds of authority claimed by the presence of a title. Printing a poem without a title or calling it "Untitled" work toward the same end. Yet these and parallel attempts actually acknowledge the built-in conditions of the interchange between a title and the poem it presents, between the titler and a reader. The traditional practices of titling that imply these inherent conditions have been extremely various; also varied, though much less usual, have been the efforts of some poets to deny, undermine, or escape them. The conventional uses of titles traced in this book have their anti-types.

The following chapters, at least the first six, are distinguished according to the nature of the question a reader might ask about the poem, which the title anticipates and purports to answer. The qualification made by the loaded word *purports* is essential to several lines of argument in the book. There are complex relationships between what titles purport to tell about poems and what they actually tell. This is true not only of titles worded so that they themselves vividly demand interpretation, but also of those that appear to be neutral or simply declarative rather than individually expressive. While some tensions between what titles purport to do and how they actually work are inevitable, the changing treatments of titling conventions in successive cultural situations of poetry can change the nature of those tensions.

Within chapters, discussions are for the most part shaped by the nature of the question the titles in each category are formulated to answer, which often turns out to be most visible in the title's grammatical form. While its grammar incorporates the fixed conventions determining the category, their changing interpretations in the history of titling necessarily make the shape of each chapter malleable and give the various chapters quite dissimilar outlines. Only Chapters 3, 4, and 6 discuss title forms that have interested poets writing in English in virtually every period from the early stages of printing to now, the territory explored in this book. By contrast, Chapter 1 focuses largely on early titling by third-person forms that tell the reader they are made by someone other than the poet; then on the revival of these forms by Ezra Pound, William Butler Yeats, Robert Frost, and Thomas Hardy, who imitated them as a means for expressing strongly felt notions about what a poem is, about its relation to its maker and to its audience. Chapter 2 begins almost a century later than the first, with Ben Jonson's discoveries in titling by first-person pronouns. Since the issues involved were taken up again with focused attention by poets only after another surprisingly long lapse, this chapter then concentrates on titling practices in the past hundred years. Chapter 5, about titling by formal categories, inevitably gives more attention than others to the neoclassical period, when generic classification was the preferred source of title forms. In Chapters 7 and 8 I talk about those nineteenth- and twentieth-century treatments of the title space that seem to deny the presentational authority traditionally claimed by wording in it.

Each chapter therefore suggests ways of thinking about the category of title it proposes for discussion, illustrated by examples from periods showing interest in that category. While the choice of examples aims at range and variety, it has turned out that certain British and American poets have been exceptionally prominent in their contributions to the course of titling in English, so that their work demanded special and repeated attention here. This seems to be so not only because they have been unusually innovative in modifying traditional title forms or inventing a variety of new ones, but because the nature of their experiments has brought into focus fundamental issues of titling. These poets seem to have thought in specially concentrated and sustained ways about such issues, even to have incorporated them into the material of their poems, and in doing so to have shaped titling practices. They are Jonson, William Wordsworth, Robert Browning, Walt Whitman, Hardy, Frost, William Carlos Williams, Wallace Stevens, W. H. Auden, and in our time, it seems, John Ashbery.

Any reader would expect to find the name Wallace Stevens on such a list, but it was a surprise to discover what concentration Jonson brought to bear on titling conventions and on reshaping them by making his own rules; or to find Hardy's unobtrusive craft in adapting traditional titles to his disguised personal intentions; or to learn how directly and widely influential Frost's innovations in idiomatic title forms have been, and how the models it seems they became for Auden spread that influence to still later poets. Surprises like these have made the terrain surveyed in this map of titling look somewhat different. Its boundaries seem to have shifted a little; its inner contours or lines of connection have been slightly redrawn.

Not surprisingly, the names on this list of titling heroes—except for Jonson's—are all of poets writing in the past two hundred years, the period when the range of title forms has been continually expanding. One explanation for this movement is that more recent poets have been able to draw from, rework, or work against a longer and therefore richer tradition of titling (in English and in other languages, only some of which it is possible even to mention in this book). A corollary reason is that poets in the last two hundred years have felt with growing urgency the need to escape the authority of generic and other traditional classifications, which are specially visible in the compressed and relatively circumscribed conventions of title formation. This movement has necessarily given its direction to particular chapters and to the design of the book.

While individual discussions try out arguments tested by a choice of exemplary titles, these local arguments do not take precedence over the larger assumption of the book. The predication of the whole enterprise is that the titles of poems are themselves inherently interesting verbal constructs working according to subtle and complicated laws virtually unique to their forms and status, and that this is true not only of idiosyncratic or attention-getting titles but of titles that seem to be neutral or merely informative. Where but in a title space would we be likely to meet self-contained grammatical units such as "Quickness," "The Tree," "A Dream," "To a Lady," "On the Death of Dr. Robert Levet," "A Night-piece"?[1] In spite of their peculiar grammatical autonomy and other special features, we tend to accept title forms unquestioningly because of their conventionality, unless they make some obvious claims on our attention. If the language of the title itself seems to demand interpretation, we read it using the same critical tools we work with when we read the text of the poem. The metaphorical suggestions of Adrienne Rich's "Diving into the Wreck," the double meanings in Hart Crane's "Modern Craft" or Derek Walcott's "A Far Cry from Africa," the more elaborate wordplay in Wallace Stevens's "Le Monocle de Mon Oncle," the clashing incongruities in T. S. Eliot's "Sweeney Agonistes" are recognizable as signals that we must ask questions about the title in preparation for reading the text. Recent titles like these, and their rare predecessors in poetry before the nineteenth century, ask for and get attention. We know what to do with them, while we ignore the vastly more common titles in forms that appear to be what is often called *straightforward*, by which we tend to mean that they demand no investigation because they can be trusted to do just what they claim.

Among titles treated in some detail in chapters to come, George Herbert's "Life," William Blake's "The Chimney Sweeper," Browning's "My Last Duchess," and Elizabeth Bishop's "Sestina" appear to answer rather than to raise questions about themselves or about the poems they present. Each seems to be declarative in function, expressively neutral, giving the reader no interpretive work to do with it or with its purported relation to the rest of the poem, when in fact each is a carefully wrought element contributing to the whole design. We need to learn how to read these titles with as much attention as more obviously puzzling ones, but reading them is a rather different process, demanding that we learn to ask new and different kinds of questions. This dimension of the study of titling asks for a variety of readings of many different sorts of titles. Exploration of a range of titles, from every period and in as wide a variety of forms as seemed feasible, will show ways of reading the title—which John Ashbery compares to "a very small aperture into a larger area, a keyhole perhaps, or some way of getting into the poem"[2]—that can raise new kinds of questions about all sorts of poems and open new dimensions to the experience of reading particular poems, even very familiar ones.

While both expressive and seemingly neutral titles can serve these interpretive purposes, they can also cast light on more general issues about poetry not necessarily visible in the same ways in its other dimensions. Then changes in titling from period to period in turn bring into focus historical changes in attitudes toward such issues. These shifts are seen most obviously in the changing preferences among title forms in different periods; in the ways traditional presentations are modified; and in the new forms that are substituted for them. More obliquely revealing are the ways conventions of titling persist in titles that remain unchanged in form but encode new meanings when they reappear in later cultural situations of poetry.

Larger issues about poetry examined here through the lens of titling are among those approached from very different perspectives in much current critical discussion. They cluster around questions of authority, as the grammar of *The Title to the Poem* signals. These are the explicit focus of Part I, "Ownership and Self-Presentation," which tracks the history of editorial third-person titles that claim authority over the poem by someone other than the poet, and the substitution, beginning in the early seventeenth century, of titles using first-person pronouns as a way to assert the poet's title to ownership of the poem. This is a vividly concentrated instance of the struggles between producer and entrepreneur made familiar in current studies of political and economic distributions of power in that period. Uneasiness about autobiographical interpretations and other intrusions by the reader into the poem, reflecting cultural changes in the relation of poet to public, are discussed in Part II, "Interpretive Fictions." Part III, "Authoritative Hierarchies," focuses on titles embodying or resisting the dictates imposed by hierarchical classifications of poetic forms and subjects, implicit analogies to other social gradations. Part IV, "Undermining Titles," explores attempts to escape the framing authority of the title over the poem in the titling experiments of poets during the past two hundred years. We can see in the powerfully compressed forms of titles how these larger issues shape poems and their histories.

Brief remarks on titles can be found in many discussions of twentieth-century poets, for instance Stevens especially since the publication by George Lensing of the notebook "From Pieces of Paper," where Stevens gathered potential titles for poems.[3] Among titles chosen by earlier poets, Herbert's (and the title for his volume *The Temple*, disregarding the strong possibility that it was not of his choosing) have been given the most critical attention, for instance by Mary Ellen Rickey.[4] Where such critical remarks have been used in this study, they are cited in the notes.

More extended separate discussions of titling are G. K. Hunter's analysis of quasi-narrative titles in sixteenth-century collections of love poetry; Helen Gardner's and John Shawcross's articles on the authorship of John Donne's titles; Geoffrey Hartman's essay about the contribution of Wordsworth's lengthy titles to his transformation of the inscription into a new kind of lyric; Marjorie Levinson's political reading of the discrepancy between title and landscape in Wordsworth's "Lines Composed a Few Miles above Tintern Abbey." Alastair Fowler's comprehensive study *Kinds of Literature* gives some attention to generic signals in titles for both long and short poems.[5]

Another kind of writing about titles has appeared quite recently, largely theoretical and drawing for illustrations more from prose than poetry. A translation published in 1988 of Gérard Genette's essay "Structure and Function of the Title in Literature" lists what it calls a selective bibliography of about a dozen such studies of *titrologie* written mainly in French and about French titles.[6] Other useful essays of the same kind should be added to the list, especially those by Hazard Adams, Jacques Derrida, John Fisher, Steven Kellman, and Jerrold Levinson.[7] These essays mainly seek to construct a taxonomy of titles by establishing their definition, often grounded in etymology from the Latin *titulus*; their status, for instance as proper name, synecdoche, or metonymy; their kinds or functions, described in such varied and sometimes overlapping ways as designation, reference, presentation, interpretation, statement of intention, contextualization, indication of form or content, seduction of the public; their effects, as of underlining, focusing, specifying, disorienting. Much the most important entry left off Genette's list is John Hollander's richly suggestive proposal for the study of the titles for shorter poems, "'Haddock's Eyes': A Note on the Theory of Titles." What Hollander outlines is the possibility of ordering titles in a "spectrum along the axis from redundancy"—what he calls "neutral" titles, which merely name the formal kind and perhaps the topic of the poem—"to maximum informativeness"—such as Stevens's titles, which seem to be an integral part of his poems. He adds that such a formalist classification can then encourage "some observations relevant to literary history as well."[8] Although I did not read Hollander's essay until I had begun working on this history of titling practices, his expressed sense of the importance and interest of the subject and the need for a full exploration of it has been an encouragement.

It will be apparent that this book has benefited by and absorbed from these valuable discussions. Its quite different arrangement of titles into categories acknowledges that the divisions among them are sometimes arbitrary in that a given title might appropriately be considered under several categories. Still, one wish is that most titles could find a fitting place somewhere in these chapters about the titling of short poems in English by British and American poets from the beginnings of printing to now. Another hope is that the shaping of categories according to the way titles purport to answer questions a reader might ask before beginning the poem may approximate the way titles themselves are made. In doing so, this approach may open new ways to think about how titles work: in association with the poems they present, in relation to the poet's other writing, and in the larger contexts of literary traditions and contemporaneous cultural situations of poetry. If the book can work in these ways, that is because it is at once a map, a taxonomy, a history, and an opportunity to explore poems in ways that may yield new or somewhat altered readings.

Part I

OWNERSHIP AND SELF-PRESENTATION

CHAPTER ONE

Who gives the title

S INCE it is a fundamental assumption in this book that the presence of a title evokes the presence of a reader, making it a form of presentation, it can be useful to begin by looking at titles that in some way point to the maker—actual or imagined—of the presentation itself. There is another reason these presentations are an appropriate place to begin. For the actual fact that early titlers were commonly not the poets themselves set conventions, shaped expectations that have been at work ever since. This starting point, then, can show with special clarity the way later titles look back at, repeat, modify, or try to reject their beginnings.

Early editorial third persons:
the author, the lover, he

Titles conferred in the early stages of printing and in contemporaneous or still earlier manuscripts are often phrased so as to announce that the words of the title are not the poet's, that the poem is presented to the reader by someone else—who might be copyist, editor or commentator, translator, printer, publisher, or bookseller—and at the time this was usually so. This circumstance is made explicit when the title attributes the poem to the poet by his proper name, as do "Horace to his booke," "Chavcers woordes vnto his owne Scriuener"; by his authorial role, for instance "The Author, of, and to his Muse," introducing a collection of verse by John Davies, or "A Hymne to Christ, at the Authors last going into Germany," presenting a poem of Donne's; or most often by third-person pronouns in titles that allude to some actual or supposed fact about the poet, such as the ones given in Tottel's miscellany of *Songes and Sonnettes* of 1557 for the Earl of Surrey's "Prisoned in windsor, he recounteth his pleasure there passed" and for Sir Thomas Wyatt's "Of his loue called. Anna."

The prerogative to present the poem, whatever the form of the title given to it, rested at the time first on the titler's possession of a copy of it. As its owner he presented it to readers in a title of his own making or one that reproduced the title given it by a previous owner, most often someone other than the poet, from whom he received his copy. The mere act of placing a title in the space above the poem made—and still makes—the added claim to authority that the giver of it must at least have read the poem in order to introduce it to the reader, who is presumed not to know it yet. Whoever gave the poem assigned as Wyatt's in Tottel's miscellany the title "Of his loue that pricked her finger with a nedle" tells readers ahead of time what they could otherwise only find out for themselves by reading to the end of the poem.

Often the wording of a title in this early period appropriated further authority for the giver by adding information otherwise unavailable to the reader even after having read the poem itself, information about its author-ship or the circumstances in which it was written. Such a title—"Sir Walter Raleigh the Night before His Death" is an example often reproduced in manuscript and in print—could give the maker of it status as an implied insider, a member of a coterie, someone closer than the reader to notable figures and events.

Other early titles make bids for the titler's entrepreneurial authority, as the knowing assessor of the wares he was in the position to offer his readers. These enticing presentations, notoriously common on title pages, began to appear in English books quite regularly by the 1530's.[1] They were often printed on separate sheets to be posted as advertisements, but the same kinds of claims were also made more succinctly in titles printed above short poems: "A goodlie balade of Chaucer"; "A sweet Pastorall"; "A Poeme both pithie and pleasaunt." Such advertising practices, often satirized, of course complicated the social issues involved in the giving of titles.

In this period it seems to have been more or less taken for granted that the titles of poems, in both manuscripts and printed books, were in fact given by someone other than the author. Probably because of this actual circumstance, titles very commonly use third-person pronouns to refer to the *I* in the poem, even when the rest of the wording makes no mention of biographical matter—like "windsor" or "Anna" in examples quoted ear-lier—that would identify the *he* or *his* of the title as the actual poet. Tottel's miscellany includes many of these: "Vow to loue faithfully howsouer he be rewarded"; "How vnpossible it is to finde quiet in his loue"; "To his famil-

iar frend." Because these three titles were given to poems among those attributed—to Surrey, to Wyatt, to Nicholas Grimald—we might conclude
that their third-person pronouns refer to the actual poets whose names are
attached to their respective sections of the volume (though only at the end
rather than where they would be read before the poem). Yet since the miscellany repeats the same title forms for unattributed poems—"To his loue of
his constant heart," "Of his loue named white"—there is usually no way
to distinguish whether the pronouns refer to the poet who wrote the poem
or to the figure using the first person in it, who is only sometimes explicitly
identified as the writer of the verses by reference to his conventional literary
form of utterance, as he is in an anonymous "Description and praise of
his loue."

Other titles in the miscellany for both attributed poems and for entries
by uncertain authors explicitly present the verses as the utterance of some
representative figure, most often the lover: "The louer comforteth himself
with the worthinesse of his loue"; "The louer sheweth his woefull state,
and prayeth pitye." It would be easy to assume that such titles reflected a
clearly formed notion of what would now be called *speaker*, *persona*,
voice, understood to be a dramatic entity distinguishable from the actual
poet. If these titles proved the existence of such a conception, they would
point to the conclusion that third-person pronouns in titles refer not to the
poet but to the distinct figure using *I* in the poem. In turn if that were so,
titles using the third person would not necessarily claim to be given by
someone other than the poet, since he—in this period when virtually all
printed poems had male authors—could then be understood to have presented the poem as the utterance of a figure not himself. This is true, for
instance, of those poems by Surrey where the verses identify the speaker as
a woman, which in Tottel's miscellany are duly given titles like "Complaint
of the absence of her louer being vpon the sea."

Yet recent critical assumptions seem inadequate to explain the confused
overlapping of both explicit and unspecified references equally to actual
poets and to figures in the poems throughout the miscellany, the most influential single English source of title forms for short poems in this early
period. The nature and prevalence of this overlapping suggest a historical
basis for the absence of a clearly recognized distinction between poet and
persona.[2] They point back to the fact that third-person title forms origi-
nated in the cultural circumstances in which titles were mostly conferred
by someone other than the poet. The recognition by readers that this was
so would have discouraged them from asking the kinds of questions just
discussed here, which arise from much later and much more clearly formulated conceptions of *speaker*, *persona*, *voice*. The articulation of these conceptions seems to have emerged in the changed cultural situation in which

the author of the poem could be taken for granted as its titler. That reduces by one the number of players in the interchange among titler, author, speaker, so that the references in the title to the *I* in the poem can be understood to be the choice of the maker of both.

In fact, the typical forms for these early third-person titles do not focus attention on the independent identity of the *I* so much as on the circumstances that provoke the complaint, or praise, vow, farewell, and often only the circumstances distinguish one of these poems from another. Wyatt's of course stand out from the many poems of the period that are as anonymous in style as in authorship, but the choice by the editor who gave to Wyatt's "They flee from me" in Tottel's miscellany the title "The louer sheweth how he is forsaken of such as he sometime enioyed" both reflected and helped to focus the interest of sixteenth-century readers more on the circumstances—actual or fictional—occasioning the poem than on the relation of *I* to author. Many titles dwell on such circumstances in narrative detail, for instance Nicholas Breton's "The Lover Beeing Accused of Suspicion of Flattery, Pleadeth Not Gyltie, and Yet Is Wrongfully Condemned."

The assumption in this period that poets were not their own titlers was compatible with what we know about the literary behavior of courtly and gentlemanly amateurs, whose social position forbade the public presentation of their own verses. Surviving manuscripts in the handwriting of poets themselves, like the Egerton manuscript of Wyatt, commonly do not have titles above the poems, perhaps because their presence would have seemed a form of self-presentation or advertisement. Simply writing down lines of verse, especially on loose sheets as was often the practice, could be a private amusement. Preceding them with a title would imitate the form of a public occasion, an exchange between the titler who introduces the poem and some actual or supposed reader. This gesture toward publicizing is one of the inescapable dimensions of titling that has continued to exercise its force long after the time when self-presentation by poets was a social stigma. The fact that Emily Dickinson's private notebooks do not have titles above the poems might be a signal of resistance to admitting the presence of even an imaginary reader.

In the period when titles were beginning to be widely used, some professional writers copied the formation of editorial titles when they saw to the publication of their own poems. Among such sixteenth-century poets the unabashed motive seems to have been to appropriate the style in which courtly verse was presented in prestigious miscellanies like Tottel's. Thomas Churchyard, who made no effort in prefaces to disguise his promotion of his own poems, nevertheless gave them titles referring to himself by proper name: "Churchyardes farewell from the Courte, the second yere of the Queenes Maiesties raigne." More numerous were titles where authors openly presented their poems using third-person pronouns, like George Turberville's "To his Friend riding to Londonwarde" or Michael Drayton's "To Himselfe, and the Harpe."

In 1648 Robert Herrick brought his own volume of epigrams, *Hesperides*, "forth like Publique Day" as he says in a prefatory poem. It includes something like one hundred and fifty titles referring to himself in third-person pronouns. In their particular forms, these associated his volume not with by then old-fashioned courtly miscellanies mainly of love poems, but with humanist editions of classical epigrammatists, especially Martial. In an edition of Martial's epigrams printed in Venice in 1475, they are presented by such abbreviated editorial glosses as *De libro suo, De suis libris, Ad sua carmina.* Herrick announces the connection clearly from the start by the titles of the first three poems in his *Hesperides*: "The Argument of his Book," "To his Muse," "To his Booke."

Besides having an allusive function, Herrick's title forms play a teasing game of pretending that is openly admitted in one instance: "The parting Verse, or charge to his supposed Wife when he travelled." Here the editorial "his" and "he" refer to the poet, to Herrick, supposing a biographical circumstance in order to write a certain kind of farewell poem. The form of the title would suggest that "he" is not to be thought of as a dramatic entity but as the poet Herrick pretending something about himself for his own and his reader's amusement. The fun depends on the reader's knowledge that Herrick is in fact unmarried, which the title makes a point of imparting.

Herrick again explicitly tells his readers how to understand this game of pretending in the closing verses of the volume: "To his Book's end this last line he'd have plac't, / *Jocund his Muse was; but his Life was chast.*"[3] The same pronouns refer to "his Muse" and "his Life"; the matters in the poems are neither biographical facts nor inventions to create a dramatic speaker or persona, as is shown most explicitly by the poem with the more "*Jocund*" title "Upon the losse of his Mistresses." Following the catalogue of their names is the complaint that they are all gone, and "Onely *Herrick's* left alone." The "his" of the title does not refer to a fictional figure of the complaining lover to be clearly distinguished from "*Herrick*," who is playing a game with his readers. They will enjoy it because they recognize that the mistresses' names are culled from literature by a poet (known by some at least to be a priest) whose poems to "supposed" ladies were bound in the same volume with *His Noble Numbers*, a collection of sacred verses.

These overt signals point in a different direction from the conceptions formulated much later of what would be called *speaker, voice,* or *persona.* Instead they tell the reader that in Herrick's epigrams and their titles his references to himself using third-person pronouns constitute a game of pretending recognizable within the conventions he plays with. This play is highlighted by two departures from his otherwise consistent practice: in a tender poem of blessing "To my dearest Sister Mistresse Mercie Herrick" and in a blast of scorn "To my ill Reader." These extraordinary first-person titles announce, *Here I am not pretending*.

The indifference still prevailing among his generation of readers to conceptual distinctions between the poet and the figure using the first person in the poem are epitomized in surviving manuscript variants of the title for Herrick's farewell poem "to his supposed Wife": "Mr Hericke his charge to his wife"; "The husband charge departing from home, to his wife"; "My charge."[4] These blurred alternatives are indicators that interest in the clear articulation of later distinctions between poet and *speaker, persona, voice* may have had to wait for the changed cultural circumstances in which the poet could be counted on to be the maker of the title.

In the period when titles began to be used regularly for short poems, the common assumption that they were literally presentations made by someone other than the author also allowed some ambitious poets with courtly aspirations to demonstrate their wit publicly in verse while pretending not to be implicated in its presentation in print. George Gascoigne seems to have intended some such hoax for poems of his printed in the 1570's, although it is hard to know how seriously he expected to be believed. To disavow responsibility for promoting his own poems, he used elaborate presentational devices including titles referring to himself by proper name or by role. Examples are "Gascoigns good morrow" and "Praise of the Authors mistresse" from *The Posies of George Gascoigne Esquire* of 1575. Something like the same unanswerable question is raised by the title "To His booke" for the opening poem of Spenser's *The Shepheardes Calendar* of 1579, a volume carefully presented with editorial commentary as a learned text in the humanist tradition. The title "To His booke" is among the devices associating the "new Poete" with classical forebears (and with Chaucer) whose works were reverently presented centuries after their deaths by learned commentators in carefully printed scholarly editions. The status granted to both the titler and the poet by the roles assigned to them in the third-person form of the title "To His booke" would exempt them from the stigma of self-presentation.

Later editorial third persons

Up through the earlier 1600's—and much later in the century for posthumous collections of short poems by a single author or for miscellanies—the fact that poets were often not responsible for the publication of their poems kept alive the practical basis for titles that identify their makers as someone other than the actual poet. At the same time, some poets exploited this fact to create in their titles the fiction that someone else was responsible for presenting their verse. So there was a period from the later sixteenth century through roughly the first half of the seventeenth century when titles that distance the maker of the presentation from the maker of the poem by use of proper name, role, or third-person pronoun reflected actual practices literally or pretended to do so, either playfully or with the intent to disguise the poet's uncourtly self-presentation.

Given the long tradition of editorial titles, combined with the vagaries of manuscript transmission and the inconsistencies of printing practices in this period, it is unlikely that readers would have been much troubled by the question whether a title's claim to be given by someone other than the author was literally true. It is more probable that the question would have been submerged by widespread inattention to the authenticity of texts, as well as by indifference to formulated distinctions between the actual poet and the figure uttering the poem. The idea that a poem could be thought of (even theoretically) as existing in some original version authenticated as the poet's and distinct from other versions seems to have been slow in exerting much force, probably because the distinction depends on the proposition that the title as well as the poem belongs to its author. The careful self-presentation of *Poems Of Mr. John Milton* is fairly unusual for a book of verse even by 1645 for its announcement on the title page that it was "Printed by his true Copies."[5] This is a decorous device allowing Milton to claim control of "his" own poems while pointing to their public presentation by someone other than himself.

The general indifference to questions of authenticity is epitomized in the phrase *a copy of verses*, widely used through the seventeenth century to mean a set of verses making up a short poem, as in Abraham Cowley's *The Mistresse; or, Several Copies of Love-verses* of 1647 (*copy* perhaps combining the original Latin sense of *copia* as fullness with the medieval Latin meaning of transcript). The absence of a clear conceptual or hypothetical distinction between original and copy until well into the seventeenth century conflated the poem with any actual copies of it, which often differed from one another in the text and even more in their titles. This conflation in turn supported the assumption that the owner of a copy was likely to have given the title to it. Whether it was of the owner's choosing or passed on by a previous holder of the same or a different copy of it was another question apparently of little interest.

The different assumption of readers beginning to take hold in the earlier eighteenth century (the act of 1709 that first defined copyright responded to multiple changes in circumstances and attitudes surrounding the presentation of poetry) was that the choice of a poem's title was the work of the poet. From that time on the grounds for this assumption have generally been factual, although of course there have been exceptions: we know that what Wordsworth repeatedly referred to as the "Poem on my own life" was posthumously titled "The Prelude" at the suggestion of his wife. Yet the publication of unauthorized texts and their titles was still notoriously common in the earlier eighteenth century, prompting poets themselves to invent satirical titles imitating the tactics of literary pirates. Some of Jonathan Swift's (probably given by him) referring to himself in the third person by name or role seem to parody the false claims to authority made in editorial titles: by the pseudo-secrecy in the title of a broadside, "D-n S—'s Answer to the Reverend Doctor SH—N"; or by the faked commentary under the title "The Author upon Himself" apologizing that "A few of the first Lines were wanting in the Copy sent us by a Friend of the Author's from London." In form they are no more preposterous than many actual editorial titles, leaving some uncertainty about the titler's identity.

As the rights of authors over their poems grew to be more strictly regulated, readers could assume that the title of a poem was the choice of the poet, except in posthumous editions and anthologies. Thomas Newton's 1761 edition of Milton attaches third-person titles to poems the author had chosen to publish untitled, such as "On his blindness," which, Dayton Haskin shows, still misleads readers who accept it as Milton's choice and therefore assume it to have interpretive authority.[6] Editors of miscellaneous volumes followed the same practices. The Book of the Sonnet, edited by Leigh Hunt and S. Adams Lee, repeats "On His Blindness" and gives such titles to Shakespeare's sonnets as "To His Lady upon Her Playing on the Virginals" (for 128), "He Laments That the Countenance of Some Great and Worthy Patron Seems to Be Diverted From Him" (for 33). The Golden Treasury, Francis Palgrave's widely read anthology first published in 1861, also perpetuates Newton's title for Milton's sonnet and adds others of Palgrave's own using pronouns in the third person or referring to authorial roles: for instance "To His Love" for Shakespeare's "Shall I compare thee to a Summers day?" and "Nature and the Poet" for Wordsworth's "Elegiac Stanzas." Dante Gabriel Rossetti's volume of translations of The Early Italian Poets, which appeared the same year as The Golden Treasury, assigns titles throughout imitating earlier presentations such as "No Jewel is worth his Lady," "He is out of heart with his Time." Even poets themselves in this period sometimes borrowed the same archaizing title forms for their own verses: for instance Robert Southey's "The Poet Relates How He Obtained Delia's Pocket-Handkerchief"; W. J. Linton's "To His Love"; Wilfred Blunt's "To One Who Loved Him" which, appearing under the heading "Juliet," links this kind of allusion to nostalgia for the Elizabethan age.

While these continuing practices illustrate the persistence of tradition in the history of title formation, they show simultaneously how the same conventional forms work very differently in the changing cultural situations of poetry. Once the poet's ownership of the poem and right to title it came to be taken for granted, third-person presentations no longer reflected the actual distribution of authority in the production and promotion of poetry, nor did they gloss over poets' socially unacceptable acts of self-presentation. By the later eighteenth and nineteenth centuries, an anachronistic editorial title could act as an allusive gesture enhancing the poem by association with the language and literature of earlier periods.

Modern pseudo-editorial third persons: Yeats, Frost, Hardy

The titles of Yeats's "His Dream" or Hardy's "He Abjures Love" copy early editorial presentations common into the seventeenth century. In doing so they work like such titles used occasionally for nineteenth-century poems as allusions evoking earlier verse, sometimes nostalgically. At the same time, poets of this generation exploit for quite other and more internal purposes the inevitable but also expressively useful differences in effect between anachronistic titles and their original models. Because it is now the poet who is the maker of the title as well as the poem, and because readers now know that this is so, a title that on the face of it pretends otherwise does not expect to be believed. Rather than abdicating the poet's authority, it allows the exercise of it by inviting the reader to respond to the expressive value of what the title pretends. Summarized in the simplest terms, what its fiction expresses is this: that the distinction in grammatical persons between the *he* of the title and the *I* of the verses is an authoritative representation (made by the author of both) of the critical distance between the actual poet and the created figure whose voice we hear in the poem.

Poems from Yeats's third book, *The Wind Among the Reeds*, are known to readers now mainly with the final titles given them by him and used with very few alterations beginning with his earliest collected editions of 1906 and 1908. At the first publication of these poems as a separate volume in 1899, many of them had different titles, among them some that were themselves revisions or substitutions for still earlier titles used when those poems were first printed individually in magazines. The fact of their successive transformations shows that Yeats gave careful attention to the choice of titles. The particular nature of some of those changes can also suggest a good deal about what may have been their intended effects as presentations of the poems.

A look at the table of contents in collected editions shows that in the final form of *The Wind Among the Reeds*, but not in any of his other volumes, Yeats makes pointed use of third-person pronouns in titles that imitate forms originally reflecting the fact that poems were then presented by someone other than the poet. One later poem, first published in 1908, then prominently placed two years after to open *The Green Helmet and Other Poems*, has the same kind of title, "His Dream." Both its title, revised from "A Dream," and its position may have been chosen by Yeats to make it serve as a link with and comment on his earlier volume.

Among the final titles for the thirty-seven poems in *The Wind Among the Reeds*, a third use "He" without a heading to locate the reference. Other wording in some of these titles identifies "He" as a poet or as a lover, or both in "He gives his Beloved Certain Rhymes."[7] These are paired or grouped in loose sequences of three or four among poems with titles that in place of "He" directly attribute the words of the poem to "The Poet," "A Poet," or "The Lover," much like the mixture of title forms in Tottel's miscellany. By contrast, no titles with *he* or *the lover* (only the same two with "Poet") are used in the original, separately printed volume of *The Wind Among the Reeds*. There the corresponding titles instead attribute the words of the poems to the named figures of invented Irish folk heroes: Aedh, Hanrahan, Michael Robartes, Mongan.

One purpose of the titles in the first printing of *The Wind Among the Reeds* must have been to give the collection of separately conceived poems a clear unity by stressing their inspiration from Irish folklore. Yeats's revision of the titles does not sacrifice the unified aspect of *The Wind Among the Reeds* nor alter its archaic cast, to which the third-person presentations contribute by adding their own allusiveness. Yet their archaizing effect could have been achieved by less special means, suggesting some other more pointed and more complex design in Yeats's revision of these titles.

Each of the figures named in the titles of 1899 was associated with the "imagination," Yeats explains in a note, which means that the name in the title refers to a poet who utters the poem but who is not the maker of its title.[8] That is, the title "Aedh Hears the Cry of the Sedge" is phrased to signal that it is the invention of someone who is not the first-person speaker in the poem: someone in the position historically occupied by the editor or commentator who knows and can explain the legend for the reader, as Yeats does in the notes to the volume. Here, then, the titles together with the notes work—as do the third-person pronouns in the later revised titles—to call attention to the fiction that the poet using the first person in the poem to tell what is in his heart is in some sense separate from the presenter of it in the title.

In the 1899 volume the notes work along with the titles to guide the reader toward Yeats's understanding of the visionary character of the poems. In them the commentator, who is also the titler, explicates the visionary experiences of the imaginary poets, in that way distancing himself from their utterances in the poems. In some other notes Yeats uses the first person to tell of his own visions: "I dreamed this story exactly as I have written it. . . . Blake would have said 'the authors are in eternity,' and I am quite sure they can only be questioned in dreams."[9] Like his visionary model, Yeats claims as dreamer to record what has been dictated to him but not to be its author. A note to another poem a few pages later casts more light on the strangely simultaneous separateness and connectedness of persons in the grammar of the titles and the texts of these poems: "Once a symbolism has possessed the imagination of large numbers of men, it becomes, as I believe, an embodiment of disembodied powers, and repeats itself in dreams and visions, age after age."[10] The legendary poets named in the titles and the actual poet who calls them by name are distinct; the visionary in the poems utters their common dreams, whose true "authors are in eternity."

The titles as revised in the collected editions do not sacrifice the definition of visionary poetry they helped to shape in their earlier forms. Yet they widen the focus of the volume by calling more attention to it also as a collection of lyrical verse richly in touch with the conventions of traditional love poetry. Some of the effects intended by this shift in emphasis in Yeats's presentation of the poems are suggested by a retrospective passage in his "Reveries Over Childhood and Youth" of 1914. In it he reflects on his evolving notions of love poetry from the time when he began writing the poems in *The Wind Among the Reeds*.

As a way into this important discussion, Yeats remembers how he first read the love poems of one of his early literary idols, Edward Dowden: "I had imagined a past worthy of that dark, romantic face. I took literally his verses, touched here and there with Swinburnian rhetoric, and believed that he had loved, unhappily and illicitly."[11] This is to say smilingly from a distance that he had once made no distinction between the poet-lover in the poems and the actual poet, whom he used to visit with his father when they first arrived in Dublin. In retrospect he is tolerantly amused by this naively biographical way of reading, but remembers the strength of his belief in it as he must still have felt it while he was writing his own early love poems, where much about his own unhappy and illicit love affairs is embedded. The sentence of the memoir continues from the same slightly mocking distance to describe the next, more literarily knowing stage in his youthful idolizing of Dowden: "and when through the practice of my art I discovered that certain images about the love of woman were the properties of a school, I but changed my fancy and thought of him as very wise."

Yet in the very next paragraph a switch of tenses as well as of tone shows that in 1914, the year *Responsibilities* was published, Yeats looked back on his youthful self in this phase as on the brink of discovering a profound truth, with sources deeper than literary sophistication:

I was about to learn that if a man is to write lyric poetry he must be shaped by nature and art to some one out of half a dozen traditional poses, and be lover or saint, sage or sensualist, or mere mocker of all life; and that none but that stroke of luckless luck can open before him the accumulated expression of the world. And this thought before it could be knowledge was an instinct.[12]

The poems collected in *The Wind Among the Reeds* might in 1914 have seemed to Yeats to be "touched here and there," like Dowden's love poems, with what in the first paragraph of this discussion he somewhat dismissingly calls "the properties of a school." Here "properties" can mean not only characteristics but also stage props. In the second paragraph, writing from his view in 1914, Yeats uses a different theatrical metaphor when he affirms that the lyric poet must be "shaped . . . to some one out of half a dozen traditional poses" such as "lover," "saint," "sage," which seems to be a kind of shaping the revised titles of *The Wind Among the Reeds* may have been designed to accomplish. The change in wording from "the properties of a school" to "traditional poses" does more than widen the range and elevate the tone of the metaphors. It marks a shift from what Yeats in 1914 remembers to have been his youthful notion of poetic conventions as stylish marks of literary sophistication to his now passionate belief in their use for the creation of a dramatic "lyric poetry" allowing the poet entrance into "the accumulated expression of the world." It seems possible that the successive revisions of titles for poems in *The Wind Among the Reeds* were an exploratory instrument used by Yeats in the early stages of his movement toward this understanding of the dramatic lyric.

It also seems possible, in light of the revisions we have traced from the early 1890's to 1910, that Yeats thought of "His Dream" when it was republished with that title in 1910 as a useful way to draw a line marking a transition to a new kind of lyric, a change he describes in a letter of 1913:

Of recent years instead of "vision," meaning by vision the intense realization of a state of ecstatic emotion symbolized in a definite imagined region, I have tried for more self portraiture. I have tried to make my work convincing with a speech so natural and dramatic that the hearer would feel the presence of a man thinking and feeling. . . . It is in dramatic expression that English poetry is most lacking as compared with French poetry. Villon always and Ronsard at times create a marvelous drama out of their own lives.[13]

The first part of the opening sentence describes "His Dream" and the poems in *The Wind Among the Reeds*; the rest of the passage characterizes what

Yeats saw himself working for in poems written just prior to 1913, which would be mainly the rest of those collected in *The Green Helmet and Other Poems*. In the revised title of "His Dream" Yeats alludes, for the only time in the volume, to his own earlier presentations that separate persons grammatically in the title from the poem. The three poems immediately following "His Dream"—"A Woman Homer Sung," "The Consolation" (later revised to "Words"), "No Second Troy"—which are about the love of woman, arise from the same autobiographical matter as is embedded in poems in *The Wind Among the Reeds*. But, as the contrast of their titles with the allusive and archaic form of "His Dream" makes pointed, Yeats's earlier need for distancing titles has disappeared. Instead of using the title to fashion the poses of the traditional poet-lover, the actual poet has now been shaped to the figures speaking in the poems, whose dramatic expression enables Yeats to join the company of poets who "create a marvelous drama out of their own lives."

When Frost, by his own accounts to various listeners and correspondents, sat by the fire one winter night soon after his move to England to sift and arrange poems for his first volume, *A Boy's Will*, he faced the same difficulties as Yeats had done almost fifteen years earlier when he gathered poems together to make *The Wind Among the Reeds*. Frost's comments tell us that he too saw the need to give unity to assorted "poems of youth," some of them already published singly, which were written separately over the decades from 1892 to 1912, "not in a design to be together."[14] He also recognized the more difficult challenge of finding ways to present poems made of "stuff . . . so very personal."[15]

According to several reports, Frost said that his way of making a unified "design" for his volume of poems was to write "some prose lines to tie them together," which he also called "marginal notes" or "'contents' notes."[16] Critics now mainly refer to them as *glosses*, reflecting their line of descent from early editorial practices. They were printed under the titles of poems in the table of contents of the first edition of *A Boy's Will* in 1913 and all subsequent editions, but were omitted when it was reprinted in collected editions beginning in 1930. Frost arranged the poems according to the design of these glosses in a three-part structure plotting an implied narrative with a loosely seasonal pattern of repeating and changing moods. Since they are mainly phrased in third-person pronouns, for instance "He sees days slipping from him that were the best for what they were," they seem pointedly to allude to titles in the revised version of *The Wind Among the Reeds*, first published seven years before Frost arranged his own book of poems.[17]

These glosses, Frost's reported comments tell us, were also designed to follow Yeats's more complex intention in using his titles to make private matter available for public presentation. One reported conversation shows Frost hinting at this need in a playfully oblique way that parallels the obliqueness of his third-person glosses themselves: "The boy in the poems couldn't be publicly a poet. He was too shy."[18] The glosses, phrased in the third person as if not by the youthful figure using the first person in the poems, circumvent his shyness to make them public. In a letter dated January 30, 1913, Frost gives a playful account of *A Boy's Will* that offers a paradigm from real "life" for the arrangement of the book:

It comes pretty near being the story of five years of my life. In the first poem I went away from people (and college); in the one called A Tuft of Flowers I came back to them actually as well as verbally for I wrote that poem to get my job in Pinkerton as little Tommy Tucker sang for his supper, and Brer Merriam read it for me at a Men's League Banquet in Derry Village because I was too timid to read it myself.[19]

Merriam is a stand-in for the maker of the glosses.

In a later account Frost is said to have remembered that he originally wrote the "marginal identifications" of "what each poem stood for" in the first person: "It seemed to me, though, that there was too personal a note in them—too much of Robert Frost. . . . So, I rewrote the marginal notes, taking the capital 'I' out, and stressing the third person, transferring them thus over to an imaginary person."[20] Whether or not he actually followed these stages in writing the prose comments, his analysis of their intended effect has an authentic ring. In a characteristically teasing tone he goes on to describe a kind of trick the glosses play on the reader: "You can never tell which person I am writing under. 'I' sometimes means 'he,' while 'he,' as in this case, means 'I.' We'll leave 'we' out of consideration." The glosses play a game of evasion with pronouns allowing poems to hint at private matter they do not disclose, an evasiveness Frost describes in a journal note made about the time of arranging the volume as making poems with doors that are not left open.[21]

The effects of juxtaposing third- and first-person pronouns, as Frost describes them, recall the way *I* and *he* are separated by the gloss-like titles for poems in *The Wind Among the Reeds*, although the mischievous tone of the description itself is decidedly not Yeats's in those dreamily nostalgic allusive titles. Allusiveness is also the first impression made by the glosses in *A Boy's Will*. Richard Poirier describes Frost's as "unabashedly in the mode of early Yeats, as in 'He Remembers Forgotten Beauty'"; yet in his finely tuned discussion of their relation to the poems themselves he describes their workings in terms that can be used to differentiate them from the Yeatsian model, because his discussion centers on the way Frost as the maker of the glosses "is mostly an older version of himself looking at a younger" in the poems.[22]

Yeats's titles in the revised forms Frost seems to have studied claim nothing about the maker of the title beyond that he is acting as the sympathetic commentator who presents the poems but is not their author or the first person in the verses. Frost's prose comments work differently. Though most refer to the figure in the poems simply as "He," they are preceded by the differently formed gloss for the opening poem: "The youth is persuaded that he will be rather more than less himself for having forsworn the world." This identifies the "I" in the poem following it, "Into My Own," and therefore throughout the volume, as "The youth," the *Boy* in the volume's title, which is itself a phrase borrowed from the refrain of Henry Wadsworth Longfellow's poem "My Lost Youth," in turn attributed by him to "the old Lapland song": "A boy's will is the wind's will, / And the thoughts of youth are long, long thoughts."[23] So "The youth" of Frost's introductory gloss is Longfellow's "Lost Youth," which he reflects on in the third person in his borrowed refrain. He is also "A shepheards swaine" of Spenser's "To His booke" and "a certain Shepherd Lad" of John Milton's "A Mask Presented At Ludlow-Castle." Perhaps most nearly he is the "uncouth Swain" in the closing lines of "Lycidas," a poem of charged significance for Frost in this period, as we shall see. In Milton's final passage the youthful poet who has sung the preceding elegy in the first person now reflects on his younger self in the distancing pronoun "he" and epithet "uncouth Swain," a layered allusion to *The Shepheardes Calendar*. There the opening word to describe "this our new Poete" is "Vncouthe" and the opening eclogue, a complaint sung in the first person by "A Shepeheards boye," closes with a stanza in the third person sympathetically describing "the pensife boy."[24]

Frost's opening prose comment, by identifying the *I* whom the other glosses call "He" as the youthful poet of pastoral tradition, shapes the volume in a chronological narrative. The poet speaking in the poems, who also gave them their individual titles, is the younger self of the mature poet who now presents them publicly in the volume by adding the retrospective glosses and the allusive title, *A Boy's Will*. Frost's accounts of the actual chronology for the making of his first volume run parallel to this pastoral narrative: he was almost forty when he arranged for publication (not in the order of their composition) poems written over the previous twenty years, which the "boy" speaking about himself "was too shy" to present to the world. Frost thought of the poems as tracing both "a life I was forced to live" for five years and also a kind of "clinical curve" of his "psychological" progress through those years: "That curve represented my flight away from and back to people, just as my second book was to be the curve of my forgiving people for being people."[25]

The glosses themselves loosely describe how the arrangement of poems in the volume represents something like such a composite curve. A selection tells this story: "The youth is persuaded that he will be rather more than less himself for having forsworn the world," and at first "He is happy in society of his own choosing," but soon "He is afraid of his own isolation." Then in another shift of mood "He takes up life simply with small tasks," and after "He sees days slipping from him that were the best for what they were," he can in the closing poem—which is given no gloss—move out from his pastoral seclusion.

The pastoral tradition evoked by the introductory gloss defines the curve of the volume also in another way. In the terms of its conventions the reader understands the youth to be not simply the younger self of the poet but his younger poetic self. In this context the gloss for "Into My Own"—"that he will be rather more than less himself for having forsworn the world"— presents the volume as the growth of the poet's mind (though in a tone of distinctly un-Wordsworthian amusement). The title "Into My Own" then also takes on a meaning that includes finding his own identity as a poet that would set him apart from Yeats, whom he admired but not uncritically.[26]

The introductory position of the poem "Into My Own" calls attention to the interplay between it and the volume's title, another turn in the game of switching between grammatical persons in Frost's arrangement of *A Boy's Will*. The use of "My" explicitly identifies the figure speaking in the poem as also the maker of its title, unlike Yeats's third-person forms, and emphasizes the chronological distance between the young author of the poems and his older self, who presents them in the volume's third-person title and glosses. At the same time the placing of "Into My Own" to start off the book deepens the sympathy between the poet and his "youth," which is not lost but tenderly preserved in the volume (and in fact Frost retained all but three of its poems in his collected editions). The title of the first poem makes a proud claim for the achievement of the young poet that his later self does not repudiate or treat ironically any more than the older poet does the "swain" at the end of "Lycidas." Instead he positions it to reinforce the boy's claim that in his poems the reader will hear him coming "Into My Own." In juxtaposition the title of the volume opens up its own double meaning. *A Boy's Will* carries the sense expressed by Longfellow's comparison to the "wind's will," freely shifting impulses and moods, but adds Frost's own reading of it: *A Boy's Will* is the youth's testament, his legacy, handing the poems on to his older poetic self.

The nature of that legacy is epitomized by the startling form of the title "Into My Own." In contrast with *A Boy's Will*, a literary allusion associating both Frost's volume and Longfellow's poem with pastoral, "Into My Own" has no prior literary associations. Instead it is a bit of common speech, breaking in on a colloquial idiom so familiar that we still hear its silent verb—*came, coming, will come*—suppressed here to lift the title out of the narrative time of the glosses. Like all such stock expressions of common speech described in Frost's famous letter of 1914 about "sentence-sounds," the fragment "Into My Own" carries a familiar combination of feelings by the tone of voice we associate with the idiom in everyday speech—confidence, self-satisfaction, triumph, some belligerence—without needing to spell out its meanings of fulfilling promise, receiving what is rightfully due, achieving proper recognition. By its form the title "Into My Own" therefore presents the opening of the youthful poet's pastoral verses as a "talk-song," a phrase Frost first used about "Mowing," his favorite poem in the book.[27]

His association of talk, speech, voice in poetry with pastoral exerted a strong influence on Frost's ideas about finding his own poetic identity in this period, an influence to which he later paid tribute in a retrospective note: "First thought I heard the voice from the page in Virgilian eclogue and Hamlet."[28] Traces do exist in his correspondence around the time of *A Boy's Will* of this link in his mind between "voice" and pastoral. In the letter elaborating his theory of "sentence-sounds" he quotes phrases illustrating the quality he aimed for in his poems, the sound of a voice "gathered by the ear from the vernacular and brought into books."[29] The examples he gives are from his own "My November Guest" and—in the middle of a hilariously motley list mainly of familiar bits of speech—a line from "Lycidas." Later speaking again on this subject, he is reported to have told an audience that Milton "caught the sound images . . . especially in 'Lycidas.' "[30]

In a letter written the year *A Boy's Will* appeared, Frost speculates about his plans for the presentation of his next volume of poems as modern pastorals: "I may decide to call it New England Eclogues."[31] When it appeared in 1914 with the title *North of Boston* (substituting for literary allusion the colloquialism gathered from a real-estate advertisement in a newspaper) he placed the pastoral love lyric titled "The Pasture" in the front of the volume. He intended it as a dedication or an epigraph, and as a kind of prologue to a new achievement in his poetry, saying: "There is a poem about love that's new in treatment and effect. You won't find anything in the whole range of English poetry just like that"; he also meant it to point back "as a link for the reader between *A Boy's Will* and say, well, a man's will."[32] To strengthen the link, a prose comment on the reverse side of the contents page of *North of Boston* says "Mending Wall," the first poem in the volume proper, "takes up the theme where *A Tuft of Flowers* in *A Boy's Will* laid it down."[33] If "The Pasture" looks back to the earlier book (the way Yeats seems to have positioned "His Dream" as a backward glance), it may be that "Reluctance," first published only the year before the volume, was given last place in *A Boy's Will* to look forward. The analogy of that closing poem with Milton's lines about the "uncouth Swain" is another expressive device tracing the poet's progress toward coming "Into My Own" as a modern pastoral.

Frost, we know, liked to recite "Lycidas" by heart, so the sounds of its closing lines may already have been constantly within hearing.[34] Their grammar is the most obvious signal of an altered voice here: the shift to the past tense and more importantly to the third person, which distances the speaker from his youthful self who "sang" the elegy. The change of perspective is also reflected in diction, here closer to speech than the earlier "strain" of the youth's "melodious tear." The directness and particularity of "th'Oks and rills" has replaced "fountain, shade, and rill." The "high Lawns" from which the young shepherd listened to nature's harmonies have turned into "Pastures" where farmers, for instance Robert Frost in Derry and the speaker in "The Pasture," leave their cows to graze. Plain nouns we ordinarily use for time—"now," "To morrow"—take the place of metaphors like "the mellowing year." Words and phrases from vernacular speech— "dropt," "stretch'd out"—are used to describe the sun in contrast with earlier mythologizing language. The tone has changed as well, has become more mixed. Traces of the swain's elegiac "mood" can be heard, but there is also a new urgency expressing his "eager thought" in "And now," "And now," "At last," building to the expectancy and excitement of "To morrow to fresh Woods, and Pastures new," a line made up of ordinary words in an uncompleted sentence.

An effect of this altered language in the closing lines is that "Lycidas" can be described in almost a literal sense as the poet's discovery of his own voice, since in the earlier stages of the elegy other voices—of Phoebus and St. Peter—break in upon the elegist to offer answers for questions he is not until the end able to resolve for himself. The distance he has come having completed the poem is precisely measured by the shift to the third person; in the poet's choice of the epithet he uses with affectionate sympathy for his younger self, the "uncouth Swain," with its echo of St. Peter's voice tenderly addressing him as "young swain." This is a paradigm for the use of the third person by the older poet in Frost's first gloss introducing the "youth" of "Into My Own."

The omission of a third-person gloss for the last poem, "Reluctance," might suggest the young poet emerging "Out through the fields and the woods" into his older self. There is a grammatical shift in the verbs of the poem, not one that distances what comes before in the simple past tense but one that traces an ongoing process "through the fields and the woods . . . I have wended," "I have climbed the hills of view." This grammar acknowledges endings, like the lines about the sun setting at the end of "Lycidas," but blending with the elegiac tone of reluctance is again a note of expectancy, for instance at the end of the first stanza, where the rather stag-ily melancholy phrase "it is ended" sounds in context also like a charged glimpse of something discovered: "I have come by the highway home, / And lo, it is ended." This movement marks the end of the volume's narrative and psychological curve and also represents the poet coming into his own.

The emergence at this point of an altered voice is analogous to the changes audible at the end of "Lycidas" and is achieved by some parallel means. Earlier, in "The Vantage Point," the young poet hies to "a slope where the cattle keep the lawn," while here there are simply "fields." In "A Dream Pang" he withdraws "in forest," but now "the woods" are particu-lar. "I have come by the highway home" is a different way of locating where the poet lives from the ballad-like opening line of "In a Vale": "When I was young, we dwelt in a vale." The change is from an allusive literary diction to a more colloquial vocabulary, and from a metrical pattern associated with traditional kinds of poetry to a line metrically varied to sound more like speech. To come "home" clearly does not mean to abandon the world of pastoral, any more than it is repudiated in "Lycidas," but to assimilate it into talk-song.

This achievement is celebrated in "The Pasture," itself a finely calibrated title that presents the poem as looking both forward and back. "Pasture" is not a word associated in English with the natural landscape of pastoral poetry. It would not be at home in a catalogue of idealized categories like the sequence in "Lycidas" of "Vales," "Bels and Flourets," "valleys low," "shades," "wanton winds and gushing brooks." "Pasture" belongs to the practical vocabulary of farmers. Yet it connects that to pastoral poetry for Frost in the last line of "Lycidas," in which Milton renders *pascua* from Virgil's eclogues.[35] In that fragment of a sentence—"To morrow to fresh woods, and Pastures new"—Milton drops grammatical persons altogether, as if the distinction is no longer necessary because the poet has fully entered into his own. What happens in Milton's line happens in Frost's poems with "The Pasture," when he no longer needs to play his game of switching per-sonal pronouns among titles, glosses, and poems in order to be "publicly a poet."

In a single sentence of the volume presented on its title page as *The Later Years of Thomas Hardy, 1892–1928* by Florence Emily Hardy, there is an extraordinary confession embedded in elaborate devices of evasion and even concealment. A retrospective entry for 1919 says:

On October 30 the following letter was written at his request: "In reply to your letter I write for Mr. Hardy, who is in bed with a chill, to say that he cannot furnish you with any biographical details. . . . To your inquiry if *Jude the Obscure* is autobiographical, I have to answer that there is not a scrap of personal detail in it, it having the least to do with his own life of all his books. The rumour, if it still persists, was started some years ago. Speaking generally, there is more autobiography in a hundred lines of Mr. Hardy's poetry than in all the novels."[36]

Something personal and revealing seems to be said here but in a contrivedly oblique and—"Speaking generally"—objectifying way, by elaborate manipulations of grammatical persons. The title page would have us believe that "the following was written" is a statement made by Florence Hardy, the purported author of the supposed biography. Yet we know that the account of Hardy's life, up to and including this chapter, was actually written by him, referring to himself—except in direct quotations from notes and from some letters—in third-person pronouns or as "Hardy." Here at what might appear to be one of the rare self-revelatory points in the autobiography, the concealment by grammatical persons is multiplied. Mrs. Hardy is presumed to have chosen this entry for inclusion in her biography of her husband, but it is an amanuensis left unspecified who uses the third person to write to an unidentified correspondent saying that "he" cannot supply "any biographical details," while appearing to admit to the presence of "his own life" in "Mr. Hardy's poetry." The admission is in fact less revelatory than it is evasive, layered over by indirections and concealments.

The uses of third-person references throughout the disguised autobiography and epitomized in this late entry might lead us to expect that titles referring to first-person speakers in the poems in third-person pronouns would have been a lasting resource for Hardy as a means of presenting personal material in his poems in oblique, generalized, and objectified ways. We have seen how variously Yeats and Frost adapted them to these ends, each in a volume available to Hardy and likely to have been known to him during the period from 1909 to 1928, when the last six of his eight volumes of verse were published. Four of the six include one such title, another has six, and the last volume, which Hardy prepared in nearly final form before his death, has two. While his interest in these title forms persisted, he used them relatively seldom and never as a shaping principle for a volume, for reasons that can be extrapolated from his other characteristic devices for presenting his poems.

The titles of Hardy's volumes all stress the "*Miscellaneous*" or "*Various*" nature of the collected verses, as do some of the headings under which poems are subdivided—again without claiming to be ordered—within the volumes: "Miscellaneous Poems," "Imitations, etc.," "Pieces Occasional and Various." The volume titles also point to their rendering of transitory "*Circumstance*," "*Moments*," "*Shows*," "*Moods*." This aspect of the collections is insistently brought to the reader's attention by Hardy's habit of framing many poems by placing them between a title in the space above the text and some sort of date below it. A single date associates the poem with a particular year, but within a volume poems are pointedly arranged out of chronological order so that, especially where more than one date is given for a poem, they point to times of composition rather than biographical occasions (with the exception, to be discussed, of "Poems of 1912–13"). They claim to be a record of his craftsmanship rather than of his life.

In yet another presentational device, the prefaces he carefully prepared for separate and collected volumes beginning with *Wessex Poems*, Hardy is still more assertive in defining them as miscellanies free of chronological or other continuities, including many poems "written down in widely differing moods and circumstances, and at various dates," recording mere "impressions" of the moment, and above all "dramatic or impersonative" in form.[37] In the preface to *Time's Laughingstocks and Other Verses* (I give the full title because Hardy complained of the misreading imposed by a reviewer who left off the second part), Hardy enlarges on the way the poems are to be read as "impersonative," even those without explicit signals such as a title or subtitle identifying the speaker—"One Ralph Blossom Soliloquizes," "The Pine Planters / Marty South's Reverie":

> Now that the miscellany is brought together, some lack of concord in pieces written at widely severed dates, and in contrasting moods and circumstances, will be obvious enough. This I cannot help, but the sense of disconnection, particularly in respect of those lyrics penned in the first person, will be immaterial when it is borne in mind that they are to be regarded, in the main, as dramatic monologues by different characters.[38]

He then adds a sentence so reticent that it seems more an evasion than a direction to his readers: "As a whole they will, I hope take the reader forward even if not far, rather than backward."[39] If this sentence is, as Dennis Taylor suggests, Hardy's assertion "that there was an important development in his poetry," in the context of this utterly characteristic preface and volume it seems likely to be about a development in craftsmanship, in the creation of unlike but equally convincing dramatic speakers.[40] Hardy seems to make the point even more directly in the "Apology" prefaced to *Late Lyrics and Earlier With Many Other Verses*, where he dismisses the possibility of arranging them as "themes in a graduated kinship of moods," which would therefore be assignable to an evolving consciousness, or to the growth of the poet's mind.[41]

The dozen third-person pronoun titles widely scattered in the last six of Hardy's volumes contribute to the impression of multiple and varied dramatic impersonations because they dramatize both the speakers in the poems and the titlers who present them. The titlers introduce the speaker of the verses as—in various degrees—naive, hapless, confused, superstitious, self-pitying, self-important, pompous, humorless: "He Inadvertently Cures His Love-Pains"; "He Abjures Love"; "He Wonders About Himself"; "He Follows Himself"; "He Never Expected Much"; "He Fears His Good Fortune"; "He Prefers Her Earthly"; "The Something That Saved Him." This sample listing of titles also suggests Hardy's originality in inventing varied roles for a titler who refers to *he* who is *I* in the poem with shadings of amusement, playfulness, hilarity, by unacknowledged techniques of deflation. The fictional maker of the title is sometimes distanced as an observer made critically aware by a sophisticated sense of incongruity and absurdity. In other instances the titler's poses are more like the posturings, including self-mockery, of the figure separated by grammatical person, who may then have chosen his own role in the poem and given its pseudo-editorial title.

Hardy's dramatic impersonations of both titler and speaker turn out to be more complex than Yeats's in the traditional editorial form of his titles; more various than Frost's in the prose glosses of *A Boy's Will* where the poet looks with steadily affectionate humor and sympathy at his youthful self. Hardy saw the possibility that anachronistic editorial titles, because they are known to be in fact the poet's own choice, can allow a dramatic interchange between the fictional titler and the imagined *I* in the poem. Examples will show some of the many subtle variations he made of that interchange.

Let us look first at what Robert Pinsky calls "the irony—comedy even" of "He Inadvertently Cures His Love-Pains."[42] Emphatically the opening "I said" attributes the song to the speaker, who is characterized by the titler as hapless. The fact that the song itself, with its exaggerated alliterative patterns and comic rhymes, then happens to parody lovers' complaints can only be known to the titler, not to the speaker:

> Thus I let heartaches lilt my verse,
> Which suaged and soothed, and made disperse
>   The smarts I bore
> To quiet like a sepulchre's.[43]

The singer is a modern parodic figure of the lover in lyric tradition, and the titler who presents him to the reader in a prosaic, straight-faced sentence said over the lover's head is a modern, satirical-minded version of the traditional editor. Both *I* and titler are "different characters" in one of Hardy's "dramatic monologues."

The stuffy solemnity of "He Abjures Love" could suggest another spoof of titles in the tradition of love lyrics, but since the lover in the verses treats himself just as seriously and in a similarly pompous, archaic style—as in "No more will now rate I / The common rare"—it is possible here to take the *I* of the poem as a figure of the author who writes an inadvertently parodic traditional farewell to love, and himself gives it a nostalgically anachronistic editorial title in the manner of early Yeats.[44] This would make the *I* a dramatic impersonation of a love poet something like the one in *The Wind Among the Reeds*. In a letter to Alfred Noyes printed in the account of his life, Hardy writes that this "is a love-poem, and lovers are chartered irresponsibles."[45]

While the title of "He Wonders About Himself" (perhaps the poem referred to in the account of his life by the title "He views himself as an automaton") is in the same archaic grammatical form, it is plainly worded, describing the speaker in an ordinary phrase with a detachment that does not oversolemnize his condition.[46] The first stanza is spoken in a similarly plain style—for instance in the opening line, "No use hoping, or feeling vext"—except for the preposterous "fantocine" ("automaton" in manuscript), an instance of what Pinsky calls "colloquial language banging against formal or archaic language."[47] The speaker and the titler seem to be the same figure. Then the speaker shifts into an exaggeration of Yeats's early style (1893 is Hardy's given date of composition)—"Shall I be suffering sorrows seven?"—followed by pompous philosophizing about "the general Will," which expresses a bitterly mocking sense of himself as a puppet manipulated by cosmic "forces." The movement of the poem dramatizes this figure's awareness of his inability to sustain the humorously detached perspective from which he presents himself in the title.

The literal absurdity of the title "He Follows Himself" matches it to the opening line "In a heavy time I dogged myself," merging titler and *I* in a single figure whose humor builds with growing self-mockery toward the bitter last stanza: "—The yew-plumes moved like mockers' beards / . . . And I seemed to go; yet still was there, / And am . . . / Thus bootlessly."[48] We cannot tell if this is again a poem where the *I* has lost his healthier comic perspective on "Himself," or if here the title is made by another figure who is a humorously detached observer of the self-pitying, self-mocking *I*.

Among Hardy's presentations using *he* for the first-person speaker, there is one where the juxtaposed tones of title and text fail to make a convincing dramatic interchange because while the contrast is grotesque, the integrity of the speaker's language in the poem, unmistakably an elegy, is not open to question. Here is the text of this elegy without the title presenting it in *Moments of Vision and Miscellaneous Verses* of 1917:

> This after-sunset is a sight for seeing,
> Cliff-heads of craggy cloud surrounding it.
>   —And dwell you in that glory-show?

You may; for there are strange strange things in being,
   Stranger than I know.

Yet if that chasm of splendour claim your presence,
Which glows between the ash cloud and the dun,
   How changed must be your mortal mould!
Changed to a firmament-riding earthless essence
   From what you were of old:

All too unlike the fond and fragile creature
Then known to me. . . . Well, shall I say it plain?
   I would not have you thus and there,
But still would grieve on, missing you, still feature
   You as the one you were.[49]

The poem expresses unspeakable grief and terrible awareness of human incapacity in the presence of the ultimately "strange," the unbridgeable "chasm." Human language has an everyday word for this absolute, but the lover cannot "say" it, a muteness painfully exposed by his outburst, ". . . . Well, shall I say it plain?"

Leaving the elegy untitled (as its great models, Milton's "Methought I saw my late espoused Saint" and Wordsworth's "A slumber did my spirit seal," were originally printed) would have pointed to this silence at its center. A simple title like "Lament," used by Hardy for another elegiac poem about his first wife among "Poems of 1912–13," would have been sympathetically reticent. Even a title referring to the speaker as "He" could have been phrased to keep a respectful distance: in another poem of this elegiac group, titled "His Visitor," the ghostly voice of the *she* mourned in surrounding poems speaks in shrouded tones of where "I lived with you."

The chronological heading makes this earlier group exceptional among Hardy's poems because it invites the reader to connect their matter with a particular period in the poet's life and to understand them as being arranged around a common center in his experience during those years. In keeping with the feelings Hardy expresses in these poems about his wife's death, their titles have no shading of the amusement, playfulness, hilarity, mockery, parody, deflation common in some degree to most of Hardy's other titles using third-person pronouns (even "His Country," a straight-faced presentation of a poem that then sardonically parodies patriotic verse).

The original title in manuscript for the later elegy quoted above without wording in the title space was "He prefers the earthly," which Hardy revised to the still more gratingly inappropriate "He Prefers Her Earthly." In the revised title "Prefers" takes on an even more unsuitably foppish social tone, something like *he prefers her in mauve*. The poem itself expresses a fathomless sense of loss fitting the actualities that the speaker's words cannot "say."

The title trivializes it by presenting it in glibly mocking and evasive language, with the result that it is only the titler, and not the speaker, who is exposed to be inadequate, whose mockery becomes inadvertent self-mockery.

In the context of Hardy's other third-person pronoun titles, this would seem to be the intended dramatic effect, supported by the placing of the poem in the later volume undated in the midst of miscellaneous poems—between the ballad-like "During Wind and Rain" and a dialogue of a little girl and her "Mammy." We recognize these devices as signals that the poem is intended as a dramatic impersonation. Meanwhile our experience of the verses leads to a different impression: that the pseudo-editorial title is not part of the poem's total design, but was tacked on in an attempt to fend off an unavoidable reading of the poem as an elegy like those headed "1912–13." There is no way to be sure whether "He Prefers Her Earthly" was separated from them because it was in fact not written until later or because Hardy chose to reserve it and to give it a title extravagantly inappropriate to an elegy out of deep uneasiness over having earlier exposed himself to autobiographical interpretation by his own invitation.

The title of "He Never Expected Much" is entirely in keeping in its tone with the comically deflating language of the "I" speaking in the poem. The alternative title in one manuscript, "A Reconsideration / On my eighty-sixth birthday," adapted in a subtitle for the published version in *Winter Words in Various Moods and Metres*, shows that the tone of both title and poem is intended to be heard as a representation of Hardy's own voice.[50] It also dates the poem among his last verses, as if to signal that he has reached an age when he is free to speak publicly about himself (a freedom satirically renounced in the poem placed last in this last volume, "He Resolves to Say No More"). This would make the presentation of himself in the title as "He" a joke with no pressure behind it to distance himself from the first-person speaker in the verses. Yet the joke turns out to be that his poem of personal reflection on his own lifelong perspective toward his experience is very like other poems by Hardy presented in third-person titles that set the speaker at a distance.

The poem belongs to the type among Hardy's dramatic impersonations where the speaker assumes a double part in a dialogue, here between "I" and "World." In it "I" reflects on his perspective, steadily held from the far distant past, of his parodically Wordsworthian childhood (which also appears earlier in "He Fears His Good Fortune" and "He Revisits His First School"): "Since as a child I used to lie / Upon the leaze and watch the sky." " 'Twas then" that the "World" first spoke to him "In that mysterious voice you shed / From clouds and hills around." The first-person speaker then puts in quotation marks the speech of that nonhuman messenger, which uses language matching Hardy's in the title of this poem and borrows also from the titles of two much-read poems printed in the opening pages of Hardy's first volume, "Neutral Tones" and "Hap": " 'I do not promise over-much, / . . . Just neutral-tinted haps and such.' " The voice of "He" then comments as "I": "Wise warning for your credit's sake! / Which I for one failed not to take."[51] This retrospective birthday poem hedges autobiographical matter by the same "dramatic or personative" devices we have seen in other poems, combined with shifts in grammatical persons comparable to those in Hardy's disguised autobiography. In an entry dated 1920 in the account of his life, Hardy says of himself: "He was not simple."[52]

Recent pseudo-editorial distances

Poets working in the decades following Yeats, Frost, and Hardy, while assimilating their achievements in distancing the poet from the poem—escaping personal revelation, confession, exposure—occasionally use the third person in titles to refer to the *I* of the poem. Typically these titles seem to act as no more than an allusive gesture toward or parody of the tradition. Some examples are: Dylan Thomas's "Poem on His Birthday"; William Carlos Williams's late "He Has Beaten about the Bush Long Enough"; John Berryman's "He Resigns"; Rupert Brooke's "He Wonders Whether to Praise or Blame Her"; Countee Cullen's "The Poet Puts His Heart to School"; Edith Sitwell's "The Poet Laments the Coming of Old Age"; John Hall Wheelock's "The Poet Tells of His Love"; David Wright's "The Poet Discovers Himself to be Infested with Lice"; D. J. Enright's "Poet Wondering What He Is Up To"; Gavin Ewart's "The Lover Complains"; Philip Larkin's "He Hears that his Beloved Has Become Engaged"; Thom Gunn's "To His Cynical Mistress"; Louis Simpson's "His Funny Valentine" (superimposing the archaic form on the borrowed title of a Rogers and Hart song).

Some other poets, not confining these title forms to allusion and parody, have adapted or revised them to fulfill different aims than the need to escape from the authority of autobiographical interpretations of their work. They devise their own formulations for titles that create the illusion of a presence, a consciousness independent of their maker, but do so by means other than the dramatic entity of speaker or persona. Differences in generations of titling between the first and second halves of the twentieth century can come into focus if Pound's "On His Own Face in a Glass" is set beside the titles of two later poems where manipulation of grammatical persons has been succeeded by their suppression: Frank Bidart's "Self-Portrait, 1969" and John Ashbery's "Self-Portrait in a Convex Mirror."

Pound's title presents a brief poem of apostrophe beginning "O strange face there in the glass!" that asks "What answer?" to the questions "I ? I ?

I ? / And ye?"[53] The grammar of Pound's title separates the maker of it from the apostrophic questioner. Meanwhile the anachronism of its form and the archaic word *glass* for mirror in the title and in the text, along with its many other archaisms—for instance the Yeatsian "O ye myriad / That strive and play and pass"—locate both titler and speaker in an antique or mythologized time. It is far removed from the actual present of 1908 when Ezra Pound published the poem (in a volume with a distancing and generalizing title, *A Lume Spento*, untranslated from Dante's *Purgatorio*, and including a poem referring directly to one in *The Wind Among the Reeds*). These devices make "On His Own Face in a Glass" a somewhat crude but therefore helpfully explicit manifesto for Pound's doctrine announced loudly by the title for a volume published the following year, *Personae* (the same year as his *Exultations*, containing two poems with these prose glosses above the text: "He speaks to the moonlight concerning the Beloved" and "He speaks to the rain").

Bidart's title "Self-Portrait, 1969," by leaving out the personal pronoun where earlier conventions of titling might predict it, is formally still more distancing than Pound's. The different choice of "His Self-Portrait" would have had virtually the same effects as Pound's traditional formulation. The reader knowing the work of poets writing in the earlier twentieth century would recognize the pronoun as the author's way of referring to the speaker or persona as a dramatic entity in the poem. At the same time the third-person pronoun would bring to the reader's attention the presence of both poet and speaker, even while masking them. Bidart's different wording of the title leaves them out, as it were, because there are no personal pronouns to evoke them. It also suppresses both poet and speaker or persona because the title is, again as it were, not made or said by anyone. It reprints a traditional museum label of a generic type, although with the specifying date "1969," anonymously copied and placed on the wall next to the painting.

Yet because "Self-Portrait" is a conventional equivalent for "Portrait of the Artist," we expect that the "Self" in the poem will be identified with the poet. Besides, readers of Bidart's volume *Golden State*, published in 1973, have been trained by poets of Pound's era to recognize a distancing title as a device separating the objective titler from the personal voice in the poem. We expect to hear a speaker using *I*, making the poet's work, a sonnet, analogous to the artist's, a portrait of himself presented to the museum visitor in an impersonal label:

Self-Portrait, 1969

He's *still* young—; thirty, but looks younger—
or does he? . . . In the eyes and cheeks, tonight,
turning in the mirror, he saw his mother,—
puffy; angry; bewildered . . . Many nights

> now, when he stares there, he gets angry:—
> something *unfulfilled* there, something dead
> to what he once thought he surely could be—
> Now, just the glamour of habits . . .
>   Once, instead,
> he thought insight would remake him, he'd reach
> —what? The thrill, the exhilaration
> unravelling disaster, that seemed to teach
> necessary knowledge . . . became just jargon.
>
> Sick of being decent, he craves another
> crash. What *reaches* him except disaster?[54]

"He's *still* young" is unexpected. The third-person pronoun where *I* would be more predictable identifies the voice with someone not the poet, not the "Self" in the portrait, but a museum visitor describing what any viewer could see in it, could say if the label gave the age of the painting's subject (as they often do), and as the dust jacket of the volume lets the reader know Bidart's age. Then immediately the portrait dissolves into "the mirror"; the present moment in the museum shifts to a past "tonight," to a recurring present of "Many nights / now," to a more distantly past "Once." The viewer now looks in the mirror, and so can no longer be the detached museum visitor. The same voice now speaks as the "Self" whose face is represented in the mirror, asking questions still in the third person that move from the reflected image to another kind of "insight" into what no other viewer could see. The voice of the poem merges with the owner of the imaged face, so that sonnet and mirror become representations of one another.

What the voice using the third person and the "he" whose face he reads in the reflection see are "just the glamour of habits," "just jargon," leaving traces on his language as on his face. "What *reaches* him except disaster?" The poem, even as the observer becomes the "Self" and therefore also the artist, is still distanced by the perspective of the inescapable third person, "he," by contrast with the exposed *I* in the poems just before and after the sonnet. This grammatical separation parallels the way the face is distanced, frozen into "something dead," by the reflecting surface of the glass. What "he craves" who represents both the poet and the "Self" of the portrait/mirror—which the poet both "stares" at and creates—is a "crash" shattering the surface, the distanced view, the "something dead" in his reflections.

The sonnet therefore becomes a portrait of the poet by indirect means very different from Pound's. To summarize the process, the juxtaposition of the anonymously worded title with the unexpected suppression of *I* in the poem creates the illusion briefly of the poet's absence from both: the visitor to the museum describing and questioning in the third person is neither the artist nor the subject of the portrait. Then the merging of the detached viewer with the gazer at the face in the mirror, who recognizes what could be seen by no one but himself, makes the reflected face and the poem stand for one another. By this indirect process the poem identifies the poet with the "Self," who is not what Pound calls a persona, not what Bidart in an interview of 1983 (where he also speaks of his early admiration for Pound, Eliot, and Frost) calls "a Yeatsian 'anti-self.'"[55] That is the phrase he does use in the interview to describe "Herbert White," the imaginary speaker given a real name (like the names in Edgar Lee Masters's *Spoon River Anthology*, for instance "Herbert Marshall") in the title of the long poem beginning the volume and immediately preceding the sonnet. The poem itself, entirely enclosed in the quotation marks of Herbert White's terrifying confession, Bidart calls the earliest of his "dramatic monologues." The voice in the sonnet is also unlike the speaker's in the long poem just after it, "California Plush," even though an *I* speaks here (and in other poems in the section it begins) from experience made out of details of a life dated and located in Bidart's autobiography: "The only thing I miss about Los Angeles" is the opening line.

  "Self-Portrait, 1969" is a different kind of poem from either of those it is carefully placed between. It is not a dramatic monologue, nor can it be called directly "autobiographical" in the same way as the "family poems" in the middle of the book, where the voice using *I* is identifiable with Bidart, who in the interview nevertheless refers to that speaker as "the son." The sonnet—the only one in the volume and in all of Bidart's work—uses the form as a kind of frame around the represented face, in something like the way it is used in Robert Lowell's "Self-Portrait," a rendering of Rainer Maria Rilke's sonnet with the title "Selbstbildnis aus dem Jahre 1906." Lowell's sonnet is the specific model for Bidart's; he says in the interview that the "great model" for the poems in *Golden State* which "think my life" is *Life Studies*.[56] The voice in Lowell's version keeps its implacable distance by impersonal articles and pronouns—"The mouth is just a mouth . . . yet it says its *yes*"—turning the face into "A still life, *nature morte*."[57] Bidart's own ways of using the title (dated like Rilke's), the sonnet form as framed portrait/mirror, the voice of the museum visitor turned mirror gazer, unfold his own intensely original process of making us believe what is imaged there to be a representation of Frank Bidart's reflection on himself at thirty in 1969.

  The title of Ashbery's poem "Self-Portrait in a Convex Mirror" works by still more devices of displacement to reflect what David Kalstone in discussing the poem calls a "state of mind . . . open to waves of discovery and distraction, and aware of the unframed and unframeable nature of experience."[58] Like Bidart's, Ashbery's title omits the personal pronoun. It also reprints an anonymous museum label for a painting, here more specifically identified in the poem as the traditional English translation of the label for Parmigianino's great work in the Vienna museum, itself derived from the account of it in Giorgio Vasari's life of the painter that is quoted in the poem. Or Ashbery's title copies a citation in a book about Italian Renaissance painting, and again a specific reference is made in the poem to Sidney Freedberg's great study of the artist's work, also a source of quoted language in the poem.

The title itself is again not traceable to any author. The "Self" it refers to is also unlocated, here ambiguous, multiple: the self represented in the convex mirror, copied in the painting; the living self of the painter from Parma named "Francesco"; a self-effacing self in the poem not identifiable with the absent poet or with a dramatic character speaking in it. There are no personal pronouns in the first nine lines, only "the face" and "the viewer," and in the next seven only pronouns quoted from Vasari about the painter. After that there are rare mentions of "you" or "we" with the sense of *one*. No "I" surfaces in the poem for more than seventy lines. The effects of these devices, working with the title, are characterized only indirectly by a description of the painting. It begins with a quotation from Vasari's words about it, themselves translated, and continues outside quotation marks in the unidentified voice that reads aloud from the translation:

> "he set himself
> With great art to copy all that he saw in the glass,"
> Chiefly his reflection of which the portrait
> Is the reflection once removed.[59]

These lines are interestingly different from the translation Ashbery gives of the same passage in a prose piece titled "Parmigianino": "he set to work to copy everything that he saw there, including his own likeness, in the most natural manner imaginable."[60] In the poem's version, "With great art" replaces "in the most natural manner imaginable"; "likeness" becomes the repeated word "reflection" (echoed also in "removed"), with its punning meaning of thoughtful examination, equally descriptive of the poem; "glass" and "portrait" are inserted; the innocuously familiar wording of "he set himself" substitutes for the equally colloquial "he set to work." This layering of representations is multiplied in the poem's version of the translation, which is itself a copy in a different language. These lines therefore reflect on and epitomize the dissolution or fracturing of traditional ways to locate the "Self" or "I" in art. The poem mirrors and is mirrored by the convex mirror that distorts "all that he," "Parmigianino," "Francesco" saw of "himself" in the "glass." The mirrored reflection imaged in the painting and its label is reimaged in the poem and its title.

Poem and title are in Ashbery's distinctive manner, yet they work in a direction followed by other poets of his generation. In a 1991 review of Ashbery's recent work John Bayley goes so far as to say that Ashbery's poetry embodies "what real achievement in a contemporary poet consists of: he has laid down guidelines and made his mark on the language of the tribe."[61] In "Self-Portrait in a Convex Mirror" the guidelines point in an altered direction from the thinking of preceding generations about *speaker, persona, voice*. In taking that direction the poem suggests why poets like Bidart and Ashbery writing in the later twentieth century, having learned from and redirected the achievements of their predecessors in creating a dramatized self, would revise title forms that are among the devices instrumental in those achievements.

Who has the title

THE QUESTION of who gives the title to the poem became highly
charged for poets once it was no longer simply assumed that the title was
one among the presentational devices put together by copyist, editor, commentator, translator, printer, bookseller—someone not the author—who
was responsible for the circulation of the poem. Ben Jonson seems to have
been the first English poet to take a public stand on this question in his own
titles. In doing so he transformed the issue, making it a question of who
has the title to the poem. For him titling assumed new and heightened value
as a means for identifying himself to be what Richard Helgerson has taught
us to call a "self-crowned laureate," with the sole authority to canonize his
own work.[1]

First-person pronouns: Jonson

We know from varied evidence that Jonson was one of the earliest
English poets to consider titles for short poems as an appropriate and
important object of attention for the poet. A sign that he gave such consideration to his choices is that the two collections of verses he is thought
to have seen through to their publication in 1616, *Epigrammes* and *The
Forrest*, are virtually unique up to that time among English printed collections of short poems by a single writer in having titles for every poem,
framed by the poet according to consistent principles. One of the clearest
of these self-imposed rules, and the most radically original for the time,
was his unvarying choice in these volumes of first-person pronouns where

third-person forms of the kind we have been tracing would have been expected.

From statements in Jonson's poems themselves we learn that, beyond being deliberate and consistent in his design for their titles, he was intensely aware of the usefulness of titling as a way of establishing the poet's authority to be both maker and presenter of his own work, and therefore to be wholly in charge of directing his readers' responses to his performance in both those roles. This authority he declares explicitly at the opening of his volume *Epigrammes*. It begins with a dedicatory couplet where the poet talks directly and commandingly in the first person "To the Reader": "Pray thee take care, that tak'st my booke in hand, / To reade it well: that is, to vnderstand."[2] Then immediately a prefatory poem tells us what is the first thing we are to "vnderstand":

> To my Booke
>
> It will be look'd for, booke, when some but see
> Thy title, *Epigrammes*, and nam'd of mee

This would now seem a surprising point for the poet to insist on first, because readers assume that of course poets give their own titles. It must have been far more startling in 1616 when it was generally assumed that they did not, and most particularly that they would not boast of such self-presentation. This volume opens with just such a boast, claiming that it is not only because Jonson is the author of it but most especially because it is "nam'd of mee"—that is, named by me but perhaps also known by my name (which Jonson signs to the prefatory letter)—that he empowers it with voice to "let men know" what should be "look'd for" in his epigrams. Built into this declaration is another claim that would also violate the expectations of Jonson's first readers: that titling is a feature of this poet's art, that the title is part of the poem's design.

The surprise would be made all the more jolting in the context of actual titling practices up through Jonson's lifetime by the very form of the title "To my Booke," radical in its pointed substitution of "my" for the traditional formulation, *his*. This declaration of proprietorship is given special emphasis because Jonson's readers would recognize the poem's announcement of his own declared choice of "*Epigrammes*" for the title of his volume as an allusion to Martial, who first used the term *epigrammaton* by which his own collection came to be known.[3] That association would have specifically raised the expectation of third-person titles because they were the form in which Martial's poems were presented, as were those of other ancient poets, in prestigious humanist editions by which they were known to English readers.

A volume of Martial's *Epigrammata* printed in Venice in 1475 separates them by an abbreviated editorial gloss above each poem: *De libro suo, De suis libris, Ad sua carmina.* These phrases may have been designed at least partly to serve a kind of typographical function: in this edition there are no other markers such as spaces, lines, or ornamental designs to divide one poem from another. The glosses may also have been useful as summaries and as aids for quick reference in such vast collections of short poems closely printed in an ancient language. Yet titles of English poems imitate this third-person form when it was no longer needed for these purposes but instead had become an allusive device, sometimes virtually a quotation linking a later text with distinguished ancestors.

In Herrick's published collection of his own vernacular epigrams he uses the third-person pronoun form for his titles, preferring the classical association before imitation of his English master, Jonson, who is lavishly acknowledged in other ways. The titles for Herrick's first three poems, quoted earlier—"The Argument of his Book," "To his Muse," "To his Booke"—are a marked departure from the Jonsonian model established in the opening three poems of *Epigrammes*: "To the Reader," "To my Booke," "To my Booke-seller." The difference points to the deliberateness of Jonson's own more radical decision and to its importance. His willingness to forgo the prestige of third-person titles, given his otherwise strong identification of himself as the heir of his ancient forebears, is a sign of the value he gave to his own reformulated titles as a means of assuming ownership of his own poems.

The traditional formulation that Jonson purposely avoided identifies the presenter of the poem as the editor, translator, commentator, rather than the poet. His right to make the presentation was predicated first on possession of or access to a copy of the poem. The authority of his particular choice for the title derived from his familiarity with it and with the corpus of the poet's work, since the poem appeared in a collection with many others similarly presented by the commentator as verses by the same *he*. The title in the third person declares itself to have been made after the poem had been written, when the *he* to whom it refers is presumably not there, to speak of present company in the third person being unmannerly (and in fact the kind of titling Jonson set out to revise was associated mainly with verses by poets long dead). Such titles are presentations by titler to reader, as it were out of hearing of the author, who is granted no part in them.

To make sure that his readers would recognize the full shock value of his opening claim to authoritative self-presentation, Jonson expands on it two pages later in *Epigrammes* 9:

> To all, to whom I write
>
> May none, whose scatter'd names honor my booke,
>   For strict degrees of ranke, or title looke:

> 'Tis gainst the manners of an *Epigram*:
> And, I a *Poet* here, no *Herald* am.[4]

This title is more arrogant about its authorship in using the first-person nominative: "I" is more assertively centered on self than "my," and the pronoun is made louder by the repetition of sound in "I write," in keeping with its bold substitution of "I" for *he*.

Then the verses enlarge on the poet's claim to be his own titler by punning expansion of meanings for the word "title." "I a *Poet* here" am "no *Herald*," a servant who would make presentations on behalf of others, at their behest; who would announce names and ranks dictated to him, not of his own choosing and ordering. Or if "*Herald*" refers also to a member of some powerful body like the College of Heralds, as Stephen Orgel suggested to me, then the claim to the poet's superior authority is even more playfully subversive. *As poet I am the bestower of titles that are my own invention.* Here Jonson attaches to the ancient meaning of *title* as inscription other senses current in his time: designation of social rank; justification of a claim; legal right to the ownership of property. As the creator and bestower of all these titles, Jonson dictates the conventions of his art, which control his readers' experience of it.

Together here, verses and title generalize about the making of poetry because to be "a *Poet*" is to address "all" readers, but to speak to them directly and immediately as "I," with no loss of vitality, because the title is brought closer to the poem through the use of "I" for the maker of both, a link reinforced by repetitions of the "I" sound in other key words: "write" in the title, "title" in the poem. The assertive first person gives the same immediacy and vitality to the sayer of the title as to the "I" of the verses, so that they sound like declarations by a single maker. Even the pattern of stressed words in the title works toward bringing it close to the poem, and contributes to their combined expressiveness as a whole pronouncement. "To all, to whom I write" consists of three iambs, giving it status as a fragment of a metrical line like those in the poem, most closely parallel to "And, I a *Poet* here," the first half of the final line. In scansion of the title by itself the pronoun would be metrically unstressed, but "I" in the last line is the most loudly heard syllable in the poem. As happens with metrical lines within such a short poem, this emphasis reflects back on the title, making "I" more emphatic than the pronoun would be if the title were "To all, to whom he writes." The combined effect is to insist on the bold unexpectedness of using "I" in a title, and on the title's part in the whole design of the poem.

The only other title in which Jonson departed as radically from traditional third-person formulation by using the nominative "I" is "Why I write not of Love." Chosen to open his other carefully arranged and titled volume, *The Forrest*, it stands even more prominently than his ninth epigram as a kind of manifesto. It announces a program for the book as well as the poem, while at the same time acting as a defense of the whole corpus of the poet's work. That is, it can be read as assuming that the reader is already familiar with this poet's verse, and therefore has doubtless noticed and perhaps wondered at the fact that he has not written the expected love verses. The title presents the poem in this way as the author's defense of his previously and continuously consistent practice, why he is still the special kind of poet he is widely known to be. In this reading the title implies that the writer has an already established reputation among readers who continue to interest themselves in his work. Like the proud address to a large audience in "To all, to whom I write," it paradoxically does some of the canonizing work of traditional third-person titles in granting Jonson the classic status usually associated at this time with ancient poets.

By avoiding pronoun forms that would separate the acts of writing and titling the verses, the title's grammar again brings it closer to the text—in contrast, for instance, with Herrick's "His Answer to a Question"—making possible more particular connections with it:

Why I write not of Love

Some act of *Loue's* bound to reherse,
I thought to binde him, in my verse:
Which when he felt, Away (quoth hee)
Can Poets hope to fetter mee?
It is enough, they once did get
Mars, and my *Mother*, in their net:
I weare not these my wings in vaine.
With which he fled me: and againe,
Into my ri'mes could ne're be got
By any arte. Then wonder not,
That since, my numbers are so cold,
When *Loue* is fled, and I grow old.[5]

Jonson's unusual use of "I" assumes a forthright posture for the poet-titler speaking in the title with the vitality and immediacy that would predict certain qualities for the poem he presents. The reader will enter it by the poet's own invitation. In it he will explain what the reader will no longer need to "wonder" about. The title therefore characterizes the poem in advance for its openness, its directness in meeting and answering the expectations readers bring to the work of this poet, and in preparing them for their first experience of these particular verses.

Instead the poem is—until the last three words—exceptionally oblique, especially among other verses by Jonson. Rather than a plain, unvarnished explanation in the manner of the poet in his title, it rehearses a mythological tale. Only in the last three words does the poet set aside the elegant literariness of his "verse," "ri'mes," "numbers" to use the present tense and plain style of his title: "I grow old." Although this direct, monosyllabic return to first-person statement is linked grammatically with the mythological tale by "and," as if they were parallel explanations, the connection so blandly offered is actually deceptive or concealed. Without comment it exposes the myth that constitutes all that precedes it in the poem as an elaborate evasion of the poet's own story. It is a disguised account of the personal pain that unmythologized "*Loue* is fled" from this aging poet's life. Leaving unspoken the analogy between him and the artisan who was the lame old husband betrayed by Venus, it avoids connecting that abandoned lover's pain with "I grow old." In this way the last line calls attention to the distance between the evasive mythological tale and the kind of poem predicted by the poet's forthright presentation of it to his readers in the title.

The text of the poem itself therefore playfully escapes the poet's presentation, both in its matter and manner, as Cupid "fled" him when he "thought" to begin his "verse." It is almost entirely filled with mythological material made familiar by "Poets" who write of "*Loue*" as this poet in the title says he does not. Jonson's specific allusion here (pointed out by Helgerson) to the opening of Ovid's *Amores*, archetypal storehouse of amatory matter, slyly underscores this contradiction.[6] The relation of title to poem is therefore much trickier here than it is made to seem by Jonson's choice of "I" to identify the poet as the maker of both.

In the title the poet tells what the reader will find him doing in the poem, but the verses do not then seem to do what the poet says they will. Here the poem acts as it were independently of its presentation, and therefore in this instance of its maker. It has its own ways of being, its "verse," its "ri'mes," its "numbers," which formal patterns contrast it with the poet's blunt address to his readers in the title. That grammatical fragment sounds more like the end of a spoken sentence than part of a line of verse, primarily because it does not scan. Its stresses are at odds with the mostly regular iambic tetrameter of the verses, making it sound like the voice of the poet telling what he is going to write. In this reading, which imagines the title to have been written *first*, the verses, by escaping the title's predictions, tease the maker for trying to bind them in advance. This seems to undercut the authority claimed for the poet's presentation of his own poem.

An alternative script supposes the title to have been written *after* the verses. This gives back authority to their joint maker, but with yet another twist because it is authority of a different kind from the right to explain his own work bluntly asserted in the title. If the poet chose the title after writing the verses, then it is he who teases his readers by its only apparently forthright address. Maker, title, and poem are then united in a conspiracy as tricky as those in Ovidian mythology, in which the poet assumes sole control over the reader's expectations. He exercises it by meeting and guiding them in the title; then violating and redirecting them in the verses; finally teasing the readers into recognition of the complex whole made by the title and the verses of the poem (in short lines to be distinguished from the elegiacs of the *Amores* and its imitations), which is after all not a love poem of the traditional sort his readers have been trained to expect. It is a poem "of *Loue*" that transforms that tradition as radically as its title alters the conventions of presentation. By combining their expressive effects, title and verses act as a manifesto for Jonson's distinctive kind of verse, in which the title is part of the whole design.

Later first-person pronouns

Milton is the seventeenth-century poet likeliest to have appreciated Jonson's insistence that the author has the sole title to his own poems. In *Poems Of Mr. John Milton* of 1645, which matches the collections apparently supervised by Jonson in self-conscious presentation, and again in *Poems, &c. Upon Several Occasions* of 1673, Milton carefully avoided titles using third-person pronouns such as those imposed on his sonnets posthumously by editors. While traditional third-person forms might have attracted him for their association with humanist editions of ancient and Renaissance authors, they would have allowed editorial authority—either actual or supposed—over his poems, neither of which he would have been likely to grant. For although his first printed collection is introduced, as Milton's gentlemanly station required, by a preface signed with the name of the "Stationer" rather than the poet (whereas Jonson's own name is attached to the dedicatory letter prefacing his *Epigrammes*), the title page announces authorial approval: that the poems are "Printed by his true Copies." This is a more decorous device for making the same claim as the first-person pronouns in Jonson's radical titles: that the poet has the ultimate authority for the form in which his own verses are presented. It was perhaps in the interests of maintaining this decorum that Milton in his published versions of titles also altogether avoided first-person pronouns, changing the original presentations of some. One manuscript title of a sonnet, "To my freind Mr Hen. Laws Feb. 9. 1645," was emended as "To Mr. H. Lawes, on his Aires." He gave another sonnet in manuscript the title "On his dore when ye Citty expected an assault," then crossed it out and replaced it with "When the assault was intended to ye Citty," but in printed editions left the sonnet untitled. Still another title using the first-person possessive in manuscript, "On ye religious memorie of Mrs Catharine Thomason my

christian freind deceas'd 16 Decem. 1646," was also simply left out when
the poem was printed.

Among seventeenth-century poets more closely associated with Jonson,
Herrick alone seems to have paid attention to the consistent emphasis of
Jonson's titling, only to reverse its direction for his own quite different purposes. The cavalier posture adopted by other sons of Ben, both in verse and
in society, would have been incompatible with Jonson's public forms of self-
presentation. Vagaries of titling in their volumes, both those posthumously
printed and those published while the poets were still alive, show that they
lacked Jonson's interest in titles, or in their pronoun forms as expressive
devices. Titles in the posthumous 1640 edition of Thomas Carew's *Poems*,
for example, follow Jonson's lead in using mainly the first-person possessive—"To my Rivall"—but also include "To his jealous Mistris" and others
in this traditional form. Even the rarer titles using the first-person nominative—"To a Lady that desired I would love her," "Song. To my Mistris, I
burning in love"—make no claims to poetic authority, as Jonson's do. With
the same indifference and inconsistency, William Habington's *Castara*,
which went through several editions within his lifetime, presents on adjacent pages "To Castara, Inquiring why I loved her" and "To Castara, Looking upon him." The preface to this volume by "The Author" opens with a
sentence designed to call attention to its un-Jonsonian air of carelessness,
to which its titling is suited: "The Press hath gathered into one, what fancie
had scattered in many loose papers."[7]

The nominative *I* that Jonson aggressively substituted for *he* in two
prominent verse statements about his poetry did not become an accepted
practice, nor has the equally rare objective form, *me*, the grammatical parallel for *him* in titles like "To his louer to loke vpon him" from Tottel's
miscellany. By contrast, authorial titles with *my* found ready acceptance
once the actual cultural conditions of presenting poems no longer supported the claims of third-person titles to have been made by someone other
than the poet.

This contrast in the histories of nominative and possessive first persons
in titling reflects differences in their grammatical status. The pronoun in
the nominative case, being the grammatical subject, focuses more emphatically on the doer, the performer, as both maker and presenter, turning titles
like Jonson's into forceful self-presentations well suited for manifestos.
Similarly the first-person pronoun in the objective case sounds more self-
assertive than the possessive, as we can hear by comparing Maya Angelou's
titles "My Arkansas" and "Woman, Me." Usually the possessive pronoun
in first as well as third person at least formally shifts attention in the title
from the maker to something in the poem: its subject only, as in D. G. Ros-

setti's "My Sister's Sleep," or as combined with its form, in Yeats's "A Prayer for My Daughter"; its occasion, as in Felicia Hemans's "On My Mother's Birth-day"; its setting, as in Samuel Taylor Coleridge's "This Lime-Tree Bower my Prison." Or the title focuses on the poem as an address to some specified audience: John Clare's "To My Oaten Reed"; Walter Savage Landor's "To My Daughter"; J. V. Cunningham's "For My Contemporaries." These possessive pronouns in the first person do not separate poet and titler as do uses of *his* in the distancing titles they parallel. Yet they still do not specially emphasize the fact of the poet acting as titler who presents his own poem. They purport to focus the reader's attention mainly on the same aspects of poems as they would if phrased in the third person.

An extraordinarily small number of titles for poems in English before the 1950's identify the titler with the first person in the poem by using the nominative *I*, unless we were to include poems where the title space is occupied by a quotation from the opening of the poem itself. For reasons that may be partly apparent here and will be explained more fully in later chapters, these self-referential opening quotations do not usually raise issues about the relation of titler or title to poet, speaker, or poem, which is the focus of this discussion. For the same reasons, titles made of quotations borrowed from an identifiable source outside the poem, like Philip Larkin's "I Remember, I Remember" (echoing Thomas Hood and Winthrop Praed) or Howard Nemerov's "I Only Am Escaped Alone to Tell Thee" (Job 1:15), will also be set aside for separate consideration.

In a few titles, again a surprisingly small number at least before the second half of the twentieth century, *I* is used outside self-referential or borrowed quotations but still without focusing on the maker of the presentation as also the maker of the poem or its speaker. One type is exemplified by Hardy's "Memory and I." It is the title for a formal dialogue between two voices marked off by quotation marks in the poem, where "I" tends to assume allegorical status like "Memory," making a pairing comparable to those in traditional titles like Marvell's "A Dialogue between the Soul and Body," or Yeats's variant of it, "A Dialogue of Self and Soul." Larkin's title "Mother, Summer, I" seems to imitate the abstracting form of Hardy's title but as a way of generalizing, of making representative and objective a poem full of particular and personal memories. The tradition is parodied in the separation of "I" from "This gentlemanly self" in Robert Graves's "My Name and I."

I has sometimes been used in another generalizing way in titles to refer to the first person in the poem who is a representative Christian. These titles achieve their generic status by echoing biblical formulas: as in William Cowper's "I Will Praise the Lord at All Times"; Christina Rossetti's "I Look for the Lord"; Patrick Kavanagh's "I May Reap." There is scarcely more pressure in the traditional phrasing of title or poem to identify the first person particularly with the poet than in titles for early religious poems naming the figure in the poem as a representative believer, like "The repentant sinner in durance and aduersitie" (presenting an unattributed poem in Tottel's miscellany), or as an abstraction, such as John Davies's "The Soule desireth to know God." The inward state of Kavanagh's speaker is defined by biblical metaphors—"I who have not sown"—while the voice in Rossetti's "I Look for the Lord" is the collective petitioner of common prayer:

> Our wealth has wasted all away,
>   Our pleasures have found wings;
> The night is long until the day,
>   Lord, give us better things.[8]

In the remaining stanzas are six more uses of both "our" and "us."

A still more minor type is constituted of titles phrased in a formula that characteristically introduces a catalogue: Hartley Coleridge's "What I Have Heard"; W. J. Linton's "What I Hate"; Muriel Rukeyser's "What I See"; Robert Duncan's "What I Saw"; Anne Stevenson's "What I Miss"; Allen Ginsberg's "What I'd Like to Do"; Julia Kasdorf's "What I Learned from My Mother"; Diane Wakoski's "What I Want In a Husband Besides a Mustache"; Hugh MacDiarmid's "The Kind of Poetry I Want"; Patricia Jones's "Why I Like the Movies." The fixed formulaic construction of these titles can itself be a means of generalizing because it commonly casts *I* in the traditional role of a maker of standards, typically by idealizing in the pastoral mode or by denigrating in satire.

First-person pronouns: Auden

Once the authority of the poet to act as titler no longer needed to be asserted, there were no cultural obstacles to the use of titles that violate tradition in using first-person pronouns not in the possessive for other expressive purposes. Even so, they are virtually nonexistent until this century, when Auden made a brilliant display of their possibilities in the titles for poems as they were printed in his *Collected Poems* of 1945.

Before that first collection, most of the poems in his individual volumes were printed without titles, which may have helped to provoke the early critical fuming about them, for instance Malcolm Cowley's in 1934, for their "damnable and perverse obscurity."[9] Later critics have responded with calmer judgments while recognizing that Auden's original avoidance of titles, though not "perverse," is a deliberately provocative gesture; a refusal to grant interpretive authority that would simplify the reader's experience of the poem. Then in *The Collected Poetry* of 1945 Auden replaced

his absent titles with what Edward Mendelson describes as "ironic and distancing titles whose tone was (depending upon the reader's point of view)
either tellingly or irritatingly at variance with the poems they headed."
Later he "replaced a few of the more flippant titles with neutral ones in
1950, and the 1966 titles were more sober still."[10]

All Auden's early titles using *I* are among those later revised from the
"brash familiarity" and "noisy" style he associates in the foreword to the
1966 collection with the "bad manners" of youth, "not to be confused with
a deliberate intention to cause offence."[11] "But I Can't" was dropped for
"If I Could Tell You," which is quoted from a repeated line in the poem; "I
Shall Be Enchanted" became "Legend"; "Which Side Am I Supposed to Be
On?" was renamed "Ode"; "Nobody Understands Me" was neutralized
as "A Misunderstanding." While the original titles are clearly meant to star-
tle and amuse, and partly by their self-assertive pronouns, they cannot all
be described as "ironic and distancing" or "at variance with the poems they
headed." Auden's titles phrased in the first person make connections with
the poems in ways as varied and complex as the third-person title forms
used by Hardy, from whom Auden may well have learned, having by his
own account begun his apprenticeship as a poet by reading no one else:
"My first Master was Thomas Hardy."[12] And like Hardy's, his titles set up
obstacles in the way of intrusive interpretations.

The pronoun in the title "But I Can't" refers to the first person in the
poem, the poet-lover of lyric tradition, cast in this role by one of its formulas
repeated in the villanelle, "If I could tell you."[13] Auden's original title completes that line outside the space of the villanelle—"If I could tell you I
would let you know [But I Can't]"—reenacting a version of the drama of
the dumbstruck lover in Shakespeare's Sonnet 23 who, "As an vnperfect
actor," cannot say his "part" except silently in his "speaking brest." Even
though Auden's title could be attached to the line grammatically, it breaks
out of the meter into fragmentary speech so that what is said in the title
space before the poem recasts the conventional situation. The common
phrase "But I Can't" is an example of the kind of language Auden may have
learned to use from his study of Frost, whose work he first met in 1923 in
Walter de la Mare's anthology *Come Hither* and continued to admire for
its mastery of "the speaking voice," "poetic speech," a "style which approx-
imates ordinary speech of a man living in the first half of the twentieth
century," for managing to "make this kind of speech express a wide variety
of emotion and experience."[14] The phrase "But I Can't" precisely fits what
Frost calls a "sentence-sound" in the letter of 1914 quoted in Chapter 1.
That is, we recognize it as a verbal package familiar to us in daily speech
that evokes a situation rich in suggestions besides those made by the opening clause "If I could tell you"—the phrase suppressed by the truncated

title idiom—when it is read as a conventional poet-lover's complaint. Now when we say *If I could tell you I would but I can't*, we might mean that we are made tongue-tied by our own passionate sincerity, but on the other hand we could and more often do mean that we know something our listener does not, a secret we are not supposed to tell but want to hint that we are in on. This makes the voice of "I" in both title and poem more vindictive than plaintive, allowing the knowing title to tip off the reader ahead of time to the possibility that the "I" it introduces may be an impudent parodist whose cynicism is calculated and mocking: "I would let you know" is flippant if it means *get the message to you* and sinister if read *allow you the information you need*.

Because the title is in the presentational position to address the reader in advance of the poem but cannot be the beginning of what the "I" says to "you," it seems to involve the reader with the poet in an alliance against an unsuspecting "you," who might be a naive reader like Malcolm Cowley, given to mistaking Auden's playful impudence for "the plain-reader-be-damned tradition that was part of Dadaism and Super-realism." Or another stand-in for the uninstructed "you" of the poem could be John Hayward, writing a critique of Auden in 1932: "Another and more obvious cause of obscurity is the exploitation of the private joke, which can only be appreciated by the initiated, that is to say, by Mr. Auden's personal friends, sometimes, perhaps, only by Mr. Auden himself."[15] In this poem the "initiated" are its readers, who are chosen to hear "But I Can't" spoken outside the closed form of the villanelle, as it were, behind the back of the listener inside it, to whom the poet cannot "tell" it or whom the poet will not "let" hear it. The original title invents a use for the space above the text that creates a tricky interplay between title and poem not allowed by Auden's later substitution of the more conventional half-line "If I could tell you."

A different kind of game is set in motion by the title "I Shall Be Enchanted," because no *I* is mentioned in the poem originally given that title. It is an address in an unlocated voice bidding "Love" to enter "These Legends" with "him," not otherwise identified. The human figure is wholly mythologized, like "Love," who guides "him" on a legendary quest described in a style as opaque as the twilight of Yeats's early poems.[16] The revised title "Legend" is toneless, merely categorizing the narrative form and mythologizing manner of the poem. Yet its effect is to lull the reader into inattention somewhat the way the hero, "when at last / These dangers past," is left unprepared to

> Find what he wanted
> Is faithful too
> But disenchanted.

The original title, by contrast, alerts the reader that the poem will offer something to be flippant about. It is another Frostian sentence-sound, this time a stock formula for accepting an invitation in affected social circles, which rubs off its silly sense of "Enchanted" on "These legends" of the poem's opening, so that the reader is from the beginning prepared for the penultimate line "But disenchanted," an ending not expected by the hero. In this parody of mythologizing poetry, "Enchanted" is the opposite of "disenchanted." More particularly the title is the solution to a riddle hinted at in the otherwise Yeatsian middle stanza. There the incantatory voice bids Love tell the answer in the questing hero's "ear" but does not say what the answer is, only that it is

> The common phrase
> Required to please
> The guardians there.

"I Shall Be Enchanted" is this magic formula, known to Love and to the poet, who has imparted it to the reader in the title but leaves the hero dumbly unenlightened. Again the authority of the title is in its knowingness, letting the reader in on what it knows in their shared space outside the poem.

The voice in the poem titled "Which Side Am I Supposed to Be On?" also uses no first-person pronouns except the collective "We," again making the "I" of the title hard to locate.[17] The poem, printed earlier in *The Orators*, untitled in a group headed "Six Odes," is a parody of a patriotic war poem (in the vein of Hardy's "His Country") where the title question "Which Side Am I Supposed to Be On?" is not "ironic and distancing," to repeat Mendelson's terms, but sardonic and sympathetic. If the "I" who asks it is the "Boy" addressed in one stanza and appearing elsewhere as the "youngest drummer" and the "recruit" (the poem's dedication in *The Orators* "To My Pupils" supports the connection), the question expresses pained bewilderment. If the "I" of the title is the poet, then it is not a question but a bitterly sardonic comment on the cynicism of patriotic fervor in war, where the outcome decides which side "fought against God." Because the title is a familiar form of colloquial sentence we recognize sometimes as a question, sometimes as a sarcastic dismissal of the question, it can be heard simultaneously as the voices of the "Boy" and the poet. Their intonations would be somewhat different, as in the phrasing from the union-organizing song suggested by Mendelson to be a possible source for Auden's title, "*Which* side are you on? which side *are* you on?"[18] In this way it illustrates what Frost admits in an interview with Richard Poirier to be the effect of using sentence-sounds in his poetry, to vary the tones of voice in a familiar phrase so that its meaning is doubled for the reader: "Yes, you could do that. Could unsay everything I said, nearly."[19] This possibility of saying and unsaying allows evasions of settled interpretations eliminated in Auden's substituted generic title "Ode," though its seemingly noncommittal form can have an ironic and distancing effect as the presentation of a poem that deflates heroic posturing.

Our instantaneous recognition of the title phrase "Nobody Understands Me" as an archetypal expression of self-pity is part of what makes it funny, along with its unabashed egocentricity, the nakedness of its demand for attention and sympathy. The title insists on the presence of someone talking to us, trying to make us feel sad, sorry, uneasy, guilty, managing to make us feel bored. It is someone dwelling, as the poem says, "on the need for stroking and sympathy" (the one line revised in the retitled version, to "the need for someone to advise"). Then the sonnet form of what follows, its opening allusion to dream visions, and the grave tone of its narrative are comically juxtaposed to the fragment of speech that precedes them in the title space but seems not to introduce them. The speaker who says the title sentence is immediately present and wholly preoccupied with himself as "Me," the direct object of attention. In sharp contrast, the narrator of the sonnet is an objective observer whose voice is distanced by past tense and grammatical person from "he" whose story he retells.[20] The shift in pronouns from title to text is loud, making the reader ask from the beginning who it is whose voice is heard in the title.

At first it does not sound like the detached narrator, but as we read on in the story the title also does not seem to belong to the dreamily passive "he" to whom the story happens. When we reach the sestet, the sayer of the title and the protagonist "he" begin to merge since in line ten the hunger "for stroking and advice," which is what "Me" of the title demands, is unlocated by grammatical person, allowing it to become a generalized and therefore generally recognizable condition. Finally the couplet seems to collapse the distance between the narrator who asks the questions and "he" who was "forced to learn" them: "Which was in need of help? Were they or he / The physician, bridegroom, and incendiary?" Both are then versions of the person who says "Nobody Understands Me" in a universal, childish voice that is the narrator's, the protagonist's, the poet's, the reader's.

With a movement paralleling some of Hardy's poems where the titler using "He" comes steadily closer to the "I" in the poem, here the distance between "Me" of the title and the speaker who uses "he" for the figure in the story narrows in the course of the poem until their final merging, in which the reader is also included. The revised title, "A Misunderstanding," by eliminating the interplay between the spoken idiom and the sonnet diminishes this dramatic development, suggesting perhaps Auden's own movement away from the early influences on his work of Hardy and Frost.

It looks toward his later acceptance of the tradition of the titler as an interpretive guide.

Auden makes a claim dissociating himself from his earlier poetry in the one title for a poem in the collected edition of 1976 using the first-person nominative, "I Am Not a Camera," printed among poems dated 1969. The title announces its distance from the early poetry because it borrows, but pointedly revises, a familiar quotation from a story by Christopher Isherwood, with whom Auden worked closely in his younger years: "I am a camera with its shutter open, quite passive, recording, not thinking."[21] Auden's title is a revision not only because it is in the negative, but because for him being a camera now means taking pictures of people when they want you not to, rather than making a record of objective observation. He associates the "Camera" in both title and poem with the qualities he also rejected in his early poetry: "It is very rude to take close-ups and, except / when enraged, we don't."[22]

The title "I Am Not a Camera" is itself a repudiation of Auden's earlier first-person titles which he eliminated by his revisions. It is not like them a fragment of speech, but a literary allusion identifying "I" as the poet in his public role, as he is known to an audience that has followed his literary career. It generalizes and distances as does the poem it heads, which consists of statements—presented almost as if they were quotations like its title and its epigraph—from which all personal pronouns except the most general "we" are excluded. The poem is formal and declarative like the title, eliminating dramatic juxtaposition or interchange between them, making them together a manifesto for his later kind of work. Here the title resumes its traditional presentational function.

Recent first-person pronouns

First-person titles (other than with possessive pronouns) are still rare, although more of them can be found for poems written in the second half of the twentieth century than in the whole previous history of titles in English. One comes across some titles, like Auden's made of Frostian sentence-sounds said by *I* or *me*, in the work mainly of American poets writing perhaps under the combined influences of Auden and Frost. Examples exist, most of them singly, in the volumes of a variety of poets: Ruth Stone's "A Woman I Once Knew"; William Meredith's "A Girl I Knew Once"; Robert Creeley's "I Know a Man"; Charles Bukowski's "What a Man I Was"; Robert Mezey's "I Am Here"; David Ignatov's "I'm Here"; Amiri Baraka's "What Am I Offered"; John Hollander's "I Was Wrong, You See . . ."; A. R. Ammons's "I Could Not Be Here at All"; W. S. Merwin's "As Though I Was Waiting for That"; Charles Olson's "I'm With You"; Philip

Levine's "I Wanted You to Know"; Stanley Kunitz's "Promise Me"; Kenneth Rexroth's "Me" and "Me Again."

Among such recent titles using idioms or clichés spoken in the first person are some that interact with the poem in ways resembling what we have seen in Auden's early titling. Theodore Roethke's "I Need, I Need" and Sylvia Plath's "I Want, I Want" are made out of idiomatic expressions of childish egoism crudely analogous to Auden's "Nobody Understands Me." Olson's "I Mean, No" and Gregory Corso's "But I Do Not Need Kindness" have the last word outside the space of the poem, like "But I Can't." John Berryman's "'*I* Know'" is another familiar spoken phrase said by the speaker as it were after the poem, but it is a response in quotation marks to another voice inside it that the speaker has heard say with a different stress "'I *know.*'" The poem appears in the same volume as "Shirley & Auden," where the figure using the first person in the poem—whose memories identify him with Berryman—recalls how he early "recognized Auden at once as a new master" for whom his "love . . . has never altered / thro' some of his facile bodiless later books."[23]

John Ashbery, also acknowledging that he "particularly admired Auden, who I would say was the first big influence on my work," shows his debt most immediately in titles, for instance: "No I Don't," "Try Me! I'm Different," "And I'd Love You to Be In It."[24] They reflect his admiration, recorded as early as 1949 in his undergraduate honors thesis, for Auden's "completely contemporary" quality, his "immediacy and concreteness," his absorption of "rhythms . . . which are very much a part of our life," the qualities common to the first-person titles of later-twentieth-century poems just quoted.[25] The impudence and energy of Ashbery's own titles, their startling and humorous juxtaposition with the form and sound of the poems they present, match Auden's early titles. Yet they serve other purposes than to make possible various kinds of dramatic interplay among title, voice, speaker, protagonist, poet, reader, although Ashbery appreciated "Auden's tremendous capacity for dramatization."[26] "No I Don't" from *April Galleons* of 1987 can bring the difference of effects into focus.

Ashbery's title phrase "No I Don't," like Auden's "But I Can't," evokes a situation we immediately recognize. Someone has asked the "I" of the title a question—either *Do you . . . ?* which is genuinely inquiring or *Don't you . . . ?* which demands agreement—and gets an emphatic, possibly impatient, irritated, or defensive response. "No I Don't" unmodified, as it stands abruptly and alone, grammatically sealed off in the title space, is less an answer than it is like "The 'closed' sign at the door" of the poem's penultimate line, put up against further intrusive questions.[27] This is an analogy for how the title's juxtaposition with the poem works, beginning with the first line: "I have no adventures, the adventurous one began." Already we are presented with two new voices that say "I" and "the . . . one," and they multiply as pronouns shift from "I" to "you," "we," "our," meaning *one* in general, to the particularized "But you—/ You cannot follow them, he said." Elsewhere pronouns are omitted in impersonal wording like "the nose" or in constructions in the passive voice, "has been duly heard," which is a grammatical joke about the disappearance of voices. The reader listening for the abrupt-sounding voice that says "I" in the title is defeated by the deliberately slow, long lines of the poem, usually enjambed to sustain thickly punctuated sentences often for five or more lines. In search next of whoever might have interrogated the title speaker, we do find many questions asked in the poem, but they never line up with the reply "No I Don't." Attempts to read the poem as an enactment of a dramatic exchange between it and the "I" who says the title are therefore thwarted by literally eccentric devices, especially uses of pronouns in both. Their effects are like that of the hypothetical vine described in the opening section, which may be an analogy for the way the poem works:

> But then, returning,
> To find some vine that has licked out over an eave
> Like an unruly eyebrow, something that wasn't there
> Moments ago, can stop you in your tracks.

This nonsentence itself epitomizes the poem by omitting the grammatical subject.

Such multiplying of voices, beginning with the form of the first-person title, which itself implies the presence of both questioner and responder, works less like Auden's earlier poems than like Eliot's. Like passages of collage in *The Waste Land* or the shiftings of "you" from single to generalized reference in the opening section of "The Love Song of J. Alfred Prufrock," Ashbery's layered voices disguise or dismantle the authoritative focus traditionally located in a central consciousness or in a title. His dissolution of such dramatic entities as voice, or speaker, or protagonist, which we have found to be multiple but discoverable in poems by Auden, also has its parallels in some poems by Frank O'Hara who, according to Ashbery's introduction to *The Collected Poems* of 1971, saw in early Auden something "like a basis for the kind of freedom of expression" O'Hara's poems strive for. (O'Hara's own tribute to this early master is to remember how, when introduced to Auden, "I almost" got sick.)[28]

O'Hara's title "I Love the Way It Goes" is of the kind we have been looking at. It is a stock expression recognizable as a rather vaguely enthusiastic, or mock-gushing, appreciation. Hearing it in a title we expect it to be about the way a poem or perhaps a piece of music "Goes." As the poem itself hilariously unfolds, it layers and eventually collapses into each other voices—quoted directly or indirectly—that would say "I Love the Way It

Goes" about "writing," a "shrub and hedge trimmer," a "ship" named "the *Pleiades*," some (probably weird) sexual act.[29] The collage of the poem makes a composition out of them that is not dramatic, that pastes radically disconnected fragments together into a mock narrative that "Goes" nowhere. The title has a special place in the paste-up because it can fit with any of the other pieces. It has a privileged status not because it has the interpretive authority of a presentation, but because it is a key shape that holds the whole design together. Although the title qualifies as a sentence-sound, its performance as part of the poem is anti-dramatic, making it work more like titles by Ashbery than like either Frost's or Auden's.

Other titles of O'Hara's in the first person are made in the same way out of fragments of colloquial language that evoke special moments, rather than stock situations associated with idioms. "Vincent and I Inaugurate a Movie Theatre" sounds like a joking caption for a snapshot in an album to be shown to friends. "You Are Gorgeous and I'm Coming" has the immediacy of slang and the intimacy of sexual joking, evoking a moment when the "I" feels like saying it to "you" in his own distinctive style of love talk. Each poem is thickly textured with particulars that give a local habitation to the "I" of the title. Because the titles are like the poems colloquial and immediate, evocative of highly particularized situations, they claim not to be presentations to readers but snatches of private talk or scraps of writing never intended to be public. Because the language of the titles is so close to the way we talk, because it catches the rhythms of what we hear every day, and because it is the same language used by the same "I" in the poem, it creates the illusion that we are familiar with the localizing details of the quotidian world inhabited by "I" of title and poem, who is like someone we know.

O'Hara describes this illusion of intimacy in a prose mock statement about his poems titled "Personism: A Manifesto." "Personism," as this parodically hideous title gives away from the start, is the name of a game, played in large part with titles and personal pronouns: "It does not have to do with personality or intimacy, far from it! But to give you a vague idea, one of its minimal aspects is to address itself to one person (other than the poet himself), thus evoking overtones of love . . . and sustaining the poet's feelings towards the poem while preventing love from distracting him into feeling about the person."[30] In the examples we have looked at, the way the poem seems "to address itself to one person" is defined by the title in which "I" says something to someone "(other than the poet himself)" who is also not a reader of the poem. The title therefore denies, or rather pretends to deny, the presentational authority that attaches to its position in the title space. The nature of the pretense is more obliquely than "squarely" described in another passage of the manifesto for "Personism": "It puts the poem squarely between the poet and the person. . . . The poem is at last between two persons instead of two pages. In all modesty, I confess that it may be the death of literature as we know it."[31]

One of O'Hara's first-person titles seems to be of a different kind, to work in a different way: "Why I Am Not a Painter." It is not an idiom from everyday language and, although it is in plain words and word order that could make it part of a spoken sentence, it does not have quite the immediacy of a fragment of intimate speech, what Ashbery calls the "instantaneous quality" typical of O'Hara's poems.[32] Its unspecified address seems at least at first to be more general, in keeping with its slightly more formal, declarative style (by comparison with what would be a typically casual, slangy bit of talk such as *I'm no painter*). For these reasons it occupies the space above the poem less incongruously than the other examples of O'Hara's titles, especially for readers who might hear in it a trace of Jonson's "Why I write not of Love."

The title seems to accept its authority to predict something about what follows. It tells us to expect a distinction between painting and poetry having bearing on the poems of the "I" who chooses the title, understood to be a poet even before the reader has been told that he is in the first line. The title therefore announces that what it presents will be some form of statement about this poet's work, which then turns out to be a casual pretense of an argument contrasting a painter—O'Hara's friend Mike Goldberg—with a poet—"But me?" It is cast as an anecdote in O'Hara's seemingly chatty style, full of local detail about how he spends his days in New York, writing a poem among other ways of passing time. The anecdote opens with a casual visit to the studio of Mike Goldberg, who is beginning to work on a new painting:

> "Sit down and have a drink" he
> says. I drink; we drink. I look
> up. "You have SARDINES in it."
> "Yes, it needed something there."[33]

As the anecdote "is going on" with its unemphatic, repetitious, but gradually forward movement, the poet drops in again on his friend, who has now "finished" the painting:

> "Where's SARDINES?"
> All that's left is just
> letters, "It was too much," Mike says.

Meanwhile the days go by and the poet at home begins to think about

> a color: orange. I write a line
> about orange. Pretty soon it is a
> whole page of words, not lines.

The two examples come together when the prose poem, like Goldberg's painting, is "finished":

> and I haven't mentioned
> orange yet. It's twelve poems, I call
> it ORANGES. And one day in a gallery
> I see Mike's painting, called SARDINES.

The point of convergence is in the relation of the "finished" work to what it is "called": in the label beside the painting, presenting it to the gallery visitor; in the title above the published poem that presents it to the reader. Yet the words Goldberg and O'Hara choose by which to "call" their works actually reveal nothing about them to the public, hide their relevance except from the artists themselves and from friends who have visited Goldberg's private studio while the painting "SARDINES" was in progress, or friends privileged to read this autobiographical account of how O'Hara chose the title for his twelve poems in prose called "ORANGES."

This anecdotal, autobiographical poem therefore blandly explains the inscrutable title of another poem by the same, apparently confiding poet, and in so doing undermines the presentational authority of its own title. It points to the fact that "Why I Am Not a Painter" does not answer the question, which it turns out must have been an intrusive request for some personal, autobiographical revelations by an unwelcome interviewer. The conclusion of the anecdote shows that it does not cast light on the poet's work so much as it implies its ultimately private quality, the core of it that remains unexplained or unexplainable.

Like the mythologized story in "Why I write not of Love," the autobiographical anecdote here both violates and unpredictably fulfills the expectations raised by the title, and in ways as complex and as playful. To summarize, for this poem O'Hara uncharacteristically seems to accept the presentational authority of a title, while in fact the poem is not what it is presented to be. It even tells a story about how titles are not presentational but secretive, at least titles in 1956 (and if this one alludes to Jonson's, then perhaps all titles). They are not clarifications of the "finished" poem for the reader but internal associations, an integral part of the making of the poem, which can no more be explained and which is no less fortuitous than the other ways the person who writes the poem experiences how the days go by. There is no answer to the poem any more than there is an answer to "Why I Am Not a Painter" but a poet. The poem, which seems like an autobiographical confidence, is therefore after all a manifesto, written three years before "Personism," representing how its apparent confidentiality about the "I" recognizable as "Frank O'Hara" ultimately "has nothing to do with personality or intimacy, far from it!"

The year 1956 when O'Hara wrote "Why I Am Not a Painter" was also the year that Allen Ginsberg, having gone back to New York from California just after publishing his first volume, *Howl and Other Poems*, began to read O'Hara's poetry. Between then and O'Hara's death in 1966, they formed a friendship grounded in shared enjoyment of the kind of city living reflected in O'Hara's poems. Ginsberg's account suggests their mutual delight in its day-by-day minutiae: "Frank taught me to really see New York for the first time, by making of the giant style of Midtown his intimate cocktail environment. It's like having Catullus change your view of the Forum in Rome."[34] They also shared literary interests (including admiration for Auden), which heightened their pleasure in the friendship each paid tribute to in a dedication: O'Hara's "Fantasy / *(dedicated to the health of Allen Ginsberg)*," Ginsberg's "My Sad Self / To Frank O'Hara." Because of the connections between them in Ginsberg's earlier years, and because his work has had an important influence on contemporary poetry, Ginsberg's ways of using titles in the first person in his later work can illustrate some new directions that parallel but also diverge from what we have seen to be O'Hara's. Together their first-person titles suggest the values of these grammatical forms for later-twentieth-century poets who were in sympathy even while being profoundly unlike.

Examples of titles using *I* from Ginsberg's volume *White Shroud: Poems 1980–1985* can point to his interests, which many poets writing since the publication of O'Hara's "Personism" share to varying degrees: "Why I Meditate," "I'm a Prisoner of Allen Ginsberg," "Things I Don't Know," "One Morning I Took a Walk in China," "I Love Old Whitman So." These titles have in common general characteristics that can be described in a critical vocabulary largely applicable also to the titles of O'Hara's previously quoted; a vocabulary we can borrow from Ginsberg's own statements about his literary (a term he would reject about himself) values.

The quoted titles conform to what Ginsberg describes as the "first necessity" of his efforts from the beginning to forge a "New Consciousness" in poetry: "to get back to Person, from public to person," and to do so by "recovery of natural tongue, of speech forms that are real rather than literary forms."[35] Although not all familiar idioms, these titles are colloquial, informal, more like what someone would say in personal talk than in a public address, or would write in a private letter or journal rather than in a "literary" presentation. Like the poems they head—four of the five are catalogues—Ginsberg's titles evoke immediate and particular experiences such as he reports to record in the journal he has kept continually since 1946, "very similar to a journal that I published called *Indian Journals*." He celebrates "little fragments" from that private record, by contrast with anything he had unspontaneously "written down or prepared and rhymed and poetised with the idea of writing poetry."[36]

The titles, as well as the poems, aim also for the spontaneous playfulness of such jottings, which Ginsberg finds supremely "interesting poetically" because they are the form of writing that is (among its other qualities) "the goofiest, and strangest and most eccentric and at the same time, most representative, most universal, because most individual, most particular, most specific."[37] Insofar as they achieve this aim, the chosen examples of his titles follow Ginsberg's prescription for the ideal exemplified for him in his favorite poem by William Carlos Williams, "This Is Just to Say": "I think that's one of his greatest exemplary poems, 'cause finally it's where life and poetry are identical, there's no separation."[38]

Of Ginsberg's first-person titles from *White Shroud*, the one that most obviously, and most endearingly, exemplifies these combined characteristics is "I Love Old Whitman So." It is a spontaneous outburst of personal enthusiasm, casually phrased, prompted by an immediate or vividly remembered experience it records in a bit of speech or a little fragment of informal writing. This title is also specially calculated to measure its distance from "literary forms," specifically from traditional poetic tributes. It intentionally violates conventional dedicatory titling of the explicit sort like Algernon Swinburne's "To Walt Whitman in America," or implicit allusive tributes like George Oppen's title "Myself I Sing" (which conflates two of Whitman's own bardic presentations, "Song of Myself" and "One's Self I Sing").

Another example, "One Morning I Took a Walk in China," less obviously embodies the same characteristics. By comparison with a title form like Wordsworth's "An Evening Walk," Ginsberg's is particular, personal, and conversational, but with a playfully eccentric tilt at the end. "China" is a very large space to take a walk in, measurable when we imagine another contrast by supposing the title were "One Morning I Took a Walk in [Midtown]." Of the other chosen examples, the title that would best meet Ginsberg's criterion of "the goofiest" is "I'm a Prisoner of Allen Ginsberg," which introduces a catalogue of grievances against himself—"Who's this politician hypnotized my life," "Why's this guy oblige me to sit / meditating"—enumerating the sorts of comical and incongruous details that fill all the poems.[39] Characteristically they create some absurd effects, for instance in "Things I Don't Know"—"Who killed Roque Dalton? What's the size of U.S. national debt?"—like the fragments pasted together in O'Hara's "I Love the Way It Goes," but with the very significant distinction that they are all details expressive of one personality.[40] The contrast is extreme between O'Hara's collage effect—which works toward dissolving, splitting apart, layering voice or speaker—and Ginsberg's focus on the creation of an identity recognizable by well-known idiosyncrasies or egocentricities of language.

While these characteristics of Ginsberg's titles describable in his own vocabulary are also typical of what we have seen in O'Hara's, more particular concentration on their uses of first-person pronouns will discover large differences. These are defined by the ways the *I* of the title is identified and the connections between that use of the pronoun and the *I* in the poem.

To begin with, Ginsberg's titles typically associate the *I* with well-publicized facts of the poet's own life: in addition to his actual name, his practice of meditating, his Asian travels, his passionate indebtedness to Whitman. These are like the personal data catalogued in the poems, so that the reader is unmistakably directed to recognize the insistent *I* of title and poem as the "Allen Ginsberg" they have heard or read about, whose "life and poetry are identical, there's no separation." This feature distinguishes his titles from O'Hara's (always with partial exceptions made for his exceptional "Why I Am Not a Painter"), which do not themselves locate the first-person speaker in a particular identity. They therefore allow the illusion that we are in the presence of "Frank O'Hara" to emerge from the poem. No formal presentation mediates between us and that presence.

A second related and even more important difference is that Ginsberg's first-person titles do not follow the moves of the game with the poem described in O'Hara's "Personism." That is, they do not address "one person (other than the poet)" as a device for escaping "personality or intimacy." In the examples given, Ginsberg's titles present "Allen Ginsberg" speaking to his audience of readers both in the title and in the poem, characteristically telling intimate details of "the most naked," "the rawest" kind, calculated to "embarrass you"—"you" being both the poet and his readers—chosen because they "are usually the most interesting poetically." The effect is again an illusion that we are in the presence of the actual person "Allen Ginsberg," but as he is baring his personality to us, his readers, in his poem, not as he is talking and writing while the days go by. The title presents the poem as public self-revelation, even though it is phrased in informal language, often using expressions we would hear in intimate conversations. Both title and poem have the status of "little fragments" the poet has culled from the intimacy of his publicly discussed—and partially published—private journals: "So it's almost like if you can catch yourself not writing poetry, but writing down what you're really thinking, actually, you arrive at a genuine piece of writing, of self-expression."[41]

The term "self-expression," by contrast with the rest of Ginsberg's critical vocabulary for his ideal of a poem quoted in this discussion, would be alien to O'Hara's, would be the point at which their parallel directions in poetry radically diverge. Both poets create the illusion of their immediate presence in their poems, of the lack of separation between their actual living selves and the *I* of the poem, but their first-person titles work to define their presence, and therefore the poems, differently. Ginsberg's vigorously claim their presentational function, doubling it by making them the presentation of both the poet and the poem. Title and poem are both forms of "self-expression," public revelations designed to create the illusion of "personality and intimacy." O'Hara's first-person titles, by the ways they appear to deny their presentational authority, are not revelations to the reader but claim the status of talk, jottings, made by "Frank O'Hara" as he goes about what he does while his days go by, *Standing Still and Walking in New York* (the title for his collection of prose pieces) or typing out a poem in an Olivetti store during his lunch hour.[42] In their different ways, though, the first-person titles of both O'Hara and Ginsberg dissolve or bypass traditional dramatic entities—persona, speaker, voice—that were a focus for earlier-twentieth-century poets in their efforts to avoid autobiographical identification with the *I* in their poems.

Part II

INTERPRETIVE FICTIONS

CHAPTER THREE

Who "says" the poem

Titles that refer to the figure who says the poem by the poet's name, by authorial role, or by third-person pronouns bring up issues that are differently charged with meanings in different cultural situations. Whether the actual giver of the title is the poet or someone else doing the work of copyist or editor is a real question only for an intermediary period between the early stages of printing, when assigning a title was a relatively haphazard practice usually carried out by someone not the author, and the time when the title to the poem and therefore the prerogative of titling it became the poet's. Third-person titles of another, more common variety give the words of the poem to a figure they unequivocally declare not to be the poet. This category has also been used since the early period of titling, evoking new responses from readers as different literary systems have evolved and as poets have made such titles work in altered contexts. For various reasons the histories of titles in this category are harder to chart than the traditions of titles using first- or even third-person pronouns.

The most obvious reason is that they are much more often used and more various; there are at least hypothetically no limits to the choice of figures who can be imagined as saying poems. They can be representative human beings identified by generic situation, class, gender, or occupation; figures borrowed from other texts, sacred or profane, or with mythological or conventionally literary names; historical persons; famous or notorious contemporaries; fictional characters with the kinds of names actual people have in recognizable times and locales. Some titles even claim that a nonhuman creature or object speaks in the poem, for instance: "A dialogue betwene the auctour and his eye" from *The Paradise of Daintie Deuises* of 1578; Anne Finch, Countess of Winchelsea's "The Owl Describing her Young Ones"; Padraic Colum's "The Sea Bird to the Wave"; Hardy's "The Aged Newspaper Soliloquizes."

Because of the virtually limitless range of possible identities in this category of third-person title, they can be given to poems of many different kinds. Or to make this point historically, by contrast with the third-person forms discussed earlier, these had many more separate starting points and so came into the traditions of titling by more varied paths, for instance: from the Bible and traditional religious writings of all sorts; from classical texts and their Renaissance presentations; from popular ballads, legends, folktales; from collections of miscellaneous shorter poems; later from the novel, the newspaper, the commercial, the movies. Because of their range and differences of origin, third-person titles of this kind work according to more varied conventions that they follow or violate in more disparate ways. Early examples from Tottel's collection illustrate some of the different ways that titles of this kind present dissimilar figures, referred to by a generic epithet or signature of class; by a literary, historical, or everyday name; by a personal pronoun. They are imagined as saying poems of the same but also of different kinds: "The repentant sinner in durance and aduersitie" and "The ladye praieth the returne of her louer abidyng on the seas" for anonymous poems; "Complaint of the absence of her louer being vpon the sea," attributed to Surrey; Wyatt's "The song of Iopas vnfinished"; "Marcus Catoes comparison of mans life with yron" and "N. Vincent. to G. Blackwood, agaynst wedding," both assigned to Nicholas Grimald.

Beyond the differences among the figures in these titles and among the forms used to refer to them, which of course multiply in later periods, what titles in this category share is the pretense—*explicitly* made but always at least *implicitly* acknowledged as a fiction—that the words of the poem are not the poet's. To illustrate this paradox of at once explicitly pretending and implicitly admitting the pretense, Wyatt's poem can be a simple model to start with. I choose it among the titles just quoted from Tottel's miscellany because it is the only one certain to derive from the poet's own choice. In the Egerton manuscript this poem is virtually alone among a hundred and twenty-four entries in having a title above the text, "Iopas Song," which like the verses is written in Wyatt's own hand. This unique feature suggests that he recognized his only poem spoken by a named figure (other than his prologues to psalms) to occupy a special category for which a formal presentation would be appropriate without opening him to the charge of uncourtly self-presentation.

As "The song of Iopas vnfinished" is printed in Tottel's miscellany, its placing and title give simultaneous and contradictory signals. Coming last in the section ascribed only at its end to "т. vviate *the elder*," it is presented as verses written by him, while the title explicitly claims that it is the song "of" someone with a different kind of name. Because "Iopas" is a figure familiar to readers of the *Aeneid* (as the bard who performs at Dido's feast), his name in the title also tells them that Wyatt has not invented the singer, unlike the title for Surrey's poem presenting the fiction of a lady in the lonely situation of her complaint. Wyatt's title signals that while the singer exists outside the poem in another text, Wyatt has imagined this song for him, elaborating on Virgil's briefer rendering of it. Paradoxically then, the explicitness of the title's separation of singer from author—by the preposition "of" and by their names—constitutes the fiction that must acknowledge its own pretense.

Any title in whatever form involves some element of fiction as it participates in the making of what Sir Philip Sidney calls the "fayned image of Poesie."[1] Still, titles of the category to be discussed here are distinct among other third-person forms in that they unequivocally deny but implicitly, or in rarer instances even explicitly, admit to pretense even as they pretend. This paradox allows such titles to raise special questions about the fictions they enact. While it seems that readers have usually been willing to enter into the pretense of believing in the imagined existence of an *I* who says the poem as if its words were not the author's, titles formulate the paradox in different ways that shape a variety of responses in their readers. Some, as examples will show, even strain the contradictory claims built into these titles so far that they also overstrain our capacity to respond as if we believed in them.

The "supposed" *I*

No title in this category can deny its presentational function or authority, since part of its pretense is to imagine that whoever gives the title acts solely as the maker of it, but not of the verses, which according to the title are in the words of someone else. The titler's only acknowledged work, then, is to introduce the *I* of the poem to the reader, except in a few relatively rare forms—Thomas Carew's "In the person of a Lady to her inconstant servant" is an example—that quite openly admit the poet's presence as both author and titler.

These explicit admissions show up first in titling practices of Carew's generation, when they suited the playful skepticism of mid-seventeenth-century poets toward their own self-conscious conventionality. A more usual formula of the same explicit kind appears in Herrick's "The parting

Verse, or charge to his supposed Wife when he travelled" and in Richard Crashaw's "Wishes. To his (supposed) Mistresse." It is a telling instance of changing assumptions on which titling practices are predicated that before the 1640's, titles did not make such explicit acknowledgments of pretense. In the sixteenth and earlier seventeenth centuries the distinctions between actual poets and their supposed identities or situations were left relatively unarticulated. For this reason, it seems, forms for presenting poems were too inconsistent, if not self-contradictory, on these questions to promote titles like Carew's, or Herrick's and Crashaw's, that explicitly comment on the distinctions involved. A later use of this title form shows how its apparently open admission of pretense loses its authority when it becomes anachronistic in a changed literary situation encouraging to autobiographical interpretation.

Alfred Tennyson in 1830 in *Poems, Chiefly Lyrical* published verses with a title imitating the formula of the earlier titles just cited: "Supposed Confessions of a Secondrate Sensitive Mind not in Unity with Itself."[2] Pointing to the imitation, Christopher Ricks writes: "'Supposed' in order to preclude an autobiographical reading of the poem—as the cleric Richard Crashaw had a poem 'Wishes. To his (supposed) Mistresse.'"[3] The comparison actually goes no farther than the borrowed word *supposed*. For Crashaw's poem, published like Carew's and Herrick's in the 1640's, does not ask the reader to suppose it as spoken by a fictional lover with an imaginary identity to be distinguished from the author of the poem. It presents the poet making verses to conjure up an ideal mistress (recalling Jonson's perfectly formed "creature" in "On Lvcy Covntesse of Bedford"). Like its title, Crashaw's poem itself is playfully but frankly open about its "(supposed)" nature, beginning with "Who ere shee bee" and closing:

> Let her full Glory,
> My fancyes, fly before yee,
> Bee ye my fictions; But her story.[4]

In combination with the fact that by the 1640's poets commonly and often admittedly used third-person pronouns in titles to refer to themselves in their authorial role, Crashaw's parenthetical "(supposed)" acts like a smiling aside to the reader about the conventional "fancyes" and "fictions" at work in both title and poem. Autobiography seems not to be in question.

Tennyson's title, by contrast, actually calls attention to autobiographical possibilities as an issue while apparently trying to forestall it. The title explicitly asks the reader to accept the figure speaking in the poem as a fictional someone distinct from the poet, who distances himself by using the third person in the title and by mocking the maker of the "Confessions" as a "Secondrate Sensitive Mind." The posture of critical distance is called into question by the bitterness and derisive precision of this epithet, which Tennyson's friend Arthur Hallam in a review of the poem calls an "incorrect" portrayal of its "clouded" mood. He also criticizes its "appearance of quaintness," which seems to refer to the borrowing of the title form "Supposed," belonging to earlier understandings of poetic fictions but by the 1830's an anachronism.[5]

The tone of bitterness in the title may be verified by Tennyson's treatment of the poem, which he suppressed after its first publication for more than half a century, even using a legal injunction to prevent its publication by a journal in 1879.[6] Yet the separation attempted in the title between the maker of it and the figure it mocks is not helped by the poem. There is nothing in it to make the confessor a dramatic fiction except the crude device of declaring his mother dead while Tennyson's in fact lived long after 1830. It therefore shows up the design of the epithet to protect the giver of the title from the charges it makes against the *I* of the poem.

This collapse of the "Supposed" distance between poet and *I* is partly an effect of Tennyson's inheritance from Romantic writers who by 1830 had effectively trained readers to expect in many kinds of poetry autobiographical connections between the poet and the figure saying it. Such expectations were very different from those readers had brought to what was admitted as *supposed* in seventeenth-century titles or in the eighteenth century, as in: the title of anonymous verses in *The Agreeable Variety* of 1717, "On Heaven, suppos'd to be written by a Nobleman"; Cowper's "Verses supposed to be written by Alexander Selkirk, During His solitary Abode In the Island of Juan Fernandez"; Philip Freneau's "To Crispin O'Connor, A Back-Woodsman, (Supposed to be written by Hezekiah Salem)"; or Charlotte Turner Smith's sonnets "Supposed to be written by Werther." Yet in spite of what Tennyson's title claims, the text of the poem does not try to distance the *I* who says it from Romantic predecessors, the way Eliot uses the opening comparison made by "J. Alfred Prufrock" of the "evening" to "a patient etherized upon a table" to attempt a surgical separation. Tennyson's "Sensitive Mind" who exclaims "I faint, I fall" in the second line sounds very like the voice crying out "I fall upon the thorns of life! I bleed!" or "I die! I faint! I fail!" in Percy Shelley's "Ode to the West Wind" and "The Indian Serenade." The weakened formula "Supposed" but not the derisively measuring epithet is dropped from Swinburne's title "Last Words of a Seventh-Rate Poet," a parody in which "pennies on" is rhymed with "Tennyson."

Another signal explicitly acknowledging the presence of the poet while supposing an independent figure who says the poem is the choice of preposition in the title. In the earlier period these grammatical signs were commonly confused, or at least hard to read in the light of later critical assump-

tions. Titles in Tottel's miscellany show a representative mix of prepositional clues: "Complaint of a louer rebuked"; "Description of the
contrarious passions in a louer"; "The louer to his bed, with describing of
his vnquiet state." "The song of Iopas vnfinished," unique among titles for
Wyatt's entries in unequivocally separating the supposed speaker from the
actual poet by name as well as preposition, escapes the common confusion.

By the mid–seventeenth century this confusion seems to disappear. An
example is a title for a poem by William Cartwright that in its own way
plays a game about supposing similar to Carew's, or Herrick's and Crashaw's, while further complicating it. The title, "For a young Lord to his
Mistris, who had taught him a Song," introduces a poem built on the fiction
of a lover saying its verses. By the third-person reference to "a young Lord,"
the titler distances himself from the suitor in imitation of editorial titles for
earlier love poems. By adding the preposition "For," the title openly admits
what the conventional form "A young Lord to his Mistris" would pretend
to the contrary: that the words spoken by the lover are not his own. The
poet has written them as a present "For" him, to advance his amorous cause
with verses "For" him to recite.

The title is playful about the literary pretense it exposes, turning it into
the lover's pragmatic deception of the lady. This is a kind of double play.
It even allows the cynical young lord to insinuate to the lady (who hears
only the verses) what the title has told the reader is untrue. In the last line
he hints that he has been "taught" not only to sing the lady's song but to
compose this one: "You, that have taught, may claim my Breath."[7] The
poet, the lover, and the reader are made co-conspirators in the lightly cynical game of seduction, the kind of conspiracy that charges many poems
of this period with their special eroticism. It translates into social or sexual terms the literary game of supposing that the *I* of the poem is not its
author or titler. Special interest in this sort of conspiratorial title in the
mid–seventeenth century may have been excited because this was the period when poets took over the title to be their own titlers.

Interest in titles playing games with the fiction of a supposed *I* revived
in the different cultural situation of poetry at the beginning of the twentieth
century, in response to new concerns about the relation between the voice
in the poem and the poet's. Eliot's finely calculated prepositions in titles are
representative of these preoccupations. His also have special effects that
depend on the self-consciously charted directions of his own poetry in its
own time and on the awareness of them he shaped in his readers.

The preposition in "Rhapsody on a Windy Night" as it appeared in *Prufrock and Other Observations* in 1917 (corrected from its probably mis-
printed form "Rhapsody of a Windy Night" in *Blast II* of 1914) leads us

to expect a traditional poetic voice, inspired to rhapsodize by contemplation of nonhuman nature. This title then clashes violently with the poem, raising the level of discomfort we are made to feel in its displacements of the human first person, grammatically present only in the "I" of lines 8 and 40–41.[8] The interpretive focus that traditionally would be centered in the inspired figure evoked by the title is replaced in the poem by the flatly commanding voice of the street lamp. Both title and text play tricks with the paradox built into third-person titles in this category, which pretend the words of the poem are not by the author of them.

"The Love Song of J. Alfred Prufrock" from the same volume involves the reader in more elaborate games of supposing, but for purposes of comparison with later poems by Eliot we will for the moment look only at the simple structure of the title. The preposition "of" draws an unambiguous grammatical line between the poet and the *I* with a different name (as in "The song of Iopas"). By a pointed shift of preposition in "A Song for Simeon," Eliot later circumvents the paradoxical pretense of this kind of title, in a direct and uncomplicated way making his poem a reverent gift *for* Simeon. It is a presentation made by the author to a figure whose existence is verified in a sacred source outside his imagination and his poem. While the pretense that "The Love Song of J. Alfred Prufrock" is not in the poet's own voice was a necessary fiction for Eliot in his early period, he had moved away from such impersonations by 1928 when he published "A Song for Simeon." The deliberateness of the change in title form is confirmed by the fact that titles for two of his other poems in the series of *Ariel Poems* published between 1927 and 1930 work in the same direction. "Journey of the Magi" uses the familiar title given to traditional renderings of the story, rather than naming the magus as a persona speaking a monologue. The title "Marina" focuses on the symbol of "grace" invoked but nowhere named except in the title of this lyrical incantation, rather than assigning it explicitly to Pericles who chants it. The choice of preposition in "A Song for Simeon" is a quiet declaration of independence from the poetic demands and doctrines of Eliot's early period, guiding readers to his evolving attitudes toward speaker or persona and the changing uses of voice in his poems. The title is a trustworthy interpreter.

Satirical names

Looking now beyond its grammar at more details of Eliot's title "The Love Song of J. Alfred Prufrock," we can consider it in comparison with titles by other poets giving the *I* of the poem similar but not quite the same kinds of name. Titles identifying the first person of the poem by a ridiculous proper name call attention to the poet using the *I* as a fictional target or instrument of satire, bathos, or parody. The compound name including the title of his own clerical office in Swift's "George-Nim-Dan-Dean's Invitation to Mr. Thomas Sheridan" seems to joke about this attention-getting kind of presentation. Tennyson appears to have a double target in the title for a poem written around 1833, "Mechanophilus (In the Time of the First Railways)." It satirizes celebrations of the mechanical age and titles classicizing mundane modern stuff. Other titles call attention to the author making satiric use of the *I* of the poem by inventing an absurd proper name out of an ordinary word or compound with comic possibilities of sound and meaning. Swift does this in "Clever Tom Clinch going to be hanged," but these titles became more common in the nineteenth and earlier twentieth centuries as the influence of novels on the conventions of titling grew stronger. Some examples are: Tennyson's "Will Waterproof's Lyrical Monologue"; Browning's "Mr. Sludge 'The Medium'"; John Davidson's "The Testament of Sir Simon Simplex Concerning Automobilism" (a satiric response to "Mechanophilus"); Stevens's "Peter Parasol"; *Alfred Venison's Poems* by Pound. It is in the context of these poems, where it does and does not belong, that we can look again at Eliot's much discussed title.

The reader is first introduced to the famous name in the presentation of the volume, *Prufrock and Other Observations*. There its status is as a title for one of the poems, besides being someone's name. As it next appears above the opening poem, "Prufrock" strikes us less as if it were the title of a poem than as if it were the name of a person singing this one. Since the poem is a "Love Song," scarcely a type noted for objective investigation or disinterested wisdom, then insofar as it qualifies as one of the volume's *Observations*, the song itself or the singing of it must be what is observed. That is, someone is making observations of or on "J. Alfred Prufrock" singing his "Love Song," presumably Mr. T. S. Eliot, whose name is the only other one on the title page. The juxtaposed titles of volume and poem position him apart from the *I* who sings the love song.

If the title were "Prufrock's Love Song," the name would predict its bearer to be a vehicle for comic observations because, as Christopher Ricks says, its silly sounding name contains "not only the play of 'frock' against 'pru'—prudent, prudish, prurient—but also the suggestive contrariety between splitting the name there, at *pru* and *frock*, as against splitting it as *proof* and *rock*."[9] Then the name could evoke responses very like those we have to the name of the singer in Tennyson's title "Will Waterproof's Lyrical Monologue." It may or may not be that Eliot had this title consciously in mind as he says he had the title of Kipling's "The Love Song of Har Dyal," or unconsciously, as Hugh Kenner tells us Eliot admitted that he may have retained the name of Prufrock-Littau, furniture wholesalers who advertised in St. Louis in his youth.[10] Still, a comparison with Tennyson's title helps to define the much more interesting effects of Eliot's.

The name "Waterproof" is made out of a word or compound like many of Dickens's names for characters, for instance "Pecksniff" (borrowed by Stevens in his heading "Pecksniffia" for a group of poems that included "Peter Parasol").[11] Since *waterproof* is a compound word formed to describe something that keeps water out, Tennyson's choice of it as the name for a singer located—first by the subtitle "Made at the Cock"—in a tavern is obviously satirical. "Will" adds, besides its alliterative sound, some vague associations with the atmosphere of Elizabethan taverns made familiar by Shakespeare (who uses the name "Will" as a punning word in his sonnets and whose surname, Eliot is likely to have noticed, is formed out of words: *shake* and *spear* or *shakes* and *peer* or *pear*).[12] These evocations are suited to a poem that makes poets, their poems, and their critics the targets of its satire and parody. Bathos is added to Tennyson's title by the generic clash in "Lyrical Monologue" (possibly recalling the earlier coinage of "Lyrical Ballads") for the boozy song of a poet with an absurd name. Tennyson's intentions are so clearly signaled in the title that it raises no questions about the fictional *I* of the poem or his relation to his inventor.

Because "Prufrock" is not quite a word (as are "Waterproof," "Sludge," "Parasol," "Venison"), and especially because it is the surname of someone who has chosen to present himself—as it were in life, before the titler introduces him to us—using the form "J. Alfred," Eliot plays a very different game. He makes it possible for us to join him in pretending belief in the actuality of this person because the formal introduction of him by name is detailed to make it socially accurate, setting it in what Pound calls "modern life," in the "discouragingly 'unpoetic' modern surroundings" that distinguish Eliot's personae from his own.[13] The name places the *I* in time and milieu as real people are—initials seem to have been used in that fashion first among the middle class in both England and America in the later nineteenth century—so that we can be seduced into further speculation, say, about the sort of parents who would choose for their son the middle name "Alfred." A socially plausible answer (since the volume was published in London), that Mr. and Mrs. Prufrock's aspirations to genteel taste in poetry led them to give their baby the name of the poet laureate, ignores the fact we are told on the title page that the choice of name is made by Mr. T. S. Eliot.

Tricking us into such speculation, the title unsettles the expectations it also raises. The name of the first person in the poem is like names made out of funny words and compounds in titles for satirical poems, but unlike them it is not an unequivocally made-up name. Though it is clearly manipulated in its pompous style of presentation, owners of actual names, including many poets, have been known to do that in their own lives. The author named on the title page as Mr. T. S. Eliot (possibly imitating the style of T. E. Hulme) is the same person who signed some philosophical pieces of this period as "T. Stearns Eliot" (then perhaps copying the poet T[homas]. Sturge Moore, brother of the philosopher G. E. Moore). Poets of the period also liked to give themselves comic pseudonyms, as Stevens early signed himself "Peter Parasol," or sillier still, "Carol More."[14]

The name "Alfred" for the singer of a post-Victorian poem is also open to the suspicion of being a satirical choice, but Eliot cannot be caught in that act since he scrupulously avoids even a much less crude combination than Pound's *Alfred Venison*. Quite possibly his speaker's middle name is a way of involving Tennyson in his poem about the attenuation of later-nineteenth-century Romanticism, as Arnold is implicated by the allusion to "The Forsaken Merman" in the closing lines or Browning, perhaps, in all the "Talking of Michelangelo." Yet the name is not uncommon, possibly even a likely choice of parents with a German family name, and besides, "Pru*fr*ock" echoes the sound of "Al*fr*ed."

Altogether we cannot be secure about what Eliot's choice of name is up to. What we can be sure of is that he does not give us clear interpretive signals in his title about how to read what it presents as "The Love Song of J. Alfred Prufrock." For the poem turns out to have in place of a beloved only a disappearing "you," and instead of a satirical mouthpiece as its speaker an "I" in a complicated, evasive, obscure relation to the poet named on the title page as the author, or rather the detached viewer and wise commentator, of *Prufrock and Other Observations*.

Pastoral names

Other forms for titles giving the poem to a figure not its author admit the presence of the poet by less direct or less obviously attention-getting means than the types so far explored. Among the most common are titles that place the first person of the poem in a generic fiction, a design clearly illustrated by the epistle and the dialogue. Some titles for those types name the kind as well as the *I*: Samuel Daniel's "A Letter from Octauia to Marcus Antonius," Francis Quarles's "A Dialogue, betweene Gabriel and Mary." Others allude to it by pairing names associated with the genre: William Drummond's "Lavra to Petrarch," Alexander Pope's "Eloisa to Abelard," Tennyson's "Hero to Leander" for epistles; for dialogues, Daniel's "Ulisses and the Syren," Sir William Davenant's "The Philosopher and the Lover to a Mistress dying," Yeats's "The Man and the Echo." Titles for these genres present the reader with two figures in an exchange that excludes the presence of the poet. At the same time that presence is evoked by the formulaic character of the presentations, which offer decoded readings of the titles: *Pope's Imitation of Ovid's Heroides in an Epistle of Eloisa to Abelard*; or *Daniel's Contest Between Honor and Pleasure in a Dialogue Between Ulysses and the Siren*.

To some degree any title by naming or alluding to a traditional kind works in this way, but the evocation of the poet's presence is stronger as the titling conventions are more formulaic, or when the *I* of the poem has an identity or is in a situation that makes the generic signal of the title especially artificial. Pope's "Ode: The Dying Christian to His Soul" announces itself as casting in a classically formal, public poem the unspoken words of someone in an intensely private moment. The juxtaposition of kind and situation, made here without tension or embarrassment, puts more emphasis on the poet's presence as performer than the title given John Davies's "A Sinners acknowledgement of his Vilenesse and Mutabilitie," since "acknowledgement" does not name a literary form chosen by the poet to shape what he gives the sinner to say. The very different traditions of pastoral poems and ballads can illustrate in other ways how generic signals in titles direct attention toward or away from the unacknowledged presence of the poet in a poem said to be the words of someone else.

The generic references in titles to the singers of pastoral poems—the shepherds, goatherds, mowers, reapers, ploughmen, milkmaids, shepherdesses or nymphs—focus attention on the poet's performance in a special way. When titles give these figures names, they are the same as or like the ones used for the prototypical singers in the idylls of Theocritus, or rather more often they imitate Virgil's names in his eclogues as he imitates Theocritus. Sometimes pastoral titles copy allusive naming in other ways: Sidney invents the name *Astrophil* to encode his own in a classical form; Spenser transfers borrowed naming into the vernacular and translates the French "Colin" from Clement Marot for his own English pseudonym, "Colin Clout."

Titles imitating each other in their repetition of fictional names copied from earlier poems trace the traditional pattern for pastoral poetry as it flourished in England in the sixteenth, seventeenth, and eighteenth centuries. Pope, who acknowledges "*Theocritus* and *Virgil*, (the only undisputed authors of Pastoral)," copies from Virgil's eighth eclogue and its other borrowers the name for one of the speakers in his "Spring, The First Pastoral, or Damon."[15] Ambrose Philips, whose rival claim is that "*Theocritus, Virgil*, and *Spenser* are the only Poets, who seem to have hit upon the true Nature of Pastoral Compositions," shows his partisan preference in borrowings like "Hobbinol" and "Cuddy" to name singers in his pastorals.[16] Three examples can show how poets have used the signals encoded in pastoral titles to exploit the pretense of separating the fictional figure who says the poem from the maker of it or of its title.

A poem by Christopher Marlowe printed in 1600 in a miscellany of pastoral verse, *Englands Helicon*, was there given the title "The passionate Sheepheard to his loue." It seems to have been the most admired pastoral song of the sixteenth and seventeenth centuries, judging by how often it appeared in print and manuscript, the many versions of it in circulation, the number of allusions and answer-poems responding to it. Admiration for its radiant and graceful presentation of the poet transparently disguised as the shepherd is easily understandable, but an added reason for its appeal may be that it is a perfect paradigm of that convention. Milton, among other poets who responded to it, uses it as such an archetype to define his own transformed versions of pastoral.

The traditional form of the title for Marlowe's poem as it is printed in *Englands Helicon* gives the *I* of the poem an identity then reflected in some details of his song and precluded by others.[17] "The passionate Sheepheard" offers his "loue" the delights that nature yields in its generic variety of landscapes. His presents to her are partly "made" out of the abundance within reach in the abode of shepherds, allowing his participation in their rural life. Even so, the rustic materials he makes into tempting gifts—"Mirtle," "Iuie," "straw," "wooll"—are opulently embroidered or buckled with "purest gold," "Corall clasps and Amber studs," becoming versions of courtly garments. Working more pointedly against inclusion of the *I* among the shepherds are his references to them, distanced in the third person like the titler's presentation of him: "And wee will sit vpon the Rocks, / Seeing the Sheepheards feede theyr flocks." Here the singer arranges himself and his love in the privileged place of a courtly audience for the rustic scene, a kind of masque in which "The Sheepheards swaines shall dance & sing" for their entertainment. His only move toward explicitly presenting himself in the role given him by the titler is also the most exaggeratedly stylized and most playful gesture in the poem. He will give his love "A gowne made of the finest wooll, / Which from our pretty Lambes we pull." As these lines picture willing nature yielding the pelts already spun and woven as if by magic into a lady's fine gown, they smilingly transform the sweaty work of shearing, the monotony of spinning and weaving, into one seamlessly artful motion. These lines and others in the catalogue of "made" gifts act out what the poem does in transforming nature into pastoral: "And I will make thee beds of Roses, / And a thousand fragrant poesies."

What this shepherd will "make"—and *maker* is among preferred sixteenth-century terms for *poet*—are beds of rose petals to lie on but also ornamental flower beds. The poet as gardener is a favorite trope, "poesies" a frequent pun on *poesy* and also a minor type of verse. His poem, then, is the singer's last and best gift, containing all the other "delights thy minde may moue," and to move or teach and delight is the true excellence of poetry. Marlowe's song is the quintessential pastoral poem in its celebration of its own conventionality. It is an elaborately simple, sensuous, and passionate game about the fiction of the *I* as shepherd, which it acknowledges to be a costume, not a disguise, for the poet to dress up in for his performance.

The title of Marvell's "Damon the Mower" also makes a display of its conventionality: the reaper in Theocritus's tenth idyll, the "Damon" of Virgil's eighth eclogue, and all imitations of them, stand behind it. It presents the "I" of the poem as a purely fictitious figure; "Damon" is not truly a proper name but a code word for the poet costumed as a rustic. The figure using the first person in the poem, by the recognized rules of the game announced in the title, is wholly the creature of its maker, who has chosen the name "Damon" for his fiction precisely as a signal for what game he is playing.

Marvell then sets it up with a framing first stanza inviting the reader to "Heark how the Mower *Damon* Sung," but this "*Damon*" will not play by the rules. He is aggressively boastful of his own identity: "I am the Mower *Damon*, known / Through all the Meadows I have mown."[18] Casting himself in the role of hero, he pits his own "hot desires" against the heat of the sun; disdains the rivalry of "the piping Shepherd stock"; refuses to be scorned by the "fair Shepheardess" who rejects his "Presents" that, following the same model as Marlowe's catalogue, include the songs "I tune my self to sing."

After eight stanzas of Damon's heroic posturing, the author who presents him in the title and first lines returns to the controlling device of a frame, which conventionally contains the speech of the *I* in the poem within the third-person commentary of its introductory and concluding stanzas. Describing in mock-heroic language how Damon flails about, "Depopulating all the Ground" with his scythe, the poet cuts him down to size:

> The edged Stele by careless chance
> Did into his own Ankle glance;
> And there among the Grass fell down,
> By his own Sythe, the Mower mown.

Following the rules of the game defined by the title, this ought to be the end of the poem and therefore of Damon's fictitious existence, over which the poet in the last two lines here speaks what sounds like a sententious epitaph. Yet this unsportsmanlike Damon will not be put down, silenced, killed off, but pops up again like Falstaff after Hal has said a farewell over his supposed corpse:

> Alas! said He, these hurts are slight
> To those that dye by Loves despight.
> With Shepherds-purse, and Clowns-all-heal
> The Blood I stanch, and Wound I seal.
> Only for him no Cure is found,
> Whom *Julianas* Eyes do wound.
> 'Tis death alone that this must do:
> For Death thou art a Mower too.

Refusing to be the poet's creature, Damon becomes his own author and titler, referring to himself in the third person—"for him no Cure is found"—and pronouncing his own epitaph in another sententious couplet that this time really is the end of the verses in which he has the last word. Marvell's poem, undermining the expectations raised by its title, collapses the convention brilliantly exploited by Marlowe of the *I* in pastoral as a poet performing in the costume of a rustic.

Milton, holding up Marlowe's song as a model in that tradition, makes a place in it entirely his own in "L'Allegro" and "Il Penseroso." His first move in this direction is his choice of titles, which have no precedents in earlier pastoral or any other English verse.[19] The unfamiliar language and form of these titles do not give the usual signals about the *I* we will hear in the poem. The Italian nouns do not work like "The passionate Sheepheard" or "*Damon*" to introduce figures made familiar by other poems and do not comfortably translate into an English epithet, by contrast with a title like Giovanni Battista Guarini's *Il Pastor Fido*, known in England in numerous translations. They are more like words for moods or ways of experiencing, though not quite the abstractions they would be without the article (as the term *allegro* names a category of musical composition). They therefore invite the question ruled out by the conventions of generic naming in titles: *how is the I to be identified in these poems?*

In "L'Allegro," placed first of the pair by Milton in his *Poems* of 1645, the answer to the question prompted by the title is buried in the grammar of the poem. Personal pronouns, and especially *I*, are suppressed as elaborately as we have seen in poems by Ashbery. The nominative surfaces only twice in "L'Allegro," for the first time not until line 37, which is part of the four-line closing of the invocation. Here "I" is linked with the first mention also of "me":

> And if I give thee honour due,
> Mirth, admit me of thy crue
> To live with her, and live with thee,
> In unreproved pleasures free.[20]

Since the lines following contain only one other personal pronoun—"And at my window bid good morrow"—the *I* disappears in a procession

of infinitives—"To hear," "to com"—and present participles—"list'ning,"
"walking"—that is followed by a catalogue of nouns naming generic pastoral figures: "the Plowman," "the Milkmaid," "the Mower," "every Shepherd." Unlike the unlocated "I," these rustics are placed spatially—"neer,"
"Under"—and in time, as the active subjects of verbs in the present tense,
while the "I" has been supplanted by verb forms without subject or tense. A
contrast is set up between the generic figures, who are those conventionally
named in titles as the singers of pastoral songs, and the almost impersonal
utterance of this poem, where the "Shepherd tells his tale" only as a figure
in a catalogue, and one that has no source except the poem itself, no identifiable singer who recites it. The nominative pronoun "I" emerges once
more, with added prominence for having been absent, in the closing couplet
("me" also surfaces one more time, the possessive only twice in all): "These
delights, if thou canst give, / Mirth with thee, I mean to live."

The two couplets in the first-person nominative frame Milton's lines as
an answer-poem to Marlowe's "Come liue with mee, and be my loue,"
which itself has a similar framing structure, moving from that opening line
to a transformed version of it at the end of the poem: "If these delights thy
minde may moue, / Then liue with mee, and be my loue." In "L'Allegro,"
which is cast as a reply to Marlowe's invitation, the grammar of the poem
takes the place, as it were, of the poet performing in the costume of the
"passionate Sheepheard." Here the "I" is present between lines 37 and 152
only as "mine eye," an instrument recording what "it measures," "it sees":
"Such sights as youthful poets dream." The nearly abstract title "L'Allegro"
matches the nearly anonymous grammar of the poem.[21]

"Il Penseroso" follows the same outline by delaying the entrance of the
"I" of the poem, here until line 64, and emphatically asserting its presence
in a final couplet that again rewrites the ending of Marlowe's song: "These
pleasures *Melancholy* give, / And I·with thee will choose to live."[22] Here
also a contrast is set up between the "I" of the poem and the poets performing in other pastorals, for whom Marlowe's "Sheepheard" is the perfect model. Within this outline the second poem departs from the design
of "L'Allegro" by allowing the "I," once introduced, to move steadily into
the foreground of the poem. A crude count of first-person pronouns can
show this difference: "I" appears only twice in the whole of "L'Allegro" but
seven times in the later lines of "Il Penseroso," which extend twenty-four
lines beyond the length of the first poem. The pronoun "me" is used four
times, the possessive five in this later part. Because the movements of the
two poems are otherwise carefully paralleled, the emerging first-person
presence is a pointed development. It seems that the "eye" of the first poem
comes into an identity that, though still experiencing "Such sights as youthful Poets dream" in pastoral verses, allows him to envision a different poetic
future that will "bring all Heav'n before mine eyes." Out of the nearly anon-

ymous grammar of "L'Allegro" and the earlier third of "Il Penseroso," the poet emerges using the first person to predict how "old experience" gained in the apprenticeship of pastoral will be transformed into a new "Prophetic strain" of poetry.

The movement here from anonymity to a poetic identity in the first person is a foreshadowing of the pattern traced in "Lycidas," where the "I" of the elegy is transformed at the end into "he," "the uncouth swain," by the distanced perspective of his older poetic self. The paired poems (which Milton's volume of 1645 prints in an earlier position than the elegy) and "Lycidas," in their parallel but distinct ways, represent stages in the growth of the poet finding an identity by working with and away from the richly conventional figure of the "passionate Sheepheard" as the poet in pastoral costume. The earlier stages are personified in the not quite abstract titles of "L'Allegro" and "Il Penseroso," naming figures that are not quite fictional versions of the poet.

The allusive repetition in titles of the names and epithets referring to the figures using *I* in pastoral poems defines their special effects among third-person title forms. It insists on the purely fictitious character of the singers in these poems; the nymphs and shepherds, Phyllises and Damons in the titles are the choices of poets or editors, culled from a large company of other poems. Since the epithets and names refer to so many places where they or others like them have already been given to pastoral figures, they actually point more to their own conventionality than to the particular identity of the *I* saying the poem. In doing so, they focus on the poet whose presence they formally deny. At the farthest extreme from them are the workings of ballad titles, because the conventions of the ballad tend to suppress attention to the poet's performance.

Ballad names

Early ballads of many sorts have anonymous origins, for instance in ancient legends or distant events, or in the public domain of village gossip and tavern talk. Later imitations of these ballads try in various ways to appropriate the authority of their anonymous beginnings, freeing the figures speaking in them from the imaginative needs of individual poets. Wordsworth seems to work for this effect in "The Armenian Lady's Love," which introduces the *I* of the poem as a ballad heroine:

> You have heard 'a Spanish Lady
>   How she wooed an Englishman;'
> Hear now of a fair Armenian.[23]

"You have heard" assumes that readers of this ballad have listened to other old stories recited by ballad singers who pass them on from generation to generation, and to drive home the point there is even a footnote to "that fine old ballad, 'The Spanish Lady's Love,' " which had been recovered for Wordsworth's generation in Thomas Percy's collection, *Reliques of Ancient English Poetry*, first published in 1765. The allusion and note associate the singer we hear in the framing lines that introduce the "fair Armenian" with bards who repeat old stories not of their own invention. The association distances this singer also from the lady whose words he brings to us only as an instrument, not as their maker. The title, copying Percy's form, identifies the poem as an antiquarian's find, a rediscovered relic from antiquity presented to modern readers. Coleridge seems to aim for this effect by the pseudo-archaic spelling of the title "The Rime of the Ancyent Marinere" in the first printed version of it in the 1798 edition of *Lyrical Ballads, With A Few Other Poems*. The generic title of this volume may also have been designed in part to suggest anonymous origins in antiquity for the poems, and no authors' names appear on the title page.

Borrowed names are the most common generic feature in titles for imitations of popular ballads. By contrast with pastoral names, they present the poems as expressions of local cultures more than as the fictions of poets. To illustrate the difference, the singer of a poem in *Englands Helicon* is not named except in its title, "*Melisea* her Song, in scorne of her Sheepheard *Narcissus*," nor would readers be likely to have heard of her from some well-known particular literary source. Yet we would be breaking the rules of the game to ask *who is Melisea?* The form of her name alone would tell us all we need to know about her: that she is a nymph or shepherdess, who exists as the instrument for the poet's performance in the kind of song he writes under the name he has presumably borrowed from other poems.

The figure we hear in Wordsworth's "The Affliction of Margaret————" is also named only in the title, and is also unknown to us from a prior literary context. Since her name gives a signal special to the conventions of the ballad, the title again precludes the question *who is Margaret?* "Margaret" is a common traditional English name; it could be the name of any ordinary woman. Still, someone knows her and has heard the story of her "Affliction," her own humble tale of old, unhappy, far-off things that were once familiar matter of today to bards who first repeated her story. The everyday proper name "Margaret" (in manuscript "Mary"), along with the dash that purports to suppress her surname ("*Melisea*" would not have one), authenticates her existence and her natural sorrow, loss, or pain outside the poem, as it were, directing attention to its roots more than to the performance of the poet as the maker of it.

Other sorts of names in ballad titles work in the same direction. Robert Burns uses regional names of actual people in "McPherson's Farewell" and "Strathallan's Lament," and Yeats imitates such proper names in the title "John Kinsella's Lament for Mrs. Mary Moore." Their homely particularity makes them seem familiar, their owners a subject of tavern talk. Yeats's speaker is identified as if we had heard of him because he is locally notorious as a bawdy old lover, not solely because he is a conventional vehicle for the poet's performance, like the speaker of "Olde *Damons* Pastorall" in *Englands Helicon.*

Yeats's titles calling the voice in some poems "Crazy Jane" in a different way also create the illusion that their source is in local culture, as if the poet were merely their titler or transmitter rather than their maker and performer. "Crazy Jane" (originally "Cracked Mary") sounds like her village epithet, the way her neighbors speak of her, not a literary epithet—contrast it with Christopher Smart's "The Fair Recluse"—and not a poet's interpretive title like Yeats's "A Crazed Girl." The heading Yeats gives to the group beginning with seven "Crazy Jane" poems seems to joke about this pretense of the poet's disengagement from them. He presents them as "Words For Music Perhaps," as if the poet had found them, collected and titled them, but could not be sure of their origins and intentions, did not quite know how to take them.

The opening poem of the group, "Crazy Jane and the Bishop," can show in more detail Yeats's uses of ballad titling to initiate the illusion of a poem that seems anonymous in origin, bringing us age-old matter transmitted, not performed, by the poet. What works most powerfully to create this illusion is what is not said, either in the title or the poem. The title pretends we have heard of "Crazy Jane," that we recognize her name from village talk (not only as a literary type of God's fool), and that we therefore know who the "Bishop" is in her story.[24] She in turn takes for granted that her hearers are of the locale, since we know the way to "the blasted oak" and therefore have listened to old gossip about her trysts there with "Jack the Journeyman" (another village epithet). The matter of the poem therefore seems to originate in local history it does not tell us because, according to the fiction set up in the title that pretends to name a nonfictional person, we already know it before the titler presents "Crazy Jane" retelling her own version of it.

Also unexplained in the poem is the mysterious, parenthetical refrain "(*All find safety in the tomb.*),"which interrupts the grammar of each stanza. This is not the way refrains usually work in ballads. The conventional form is more nearly approximated in the other repeated line of the poem, "*The solid man and the cockscomb,*" which completes the grammar of each stanza in the speaker's own voice, commenting on her own story. By contrast, the parenthetical line is a sentence unto itself, and a sententious truism, which comes as if from nowhere, perhaps as if its source were deep in folk wisdom or—since its appositeness in each stanza is ambiguous— in folk superstition. Because the sentences of "Crazy Jane" continue uninterrupted around it, she seems not to hear or notice it, enlarging the possibility that it is unspoken utterance from some unlocatable depths. It is certainly not the same casually amused modern voice that calls the group of poems "Words For Music Perhaps," and not the titler's echoing village talk about "Crazy Jane and the Bishop." It therefore contributes to the fiction that the poem comes to us from a remote source, beyond our knowing or the poet's.

Proper names

Poets in the nineteenth century were attracted to a new kind of title, different from pastoral forms but also giving the *I* of the poem a name borrowed from ancient literary sources. Tennyson's (and Swinburne's) "Tiresias," his "Ulysses," Browning's "Ixion" illustrate the type. Since they share some obvious features with names conventional to pastoral titles, how they are unlike can show up more sharply the differences in effect in their pretense that the named speaker of the verses is not the poet who gives the title.

The way pastoral naming is woven into an intricate net of allusive repetitions, the names are treated as purely fictitious and therefore easily interchangeable, which proper names are not. In most instances the same shepherd can as well be called *Corydon* as *Damon*, *Tityrus*, or *Narcissus*. "Astrophell," Sidney's pastoral pseudonym encoding his own actual first name, is also used in *Englands Helicon* for the singer of a poem attributed there to Nicholas Breton. Each name focuses attention on the poet performing in pastoral costume under what is not a proper name but a name of an appropriate type, so that titles using them put little pressure behind their formal claim that the singer of the poem is not the author.

The nineteenth-century titles "Tiresias," "Ulysses," "Ixion" work differently though they also cite names for the figures saying the poems, who have multiple literary sources. One reason these titles have other effects is that they consist of names not in the pastoral network (unlike the names still used in the nineteenth century as titles for tributes to dead poets, like Shelley's "Adonais," an elegy on Keats, and Arnold's "Thyrsis," a monody on Clough). Not being conventional to pastoral, they do not signal us to think of them as names for the poet in transparent disguise. Another reason is that the poems treat the figures named as if they were not literary fictions but people who actually lived, so that they invite us to think of the titles as having the status of proper names claiming the independent identity of the *I* in the poem, which it is interested in maintaining. In this respect they are unlike pastoral titles but very close in their workings to another kind that interested the same poets: Tennyson's "Columbus" and "St. Simeon Stylites," Browning's "Cleon" and "Fra Lippo Lippi" are examples of titles calling the *I* of the poem by the proper name of an actual historical figure.

Typically, nineteenth-century titles of this kind consist only of the name (unlike "Iopas Song"), which focuses them on the figure who says the poem and on the title's status as a proper name. It suppresses identification of the *I* with the poet's performance, or of the poem as that performance in a recognizable literary kind. When detail is added to the name, as in the full presentation of Browning's "Abt Vogler (After He Has Been Extemporizing Upon the Musical Instrument of his Invention)," it more firmly places or characterizes the figure we hear in the poem, widening his separation from the poet. The effect is like that of the final title for the poem originally called "The Tomb at St. Praxed's," which Browning revised as "The Bishop Orders His Tomb at St. Praxed's Church" to focus it on the speaker it particularizes: that one bishop, not a representative cleric, and not a poet. The title places the *I* of the poem as that one bishop speaking to someone on a special occasion, not shaping his speech into a generic form of verse like a ballad, a pastoral song, an epistle, an ode.

Such titles allow possibilities attractive to poets of this period. Most obviously, by their emphasis on the independent existence of the *I* in the poem from the author, they challenge the authority of autobiographical readings such as seem to have provoked Tennyson to suppress his "Supposed Confessions of a Secondrate Sensitive Mind" and Browning his first publication, *Pauline*, printed anonymously in 1833 with the subtitle "A Fragment of a Confession."

Tennyson thwarts what he calls the "absurd tendency to personalities" of "almost all modern criticism" in titles like "Ulysses," although elsewhere he admitted privately to have included "more of himself" in the poem than it or its title acknowledge.[25] Browning uses not only the titles of poems but the titles of volumes and their prefaces, or poems placed in them as prologues or epilogues, to hold off identifications of himself with the figures named in the titles. The advertisement to *Dramatic Lyrics*, published in 1842, describes the volume in terms Hardy later adopts from Browning for the prefaces of his quoted in Chapter 1: "Such Poems as the following come properly enough, I suppose, under the head of 'Dramatic Pieces'; being, though for the most part Lyric in expression, always Dramatic in principle, and so many utterances of so many imaginary persons, not mine."[26] Browning's own model for the leap the title of this volume takes over generic barriers may have been *Lyrical Ballads*. His later *Dramatic Romances*, *Dramatic Idyls*, and *Dramatis Personae* drive home the same point.

The volume published in 1855 with the still bolder title *Men and Women* emphasizes dramatic characterization even more strongly. The final poem, dedicated "To E.B.B." with the title "The Last Word," later changed to the more intimate spoken phrase "One Word More," acts as epilogue and manifesto. The poem opens with Browning presenting the book to his wife, imagined as a private moment between them taking place outside the covers of the volume: "There they are, my fifty men and women / Naming me the fifty poems finished!"[27] These are figures named in the titles of the poems they speak, whom he sets apart from his own "person" intimately saying this "One Word More" to his wife:

> Love, you saw me gather men and women,
> Live or dead or fashioned by my fancy,
> Enter each and all, and use their service,
> Speak from every mouth, — the speech, a poem.
>   . . .
> Let me speak this once in my true person,
> Not as Lippo, Roland or Andrea.

What Browning's presentational devices show is that poems of this kind, besides fending off autobiographical readings of them as confessions, at the same time open an escape from other generic categorizing. If what is spoken "from every mouth" is—and Browning's wording is meticulous on this point—"the speech, a poem"—then it takes its form from the character of the speaker, past experiences and present circumstances, occasion, listener, all of which inform the moment of speaking and therefore the shape of the speech. Contrasts would be with Pope's "Ode: The Dying Christian to His Soul" or Wordsworth's "The Complaint of a Forsaken Indian Woman." Since these like all title presentations precede the poems, they predict features that they announce are predetermined by the poet and that acknowledge other poems as generic models for this "Ode" or this "Complaint." Titles that merely give a proper name or add details that further support its status *as* a proper name do not make the same predictions. Even "Ulysses," which presents a poem having something to do with heroic adventure, does not raise more particular expectations than that, in contrast with Daniel's title "Ulisses and the Syren," which predicts the form of an allegorical dialogue.

We can use "Ulysses" to explore more fully the freedom from established literary kinds allowed to poems with this form of title. Tennyson's presents what follows as the speech of a hero known to all his readers but, as is often true of poems of this kind, the poem enters his story long after his recorded epic actions. It therefore treats him as an actual person like Columbus, with a personal history extending beyond what we know from literary sources, but not like Allen Tate's "Aeneas at Washington," who is a legendary hero transported into the unheroic twentieth century. For this poem Tennyson had a literary model for imagining the hero's story after the *Odyssey* is over in Dante's *Inferno* xxvi, but as Robert Langbaum points out, Ulysses' old age "is incidental" to Dante's version, crucial to Tennyson's.[28] Tennyson gives the same structure to several poems of this kind: the figures of "Ulysses," "Tiresias," "Columbus" all speak as weary old men looking back from a diminished present at their famous pasts. This pattern begins in the titles, which free the poems from kinds associated with celebrations of heroism, making them seem to be shaped instead to the pressures brought to bear by the present circumstances of the speaking figure and by the responses of his fictional listener.

The freedom achieved in this way of titling and shaping his materials opened for Tennyson another possibility allowed by the titles for this kind of poem: the impersonation of character in greater psychological detail. Something like this intention is implied by his son in *Alfred Lord Tennyson: A Memoir* when he describes these poems: "He purposely chose those classical subjects from mythology and legend, which had been before but imperfectly treated, or of which the stories were slight, so that he might have free scope for his imagination."[29] A result, Hallam Tennyson recognizes, is that a "modern feeling was to some extent introduced into the themes" by the encouragement these treatments gave to particularity of detail (here the relevant nineteenth-century sense of "modern").

Browning's poems spoken by figures whose names constitute their titles are more often historical than mythological. They circumvent generic expectations as well as autobiographical readings mainly by inventing and elaborating on specific settings and occasions in copious atmospheric detail. This shapes the speech of the *I* whose character is at the same time dramatized by his response to the place and occasion. In doing this the poems also make the most of the opportunity for the exploration of particularities. In Browning's work the circumstances that give rise to the speech of his "men and women" are epitomized by what "Fra Lippo Lippi" calls "a string of pictures of the world."[30] The details that fill these "pictures" are of course the very particulars that fill this and other similar poems by Browning. Because of their dramatic immediacy, because the language to describe them is often casual and colloquial, they are, like Tennyson's characterizations, infused with a "modern feeling" that coexists with their detailed evocation of an imagined past. "Fra Lippo Lippi," fully embodying these features, is a manifesto for this kind of nineteenth-century dramatic poem, in the way the painter's descriptions of his "pictures of the world" are made analogies for the manner and matter of the poem itself and of the volume *Men and Women*. It seems that another great Victorian master of particularity, George Eliot, appreciated the poem as such a dramatization of Browning's position when she wrote about it in a review dated 1856: "we would rather have 'Fra Lippo Lippi' than an essay on Realism in Art."[31]

Pound imitates this title form for a number of shorter poems: "Cino" and "Plotinus" will be examples here. He also borrows Browning's term *Personae* (from *Dramatis Personae*) for the title of his own 1909 volume where these poems are included with others of the same type. He describes that type in a letter to Williams of 1908 as "the short so-called dramatic lyric," where again the defining term is copied from a title of Browning's.[32] These are among many tributes to his "Master Bob Browning" (saluted that way in the poem with its title, "Mesmerism," borrowed from Browning) that appear repeatedly in his poetry and prose writings.[33] In a letter of 1928 he proclaims his lineage in two of his languages: "Und überhaupt ich stamm aus Browning. Pourquoi nier son père."[34] Like so many declarations of indebtedness, Pound's borrowings from Browning point to very real connections while at the same time signaling differences.

The title of Pound's 1909 volume looks back to *Dramatis Personae. By Robert Browning*, published in 1864. Pound's title page reads *Personae of Ezra Pound*. The finely made adjustments of prepositions and punctuation give instructions to readers that Pound's personae are, in Donald Davie's words, "less *dramatis* personae than they are embodied aspects of his own situation and his own personality (though this is truer of some poems than of others)."[35] The distinction rests on identical terms with different meanings. *Dramatis Personae*, the traditional heading above a theatrical cast of characters, presents Browning's volume as if it were a collection of speeches by dramatized figures separate from the author. Pound's title page erases the separation grammatically with *of* to fit the new meaning it gives to the theatrical metaphor. Richard Blackmur comments on its significance as Pound uses it in a review of the 1926 edition of *Personae: The Collected Poems of Ezra Pound*:

The nub of the matter is in the title. . . . *Personae* were the masks of Roman actors. But they were not masks worn to hide character but to show its clearest face. They hid only the irrelevant and unseemly, the unreality of the private individual under the definition and the clarity of a symbol. So Ezra Pound has supplied a variety of masks—some beautiful, some malicious, some ironical—and all better made than any in our generation.[36]

Pound himself comments directly on this understanding of the title for his volume *Personae* in one of its poems called "Masks," in which he recites a catalogue invoking "Strange myths of souls":

> Old singers half-forgetful of their tunes,
> Old painters color-blind come back once more,
> Old poets skill-less in the wind-heart runes,
> Old wizards lacking in their wonder-lore.[37]

Except for the "painters" (perhaps a reference to Browning's), these "singers," "poets," "wizards" are personae, "old disguisings," of Ezra Pound in other poems.

Pound's "Scriptor Ignotus," dedicated "To K. R. H. Ferrara 1715" in *A*

Lume Spento of 1908, copies and revises Browning's "Pictor Ignotus" sub-scribed "Florence, 15—" in directions typical of the way many of Pound's presentations work. Both titles refer to the *I* of the poem in the anonymous formulas for the signature in a poetic miscellany or the attribution in a museum label for a painting, but the subscriptions giving local habitations and dates claim that the unnamed speakers are not fictions but actual per-sons who lived in times and places at a distance from the authors of the poems. Pound even adds a note to tell us what we would surely not know otherwise, that the title has in mind Bertold Lomax, "English Dante scholar and mystic," that he died in 1723 with his "'great epic'" still "a mere shadow," and that the poem is his address to a lady organist of Ferrara.[38]

Browning reinforces the separation between the *I* and the poet by choos-ing a painter to say the poem, which is a defense of his "pictures" to an unappreciative listener. The occasion allows a detailed evocation of what Browning imagines to have been the atmosphere of sixteenth-century Flor-ence in which the painter works. Pound narrows the distance between him-self as author and his persona: by making him an artist who is specifically a poet, who is like Pound himself a scholar of Italian poetry, who has not written an epic, whose vow to his beloved to "make . . . / A new thing / as has not heretofore been writ" would remind readers of Pound's often re-peated call to arms for poets of his generation to "Make it new!" The poem itself does not weave particulars of setting or occasion into the speech of the unknown scriptor that would identify him with the actual person de-scribed in the note. He compares himself to Dante but also to Pierre de Ronsard, his lady to Iseult as well as to Beatrice. His speech is in the tradi-tion of promises to immortalize the beloved; he is the mask of the poet-lover, and of Ezra Pound who wears it to write "Scriptor Ignotus." The poem therefore makes only the slightest gestures toward the detailed treat-ment given to Browning's *dramatis personae*. Browning's closest imitator of such treatments is not Pound but Edwin Arlington Robinson, for in-stance in "Rembrandt to Rembrandt (Amsterdam, 1645)," published in 1927.

Pound's poems are often spoken under the masks of "Old singers," "Old poets," "Old wizards," and they are often presented by titles in the same form as Browning's "Fra Lippo Lippi" that consist only of the proper name for an actual person who lived in a distant time and place. An example is "Cino," with the subscription "(*Italian Campagna 1309, the open road*)." This presentation and some brash colloquial lines like the opening—"Bah! I have sung women in three cities"—are like Browning in particularity and immediacy, but the poem as a whole is less a burst of speech than an incan-tation full of "Strange spells of old deity" and "the souls of song."[39] The title for a sonnet of the same period names the "I" of the poem "Plotinus,"

who seems to be another mask of the poet, a visionary who makes "images"
of the self:

> I cried amid the void and heard no cry,
> And then for utter loneliness, made I
> New thoughts as crescent images of *me*.[40]

In a poem of the same period Pound again salutes Browning by borrowing
from his title "Paracelsus" but making it new as "Paracelsus in Excelsis."
Browning's is a dramatic poem in five scenes adding up to more than four
thousand lines; Pound's is thirteen. Its stripped form is fitted to the wizard-
persona's stark vision: "Being no longer human, why should I / Pretend humanity or don the frail attire?" He sees himself among beings who rise
above "the world of forms" to become like works of art:

> We seem as statues round whose high-risen base
> Some overflowing river is run mad,
> In us alone the element of calm![41]

The "I" is another mask for the poet whose vision is the poem. Its title,
incorporating "Paracelsus" into a rhyme with "Excelsis," treats the proper
name as a word in the game of poetry, abstracting it from historical context
and dramatic impersonation.

Although the titles that present these personae are often in the same form
as "Fra Lippo Lippi," in relation to the poems they head and the contexts
in which they appear they work quite differently. Pound himself explains
what these differences are in the previously quoted letter to Williams of
1908:

To me the short so-called dramatic lyric—at any rate the sort of thing I do—is the
poetic part of a drama the rest of which (to me the prose part) is left to the reader's
imagination or implied or set in a short note. I catch the character I happen to be
interested in at the moment he interests me, usually a moment of song, self-analysis,
or sudden understanding or revelation. And the rest of the play would bore me and
presumably the reader. I paint my man as I *conceive* him. Et voila tout![42]

His terms fit the poems. They are "song" or "revelation." They "paint" as
they "*conceive*" (in both senses of apprehending and bringing to life), not
what they see, as does "Fra Lippo Lippi" in the artist's "pictures of the
world." In that poem the painter's art is an analogy for Browning's kind of
poem, but the figure of the artist himself is not a mask for the poet in
Pound's sense. The painter is a particularized dramatic character who is
given lines to speak with which their author, the poet, is in sympathy. By
contrast, "Scriptor Ignotus," "Cino," "Plotinus" are personae who represent the poet, to quote Blackmur again, "under the definition and the clarity
of a symbol." Although the poems are presented in titles of the same forms

as Browning's, they do not ask for the same complicity in pretending to accept the independent existence of the *Personae of Ezra Pound* that is asked of Browning's readers in the instructions of his title page, *Dramatis Personae. By Robert Browning.*

Elizabeth Bishop in the title "Crusoe in England" gives the figure whose voice we hear in the poem a name that confers on him a multilayered identity shaped by his relations to twentieth-, nineteenth-, and even eighteenth-century first-person speakers. Like "Ulysses"—and Tennyson's poems were among books of her aunt's that Bishop read as a child[43]—the title "Crusoe in England" identifies the *I* of the poem by a proper name famous as the name of a seafaring adventurer in a literary narrative that is also known by his name. But then, unlike Homer's hero or Tennyson's, the narrator of Daniel Defoe's *Robinson Crusoe* of 1719 had an actual, contemporaneous prototype, the Scottish sailor who lent his name to the admittedly pretended "I" of Cowper's "Verses, supposed to be written by Alexander Selkirk, During His solitary Abode In the Island of Juan Fernandez," first published in 1782. Bishop's "Crusoe" is related to Defoe's fictional and to Cowper's "supposed" first-person speaker, each in some sense authenticated by Selkirk's well-known history, which was recounted in various prose reports of the time including one by Richard Steele, who "had the pleasure, frequently, to converse with the man soon after his arrival in England in the year 1711."[44] Among the other reports of Selkirk, one claimed to be "Written by his own Hand," while the many reprints of Cowper's poem included an attempt, in 1787, to pass it off as "an original composition of Selkirk during his solitude."[45]

Something like this conflation of the actual and the imagined is reflected in special ways in the precise final form of Bishop's title "Crusoe in England," revised from "Crusoe at Home." Locating the figure with a fictional name in a real place treats him as an actual person like Selkirk or like the prototype of Tennyson's "Columbus," not a legendary but a historical seafarer, adventurer, discoverer. Bishop's title also points to the way the poem shapes his story. He tells it when he is "old" and "bored," when his famous voyage is only a memory to dwell on in the "uninteresting" present, which is located after the conclusion of Defoe's written account but parallel to the years Selkirk lived, according to Steele often bewailing the lost "tranquillity of his solitude," beyond his return to England.[46]

Defoe's hero is of course Bishop's immediate model for a fictional *I* with a supposedly true history, which his narrative recounts in such bewitchingly minute detail that the illusion of reality is irresistible. Bishop's revised title "Crusoe in England" lays claim to an illusion of reality like Defoe's, but when set beside Defoe's *The Life and Strange Surprizing Adventures of Robinson Crusoe*, her title shows its own different directions to the reader. The *I* of her poem is not *Robinson Crusoe*, what he would be called in the title of an autobiographical narrative by its editor, likely also to be its publisher, whose entrepreneurial enthusiasm Defoe's title imitates. In Bishop's title the speaker is more familiarly named just "Crusoe," someone we need no editor to introduce us to, someone we already know or know of. This adjustment in the title is pointed, especially where naming is a recurring interest in both the poem and the narrative.

What Defoe's narrator tells us most about in the opening paragraph, which begins the transformation of his fictional story into history, is his name:

I was born in the year 1632, in the City of York, of a good family, tho' not of that country, my father being a foreigner of Bremen, who settled first at Hull . . . afterward at York, from whence he had married my mother, whose relations were named *Robinson*, a very good family in that country, and from whom I was called *Robinson Kreutznauer*; but by the usual corruption of words in England, we are now called, nay, we call our selves, and write our name *Crusoe*, and so my companions always call'd me.[47]

Bishop's title takes pleasure in its pretense as Defoe's does, but she invites us to join her in playing a more complicated game with it. By naming the *I* of the poem what his "companions" always called him, her title refers to him not as he is presented to readers of a printed account like Defoe's, but as he is spoken to *in real life*—that is, in the life of Defoe's fictional hero outside his written narrative. This asks us to imagine that we are familiar with "Crusoe"—we do not ask *who is Crusoe?*—as if he were a person we might know, as if we had not in actual fact heard of him solely because he is the famous hero of a literary narrative, an eighteenth-century *Odyssey*. At the same time the title treats him as a celebrity whose return to England we might learn of in the news, someone we know to have been elsewhere.

The layering of representations that begins in the title with the third-person naming of the *I* of the poem raises a question "Crusoe" himself asks in many forms, but nowhere as explicitly as it is asked in a poem also from Bishop's culminating and retrospective last volume, *Geography III*. That poem, which has the archetypal title "Poem" and occupies the central space in the volume, explores the nature of representation questioned throughout Bishop's work, beginning with "The Map," which opens *The Complete Poems*. In "Poem" the "I" who contemplates a dim little painting, "but how live, how touching in detail" (like Defoe's narrative), asks:

art "copying from life" and life itself,
life and the memory of it so compressed
they've turned into each other. Which is which?[48]

The complicated design we have seen in Bishop's third-person title "Crusoe in England," naming a famous fictional *I* treated as an actual person, also raises this question, which is not asked in poems with such titles by Tennyson, or Browning, or Pound. It troubles her "Crusoe" but not Defoe's *Robinson Crusoe* or Cowper's supposed "Selkirk," and troubled questioning is the mode of her poem.

The issue of "art 'copying from life,'" of representation, is concentrated in the title: on the name the poet gives her speaker, and therefore on how she names her poem. For "Crusoe" himself, the confusion of representations around the act of naming gathers like the clouds over his island. He begins by contrasting a newly discovered island he has read about—"They named it" he does not say what—with the island in his memory, which is "unrediscovered, un-renamable. / None of the books has ever got it right."[49] His own effort was and is to get it right, which he tried and tries to do by endlessly varied acts of naming, like a twentieth-century Adam cast away in an unrecorded world. He remembers how he named—by word or epithet but more often by comparison—everything about the island, but there is a strange silence in the poem about whether or not he gave a name to the island itself (would it be "un-renamable" either way?). By contrast, Defoe's narrator begins the journal he keeps after being shipwrecked on his island with his first act of naming it "the *Island of Despair*, all the rest of the ship's company being drown'd, and my self almost dead."[50]

Bishop allows "Crusoe" to borrow from this christening with revealingly different effects, beginning with his application of the name just to a part of the island:

> One billy-goat would stand on the volcano
> I'd christened *Mont d'Espoir* or *Mount Despair*
> (I'd time enough to play with names),
> and bleat and bleat, and sniff the air.

Here getting it right is not finding the right name for fact and feeling—Defoe's narrator has no hesitation in calling his "dismal unfortunate island" simply "*Despair*"—but playing with names like a poet. (Who else, besides someone stranded on a desert island, would have a lifetime for word games?) By such play "Crusoe" discovers that two epithets contradictory in meaning are meaninglessly, or significantly, alike in sound. Then are words real things insofar as they are sounds, or are they names for real things that do not fully exist until they are named?

The same game is played more obliquely in this passage with the nickname "billy-goat" (boy-goat, but *billy* as noun once meant *fellow* or *mate*) for the creature whose eyes "expressed nothing, or a little malice." The familiar, friendly epithet contrasts with the creature's strange bleating noises:

> The goats were white, so were the gulls,
> and both too tame, or else they thought

I was a goat, too, or a gull.
Baa, baa, baa and *shriek, shriek, shriek,*
baa . . . shriek . . . baa . . .

The passage is again revealingly reshaped from its source, this time lines
spoken by Cowper's supposed "Selkirk":

The beasts that roam over the plain,
  My form with indifference see,
They are so unacquainted with man,
  Their tameness is shocking to me.[51]

"Crusoe" ignores Cowper's particular satiric point here that the insulting
"indifference" offensive to the dignity of "Selkirk" comes from the beasts'
ignorance of human cruelty. His interest is again in questions of naming:
are the goats' bleats like words in being sounds or like words in being animal names for *goat* and *gull* that they misapply to man, as he may misapply
"billy-goat" to some radically other thing?

Defoe's narrator applies hilariously inapposite names to make himself
at home on his island, but he does so with cheerful bravado. Describing his
efforts to secure himself from "savage wretches," he tells how he "kept close
within my own circle": "When I say my own circle, I mean by it my three
plantations, *viz.* my castle, my country seat, which I call'd my bower, and
my enclosure in the woods." He titles himself "My Majesty, the Prince and
Lord of the whole island," perhaps a source for Cowper's famous line, "I
am monarch of all I survey"; in time he calls his "castle" his "home."[52]

At least as hilarious but much more troubled, sadder, are the efforts of
Bishop's "Crusoe" to transplant an Englishman's home to his island by the
power of renaming. He sees piles of "Snail shells" that "at a distance" look
like "beds of irises":

        —well, I tried
    reciting to my iris-beds,
    "They flash upon that inward eye,
    which is the bliss . . ." The bliss of what?

Is the missing word from Wordsworth's line the counterpart of the island
name missing from this poem? Could "Crusoe" not remember "solitude"
because questions disturb him about words' worth as names for either fact
or feeling: "The bliss of what?" Or was his memory receiving interference
from Cowper's supposed "Selkirk," who asks a different question: "Oh Solitude! where are the charms / That sages have seen in thy face?" Or could
he not finish the line from "I wandered lonely as a cloud" because Wordsworth had not yet (not by 1709 when Selkirk was rescued, not by 1719 or
1782 when Defoe's and Cowper's renderings were published) written the
book of poems where "Crusoe" back in England could "look it up"?

"Crusoe," like "A poet" who is the "I" of Wordsworth's poem, "wandered lonely," but in a space that "seemed to be / a sort of cloud-dump" offering "not much company" except the goats whose "questioning shrieks, . . . equivocal replies" might be dubiously analogous to language insofar as they are unlike, or like, human names in relation to the things they do or do not represent. His island, itself rediscovered but not renamed in his memory, seems to his imagination more real (though not nameable "the bliss of solitude") than the island he lives on. Unlike Bishop in the title, he does not say that it is "England," nor does he call it "Home," as the original title named it with pained inappropriateness, but only "another island, / that doesn't seem like one, but who decides?" Who decides to call it an "island"? to name it "England"? to say it is more real than "my poor old island" because it is so named officially in the same "books" that have never been able to get his "un-renamable" island right?

Starting with her title, Bishop creates an *I* with a unique identity apart from her own, shaped by her uses of his remarkable origins. "Crusoe," we have seen, has special status as a fictional figure with an actual contemporaneous prototype who is spoken of in the title as he would be by his familiar friends. And this is how the poem treats him. Bishop's attitude toward him is above all friendly, which narrows the distance between them while maintaining it. Friendliness, unlike pity, does not "begin at home" (where it begins for "poor miserable Robinson Crusoe" in the opening sentence of his journal). We feel friendly toward others, not ourselves. The poem makes us feel that way toward "Crusoe," who is likeable for his inventiveness and practical energy, his humorous capacity to make up, to make do, to make things: "Home-made, home-made! But aren't we all?" The affection the poem expresses for these qualities matches "Crusoe's" for the results of his contrivings: "I felt a deep affection for / the smallest of my island industries." It is also matched by Bishop in a notebook entry dated 1934 about a stay on Cuttyhunk Island: "on an island you live all the time in this Robinson Crusoe atmosphere; making this do for that, and contriving and inventing. . . . A poem should be made about making things in a pinch."[53]

The companionable distance created by the poem's friendliness toward "Crusoe" is supported by its anachronisms, which make him a contemporary of the author and the reader. His speech is wholly modern, with none of Pound's archaisms. It has none of Browning's names, dates, and historically reconstructed details to set him at a distance, for instance in Defoe's or Selkirk's early eighteenth century. On the contrary, "Crusoe" can—almost—quote lines (then not yet written) by Wordsworth, whose language is echoed everywhere in Bishop's poem. This makes the "I" and his author alike and sympathetic, and yet keeps them separate; she could supply "Crusoe" with the word missing from his quotation.

Both the title and the poem humorously keep their balance in treating the first-person speaker as someone who is not the author but like her, someone she would enjoy as a friend. Both are modern poets, which for them means post-Wordsworthian poets who playfully ask disturbing questions about representation, about the connections among words, things, meanings. "Crusoe" is a free-standing figure with an identity distinct from Bishop's, yet is her fictional representation of that real presence, "art 'copying from life.'" The illusion invites us to ask "Which is which?" This question, at the center of "Crusoe in England," the volume *Geography III*, and *The Complete Poems*, is not raised by Defoe or Cowper. Nor is it asked about the presentations of the historical or mythological figures named as speakers in later-nineteenth-century impersonations or as personae in earlier-twentieth-century symbolic monologues.

The inclusive *man*

The nineteenth- and twentieth-century titles that consist of a proper name for the first person we hear in the poem pretend to exclude the presence of the author but acknowledge us as listeners. Another kind of third-person title, mainly appearing soon after Pound's early recastings of the dramatic monologue as the mask, presents the first-person speaker in a form that ultimately includes both the poet and the reader in its reference.

The group of D. H. Lawrence's poems published in 1917 was begun about five years earlier, when he was reading Pound, whom he had met in London. Its original title was to be *Man and Woman*. Setting it beside Browning's *Men and Women*, a comparison Lawrence is likely to have intended, we see that the everyday social particularity suggested in Browning's title—one we might expect for a Victorian novel—is transformed into an archetypal formula with mythic and biblical associations. The more provocative title Lawrence finally gave to the volume, *Look! We Have Come Through*, emphasizes the intimacy of these love poems and their status as what in the foreword to them he calls "confession," but it also focuses the volume on the poem in it with a title it borrows from, "Song of a Man Who Has Come Through."[54] This combines the immediately personal idiom of the revised volume title with the general and archetypal epithet of the original. It refers to the "I" of the poem in mythic outline as "a Man," who is modernized by the colloquialism describing his heroic achievement as having "Come Through."

This title and others in the volume of the same pattern like the one for the poem immediately preceding, "Song of a Man Who Is Loved," are designed to include an archetypal reader with the poet in the form of reference to the *I* whose personal history is told in the poems. Again more particularly the archetypal woman reading the poems is specified both as listener and participant in the experience of the first person speaking the poem immediately following. It is titled "One Woman to All Women," another echo and alteration of a title of Browning's, "Any Wife to Any Husband," from his volume *Men and Women*. These transformations of Browning's titling are like Pound's in transcending everyday particularity, an effect supported by the combination of archaic with colloquial language in the poems. Yet Lawrence's presentations of the *I* are very different from Pound's symbolic masks of the poet. Lawrence's archetypes are ideal images of the unity of experience in which both poet and reader participate.

Hardy's *Moments of Vision and Miscellaneous Verse* was also published in 1917, with two poems titled to refer to the first person who says the poem in something like the same mixed way, but with different effects. "The Man with a Past" conjures up a figure on a large scale or in imposing silhouette by its echo of epic openings: the first words of the *Aeneid* as in John Dryden's translation—"Arms and the man I sing"—or of *The Faerie Queene*—"Lo I the man." (Robinson's title "The Man Against the Sky" of 1916 has the same reverberations.) Yet Hardy's added colloquial idiom "with a Past" evokes instead of suitably heroic memories a skeleton in the closet, some melodramatic secret. Here the clashing of styles in the title both matches and mocks the speaker's reading in the text of the "blows" that "time" dealt him "long ago."[55] If the title were "He Laments His Past," on the same model as the two following, "He Fears His Good Fortune" and "He Wonders About Himself," it would distance the poet and the reader from the speaker and would direct us to read the poem without much hesitation as another instance of what Hardy calls "dramatic impersonation." By referring instead to the first-person speaker as "The Man," the title mythologizes the feelings expressed in the poem much as they are enlarged by the protagonist himself. It therefore equivocates about who after all the mythmaker is, allowing that we—who are included in "Man"—along with the giver of the title may be implicated in this essential human self-delusion.

"The Man Who Forgot" from the same volume could be the title of a tragic legend, but it also sounds rather like a limerick—*There once was a man who forgot*—or a title in a collection of light verse, like Ogden Nash's "The Man Who Frustrated Madison Avenue," or Louis Simpson's "The Man Who Married Magdalene," or the potential title in Stevens's *Schemata* notebook, "The man who could not sell even nectarines." The clash of associations in Hardy's title becomes more sharply mocking in its relation to the poem, where we learn what the title holds back: what it is that "The Man Who" says the poem "Forgot."[56]

One reading of the answer is that the speaker in remembering his past has forgotten that it is past, that "Forty years' frost and flower" have rotted what his memory keeps deceptively alive. Another way to read this answer to the title is that he forgot to forget. He alone remembers as real and sees in seductively "fair" moonlit imaginings what is no longer an actuality—"Nothing stands anywhere"—to "brains" the less deceived. This reading recognizes a hint that the "I" of the poem is everyman and also more particularly a late-Romantic poet. To this figure, what Hardy in "Shut Out That Moon" calls "that sad-shaped moon" (revised to "stealing moon") is an insidious muse inducing memories "almost forgotten" except by poets writing in the "decline" of daylight, yet still indispensable to their imaginations: "My right mind woke, and I stood dumb." Since the poem "The Man Who Forgot" allows both answers to the question left open by the title, it includes the reader as well as the poet in the experience of the protagonist named by the titler as "The Man." That form of reference identifies the "I," the poet, and the reader all as modern versions of the epic hero struggling to keep alive what is "almost" but not wholly "forgotten," at the same time that we are suitable figures for nonsense verses who are not in our "right mind."

We and the poet meet again as we are implicated in the way the title refers to the speaker of Stevens's "The Man Whose Pharynx Was Bad," another epic-limerick hero. The poem is included in Stevens's first volume, *Harmonium* (in the edition of 1931), but was projected as early as 1905, when his journal records that he was reading Hardy. An entry for December 31 of that year reveals what he recognized as their kinship of feeling: "A weighty day of course. . . . read a little of Hardy's 'Trumpet Major' and after dinner read more. Pulled my curtains shortly after four and lit my lamp, feeling rather lonely—& afraid of the illusions and day-dreams that comfort me."[57] The scene and mood are an almost uncanny prediction of Hardy's "Shut Out That Moon," dated 1904 and published four years later in *Time's Laughingstocks*, confirming the rightness of the sympathy Stevens early felt between them:

> Close up the casement, draw the blind,
> Shut out that sad-shaped moon,
> She wears too much the guise she wore
> Before our lutes were strewn
>
> . . .
>
> Within the common lamp-lit room
> Prison my eyes and thought;
> Let dingy details crudely loom,
> Mechanic speech be wrought.[58]

Hardy's grimly dismayed self-mockery in this and the other poems discussed here is very close to the quality of feeling in Stevens's early poem

"The Man Whose Pharynx Was Bad," in which the first person of the opening stanza—"I am too dumbly in my being pent"—lives in a late-Romantic version of the world where Coleridge and Wordsworth were "in the great City pent":

> The wind attendant on the solstices
> Blows on the shutters of the metropoles,
> Stirring no poet in his sleep.[59]

The figure speaking "dumbly" is the modern "no poet" but, as the pronoun "I" disappears after the first stanza to become "One" in the last, "The Man Whose Pharynx Was Bad" finally stands obliquely for the reader as well as the poet.

There are three other poems by Stevens with titles presenting the speaker as absurdly heroic or heroically absurd *man* who speaks in the poem as *one*: "The Snow Man," also in *Harmonium*; "The Man on the Dump" and "The Sense of the Sleight-of-hand Man," both in *Parts of a World* of 1942. The specially charged connection between their form of title and their pivotal pronoun is confirmed by the fact that in *The Collected Poems* there are only two other poems built around the speaker's use of *one*.[60]

Generic one is what grammars also call an indefinite pronoun. They describe it as the formal equivalent of generically used *you, we, us*, but with the difference that these are personal pronouns collectively referring to "people in general" but still with traces of their personal origins. This terminology describes what we know from our experience of both written and spoken language, that *you, we, us* work dramatically, as a sort of appeal by the speaker to the listener, an evocation of shared experience, a reminder of some common bond. *One*, somewhat more usable in writing than in speech, has no personal roots but includes all persons impersonally, grammatically, in what Otto Jespersen terms the "generic person." It is the English equivalent of *on* in French, *man* in German, linguistic parallels not likely to be lost on Stevens. *One* suppresses connections between the speaker and someone else listening because of its impersonal oneness, avoiding dramatic interchange or expression, like a blank mask. It is used, as Jespersen says, "often as a kind of disguised *I*."[61] In "The Man Whose Pharynx Was Bad" the disappearance of "The Man" who speaks as the first-person singular nominative "I" into the generic indefinite pronoun "One" is the grammatical record of his grotesque "malady," an absurd analogy in its blank inexpressiveness for the "dumbly pent" condition of the generic person, "one." It includes "no poet" and indefinite reader in a nonconnection between speaker and hearer.

"The Snow Man" is another title presenting "Man" in an aspect at once ridiculous and archetypal, by conjuring up the image of a cheery, childish, perishable artifact, the snowman, and also an elemental, mythic being, the man of snow (who might be compared with "The man of autumn" of "Secret Man" in Stevens's *Opus Posthumous*). In the poem the snowman is immediately dissolved while the man of snow emerges gradually. The process is recorded grammatically as the "One," who opens the poem-sentence guardedly regarding, disappears into the other-than-humanly personal "listener" who, "nothing himself," is receptive to "Nothing that is not there and the nothing that is." Although the grammar of the sentence makes no dramatic interchange between speaker and hearer, "the listener" obliquely allows the possibility of our representation with the poet in the generic man of snow.[62]

Differences between these presentations of "Man" and the absurdly grand figures who speak the two related poems in the later volume *Parts of a World* are again guardedly recorded in the grammar of the speakers, beginning with the pronouns they choose to speak in or behind. Both still prefer the indefinite *one*, even using it more often, but that repetitiveness itself charges *one* with a new expressive energy: in "The Sense of the Sleight-of-hand Man" "One's grand flights, one's Sunday baths, / One's tootings at the weddings of the soul"; in "The Man on the Dump" "One sits and beats an old tin can, lard pail. / One beats and beats for that which one believes."[63] Also in each of these poems, unlike the earlier two, there is a moment when "One" speaks as "you," still a generic pronoun but with personal roots, acknowledging a bond between speaker and hearer, creating a dramatic connection grounded in shared experience. The "Sleight-of-hand Man" asks, "Could you have said the bluejay suddenly / Would swoop to earth?" Questions, which even when verging on the rhetorical imply at least some unspoken response, are another grammatical gesture not made by either *one* in the earlier poems. The identification with "you" happens for "The Man on the Dump" when "One rejects / The trash"

> and the moon comes up as the moon
> (All its images are in the dump) and you see
> As a man (not like an image of a man).

"One" becomes "you" and "a man" at the same "moment," connecting "The Man" heroically alone on his grotesque promontory with someone listening. The acknowledgment is more direct, grammatically but also feelingly more personal than in "the listener" at the end of "The Snow Man." The presence of the poet speaking to the reader is therefore closer to the surface in the interplay between the title and the grammar of the poem, which includes us in the figure of "a man" now not so "dumbly pent" that his language cannot include "you."

The title of John Ashbery's "A Man of Words" in *Self-Portrait in a Con-*

vex Mirror evokes memories of these titles, but more especially of Stevens's "Men Made out of Words," which ends with a chillingly inclusive aphorism: "The whole race is a poet that writes down / The eccentric propositions of its fate."[64] Ashbery's title at the same time echoes in disturbingly revised form the familiar idiom *a man of few words*, which brings to mind the traditional hero, the strong silent type, the doer of deeds, for whom "A Man of Words" is the anti-hero. The "Man" the title deconstructs to "Words" is shrunk further in the opening lines to become "smaller / Than at first appeared," the maker only of "a skit," dry, brittle "grass writing," as chillingly lifeless as a weather report "with / The outlook for continued cold."[65]

This disembodied figure is isolated in the third person of the title and the clinical opening phrase, "His case," and by the almost implacably steady avoidance of other personal pronouns, which gives the poem itself an impenetrably cold, dry surface. A more direct hint that "His case" is the malady this poet fears he may suffer from, that this poem is another *Self-Portrait*, escapes midway in the first-person pronouns that slip out in a parenthetical negative: "not the metallic taste / In my mouth as I look away." The reader, who has been kept from discovering the first person "Behind the mask" of grammar worn by "A Man of Words," has only this glimpse until the closing lines, where one more personal pronoun surfaces, but with more controlled obliqueness: "Just time to reread this / And the past slips through your fingers, wishing you were there." Here "you" is a grammatical mask for the first-person singular, but unlike "He" does not isolate the hidden *I* from the reader. Generic "you" includes us grammatically and dramatically in the appeal it makes to shared experience, which here seems to be the experience of absentness and separateness expressed by another rewritten idiom, the transformed version of the postcard cliché *wishing you were here*. The pronoun "you" also includes the briefly exposed "I," expressing this later-twentieth-century poet's sense of connection with poets of the "past," "you" who shared his fearful recognition that "All diaries are alike, clear and cold." It is a gesture of kinship with poetic forebears, perhaps Stevens particularly under the guise of heroically absurd "Man," who struggled to make new "The story worn out from telling." That figure seems not as much to be a fictional person here as, more precisely, a grammatical person.

CHAPTER FOUR

Who "hears" the poem

ANY TITLE presupposes the existence of an audience for the poem by its status as a presentation. The category of title to be discussed here acknowledges this by some sort of reference to what is now often called by the linguists' term the *addressee*. By explicitly acknowledging this fictional presence—in the vocabulary of grammar, the second person—all such titles create versions of the actual circumstances built into the existence of a poem: that it is made by the poet and to be experienced by some *you*. While they all refer to this literal situation, their representations of it differ in their distances from it. That is to say, they differ in the kinds of fictions they inevitably cast it in.

Like third-person titles naming a figure who says the poem but is not the poet, titles in this category have hypothetically no limits to the choice of presences a poem can be addressed to: a particular person or group— present, absent, dead, or yet unborn; a particular person identified by proper name, gender, occupation, country, race, kinship to the poet, or personal pronoun. The title can present the poem as an address to a category of human being or an unspecified *one, anyone*, or, as in a title of Richard Wilbur's, "Someone Talking to Himself." The fictions at the farthest remove from the actual situation of reading are titles imagining that the figure addressed as *you* in the poem is a nonhuman presence: some work of art or made object; a natural creature or force; a place; a mythical being; an abstraction; a deity. Among the many varieties of title purporting to answer the question *who hears the poem?* some have continuous histories that show stages of transformation like those in categories already discussed, when the same formulations or modified versions of them emerge in new cultural contexts. Others crop up only intermittently; still others appear not earlier than in the past hundred years or less.

To *the reader*

Ben Jonson can begin to teach us about the workings of titles in this category, appropriately since he seems to be the earliest English poet to have thought about the pedagogical authority of titling. He addresses us as teacher in the two-line dedicatory poem that opens his *Epigrammes*:

> To the Reader
>
> Pray thee take care, that tak'st my booke in hand,
>   To reade it well: that is, to vnderstand.[1]

The poem is immediate, even bluntly so. It talks to each of us directly—not as *he* or *one*—and individually—as "thee," not *you*—charging each of us with personal responsibility for being a fit reader, the burden each must accept as receiver in the exchange transacted in the title. Meanwhile the title itself does not address us in the same direct second-person singular as the verses. Since Jonson makes a point of telling us in the very next epigram and again two pages later in the ninth that he is the maker of both, we are to understand that "To the Reader" is in a form of address as carefully chosen as his first-person titles, beginning with his next two epigrams printed on the same page, "To my Booke" and "To my Booke-seller," and repeated throughout the volume.

If he had chosen to establish this pattern in the opening title, making it "To my Reader," the presentation of the poem would have come a step nearer grammatically to the way the verses themselves address "thee . . . that tak'st my booke in hand." As the actual title is phrased, its more distant reference to "the" reader exaggerates the differences between the poet's forms of address in verses and title, all the more noticeable in such a very short poem, which leaves no space for the impression of contrasting forms of address to fade. This shift in grammatical reference is by now so familiar a convention that we tend to take it for granted without questioning its inherent oddness. It will be questioned here because the juxtaposition of Jonson's carefully chosen title with his opening verses can be a useful paradigm to introduce some fundamental features of titles alluding to the second person addressed in the poem. It can serve this purpose because Jonson's shift from "the Reader" in the title to "thee" in the line just below it is a grammatical diagram of the relation between the situation imagined in the title—*this is a poem in which the second-person pronoun refers to the reader*—and our actual experience of reading.

That is, each one of us quite literally takes Jonson's book in hand to read first the title and then the verses, and they pointedly define our situation by those physical acts. We can therefore be directly and individually addressed in the second-person singular since we are immediately present to the poet in the sense that he reaches each one of us through his words on the page open in front of us. Yet in the title the second-person singular of the poem is referred to as a collective or generalized person, not as *thee* or *my reader* or even *a reader* but "the Reader." Because the reference is in the third person, it is as if the title were presenting "thee" of the verses to some other presence, a kind of meta-reader, since the poet would not use *the reader* to address one of us directly, as we are each spoken to face-to-face by the pronoun "thee" in the poem. Because in fact we read both the title and then the verses, our presence is acknowledged equally as the listener in the poem and as the meta-reader the title presents it to.

Both "the Reader" and "thee" are fictions useful to Jonson in defining himself as a poet by articulating what kind of poem he writes, and "To the Reader" is a carefully placed example of that kind. Its double address to the immediate, singular "thee" and to a distanced and generalized audience called "the Reader" constitutes a kind of manifesto for the volume. The poet's directness reaches the moral center of each "thee" who takes up his book by the plain speaking—"Pray thee take care"—of his verses. At the same time their broad discriminations—what it is to read "well"—establish a cultural ideal that the poem transmits to "the Reader" in every generation.

There is no contradiction here between these simultaneous fictions of "thee" who listens in the poem and "the Reader" the title presents it to. If the conflict much discussed in recent criticism between the competing claims of voice and writing ever originates in poems rather than in theory, that originating event happens only in a much later situation of poetry than the cultural moment when Jonson staked out his own claim to being titler as well as author of his verse. Jonson's kind of poem as manifested by him in "To the Reader" embraces the immediacy of voice and the permanence of writing claimed by the title's generalized address "To the Reader," who is the timeless contemporary of all readers. Nor is there implied here the sort of division between poet and speaker assumed by criticism that applies modern understandings of the term *persona* to Jonson's poems.[2] The effect of Jonson's performance as both author and titler is rather to make poet and speaker work together in defining himself as the poet who speaks in his poems—where he sometimes calls himself by his actual name—presented by him in his titles.

Jonson found a way of combining his title and verses in this dedicatory epigram "To the Reader" to articulate his ideal of a poem by exploiting the parallel between the fictional situation they create and the inescapable condition that a title represents a transaction between author and reader. Although we might expect titles representing this exchange to be an opportunity attractive to poets, such titles are historically quite rare, for reasons to be suggested. Insofar as their intermittent appearances belong to a tradition in English, it originates in epigram forms used especially by seventeenth-century poets.

Titles addressing the poem in some form or other *to the reader* often define the ideal of reading well by treating the imagined listener in the verses as an anti-ideal. Jonson's "To my meere English Censvrer" satirizes "thee" as the antithesis to the fit reader addressed in the preceding epigram, "To the Learned Critick."[3] Herrick's "To the soure Reader" openly reviles "thee" as "O Perverse man!" allowing the possibility that all fallen readers may sin in sourness; his apparently contrasting epigram, "To the generous Reader," hints at the same judgment, that all readers must "doe our best" to correct our corrupted taste. The slyly satirical undertone in this epigram prepares for his next, "To Criticks," which threatens "You" with extinction.[4]

These seventeenth-century satirical epigrams are shaped to make us question our likeness to the target of satire, the bad reader addressed in the poem in second-person pronouns that by their grammatical nature can include each of us who reads it. At the same time the title, by its third-person reference, appeals to another audience, the meta-reader, who can share the poet's scorn for the offender in the poem. If uneasiness is produced by the juxtaposition, it is not the poet's but ours; the shift in address between title and text is the author's reminder that our likeness to or distance from either fiction is our own moral responsibility.

It seems paradoxical that in the later seventeenth and eighteenth centuries, the period showing the most interest in didactic verse including many specially admired poems on the subjects of writing and reading well, poets did not choose to imitate the traditional title forms for epigrams addressed to the reader. Instead they turned to the verse epistle as the preferred kind for such poems. Representing the literal exchange between the writer of a letter and the person it addresses, this fictional transaction calls for titles naming the second person of the poem as the particular correspondent. The title is therefore a kind of analogy for the envelope that tells who the letter is meant to be read by. When, as is often true, the *you* of the poem is in the title given the name of a living prototype the writer might otherwise address in an ordinary letter, the fictional presence appears as solidly grounded in the poet's actual society as the name on an envelope. Still, because the title refers to the second person of the poem by proper name in the third person, another audience is silently acknowledged, as we have seen in poems addressed more generally to the reader. This implied meta-audience is also closely approximated to the poet's actual, contemporaneous readers because the proper name in the title presentation is assumed to be recognizable, as it would be in the right social circles. The title "An Epistle from Mr. Pope, to Dr. Arbuthnot" is worded in a way meant to imply that readers will know of the friendship between these two men, whose association in the Scriblerus Club signals their shared literary tastes and therefore casts *you* in this epistle as the poet's ideal reader. The title "A Letter From Dean Swift to Dean Smedley," assuming that its readers will know of the *Satyr* on Swift published in Dublin in 1725 by Jonathan Smedley, presents a satire with the receiver of the "Letter" in the role of the anti-ideal, the bad reader. The larger fiction implied by these titles is that there exists a community of like-minded writers and readers. This in turn supports the more particular fictions of *you* in the poem as an identifiable living person and of the reader as an insider.

Perhaps largely because cultural circumstances allowing poets to imagine such a society had changed by the early nineteenth century, titles in the traditional epigram forms of address to *you* of the poem as the generalized or collective reader surfaced again, for instance in Shelley's "Lines to a Critic" published in 1823. Now the satirized target is somewhat differently defined than by Jonson or Herrick, even when their terms—like *critic*—may be the same, reflecting changed conditions of the literary system within which earlier-nineteenth-century poets worked. Shelley uses the vocabulary of money—"equal," "repay," "gold," "dear"—to address "thee" in "Lines to a Critic,"[5] defining *critic* more specially than it was meant in seventeenth-century poems for the reader who judges sourly or—in Jonson's ideal culture—"well." For Shelley, to be "a Critic" is to follow a lucrative occupation, to judge poems for pay, which is also true of the second person addressed in Shelley's "Lines to a Reviewer" (a term and occupation unknown in the early seventeenth century). To this reader Shelley also applies the vocabulary of the market, asking "what profit can you see / In hating such a hateless thing as me?"[6] Because the second person satirized in each of these poems is given a more specialized role than in the seventeenth-century epigrams quoted, the shift in address between title and text has a somewhat different effect. While the title assumes that the offender will be among readers of the poem, the poem itself does not ask the rest of us to see ourselves represented by the debased reader it speaks to as *you*, but rather to hold ourselves aloof with the poet from the mercenary world that produces bad readers by paying them.

Such changes beginning in this period in the production and reception of literature, long ago made familiar to us by writers like Raymond Wil-

liams, are reflected not only in new meanings for terms but in modified
versions of established title forms referring to the second person in the
poem as the reading audience for it. For instance, the traditional generalized "To the Reader" begins to be readdressed "To the Public," as in a poem
with that title published in a volume of verse by Philip Freneau in 1795,
making fun of the habits of his own newspaper readers. That target precisely embodies what Williams describes as the emerging middle-class
readership toward which—he shows in quotations from Shelley, Keats, and
Wordsworth—poets expressed their contempt by lumping together a noisy,
undifferentiated crowd as *the Public*.[7] Titles in that form separate the mass
directly addressed by second-person pronouns in the poem from the implied
other audience to whom the title presents it, which is assumed to share the
poet's scorn for the mob. Freneau's poem, first printed in 1791 in the opening number of the *National Gazette* under the title "Poetical Address to
the Public of the United States," implies that his direct speech to his listeners
in the poem will lift them out of the mass to become the discriminating
meta-reader implied to exist by the title.

Titles in this form given to poems written in the earlier twentieth century
reflect a somewhat different sense of the separation between the fictions of
the debased modern reader who is the *you* in the poem and the possibly
sympathetic meta-reader to whom the title presents it. The second person
in the poem is still more scornfully dismissed, as in John Gould Fletcher's
"To the Public"—"I do not condescend to you / . . . For you are not"—or
in a poem by Louis MacNeice with the same title—"We do not need your
indulgence, much less your pity."[8] At the same time the existence of the
potentially sympathetic reader is imagined more tenuously. In MacNeice's
"To Posterity" the poet predicts a future when "reading and even speaking
have been replaced / By other, less difficult media."[9] In addressing this
world of dehumanized, nonverbal beings, "To Posterity" foretells destruction for its own fictions of *you* and *the reader*, which would mean the end
of poetry.

Robert Graves's "The Reader Over My Shoulder," written around 1930,
positions itself among earlier-twentieth-century poems like those just
quoted, and within the tradition they carry on. The poet attacks the "You"
addressed in his poem in terms and tone recalling earlier satirical epigrams:
as "old enemy," "judge and patron." The poem also expresses the contempt
heard in other poems of its period toward the modern reading audience:
"I am a proud spirit, / And you forever clay."[10] At the same time Graves's
allusions to these contexts modify the conventions they evoke, allowing a
shift in focus. His poem concentrates attention on the fictional status of
you and *the reader*, which is implicit in the other poems but not treated as
their explicit concern.

The title "The Reader Over My Shoulder" (revised from "To the Reader Over My Shoulder") is a radical reshaping of the traditional form of address. Because it leaves off the usual preposition *to*, it does not raise the expectation of the conventional shift to the second person in the poem. Besides, the imagined figure is located, as it were, in a space outside the poem, standing behind the poet and looking over his shoulder. There is an intimate quality to the scene, but a hostile atmosphere because the idiom *looking over my shoulder* implies that the person reading is peering furtively at secret matters and that the person writing is uneasily, perhaps guiltily aware of an intrusive presence, but is not directly responding to it. This fiction makes the traditional shift to direct address that happens abruptly in the first word of the opening line "suddenly" more noticeable: "You, reading over my shoulder, peering beneath / My writing arm—I suddenly feel your breath." This intrusive entrance of "You" into the poem forces the poet to break it off, only to scratch a few "Words on the margin for you, namely you, / Too-human shape fixed in that shape." This "Reader" exists merely as marginal "Words," "namely" the pronoun "you," or as an insubstantial "shape" delusively representing the "Too-human" actual reader while in reality embodying nothing but a fiction of the poet's, "this other self of me," "In damned confusion of myself and you."

Graves's "The Reader Over My Shoulder" goes beyond traditional satirical attacks fending off sourly critical or mercenary readers and reveals more than the contempt expressed by poets contemporary with him toward the incapacities of their reading audience. His poem reflects deeper uneasiness that the poet works in absolute isolation, has no one to address face-to-face, and therefore can write only in secret, only under the self-delusion of a fictional presence—"this other self of me"—lurking behind its author's back, in order to have anyone to write the poem to. Fearing that poets can no longer trust their own fictions, Graves struggles, not entirely successfully, to make the open admission of their fictiveness do the work of the conviction now lost.

Uneasiness over the efficacy as fictions of *you* and *the reader*, strongly felt in "The Reader Over My Shoulder," is differently and more obliquely expressed in Ashbery's "But What Is the Reader to Make of This?" included in *A Wave* of 1984.[11] The question asked in the space above the poem could be the baffled response of "the Reader" trying to soothe wounded self-esteem by claiming kinship with any sensible person who would surely be as bewildered. It could be the frustrated poet's expression of self-mocking dismay over the difficulty in writing to "the Reader." Whoever asks the question in the title space is clearly at a loss how to present the poem, what proper title to give it, while the poem itself reflects the difficulty it causes for both poet and reader because it has no *you* to address in it. Meanwhile the slightly irritated question "But What Is the Reader to Make of This?" jokes about the stubborn persistence of belief in the fiction of a second person present in the poem to whom it must be addressed, despite what complicated evasions, what verbal obstacles the poet's differences from the commonsensical "Reader" may set up to the contrary.

The idiom *what to make of* borrowed for Ashbery's title has the double meaning it also has in the last lines of Frost's "The Oven Bird": "The question that he frames in all but words / Is what to make of a diminished thing." That is, Ashbery's title can be read to ask not only *what is the reader to understand from this poem?* but *what is the reader to make it into?* The oblique answer implied in all but words by the juxtaposition of title and text is that we will inevitably expect this poem to represent the literal circumstances that it is made by a poet and to be experienced by some second person. To *make it into* a poem that fulfills these expectations, we look for—and in looking assume the existence of—the missing *you*. The question in the title space frames in all but words that the presence we supply is not in the poem itself but in our own search for it, and that the diminished thing is the fiction of *you*.

To *you*: Whitman

In 1888 Whitman took "A Backward Glance o'er Travel'd Roads" in the preface to *November Boughs*, which was then used as "my concluding words" at the end of his preferred last arrangement of *Leaves of Grass*. In it he describes that life work as "a *sortie*—whether to prove triumphant, and conquer its field of aim and escape and construction, nothing less than a hundred years from now can fully answer."[12] He does not say here who were the volume's besiegers, but like many of its metaphors, this one recurs all through it, beginning with a poem in the opening section that asks but does not answer "What Place Is Besieged?" He uses such repetitions, making connections among parts of the volume, to support his claim for its living, organic wholeness, also insisted on in the title *Leaves of Grass*.

The final version opens with twenty-four introductory poems gathered together as "Inscriptions." Whitman probably took this heading directly from his title for an unpublished prose preface to the volume, "Inscription To the Reader at the entrance of Leaves of Grass," but it derives ultimately from the Latin word *inscriptio*, translating the Greek *epigramma*. The last four of these "Inscriptions" together form the dedication of the volume, suggesting a parallel with Jonson's beginning sequence in his *Epigrammes*—"To the Reader," "To my Booke," "To my Booke-seller"—or Herrick's opening group, which includes "To his Muse," "To his Booke,"

"To the soure Reader." Whitman's dedicatory inscriptions are addressed to "proud libraries," to "Poets to Come," "To You," and to "Thou Reader."[13]

The first two of these poems reflect directly on Whitman's metaphor for the volume as "a *sortie*" against besiegers that can only "prove triumphant . . . a hundred years from now." The verses with the admonition "Shut Not Your Doors" in the title space instruct "proud libraries" that what "your well-fill'd shelves" most need "I bring, / Forth from the war emerging, a book I have made." The next poem summons his troops: "Poets to come! orators, singers, musicians to come!" He is the vanguard of the sortie—"I but advance a moment only to wheel and hurry back in the darkness"— calling up his poetic followers: "Arouse! for you must justify me." The enemy, it seems, is tradition, which has up to now trained readers as well as poets to expect what in his "Backward Glance" he calls the "conventional themes," the "stock ornamentation" of "establish'd poems."[14]

In the final "Inscriptions" Whitman rewrites traditional addresses to the reader as the climax to his definition of his battle with "establish'd poems," the besiegers he leads his sortie against. The closing pair among the "Inscriptions" are the only two-line poems, sharpening their allusion to the tradition of the epigram, which is even more pointed in their titles. The first of the pair is:

To You

Stranger, if you passing meet me and desire to speak to me,
    why should you not speak to me?
And why should I not speak to you?

The title imitates the expected prepositional form of address but breaks its rules by shockingly substituting "You" for the conventional, distancing third-person reference to the listener in the poem. Here the relation between the exchange defined in the title and our actual situation as readers of the poem is radically reimagined: *this is a poem to you.* That is to say, with electrifying simplicity, that it is not a poem in which another audience, the meta-reader, will read what the author says to *you* only after the title's mediating presentation of those immediately spoken words. The address in the title space is continuous with the speech in the poem, equally and, as it were, literally directed to "you."

In the verses the listener is also invoked as "Stranger," which, if the title were in traditional form, would be recognizable as the figure hailed—*stay traveler (siste viator)*—by the poet from the gravestone in the conventional opening of an epitaph, a type closely related to the epigram. By pointed contrast, Whitman's radically innovative revision of the title form—so far as I know, no epitaph, epigram, or any other poem in English was ever before titled "To You"—announces a different kind of exchange. The shared use of the second-person pronoun in both title and verses is a vehicle for delivering the poet's new message to the listener who hears both utterances: that the exchange is immediate, intimate, mutual, spoken; that it narrows the traditional separation of poet and reader in the epitaph marked by the gravestone; and that it dissolves the distinction between the fictions of *the reader* and *you*.

Whitman takes another giant stride in his sortie against established poetry in the very last inscription, a new poem added to the group in its final arrangement of 1881, which makes a vivid contrast with Jonson's verses "To the Reader":

Thou Reader

Thou reader throbbest life and pride and love the same as I,
Therefore for thee the following chants.

The wording above the poem here is not a true title, that is, not a presentation. It redefines what transpires in the title space because it is a vocative, an evocation, and identical with the first words of the first line so that together they are the invocation to "the following chants." Such self-referential quotation in the title space is a favorite device of Whitman's to be discussed further in the last chapter. He uses it for sixteen of the twenty-four "Inscriptions," transforming traditional presentations of the poem to the reader into salutations to the listening *thou* or *you*. Here the vocative form, with its immediate repetition in the poem, emphasizes its different status from traditional titles, which Whitman had originally avoided altogether in the first edition of *Leaves of Grass* of 1855, leaving the spaces above the poems in it unfilled.

"Thou Reader" makes us see that its startling form of address is as calculated and as bold a revision of titling conventions as were Jonson's in his own time. Whitman's most aggressive attack on tradition in this final inscription demolishes the double fiction of *you* and *the reader*, evoking in its place the single, inclusive "Thou," wholly present in the title space as well as the poem, at once immediate listener and timeless, mythic evocation. There is no third-person reference to the second person implying the traditional meta-reader. Instead the fictional situation is of the unmediated presence and organic oneness—"Thou . . . the same as I"—of the poet and the listener, both mythologized and therefore generalized by the "chants" that bind them to one another.

In the body of the volume in its final arrangement, "To You" is repeated as the title for a much longer poem that fills out the fiction compressed in these dedicatory "Inscriptions":

> Whoever you are, now I place my hand upon you, that you be
>   my poem,
> I whisper with my lips close to your ear,
> I have loved many women and men, but I love none better than
>   you.[15]

Whitman imagines our situation in two metaphors, both altogether different from Jonson's picture of us facing the page from which the poet's words address "thee." Our reception of the poet's gift "To You" is a mystical laying on of hands, by which we are transubstantiated as the poem, and it is the secret communication between lovers. These metaphors, both suggesting mysteriously spiritual physical touch, are blended together into a seamless incantation reimaging the fictional exchange represented in traditional addresses "To the Reader."

The hundred years have passed that Whitman believed were needed before we could judge whether his sortie had proved triumphant. From this perspective, it seems that Whitman's "Thou Reader" and "To You" are even now almost as radical among title forms as they were a century ago. Still, his grammatical inventiveness in these forms helps to shape the sense of unmediated presence that he declares to be at the very heart of his poetry and that has since become for many and diverse poets an ideal to work for in their own poems: "I and mine do not convince by arguments, similes, rhymes, / We convince by our presence."[16]

To *you*: Auden and after

The practice of using second-person pronouns in titles to support the illusion of immediate presence continues in some—but still surprisingly few—twentieth-century poems. Closest among them in form to Whitman's addresses are tributes to other poets: Archibald Macleish's "You, Andrew Marvell" and "You Also, Gaius Valerius Catullus"; Charles Olson's "You, Hart Crane" and "A Lustrum for You, E. P." In these titles the proper name is not a third-person reference to the imagined listener in the poem, as it would be if they were worded in traditional forms: "[To] Hart Crane," "[For] E. P." Instead the name is a vocative directly summoning up the absent poet with the name he would be addressed by in life (not a literary name like "Adonais" or "Thyrsis" used in nineteenth-century tributes to dead poets).

Whitman may also have suggested the use of titles with this pronoun form for love poems by his recurring metaphor of the lover-like relation of poet to reader, already seen in the longer poem "To You." The appropriateness of "To You" as the title for a love poem seems obvious at least in the abstract, but in actual practice only to a very few poets so far in this century. Frank O'Hara, for whom "after all, only Whitman and Crane and Williams, of the American poets, are better than the movies," copies Whitman's precise form "To You" for a love poem we will return to.[17] So does his friend Kenneth Koch. Auden, another hero of O'Hara's, seems to reflect on the simple appropriateness of this formulation for love poems in one of his own, "To You Simply." His title quotes from lines in the poem—"To you simply / From me I mean"—that invite two readings of it.[18] First is: simply to you alone from me, simply here making love to you while "Who goes with who / The bedclothes say." The line also asks to be read: to you directly from me in a simple way of talking. The unmediated title address "To You" represents that direct simplicity, which its added "Simply" comments on.

Many of Auden's titles as originally printed in *The Collected Poetry* of 1945 seem to have been the ultimate source of another distinct style of title for more recent poems using second-person pronouns built into familiar idioms and clichés. Here are some examples—among them titles for love poems—still as fresh and funny as they must have seemed to readers when they were first published and to the poets who have since used them as models: "Make Up Your Mind"; "Are You There?"; "Please Make Yourself at Home"; "Shut Your Eyes and Open Your Mouth"; "What Do *You* Think?"; "Leap Before You Look."

This style of title, virtually nonexistent in English before Auden, is used more often by later-twentieth-century poets than Whitman's bardic forms of address. Here are some more recent examples in something like the style and spirit of Auden's: O'Hara's "What Appears to Be Yours"; Ashbery's "And You Know"; Koch's "In Love With You"; Ginsberg's "'You Might Get In Trouble'"; Tom Sleigh's "You Have Her Eyes"; Paul Blackburn's "You Ask Me Why"; Robert Creeley's "Thank You"; Stanley Kunitz's "'What Have You Done?'"; David Wright's "As You Were Saying"; Mark Strand's "So You Say." They preserve the immediacy of the personal pronoun, a purpose crucial also to Whitman's innovative uses of the title space, while generalizing the presence in the poem in ways different from his mythic evocations. The fact that the radical titling practices of Auden and Whitman serve these parallel ends can help to explain how two such wholly dissimilar poets (and Auden's distaste for Whitman's poetry is well known) could both take their places among the heroes of a more recent and himself innovative maker of titles, Frank O'Hara.

Mark Strand's *The Late Hour* of 1978 includes a poem representing part of an exchange between lovers, "So You Say." Beginning with that familiar phrase in the title space, the speaker expresses the seemingly casual but troubled skepticism conveyed by the idiom, here brought to bear on love's idealisms:

It is all in the mind, you say, and has
nothing to do with happiness. The coming of cold,
the coming of heat, the mind has all the time in the world.[19]

The title is a casual, spoken idiom in the same style as the text, making them
a continuous response directly said to "you" present in both. Although "So
You Say" pretends that the exchange takes place only between the lovers,
it uses grammar and idiom to generalize the immediate, private situation
imagined in poem and title. The simplest means, common to titles of this
kind, is to exploit the capacity of second-person pronouns to have more
than one reference. The sequence of pronouns in Strand's poem—"You,"
"you," "you," "we," "us"—makes this happen by including first love poets
(evoked by allusions to Donne's "The Sunne Rising" and Marvell's "To his
Coy Mistress") who recite hyperboles like the lover's claim that "the mind
has all the time in the world," that it has power over "the sun arriving after
a day in Asia." Since their hyperboles are repeated in this love poem in everyday idioms like "So You Say," which we have all heard and may sometimes have said however skeptically, we also become implicated in a generic
"you" and then in "we" and "us." We, the lovers, the poets are bound together by our common human fallacy: we cannot or do not wholly admit
that "the mind" holds what it loves only in such brief measures as a late
hour.

Returning now to O'Hara's poem "To You" dated 1959, we can recognize that it not only embodies but reflects on—or as it says, "sheds a little
light" on—the ways titles spoken to the second person in the poem use the
multiple references possible for the pronoun *you*. Like poems by Ashbery that these chapters read as implied comments on traditional titles
and their anti-types, O'Hara's plays a witty game with some of the theoretical or conceptual implications of second-person title addresses for a
poem between two lovers. A line of O'Hara's poem in one manuscript
(but not in the first published version in *Poetry*, May 1960) makes a kind
of riddle out of this grammatical happening: "The you is you. As you
may know."[20] The play is with *you* as an instance of the grammatical class
for which Otto Jespersen invented the name *shifters*. In Roman Jakobson's later analysis of their workings, *you* in one sense depends for its
meaning on the "existential" or "physical" presence of its reference,
whatever it points to in its capacity as an "index," which in O'Hara's
poem is the other lover in the moon-lit bed who is the "You" spoken to
in the title. At the same time, like all shifters, *you* acts also as a "symbol,"
because it "possesses its own general meaning. Thus 'I' means the addresser
(and 'you' the addressee) of the message to which it belongs."[21] O'Hara's
love poem both embodies and reflects on this double status of its title,
"To You":

> What is more beautiful than night
> and someone in your arms
> that's what we love about art

(which turns into "the moon")

> because it stands for all to see
> and for a long time just as
> the words "I'll always love you"
>
> impulsively appear in the dark sky
> and we are happy[22]

The shifting pronouns, circling around the familiar idiom "I'll always love you," represent the power of art to generalize and give permanence to the immediate, a connection made perhaps too flatly obvious by the poem's canceled earlier title, "Painting." The revised title works better to sustain the fiction of the existential or physical presence of "I" and "you" all the way to the end of the poem, as lovers in bed looking out their window "like a couple of painters in neon allowing / the light to glow over the river." The title together with the poem "sheds a little light" on the ways these second-person forms of address make special use of grammar and idiom to escape the traditional separation of the meta-reader from the listener in the poem. In doing this they preserve the immediacy of the personal pronoun while making it inclusive.

To a secret third person

The anxieties of more recent poets about the relation of the poem to the reader find their most famous expression in *The Waste Land* in the last line of "The Burial of the Dead": "'You! hypocrite lecteur!—mon sembla-ble,—mon frere!'" It has everything to do with what has been said in this discussion of titles that Eliot's violently direct address is not a title (which would constitute a presentation of poem to reader); that it has no locatable speaker because it is a fragment with no defined dramatic context; that it is itself in quotation marks and contains an unmarked, untranslated quota-tion within a quotation from Charles Baudelaire's poem—devices making it simultaneously immediate and oblique. These qualities attach to the anx-ieties already shown in other twentieth-century poems focusing on issues of presentation and reception, which are unusually explicit in poems ad-dressed to their readers. Yet of course questions of presentation and recep-tion are not exclusively modern sources of unease, but have been met in every situation of poetry, and must raise some concern in authors of any period. Richard Helgerson and others following his lead, for example, have exposed uneasiness beneath Jonson's authoritative self-presentation.[23] This tendency among poets suggests one reason why titles belonging to the types explored so far in this chapter are relatively rare.

Another way of thinking about that historical circumstance is this: besides the natural uneasiness poets must feel about the issues of presentation and reception explicitly raised by such poems, they must overcome the literary problem built into them. That is to find a way of imagining and addressing a presence that inherently has no more "shape," to borrow Graves's ghostly metaphor, no more explanatory context, than as an undefined someone reading the poem.

Much commoner are titles that identify the second person in the poem by what seems to be a more detailed or more specifically defined third person than *the reader* or *you*. In these titles the reference to the listener points to a fictional presence that in the poem is given a more clearly separate existence from the meta-reader to whom the title presents it. Here are some examples to illustrate the variety of titles in this category for different kinds of poems and from every period: "To a ladie to answere directly with yea or nay," assigned to Wyatt in Tottel's miscellany; Richard Lovelace's "To Chloe, Courting her for his Friend"; Swift's "To Mrs. Biddy Floyd"; Wordsworth's "To ———, on Her First Ascent to the Summit of Helvellyn"; Walter Landor's "To My Daughter"; Whitman's "To a Common Prostitute"; Robert Lowell's "For Elizabeth Bishop"; Phoebe Cary's "Advice Gratis to Certain Women"; Diane Wakoski's "Ladies, Listen to Me."

Any of these and numberless other title forms are devices for shaping the poet's mode of address. They do this by raising more or less detailed expectations of how the *you* in the poem will be imagined, therefore in what relation to the poet and, in a different sense, to the reader. The poem may then fulfill, modify, or violate these expectations in all sorts of ways. In comparison, a title addressed only to someone reading the poem is relatively spare in its shaping associations, and increasingly so in recent periods when generic expectations like those Jonson and Herrick could count on have steadily weakened.

The list of examples just cited makes the obvious point that this ubiquitous category of titles does not constitute a tradition but incorporates many. As previous discussions would predict, some of their conventions reappear in identical forms in different periods, but with changing effects. For instance, the title "To a Lady" in Hardy's first volume of 1898 has, if not an edge of mock formality, at least a deliberate air of old-fashioned or stilted politeness that it would not carry in a sixteenth-century miscellany. Also predictable is the steady appearance in successive periods of titles referring to the same kinds of figures imagined as the second person addressed in the poem: a fellow author or artist; an admired or hated public figure; a representative or collective figure encoding literary associations or social attitudes; someone intimately dear—lover, child, parent, sister, brother, friend. The forms and styles of reference to the same kind of listener can persist or they can be deliberately revised or revolutionized: compare among tributes to dead poets Dryden's "To the Memory of Mr. Oldham" with Ginsberg's "To Poe: Over the Planet, Air Albany-Baltimore." Sometimes titles refer to kinds of figures imagined as listeners only in one period and not in others: Rudyard Kipling says this loudly in his title "To Motorists" for a parody of Herrick. Other recent title addresses are cast in grammatical forms and styles unimaginable before the later twentieth century, making them act as manifestos for the poetics of their generation: John Berryman's "Damn You, Jim D., You Woke Me Up"; Paul Blackburn's "I'd Call It Beggary, Corso"; Frank Lima's "Mom I'm All Screwed Up."

In poems where the listening figure is addressed as if on a public occasion, for instance in Jonson's "To King Iames" or Dryden's "To the Pious Memory Of the Accomplisht Young Lady Mrs. Anne Killigrew, Excellent in the two Sister-Arts of Poesie and Painting. An Ode," we are not represented by the name or noun in the title, but we are nevertheless present as part of the public audience for the address. No particular tension is caused by the switch from the third-person form of the title to the second-person pronouns in such a poem.

The kinds of titles chosen for more discussion here evoke figures who would be more intimately spoken to. They imply our exclusion from the private situation between speaker and listener in the poem; our presence is admitted only in the title. This would then seem to create the effect described in a well-known aphorism of John Stuart Mill's as the distinguishing illusion of poetry, that it is not "*heard*" but "*over*heard."[24] His formula, applied to distinguish the lyric from other genres, has often been quoted in recent criticism, for instance in an influential discussion by Northrop Frye in the *Anatomy of Criticism*: "the concealment of the poet's audience from the poet, is presented in the lyric . . . preeminently the utterance that is overheard. The lyric poet normally pretends to be talking to himself or to someone else: a spirit of nature, a Muse . . . a personal friend, a lover, a god, a personified abstraction, or a natural object. . . . The poet, so to speak, turns his back on his listeners."[25] Frye's analysis of Mill's formula shows that his own application of it is actually narrowed still further than to the lyric. He uses it mainly to describe the kind of poem that, in the terms used in this chapter, turns its back on the meta-reader implied in the third-person title to address the fiction of an independent presence spoken to in the second person in the poem.

Some senses in which the poem may be said to be "*over*heard" or the poet imagined turning "his back on his listeners" seem actually to be acknowledged in several traditional kinds of titles. They are addresses that pointedly keep secrets by their very forms, even as they represent the transaction between poet and reader that is built into all titles. Their uses in English begin in the earliest period of titling, when shielding the identity of the *you* in the poem could be a very real necessity, or when doing so was a pretense imitating that social requirement. For quite obvious reasons these secretive titles were specially helpful for poems addressed by male poets to female figures, and that convention has persisted.

Titles that name the *you* in the poem by what is recognizably a pseudonym, like Edmund Waller's "To Amorett" or Landor's "To Neæra," predict our exclusion from an exchange between the speaker and the listener who is known to him by another name. The fiction is that we are made outsiders by the secrecy of the title form. Initials or a conventional epithet replacing the actual or supposedly real name of the figure addressed in the poem have the same effects, illustrated in revisions of the presentation for a poem by Pope, which in manuscript originally read in the title space "Written, June ye 15th. On Your Birth-Day, 1723." This personal note was then revised for publication in titles that substitute either a disguising epithet—"to a Young Lady"—or initials—"Sent to Mrs. M. B."—for the original second-person pronoun.[26] Both public versions stress the separation of the particular person who is the *you* addressed in the verses from the meta-reader of the title who is not allowed to know her name.

Some effects of secret-keeping can best be seen in the kind of title that insists most strongly on it. These leave a startling blank to mark the omission where readers would expect a name or noun alluding to the *you* in the poem. Wordsworth can show the workings of such titles in his uses of them for a number of poems composed in 1824 and published in 1827. Three give nothing away in their titles, all of which are addressed "To ———," except that they are designed actually or as if to keep a secret from the reader. In one of them the poet speaks to the listener in the verses with playful affection, by her name: "Heed not tho' none should call thee fair; / So, Mary, let it be."[27] Calling her by the name (and it is pointedly not a literary pseudonym) held back in the title, he makes the pretense that the poem is only for her. It is as if the verses, needing no title when the poet spoke them directly to the real "Mary," had been pirated and publicly presented by an editor who, like his readers, does not know the actual circumstances behind them (as was true of some much earlier poems with this title, to which Wordsworth's alludes). Here the form "To ———" playfully supports the fiction that a conventional love song masks the poet's affection for a real woman.

Another of these poems opens as a meditation on "the fate of summer flowers."[28] Its generality implies an audience wider than the "thee" singled out in the later stanzas of the poem, but the withholding of her name from the title creates a private drama. She alone among its readers is allowed to know that she is the "soul-gifted Maid" asked by the poet who knows and cares for her to apply his meditation to herself. Here the effect of the secretive title is to charge general language with a personal quality of feeling, which is also the way it works in "To ———, In Her Seventieth Year." It is a sonnet in a Spenserian manner evoking a presence—"O Lady bright"— to praise so that all may envision her.[29] Yet holding back her name creates the impression that the poet is tenderly protecting the old age of a woman dear to him from the public gaze attracted to her evocation in the poem. That delicate personal situation would not be implied by a title naming the lady or calling her a lady. Wordsworth here uses the title form to make public language more intimate, withholding the name of the "Lady," although we are present as audience for her praise in the sonnet.

Such titles, by keeping secrets, prepare for the switch in grammatical form from title to verses that situates the poet with back turned to the implied first audience. In these ways they create fictions that fit the definition of poems the reader does not hear but overhears. At the same time their very insistence that they are hiding something from their audience makes its continuous presence felt. That is to say, a secretive presentation like "To ———" creates more tension between title and poem than if it did not withhold the identity of the figure addressed in the poem, for instance if Wordsworth had left off the title of his song, as he did earlier for some of his love poems, or if he had titled it "To Mary."

What Frye's discussion ignores—and this is far from uncommon in considerations of poems on almost any plane of abstraction, or for that matter of particularity—is that poems have titles, which at least since the seventeenth century have usually been designed by poets to make connections with the poem. This omission is specially unhelpful in a discussion where the issues are what "is presented" and to what "audience," since titles are quintessentially presentations to some identified or implied audience or to both. Title forms that allude to the listener by a seemingly more detailed or more specifically characterized third-person reference give that imagined figure still greater separateness from its implied other audience and a more defined relationship to its speaker. The questions to be asked about these titles are how far and in what ways they work toward the "concealment of the poet's audience" or match Mill's definition as "*over*heard" utterance.

Marvell's poem with the title "To his Coy Mistress" is a favorite choice of critics to illustrate the kind of dramatic lyric said to make us feel we are eavesdropping. Here, for example, is the way J. B. Leishman begins his still often-quoted discussion of it: "Where this poem most resembles Donne, and is perhaps more fundamentally indebted to his example than any other of Marvell's poems, is in its essentially dramatic tone (more dramatic than anywhere else in Marvell), in the way in which it makes us feel that we are overhearing one of the speakers in a dialogue."[30] Mill's formula, made so familiar in critical writing of this century that Leishman does not give its source, is the predication for his discussion of the poem. Like the way of reading compressed in the formula itself, it pays no attention to the title, although that is our first encounter with the poem and finally inseparable from the whole of our experience of reading it.

"To his Coy Mistress" was not printed until 1681, three years after Marvell's death, but recent scholarship has uncovered that his nonpolitical poems circulated in manuscript among various groups of readers while Marvell was alive, a form of publication that had by then begun to predict the use of titles among other presentational devices. This circumstance makes it likelier that he originally gave them the titles printed in the volume of his *Miscellaneous Poems* in 1681, where Mary Marvell certifies "To the Reader" that "all these Poems . . . are Printed according to the exact Copies of my late dear Husband, under his own Hand-Writing."[31] At any rate, since by Marvell's generation the use of *his* no longer necessarily signaled editorial imposition or even the serious pretense of it, it could be freely chosen by whoever was the titler for its inherent distancing power.

The title by which we know Marvell's poem, like Carew's "To my inconstant Mistris," combines a personal pronoun with an epithet, but with special adjustments that make its effects distinct even from those of Carew's nearly parallel form. It conveys a greater sense that the speaker can look at "his" mistress with some detachment than would *my mistress*, and it pointedly holds "his" persuasion up before the reader as a performance of "I" addressing "you." We are distanced as an audience, but we are invited to be present.

The other specially calculated detail in the title is the choice of adjective. Countless mistresses besides Carew's are accused of being "inconstant" or praised sarcastically for exemplifying "Womans Constancy," as in a title given to one of Donne's poems in the edition of 1633, but few are called "Coy."[32] As the *Oxford English Dictionary* defines the adjective for this period, it could mean displaying shyness, modesty (like Milton's Eve who gave herself to Adam "with coy submission, modest pride"), or making a display of it, so that the most striking word in the title has a double edge like many expressions in the verses. By that adjective in the title, we are let in on the speaker's rhetorical strategy. We are told in advance that he will appeal to the listener as if she were truly shy and modest, while allowing that she may be only putting on a show of reluctance. As a result, there is a kind of complicity between the titler and the reader already seen among titles of this period, which excludes the *you* of the poem who hears only the verses; we approach them from that privileged position. While it can be said that the poem makes us feel we are listening to one of the speakers in a dialogue, we have been prepared to hear it from that speaker's perspective. The title therefore does not precisely conceal or ignore our presence in the poem, but draws us into it as an audience ready to listen to the lover's dazzling argument with an informed appreciation for its fusion of passionate intensity and witty detachment. This would not be the lady's likeliest response to it, either if she were genuinely or affectedly coy.

Matthew Arnold's title for the poem known as "To Marguerite—Continued" since its publication in the first collected edition of his verse, *Poems* of 1869, arrived at that awkward title form through a revealing succession of revisions. The poem first appeared in 1852 in the volume *Empedocles on Etna, and Other Poems*, which acknowledges his authorship on the title page only as "By A." There the poem has the title "To Marguerite, in Returning a Volume of the Letters of Ortis"; in 1853 it was "To Marguerite"; in 1857 it became "Isolation." These changes trace a movement away from particularity. Even the final reappearance of the name in "To Marguerite—Continued" has a different effect from its use in either of the first two versions because it links directly with the poem just before it, "Isolation. To Marguerite," making the titles together more an argument on a theme—*Isolation. Continued*—than a direct address to an intimate listener. As the use of the name hints, there was a personal history behind the changing title. The flowery French pseudonym (with its German connection to Goethe's *Faust*) was Arnold's disguise for an actual woman named Mary Claude whom he knew in Switzerland (the place-name became the heading for the group that includes the poem). The pseudonym associates her with the sort of continental literature exemplified by Ugo Foscolo's "Letters of Ortis," which she liked to read and imitate in her own writing.[33]

The original title, "To Marguerite, in Returning a Volume of the Letters of Ortis," while calling attention to its secrecy about the woman's real name, fills in other details that give her an identity as listener independent of the meta-reader and construct an intimate connection between her and the speaker of the poem. She has lent him a book they have talked about; he in returning it picks up their conversation with the abrupt opening word expressively punctuated, "Yes:" he has felt and found echoes in the book of what he knows she also feels. The poem begins as if in the middle of their talk, with a dramatic immediacy especially startling when it was surrounded in the 1852 volume by poems with contrastingly generalized or abstract titles: "Absence," "Destiny," "Human Life," "Despondency." Yet what follows that conversational opening (in all printings) is a sequence of distancing pronouns in place of the expected *you*:

Yes: in the sea of life enisl'd,
With echoing straits between us thrown,
Dotting the shoreless watery wild,
We mortal millions live *alone*.
    The islands feel the enclasping flow,
And then their endless bounds they know.[34]

The first instance, "between us," could be personal but it is quickly generalized by "We mortal millions," then "they," which are the islands metaphorically displacing their "mortal" subjects. The absence of *I* and *you* and the
movement from the directly spoken opening to the final description of the
islands—"betwixt their shores . . . / The unplumb'd, salt, estranging sea"—
are paradoxically given personal weight by the presence of the title as it was
printed in 1852. In that form it makes possible a reading of the poem's
inability to sustain immediacy as an expression of its meaning more than
as a sign of its failure: "Yes:" it is true that even sympathetic spirits such
as we two cannot reach each other in the world of the later nineteenth century, or in its poems, where the "moon" of earlier romanticizing poetry
now only sheds its light in "hollows."

By diminishing the particularity of the title's reference "To Marguerite,"
or in "Isolation" canceling it altogether, the revised title forms weaken the
sense of a *you* in the poem being spoken to in a strained sequence of impersonal pronouns and metaphors that expresses the unbridgeable distance
separating the lovers. In doing so, the changed titles narrow the space between the listener and the other audience implied in the third-person title,
making "us" and "we" seem to be directed at readers of the poem. We become at once its acknowledged audience and the reference for its pronouns
and metaphors. This movement away from particularity in the successive
revisions of the title shows Arnold's uncertain efforts to fend off the kind
of autobiographical reading we have also seen Tennyson, Browning, and
Hardy working against in their various ways. As the illusion of a real
woman behind the pseudonym is weakened or canceled, her disappearance
collapses the fiction of *I* only indirectly able to address *you* in the poem.
This rules out the possibility of reading it as if we were hearing one speaker
in a dialogue between lovers. It becomes instead the poet's address to the
reader on the theme of isolation. The pseudonym in the final version of the
title, "To Marguerite—Continued," is an unconvincing device for creating
a fictional drama in which the woman listening is not the reader and her
lover speaking is not Arnold. The attempt to escape from autobiography
here pays a price.

Robert Lowell's *Life Studies* of 1959 is a declaration of independence
from the dread of autobiographical interpretation that had powerfully

shaped the course of much poetry written in the later nineteenth and earlier twentieth centuries. It is a revolutionary book that marks the passing of what Donald Davie calls "the heyday of the *persona* and of impersonality in poetry."[35] The volume, drawing on Lowell's experience of trying to write his prose autobiography, in its way embraces the directness that Hardy's disguised autobiographical account of his life goes through its third-person contortions to guard against: "In *Life Studies* I caught real memories. . . . I wrote about my marriage and parents; I didn't see them as desperate— though life must be askew. When I wrote, most good American poetry was a symbol hanging like a gun in an armory. Many felt this."[36]

Elsewhere in this interview with Ian Hamilton published in 1971, and in another given ten years earlier with Frederick Seidel, Lowell makes distinctions between the "personal poetry" or "autobiographical writing" of *Life Studies* and some of his later work.[37] Even so, the title *Life Studies* itself defines personal or autobiographical poems as drawings made from life but studied, the practice of an artist (as in James Russell Lowell's title "Studies for Two Heads"), not jottings in a diary or scraps of personal correspondence. This means that what is taken from life is not in any simple or ordinary sense "confessional" (a term used in the interview by Hamilton but not by Lowell). The poem for discussion here is from the volume of 1973 with the title *History*, presumably chosen to suggest changes in the scope and style of the poems in this volume by contrast with those in *Life Studies*. Still, the distinction is more of degree than of kind, since the title of the poem itself presents it as "personal," "autobiographical" in reference: "For Ann Adden 1. 1958" (the sense of personal history being extended by the three poems following, addressed to the same named figure over a period of time).

The style of the name "Ann Adden" in the title, not a literary pseudonym or the glamorous name of a public figure, tells us the poem is about the poet's private connection with an actual woman. Our acceptance of that claim does not depend on our knowing who she is (Lowell's affair with her is recounted in Ian Hamilton's biography) but on the kind of name and on the unexplained date hinting at a shared memory of some privately important time.[38] Because the title tells us this much, it prepares for the traditional shift from its public third-person reference to the direct address of the poem, which begins:

> Remember standing with me in the dark,
> Ann Adden? In the mad house? Everything—
> I mad, you mad for me?[39]

The personal pronouns continue to pile on to the end of the poem: "me," "I," "you," "my," "your," "our," "we." The lines are also thickly textured with remembered details of personal objects and experiences that, since we are not in a position to get all the references, strengthen the impression that the poem draws on intimate memories and private associations. So does the repetition of the listener's name: at the beginning "Ann Adden," the same form as in the title but become playfully affectionate address; then in the last line, with graver intimacy, simply "Ann."

The poem might seem to fit the definition of overheard speech, but again the presence of the title and its particular form invite questions about the application of Mill's famous formula. "For Ann Adden" rather than *to* her gives the title a formal style of presentation appropriate to this sonnet's traditional form (its interlocking rhyme scheme is especially noticeable among the many unrhymed sonnets in the volume). "For Ann Adden" announces: *this is a poem written for Ann Adden*, not a representation of a fragment of speech said *to* her (in *History* only "To Daddy" and a sequence of four poems "To Allen Tate" use that preposition). While the beginning of the poem is written in informal half questions and broken phrases, it expands toward the end into allusive, metaphysical love poetry: "Pascal's infinite, perfect, fearful sphere—/ the border nowhere, your center everywhere. . . ." Then the last line, hyperbolic in the tradition of the sonnet (but wilder, nearly blasphemous in its echo of Psalm 137:5—"If I forget thee, O Jerusalem, let my right hand forget her cunning"), is a version of the poet's vow to immortalize. "And if I forget you, Ann, may my right hand . . ." has a double address to "you, Ann" and to the readers for whom the poet's writing hand will preserve her in his sonnet.

The title of the poem presents it as a life study, which insists on its status as both autobiography and art. As Lowell describes this kind of poem to Seidel,

if a poem is autobiographical—and this is true of any kind of autobiographical writing and of historical writing—you want the reader to say, This is true. In something like Macaulay's *History of England*, you think you're really getting William III. That's as good as a good plot in a novel. And so there was always that standard of truth which you wouldn't ordinarily have in poetry—the reader was to believe he was getting the *real* Robert Lowell.[40]

This definition of an autobiographical poem like "For Ann Adden 1. 1958" is very far from imagining the poet with back turned to the reader. There the focus is on the separation of the reader from the listener in the poem and the concealment of that other audience from the dramatic fiction of *I* speaking to *you*, as if the poem had no title. Lowell's definition shifts its focus to a different fiction, which is not meant to persuade us, to repeat Leishman, "that we are overhearing one of the speakers in a dialogue," but rather to encourage in us the sense that what "the *real* Robert Lowell" says in a poem written "For" an actual person in his life "is true" experience made into art.

To a nonhuman listener

Jonathan Culler quotes Frye quoting Mill as the starting point for his own discussion of poems "which turn away from empirical listeners by addressing natural objects, artifacts, or abstractions." He locates such "invocations" at the center of a "poetics of the lyric" that considers them under the aspect of apostrophe, the figure of "embarrassment."[41] It is chiefly literary critics and their audiences who in Culler's view are embarrassed by the extravagance of apostrophe, but if we look among title forms for this kind of poem we can see signs of some corresponding uneasiness in their makers. The titles of poems that turn their backs on the empirical listener to address a natural thing—Herrick's "To Meddowes," Swinburne's "To a Seamew," Longfellow's "To the River Rhone"—or a work of art or man-made object—William Walsh's "To his book," Marianne Moore's "To a Steam Roller"—very often use only the simple prepositional form traditional also for poems that imagine a human listener. Poems addressed to abstractions less often do: John Keats's early "To Hope," Wordsworth's feeble "To Enterprise," Moore's satirical "To Statecraft Embalmed" are exceptions. Instead poems of this type are much more commonly presented as instances of a literary kind, almost invariably the ode or hymn: Thomas Gray's "Ode IV. To Adversity"; Mark Akenside's "Ode VI. Hymn to Cheerfulness"; William Shenstone's "Ode to Indolence"; Laetitia Barbould's "Hymn to Content"; Shelley's "Hymn to Intellectual Beauty"; George Meredith's "Ode to the Spirit of Earth in Autumn"; Ginsberg's "Ode to Failure." Even Wordsworth, who determinedly does not name the genre in his titles for poems to natural objects (though there are eighteenth-century precedents like Richard Polwhele's "Ode to a Red-Breast"), follows the common practice for apostrophizing abstractions in the title of "Ode to Duty."

These contrasting patterns in titling suggest that poets themselves may feel some risk of embarrassment in addresses to abstractions, because of all forms these come closest to what Culler calls "the pure embodiment of poetic pretension: of the subject's claim that in his verse he is not merely an empirical poet, a writer of verse, but the embodiment of poetic tradition and of the spirit of poetry."[42] It may be to justify what might otherwise seem an embarrassingly pretentious posture that poets tend to evoke generic authority in such titles: this poem is an ode; it has the license allowed by its genre; its tradition sanctions the claim to prophetic power calling into being an abstraction to hear and potentially answer the bardic utterance.

A title that identifies the listener in the poem as a nonhuman presence is at the farthest remove from the literal situation of the reader with book in hand open to the poem, where this chapter started. Still, since a title that says the poem is heard by some thing is a form of personification, its personifying act can in various ways blur the distinctions between the nonhuman *you* and what Culler calls "empirical listeners."

In titles that say the listening object is the book or poem, a convention stretching back to manuscript and early printed books and still alive in this century, the separation between the nonhuman listener and the reader is least emphasized. The reason is that the book or poem addressed is a linguistic object made by the poet and experienced by the reader and can be used metonymically for either or both. That possibility is expressed in conventional phrases as old as the title form itself. First is the use of the author's name in place of the title for the work, for instance when Milton writes of reading about the sublime art of poetry "in *Horace*," as if book and author were one (reflected also in the grammar of early titles for volumes like *Horace his epistles*).[43] Second is the equally conventional phrasing empowering the conflated poem-poet with speech: Keats's "Till I heard Chapman speak out loud and bold." Here not only poet and poem but poem and reader are bound together, because whenever the poet-poem speaks, even if explicitly in self-address, there is the reader whose presence is implied by the title as ultimate audience.

The assumptions on which these conventional expressions are predicated are the same as those that inform titles addressing the poem itself or the book. Jonson's "To my Booke" makes the point by charging the personified object-book "Thou" with the poet's role to "let men know" what constitutes the kind of "honesty" in speech that raises poet-book above the reach of "vulgar praise." In Roy Fuller's sonnet "To a Notebook," written around 1950, the text is a hostile reminder—"You always open at unfinished pages"—of the poet's precarious immortality: "Will you survive me? That's my constant care, / Living a miser for a doubtful heir."[44] Because the object-book is linguistic, it can also be identified with the reader capable of listening and responding to what the poet says to *you*. This identification is embedded in O'Hara's "To the Poem," which in manuscript had an earlier canceled title, "To a Reader." Its opening—"Let us do something grand"—is an invitation to "be"—"In a defiant land / its own a real right thing," which "thing" is the doing and being that unite poet, reader, and poem.[45]

Like titles imagining a book or poem as the listener, titles addressed to natural things seem to turn away from the reader while using that gesture to raise issues about the relations among poet, reader, and the fiction of the listening object. Herrick's title "To Blossoms" addresses an unlocated, collective natural object that exists as imagined listener only in the poet's personification. After it invokes this listening presence, the personification is then elaborated in the first two stanzas, where blossoms are spoken to as blushing beauties and asked questions as if they could speak the answers. Here the fictional situation is that the poet turns to address the personified presence of the collective blossoms. Then the last stanza redefines the listening object by transforming blossoms into a verbal artifact, the book or poem:

> But you are lovely Leaves, where we
>   May read how soon things have
>   Their end, though ne'r so brave.[46]

With this transformation the poet begins to turn away from the natural object in shifting pronouns, as "you" become "things" that have "their" endings, while "we" refers to the poet and the reader standing for all human beings as distinct from natural objects. Here the poet faces the other audience only implicit in the title, holding up the metaphorical book where "we" can read the lesson that blossoms have been made to serve in the poem:

> And after they have shown their pride,
>   Like you a while: They glide
>   Into the grave.

Now "we"—the poet and the reader—have been drawn grammatically "Like you" into a comparison with "things," so that we "read" our life as brief and our death as the falling of blossoms. Herrick's grammatical design of the title working with the poem charges, complicates, and finally dissolves the separation between the metaphorical natural object that is the poet's imagined listener and the reader whose presence is implied by the title.

Wordsworth's titles for his many poems addressed to things in nature include only one in the plural, not in Herrick's unqualified collective noun form but "To the Clouds," those "Ascending from behind . . . that tall rock." All his other addresses are defined by singular nouns further defined by *the* or—not as often—*a*. The choice between definite and indefinite articles, while less obviously important to us than the differences between singular nouns and their plural forms, was of "mighty" weight to Wordsworth, he writes in a letter of 1808. Quoting a careless reader who had referred to his poem "on a Daisy," he strenuously corrects the mistake: "it is on *the* Daisy, a mighty difference."[47]

In the same year as his three daisy poems, 1802, Wordsworth wrote the first and greater of his two poems "To the Cuckoo," using his preferred grammatical form of title address. What a dictionary says about *the* can go some distance in explaining its importance to Wordsworth. It is categorized as both definite article and demonstrative adjective, "used chiefly before a noun to individualize, specialize, or generalize its meaning."[48] It can point to a particular—*the cuckoo I hear*—as distinct from the possible "indefinite distributive force" of *a*—*I long to hear a cuckoo*—and from the "abstract force of the unqualified noun"—*cuckoo*. It can also generalize by pointing to a genus or species: *the cuckoo is a bird one hears in the spring*. Built into the title "To the Cuckoo," then, is the question whether it individualizes or generalizes the natural object addressed in the poem, which itself explores the same question in the form of what to "call" the bird.

Hearing the cuckoo's "shout" is an intensely personal experience for the poet, who addresses it intimately in the second-person singular and in endearments—"Darling of the Spring!"—calling attention to his own presence by repeated first-person pronouns.[49] "I" is used five times in the opening eight lines. Insistent repetitions of "thee," "thou," "thy" and "I," "me," "my" through the penultimate stanza work to will into being recognition, response, an intimate message from the cuckoo to the poet. The exclusion of any other audience comes close to being asserted in the original third stanza (by contrast with its more equivocal revised version):

> To me no Babbler with a tale,
> Of sunshine and of flowers,
> Thou tellest, Cuckoo! in the vale
> Of visionary hours.

The exchange imagined between "Thou" and "me" individualizes *the* cuckoo as if it were a human being, but the intimacy is more "long'd for" than achieved because the cuckoo is to the speaker an "invisible Thing." It is evasive because not located like the poet in a body or in time; it is a "Newcomer" and yet "The same whom in my School-boy days / I listen'd to." Because it is a "Thing," it has no individuality to separate it from the species, which is how the generalizing force of the definite article defines it.

The effort to will a response turns into a different kind of apostrophe in the last stanza:

> O blessed Bird! the earth we pace
> Again appears to be
> An unsubstantial, faery place;
> That is fit home for Thee!

The "Bird" is elevated above the human sphere almost as an abstraction. The poet is separated, ontologically, from the cuckoo, which does not pace the earth, and now the pronoun "we" in place of "I" acknowledges the reader in a common humanity with the poet as the ultimate audience for the poem. The title "To the Cuckoo" simultaneously particularizes but also generalizes the natural object so that the imagined possibility that the cuckoo can listen and respond to the poet is seriously called in question, as Herrick's address to the personified collective "Blossoms" is not. This is a "mighty" purpose served by Wordsworth's precisely considered title form.

Also in 1802, Wordsworth wrote the second and greater of his two poems with the title "To a Butterfly." A dictionary description of the multiple uses for the indefinite article *a* can again suggest what Wordsworth saw as its special expressive powers. Before a noun, *a* can point to: one particular of a class; some undetermined or unspecified particular; some certain one; someone or another; one of a kind; any, each, every. It therefore combines the power of particularizing with its indefinite distributive force. Both are at work in Wordsworth's poem.

The first stanza insists more than "To the Cuckoo" on the immediate presence of the natural object directly in front of the speaker in a concretely detailed setting: "I've watched you now a full half hour, / Self-poised upon that yellow flower."[50] The butterfly has individuality because the speaker can see it as its separate self, which makes it more accessible to personification. His question is not here what to call it. He more easily uses the conversational pronoun "you" rather than *thou* to speak to it, and instead of the epithet "Darling of the Spring!" calls it more simply "little Butterfly," struck by its physical smallness.

All these features serve the particularizing aspects of the title but already "little Butterfly" predicts changes to come. It can mean that the watching poet is struck with the specially diminutive size of this butterfly in contrast with butterflies of other types, or with the smallness of all butterflies next to human beings, and in comparison with grandeurs of nature like "frozen seas," which this "little Butterfly" in its impenetrable "motionless" being brings to mind. The thought causes a disturbance in the speaker, silently marked by the stanza space and expressed by the change in pronouns as "I" is replaced by "we," "our," "us." They first refer to himself and his sister—"This plot of Orchard-ground is ours"—and then attempt to include the butterfly. David Ferry, to whose discussions of this poem and "To the Cuckoo" mine are much in debt, hears in those lines a "jauntiness" that exposes the personification as "a piece of wishful thinking":[51]

> Come often to us, fear no wrong;
> Sit near us on the bough!
> We'll talk of sunshine and of song;
> And summer days, when we were young.

Like the cuckoo, a butterfly has no youth or memory of it, but here "We'll talk" more pointedly calls attention to the fact that it has no language—butterflies do not even make a sound that could be construed as voice, song, shout, cry—and therefore undermines more unambiguously its imagined presence as the personified listener in the poem. Here "we" become the human audience, represented also by the poet and his sister, who share the language that records our individual existence in time. The indefinite reference of *a* combined with its power of greater particularity allows the title "To a Butterfly" to serve a more disruptive purpose than "To the Cuckoo." It works with the poem to expose to the reader the collapsed fiction of a personified natural creature as the listener in the poem, a fiction the "I" cannot let go.

Twentieth-century poets find their own ways of exploring the issues raised by such personified listening objects. An instance is Williams's poem in *Pictures from Brueghel and Other Poems* of 1962 with the title "Bird." The choice of natural object makes a place for the poem in the tradition of Wordsworth's addresses to things in nature, the greatest number of them being to such winged creatures—"Cuckoo," "Skylark," "Redbreast," "Butterfly"—a choice also inspiring some of the greatest poems (and many lesser ones) by other nineteenth-century poets. While Williams's title alludes to that tradition, it recasts it by stripping down to the unqualified noun with a peculiar abstract force, freestanding as a purely grammatical entity. It suggests the essence of "Bird," birdness, after the model of titles for abstract paintings and sculptures. In keeping with that analogy, Williams's title form seems to reject the tradition of an address *to* a bird that would inevitably personify it. Such an imposition of human language on it would violate its birdness.

This prediction of the title is lived up to by the first stanza—

> Bird with outstretched
> wings poised
> inviolate unreaching[52]

—especially in allusive contrast to Wordsworth's personification of the "Self-poised" butterfly whose inviolate "motionless" being the speaker tries to reach by talking to it. Then Williams allows a special form of address, grammatically direct but otherwise indirect, displacing "Bird" with "your image," which is not "fixed" *by* the imposition of a personifying interpretation, but "in" the poet's "eyes." They are "arresting" as a present participle that respects the timeless immediacy of natural process. If the language were troubled, as it is in "To a Butterfly," these stanzas could suggest the poet's helplessness to resist "reaching" out by personifying a nonhuman listener. In their own poised clarity, imaging the bird's, the lines point instead to the way "your" is attached only to "image," the painting or sculpture or poem that "miraculously" represents birdness, leaving the natural object "inviolate."

Marianne Moore's title "To a Giraffe," from the volume *Tell Me, Tell Me: Granite, Steel, and Other Topics* of 1966, follows the grammatical form of "To a Butterfly" but her choice of natural object is a comical departure from the tradition. It depends for its humor partly on the way it is unlike but also like winged creatures that can ascend to a sphere—Moore's animal "can live only on top leaves"—not "reachable" by human beings.[53] The title is amused at itself also because it predicts a poem directly addressed to a "beast" very awkward to speak to because it is so inhumanly "tall," and hard to get an answer from because for all its size it can only make a barely audible sound.

Then the poem itself goes its own way apart from tradition because it turns out not to be addressed to a giraffe or to any *you*, but meditates to itself or to some unspecified, unlocated audience on "the giraffe" as "the best example" of the poem's topic. What the topic is the poem never defines except obliquely, by its refusal to personify "the unconversational animal" it also refuses to address. Instead of making it human, the poem treats the giraffe as an escape from the "personal," the "psychological," the "conversational" that plague "some emotionally-tied-in-knots animal." The implication is that "the giraffe" is an "example" of the state of being the title poem of the volume pleads for—

> Tell me, tell me
> where might there be a refuge for me
> from egocentricity[54]

—and more particularly it is a model for the poet who can write "To a Giraffe" without using the address of *I* to *you* that imposes a personification on what is, "to be exact," a fellow "creature."

To *one*

In Wallace Stevens's *Adagia*, his mastery of the indefinite pronoun *one* is at play in a gnomic pronouncement on what this chapter is about: "One does not write for any reader except one," a sentence as relevant to the kinds of titles discussed here, and as riddling, as O'Hara's "The you is you. As you may know."[55] The first "One" can be taken as a disguised *I*, as the poet, but the second "one," itself more evasive, complicates that reading with overlapping possibilities. Taking "one" as a reference to a disguised someone, the adage jokes about another convention of secretive titles like those discussed earlier, for instance: Thomas Randolph's "To one admiring her selfe in a Looking-Glasse"; Edgar Allen Poe's "To One in Paradise"; Arthur Symons's "To One in Alienation." While the exaggerated obliqueness of the doubled "one" in Stevens's sentence hints of some such secret reference, other readings working together take precedence: one does not write for any reader except oneself; except for some single intelligence, another self; except for a reader who is also a poet or for poets like ourselves; except for you. With characteristic evasiveness, they constitute a reflection true to much earlier-twentieth-century poetry, and especially of course to Stevens's own.

In the whole of *The Collected Poems* there is only one title addressing the poem to a human listener, "To an Old Philosopher in Rome," and one to something in nature, "To the Roaring Wind," which is the four-line envoy to *Harmonium*. Neither type appears in *Opus Posthumous* or among the potential titles written in the notebook "From Pieces of Paper." The implications of this virtual exclusion, which the adage is a kind of comment on, are also reflected in Stevens's only other title for a poem using the prepositional form of traditional addresses, "To the One of Fictive Music," in *Harmonium*.

The complex route by which Stevens arrived at this precise—but awkward and oblique—wording is mapped on a manuscript copy of the poem described in an article by Louis Martz:

At first Stevens gave the poem the typed title, "To the Fictive Virgin". . . . This title is crossed out, and pencilled above and around it are varied suggestions: "Souvenir de la Muse De la Belle Terre," or "De la Terre Belle et Simple"; "Souvenir of the Muse of the Earlier, Simpler Earth"; "Souvenir of the Muse of Archaic Earth"; "Souvenir of the Archaic Muse"; "Souvenir of A Muse"; "To the ["Fictive" *crossed out*] One of Fictive Music."[56]

Surviving from the first version to the last are the form of address "To" and the adjective "Fictive"; added are "the One" and "Music" to replace "Virgin" or "Muse."

"The One," especially modified by the tentatively added but then canceled "Fictive," has all the evasiveness of the indefinite pronoun in the adage with some different definitions as well: an entire being or thing, or single in kind; a thing conceived or spoken of indirectly; a certain thing or person not specified; any person or thing whatever; in philosophy, the first principle or ultimate being. This proliferation of possibilities, combining particular but unspecified references with large abstractions, works to charge "The One" with paradoxically precise but all-inclusive meanings, enhanced by the awkwardly attached phrase "of Fictive Music": "The One" composed "of Fictive Music"?; the oneness "of Fictive Music"?

"Fictive" in the title makes connections most directly in the poem with

"Our feigning"—the imaginings of human beings, of poets, of modern poets—and with "Unreal"—the final invocation of the "Fictive Music": "Unreal, give back to us what once you gave: / The imagination that we spurned and crave."[57] Still, that "Fictive Music" is not quite what the final version of the title says the poem is addressed to, as Wordsworth's is "To the Cuckoo" or as Stevens's first version of the title was "To the Fictive Virgin." It is addressed instead to "the One," which includes the Virgin-Muse but also all the possible references of the indefinite pronoun, among them "us"—human beings, poets, readers—a connection made more explicit in the manuscript copy of the poem, where the penultimate line reads "Unreal, give back to us what once we [not "you"] gave." The "Fictive Music" is an imagined absolute one craves as the "I" of "To the Cuckoo" once longed to see the invisible source of the bird's disembodied cry, but the source of "Fictive Music" is "The One," a supreme fiction. Addressing it, as Stevens does in this poem, one does not need to write for any reader except one.

Part III

AUTHORITATIVE HIERARCHIES

CHAPTER FIVE

What kind the poem belongs to

QUESTIONS about *kind*—a term with a much longer history in English than the equivalent nineteenth-century French import, *genre*—are inextricably bound up in titling, since a title gives the reader directions about what to make of the poem, and so does its kind. For this reason a title, without naming what the poem is, can have other ways of identifying its formal kind. A formulaic phrase like Jonson's "To the Reader" can announce an epigram. Williams's "Bird" names a traditional poetic image but in a stripped modernist form presenting the poem as a revision of the Romantic ode. The pronoun in Yeats's "He Remembers Forgotten Beauty" is a code word signaling a love poem. The name of the singer in Marvell's "Damon the Mower" locates him in a pastoral, while Wordsworth's naming in "The Affliction of Margaret ———" shapes responses appropriate to a ballad. Without explicitly stating the kind—"Damon the Mower['s Song]," "The Affliction of Margaret ———[: A Ballad]"—these titles act as generic signals for how to read the poem. Titles in the different category explored in this chapter do explicitly present the poem as a member of a formal kind. While giving these sorts of signals, they can also do other work—generating different kinds of expectations, exploiting new expressive possibilities.

A title that states what kind the poem is calls attention first to the poem's existence as a discrete entity. It is presented above all as an object more than as someone's utterance or as the representation of some other object. It is a thing existing independently, constituted of language, but with a special identity because the words it is made of are arranged according to some linguistic design or function that its kind expresses and that its title naming that kind directs the reader to look for. The very fact stated by the title that the poem has identifiable formal features—even titling a poem a "Fragment" announces a form recognizable for its fragmentariness—emphasizes its freestanding status, distinguishing this category of title from those already discussed, where the emphasis of presentation is on the titler, the author, the speaker, the listener. The distinction constitutes one among several reasons why titles presenting the poem by kind are preferred in some periods more than in others.

Traditional terms

The focus on the poem as a formal entity is sharpest in titles that say nothing but what kind the poem is. John Hollander, in the article cited in the Introduction, uses "Sonnet" as his example of "the completely redundant title." He places it on a "spectrum along the axis from redundancy to maximum informativeness" at the opposite pole from a title performing a "much more analytic or interpretive role," like "Le Monocle de Mon Oncle."[1] No one would disagree that "Sonnet" is likely to strike the reader as relatively inexpressive compared to Stevens's attention-getting, idiosyncratic title. In fact, in the early period when the presence of titles for short poems was unpredictable, collections both in print and manuscript often used terms like *sonnet* (which could at that time have a meaning as vague as *poem*) to do the same work as a blank space, an ornamental design, or a line above the poem dividing one entry from another. In *Brittons Bowre of Delights* of 1597, "A Sonet" fills the title space above a stanzaic poem followed by "A Poem" of fourteen lines in rhymed couplets. Once the presence of a title given by the author came to be expected, then even a seemingly neutral label like *sonnet* or *ode*, which does little work of interpretation itself and seems to demand none of the reader, can be expressively charged. Sometimes the very show of neutrality in titling by formal kind is a device for insinuating an interpretive characterization of the poem. In other instances, the naming of formal kind in the title is an active element in the whole expressive design of the poem.

A title naming the poem's kind, even one saying nothing but that, must recognize though only implicitly the reader whose response it directs. This is to some degree true of any title—even if it seems like a neutral label—since any title is a presentation of the poem to someone. Beyond that recognition, a title naming a formal kind, and this is specially true of traditional kinds like the sonnet and the ode, implies more about who the someone is. Wordsworth made the uncharacteristic choice of simply "Ode" for his poem given the privileged last place in his *Poems, in Two Volumes* of 1807, to which he later added, below the formal term in the title space, the subtitle "Intimations of Immortality from Recollections of Early Childhood."[2] The original title, aided by a separate title page saying only "ODE." (with a quotation from Virgil on the reverse side—*Paulò majora canamus*, "let us sing a greater song"), focuses attention on the poem as an object belonging to an elevated formal kind and empowered by it. It makes the poem's identity as "Ode" part of its lofty argument or theme: its intimations of immortality. The title could not work as a generic signal unless it assumed the status of a presentation to readers educated in poetic traditions and sensitive to distinctions of kind. This classical literary education is not demanded of readers by titles like "To a Butterfly" or "To the Cuckoo" for poems that Wordsworth's contemporaneous critics liked to ridicule as celebrations of minutiae by calling them "his odes to '*Small* Celandines,' 'Daisies,' and 'Butterflies,'" in defiance of his own pointed decision not to title them by formal kind.[3] His choice of the simpler title form, while it purports merely to name the listener in the poem, implies his ideal audience for it, readers who will respond freshly, without the conventional expectations dictated by the authority of generic classifications. Keats makes the same choice, with the same cultural implications, in "To Autumn," by contrast with his use of the traditional term in the titles for his other odes.

Any title that focuses on what kind the poem belongs to must of course also acknowledge implicitly that the choice of kind was the poet's, who then performs in it. Given this implication, a title saying nothing but what kind the poem belongs to, like Wordsworth's "Ode"—not *Ode to* some listener or *Ode on* some topic; not even *An Ode*, one performance in its kind—keeps the poet's presence separate, as it were, from the finished object by its unqualified noun form. A contrast would be with Keats's "Ode to a Nightingale," where the attached prepositional phrase brings the poet's act of addressing into the title, and where "a" in this instance comes close to particularizing that address as the representation of a single utterance in time and place. The title form "Ode" contrasts in a different way with Keats's "Ode on a Grecian Urn," with its combined emphasis on the poem's membership in a formal kind and on its status as a representation of some object other than itself, bringing closer the presence of the poet who observes and represents that object. The simple grammar of "Ode" makes the title a freestanding entity, like the poem. Because it is an unqualified noun, it is not part of a sentence, not part of someone's utterance, not potentially dramatic. Nothing mediates, so to speak, between the poem and its noun title.

In such a presentation there is a perfect coincidence of what John Hollander, borrowing terms from René Wellek and Austin Warren, calls "outer form (specific meter or structure)" and "inner form (attitude, tone, purpose—more crudely, subject and audience)." He associates titling that aspires to this coincidence of inner and outer form with the practice and ideals of neoclassicism, reflecting "a longing for a great golden age in which poems needed no titles whatsoever. Being entitled, as it were, by birth to their genre and authority, they were like an aristocracy that preceded an arriviste nobility."[4] Such nostalgia he finds embodied in the neoclassical preference for titles combining a "topic label" with "a usually redundant" term for a traditional formal kind. This title form—Dryden's "An Ode, on the Death of Mr. Henry Purcell" is an example—is markedly more common in the late seventeenth and earlier eighteenth centuries than in other periods, a sure sign that it reflects some deeply held cultural attitudes such as Hollander suggests.

Earlier, generic terms like *sonnet* were used in titles for volumes, for instance George Turberville's *Epitaphes, Epigrams, Songs and Sonets* of 1570, and this practice continued well into the seventeenth century, as illustrated by the 1649 edition of Richard Lovelace's *Lucasta: Epodes, Odes, Sonnets, Songs, &c. To Which Is Added Aramantha, A Pastorall*. Headings within volumes also took this form: the 1602 edition of *A Poetical Rapsody* includes a separate title page introducing "Sonnets, Odes, Elegies, and Madrigalls." Yet poems under those classifications do not necessarily repeat the generic term in their titles and often do not belong to the kinds specified in the heading. The loosely fitted heading "Songs and Sonets" for Donne's love poems in the 1635 edition is a later example imitating the title of Tottel's miscellany. Up through the earlier seventeenth century, short poems were sometimes given a double title like "Elegie II. Or Letter in Verse" from *A Poetical Rapsody*. Such linkage of alternatives by *or* may have been borrowed from title pages where the entrepreneurial advantage of presenting a volume under as many addenda to the title as possible led to abuses often satirized, as in the title *Twelfth Night; Or, What You Will*. In the poem title just cited, the addition of a second generic term in the subtitle suggests deference to and possible vagueness about the proper kind to name the poem, along with uncertainty about the generic sophistication of the audience for it. Subtitles in this period were useful in meeting such concerns.

Toward the end of the seventeenth century, titling according to kind began to sort out these confusions as it became the preferred style of presentation, but even at this time definitions describing characteristics that separate one kind from another often overlapped, so that they blurred those distinctions. To state the point another way, definitions of kind were various enough and flexible enough even in this period, when taxonomies were specially valued as ways of ordering the reader's understanding, that a title could be chosen from a variety of more or less precisely applicable generic terms. While in theory such a title purports to reflect an objective correspondence between the particular poem and its established kind, making inevitable the choice of the generic term to present it, in practice that choice has a range of signifying possibilities. It may be true that in this cultural situation of poetry, when titling by kind was preferred, the question of which formal term to use in the title was most particularly weighted. Evidence of this pressure seems to be reflected in various aspects of titling in the later seventeenth and eighteenth centuries.

John Dryden's reception of the newly official English title of poet laureate in 1668 coincides, not altogether coincidentally, with his emerging influence on the titling of poems in this period. He seems to have set a prestigious example by giving order and prominence to titles naming the kind and topic of the poem, a form used before in English (especially for epigrams and epitaphs) but less often, and typically with less careful attention to the wide range of possibilities in the naming of kinds. Dryden's characteristic titles, often aided by subtitles, encode a program for invoking the authority of ancient generic terms to give official sanction and social acceptance to current matters in modern poems. In other titles he uses presentations by formal kind to shape interpretive characterizations of the poems. Both functions suited the interests of poets who followed him.

To begin where Dryden seems to have discovered the usefulness of finely tuned titling by kind, one of his earliest poems was published in 1659 with the title "Heroique Stanza's, Consecrated to the Glorious Memory of his most Serene and Renowned Highnesse Oliver Late Lord Protector of this Common-Wealth, &c." The precision in his choice of "Heroique Stanza's" can be measured by the substituted titles given to this poem when it was later put into print by enemies of Dryden to attack his political allegiances. In 1681 it was published as "An Elegy on the Usurper O.C."; in another reprinting the suggestive possibilities of "Heroique Stanza's" are further reduced by the substitution of "A Poem." These changes of formal classification show that the hostile titlers saw the intentions of Dryden's original choice.

He uses a term to describe his lines with the neutral meaning explained in the dedication to his translation of Juvenal: "The English Verse, which we call Heroique, consists of no more than Ten Syllables."[5] Similarly, "Heroique Stanza's" is a formal technical term for cross-rhymed iambic pentameter quatrains; it does not overtly make the inflated claim of a more elevated generic classification like *heroical poem*. At the same time Dryden allows the charged adjective "Heroique" and the recent association of the stanza form with Davenant's *Gondibert* of 1651 to attach to his subject because his verse form, being designated for the celebration of heroes, elevates Oliver Cromwell to their stature, which is disallowed by the generic terms in the titles substituted by his enemies. Meanwhile the same associations elevate his poem itself, although his title cannot be accused of saying so, by linking it to the kind traditionally recognized as highest or greatest in the generic hierarchy. The purportedly neutral formal term "Heroique Stanza's" molds ancient and modern precedents to serve the social and political needs of a highly charged contemporary topic.

Dryden finds ways to use the possibilities for insinuation in an apparently neutral, traditional vocabulary for naming kinds in other titles, sometimes reinforcing them with explanations of their design that seem matchingly forthright. An early example is "Annus Mirabilis The Year of Wonders, 1666. An Historical Poem." It was printed the following year with "An account of the ensuing Poem" that is also an account of its combined topical title and generic subtitle: "I have call'd my Poem *Historical*, not *Epick*, though both the Actions and Actors are as much Heroick, as any Poem can contain."[6] The reasons he gives are that "the Action is not properly one" because "ti'd too severely to the Laws of History," and that "*Epick*" would be "too bold a Title for a few *Stanza's*, which are little more in number then a single *Iliad*, or the longest of the *AEneids*." The protagonists of his poem who are named by their titles on its title page, "His Highness Prince Rupert, and His Grace the Duke of Albemarl," are here characterized at once as epic heroes and as actors in the great events of ancient Rome. His poem is made equivalent to a book of the *Iliad* or *Aeneid* while being honorably bound to historical truth. In turn the poet is defended by the title's modest generic claim from accusations of boastful self-presentation, and by its precision from charges of ineptitude for failing to follow the rules of epic unity.

The sophistication and complexity in Dryden's ways of using these generic terms in titles and subtitles show up by contrast with how earlier poets cite prestigious precedents to justify their use of formal terms, often new in English. Michael Drayton explains his title *Englands Heroicall Epistles* of 1619 by deferring to "OVID (whose Imitator I partly professe to be)"; *The Legends* he claims precedent for in Spenser, the first in English who transferred *legend* "from Prose to Verse"; for "the title of Ballade" he invokes the double authority of "*Petrarch*, and our *Chaucer*."[7] Such appeals seek respectability for the generic term itself and therefore credentials for the poet, without using the term in suggestive connections with the poem. When alternative terms are weighed, the balancing *or* makes a typically loose rather than a purposeful distinction, as when Drayton refers to his "last Ode . . . or if thou wilt, Ballad in my Booke."[8] Dryden's more finely honed discriminations within a much wider range of generic terms make that vocabulary serve the subtle designs discovered so far in two of his early presentations.

He attaches the most neutral seeming of all formal terms to a title in the boldly simple subtitle of "Absalom and Achitophel. A Poem." There is something magisterial in this presentation, as if by 1681 John Dryden did not need even the sanction of classical precedent to lend authority to his verse; as if an audience were prepared and waiting for "A Poem" from him of any kind, and on whatever topic he might consider worthy of his art. Yet none of this is said or can be charged to his titling, which makes no inflated claims for the poem's kind. Nor does the epistle "To the Reader," which opens in the same tone of magisterial calm: " 'Tis not my intention to make an Apology for my *Poem*: Some will think it needs no Excuse; and others will receive none. . . . Yet if a *Poem* have a *Genius*, it will force its own reception in the World," and in this instance it does so by means of its subtitle, which gives independent authority to the poem to "force" appropriate responses from its readers.[9] More deeply embedded in this non-apology, though, is a hint that "A Poem" is not a neutral but a calculatedly loaded term used as a pointed substitute for the expected "Satyre" (the kind named in Dryden's subtitle for "The Medall. A Satyre Against Sedition," published the following year). The substitution of "A Poem" is a proud claim to rise above the meanly partisan expectations of "a Malitious *Reader*," which are unworthy of the "Impartial" honesty to be met in the work of this "Historian" in verse. The choice of formal term supports that large-minded claim to be above mere party.

When in 1682 Dryden adds the same neutral formal term in the subtitle to "Religio Laici Or A Laymans Faith A Poem," he adopts the same authoritative manner, again for submerged and complex ends. The subtitle "A Poem" is a dignified disguise for an advertisement telling his ready audience of potential buyers for the volume that they will find in it the mode of writing they look for from the poet they know and admire though, "The Preface" says, "so serious a Subject wou'd not be expected" from him. The formal term is also a critical defense of the poet's authoritative choice to treat "Speculations, which belong to the Profession of *Divinity*" in verse.[10] That is to say, embedded in this broad generic subtitle is a manifesto for didactic poetry, which continued to grow more interesting to poets following Dryden.

His titling practices lent glamor to presentations of poems by kind and showed their shaping power by exploiting their range of signifying possibilities under a mask of neutrality, all at a time when attention to the fiercely hierarchical classification of kinds was intensifying. Dryden was the refiner of generic titling as a device for adjusting the reception of a poem, though not of course the discoverer of it. There was the precedent of Jonson, especially in his appropriation from Martial of the generic term for the title of his *Epigrammes*, supported by a prefatory account advertising the volume as "the ripest of my studies." Typically, later seventeenth- and eighteenth-century titles follow the practice of naming kinds that appeal to the authority of classical models. This form of presentation evokes an ideal society to which poets and readers equally belong because they share educated familiarity with the same texts and with the traditional vocabulary for classifying and ranking them. By contrast, these assumptions seem not to have been counted on by sixteenth- and earlier-seventeenth-century poets, Jonson being the self-appointed exception. They tend to give signs of uncertainty, like Drayton's, about their audience's familiarity with the generic terms they invoke in the presentations of their poems.

In the later period, traditional terms for formal kinds of verse can be relied on as a device for declaring hierarchical standards—aesthetic, moral, social—even in titles where they are used partly for comic effects: as in Thomas Gray's "Ode on the Death of a Favorite Cat, Drowned in a Tub of Gold Fishes"; Anne Finch, Countess of Winchelsea's "The Spleen A Pindaric Poem"; John Gay's "The Toilette. A Town Eclogue." Other titles can strike us now as inadvertently comic misfits but must not have had that effect in their own time. Examples are John Norris's "The Passion of Our Blessed Saviour, Represented in a Pindarique Ode" or John Wesley's substitutions of "Anacreontick" for Herbert's titles "Life" and "The Rose."[11] In their original context these neoclassical titles and subtitles reflect an assumption shared widely by poets and readers that ancient kinds correspond objectively to the whole range of verse forms, making them capable of representing all topics appropriate to poetry.

Unsettled traditional terms

In any period the active vocabulary of formal kinds, because it describes features reflecting shared standards among members of the same kind, can be used to measure adjustments of the norm or departures from it. In the late seventeenth and eighteenth centuries when generic classification was specially valued as a way of invoking a hierarchy of norms, it could work as a particularly sensitive gauge. Some poems in this period exploit a generic title as a way of pointing to the poem's special situation in its kind, or as an attack on its kind, even as a critical comment on generic classification itself. Like the titles where a neutral formal term is a mask for an interpretive characterization of the poem, the examples to be considered also use the vocabulary of kinds as complex signals, but these give more particular directions that allow the wording of the title an active role among the other expressive details that make up the design of the poem.

Here is an epitaph of Pope's published by him in 1738, six years before his death. As it appears on the page, the whole presentation is at least as

prominent as the verses, if not more, and takes up almost as many lines.
It calls attention to itself that its wording, as carefully calculated as the
poem's, repays:

EPITAPH
For One who would not be buried in
Westminster Abbey.

Heroes, and Kings! your distance keep:
In peace let one poor Poet sleep,
Who never flatter'd Folks like you:
Let Horace blush, and Virgil too.[12]

Poem and title together make a shape on the page that looks the way an
epitaph should, imitating in its typographical design the carving on a burial
monument. Pope's readers would respond to this visual representation of
its formal kind because they could be counted on to know the antique
origins of the term from the Greek meaning an inscription *on* [*peri*] *a tomb*
(by contrast, Wordsworth's title for his sixty-line stanzaic poem "A Poet's
Epitaph" does not demand this recognition but instead exploits the separation of the term from its literal root meaning). Pope's title, naming the kind
and beneath it the topic of the epitaph, imitates the identification of the
person buried under the carved stone, followed by praises of the deceased
below that name. This epitaph looks at first glance the way it should, but
its looks are satirically misleading. They raise expectations immediately
unsettled by the wording below the neutral generic term, in its every detail
and then in its equally detailed connection with the language of the verses.

Most arrogant of Pope's departures from the conventions of the epitaph
in the presentation is the substitution of "*One*" for the name of the honored
dead. It calls attention to the poet who deliberately withholds the name
and to his estimate of the unnamed subject. In some contexts *one* could be
a contemptuous dismissal—*some one or other, some nobody, someone
not worth naming*—but the finely calculated choice of the preposition in
"*For One*" sets a different tone. That is, the preposition normally expected
to precede the inscribed name of the deceased is *on*, not *for*. Pope uses this
traditional form in the titles for virtually all his epitaphs, the other exceptions being the "Epitaph Designed for Mr. Dryden's Monument" and the
"Epitaph. Intended for Sir Isaac Newton," both plans meant *for* actual
monuments. In the title of an epitaph, *on* can be neutral, meaning simply
inscribed upon, but in Pope's different wording "*For One*" the tone is more
personal, sympathetic. It implies some complicity between the maker of
this epitaph and the person *for* whom it is meant, who is presumably not
yet dead and therefore does not have a tombstone to inscribe *on*. The poet,
the title implies without admitting, withholds the name from motives of

allegiance to *one set apart, one alone, the only one* who, the title tells us, has chosen this separateness: "*who would not be buried in Westminster Abbey.*" This refusal constitutes grounds for sympathy from the poet who, in turn, refuses on behalf of "*One*" to meet the formal demands of the epitaph, the kind by definition meant to preserve and publish the name, as Samuel Johnson declares in "The Criticism upon Pope's *Epitaphs*," first published in 1756: "The end of an epitaph is to convey some account of the dead; and to what purpose is any thing told of him whose name is concealed?"[13]

Although the poet's presence is formally kept out of Pope's title by the preferred neoclassical combination of generic term and topic, his violations of the expectations raised by that form make an issue of the author's relation to the subject whose name is withheld, and to the readers from whom it is hidden. The title in this way creates special expressive possibilities then developed in detailed connections between its wording and the language of the verses. They make a kind of drama out of the tensions among the participants whose presence is suppressed in the title. It is of course because of the recognized prescriptions built into the term *epitaph* that violations of them can be expressively charged.

The "*One*" of the title emerges as the "one poor Poet" of the poem who is the defiant maker of both, writing his own epitaph to prevent the inscription on the tomb he refuses to be buried under. He calls himself the "one poor Poet" in several proud senses: that he is the one poet to be pitied because he is besieged by honors he alone despises; that he wants to be the one poet to escape the discredited distinction of being buried in the overcrowded Poets' Corner of Westminster Abbey; that he is the one poet who is poor because he alone has "never flatter'd" the rich and powerful and so will not be buried among their sycophants. Matching the arrogance of "*One*" in the title in place of the name is the poet's substitution in the first verse for the expected opening of an epitaph. The traditional choices—*here lies* (*hic jacet*) or *stay traveler* (*siste viator*)—invite the imagined audience to draw near, that they may read or listen to the name and praises of the dead. Here the poet reverses these commands—"your distance keep"—holding his name and reputation aloof from inferior "Folks," the "Heroes, and Kings" and poets who are or "*would . . . be*" (*will be, want to be*) buried in Westminster Abbey.

This command, together with the equally defiant withholding of the name in the presentation of the subject, shapes the defining features of the kind to an attack on it, voicing the same scorn Pope heaps on it in a letter dated 1736: "*Epitaphs* (that is to say, Flatteries and False History) . . . the Burden of Church-walls, & the Shame, as well as Derision, of all honest men."[14] Presentation and verses work together expressively to make a special space for the poem within its kind: it is an anti-epitaph.

Beyond that self-definition, the poem is a critical comment on how generic classification itself can be made to condone abuses of poetry. One way the epitaph makes this criticism is by its choice of target, not some unworthy modern invention like the sonnet but a respected ancient kind. Johnson says of it in "An Essay on Epitaphs" published two years after Pope's anti-epitaph: "If our Prejudices in favour of Antiquity deserve to have any Part in the Regulation of our Studies, Epitaphs seem intitled to more than common Regard, as they are probably of the same Age with the Art of Writing."[15] It is precisely these "Prejudices" that Pope's attack on the epitaph exposes, and not only because his subversion of the kind depends on its recognition and respectability. In the last and boldest stroke of his anti-epitaph he takes aim against heroes admired in earlier Augustan England for establishing standards by which modern poets might be judged worthy of an epitaph in Westminster Abbey. "Let Horace blush, and Virgil too" is a judgment on abuses of kind, the "Flatteries and False History" perpetrated by all poets but "one" when they hide behind the authority of classical kinds and names to exonerate themselves for their lies. It is also a castigation of readers who accept such manipulations of their "Prejudices" as substitutes for the standard of truth in poetry.

In its different ways the title of William Collins's "Ode, Written in the beginning of the Year 1746," appearing in December of that year in *Odes on several Descriptive and Allegoric Subjects*, makes connections with the language of the poem so that their combined effects place this ode in a special situation within its kind. The title is curiously worded so that a couple of details locate the poem centrally in a recognizable tradition while others displace it. In this way the title presents the poem in a different relation to its kind than Pope's anti-epitaph, not as an attack on it but as a modification of it. It is a reflection *on* the conventions of the ode rather than what would be traditional, a reflection *of* the standards embedded in them.

Because it includes a date, Collins's title purports to classify his "Ode" as belonging to a traditional type within its kind: a public commemoration of an event recorded in recent history, like Marvell's "An Horatian Ode upon Cromwell's Return from Ireland." By associating the poem with this type of ode, the unexplained date asks to be read as hyperbole because it implies that the topic of this poem is a public happening so famous it needs no further identification than by year and season. Since "the beginning of . . . 1746" is in the immediate past of the volume's first audience, the date is assumed to be vivid in their memories and will be kept so for posterity by the ode, which begins its work of commemoration in the opening couplet:

"How sleep the Brave, who sink to Rest, / By all their Country's Wishes blest!"[16] This hyperbolic exclamation, following the presentation of the poem by topical date, meets the expectations raised by associating it with the tradition of odes celebrating public events.

Other details in the formation of Collins's title set the ode apart from more conventional members of its kind. An example for comparison is his "Ode to a Lady on the Death of Colonel Ross in the Action of Fontenoy," the only other commemorative ode in the volume.[17] The comparison points to the omission from the gloss in "Ode, Written in the beginning of the Year 1746" of more information about the event to be celebrated than the time it was written *in*, while nothing is said about what topic it might be *on* or who might be the imagined listener *to* it. This oddity turns out to be a prediction of others to come.

After the public commemorative opening couplet, which suits the kind of topic hinted in the title, the remaining ten lines turn away from the conventions of poems like the "Fontenoy" ode. There a procession of mourners coming to "bless the Grave" passes before the listening "Lady" and the poem's readers, who are the public audience at the ceremony. The mourners are "*Britannia*'s Genius," "His Country's Vows," "*Honor*," "The warlike Dead of ev'ry Age." They constitute a heroic pageant of "pictur'd Glories" painted by "The Muse . . . with social Grief." In the "1746" ode, which does without the cumulative force allowed by length (all but three of the other odes in the collection are more than forty lines, none is less than twenty-four), the mourners are of a different order: "*Spring*, with dewy Fingers cold," "Fairy Hands," "Forms unseen," "*Honour* . . . a Pilgrim grey," and "*Freedom* . . . a weeping Hermit." If these allegorical figures are meant to recall carvings on burial monuments, they point to the circumstance that here only "Sod" covers the tombless dead. No spectators witness the procession, as there is no listener named in the title *to* whom the ode is addressed. No public commemoration is recited over the fallen heroes as in the other poem or as the opening couplet of this one predicts. There is only a strangely unattended marking of the event that shrouds it in a kind of privacy, even in the poem commemorating it, as there is no nameable topic in the title *on* which the ode can heap public tributes like those traditionally spoken before the gilded monuments of England's heroes. This "Ode," like its title, is restrained, almost secretive, by contrast with others of the kind it both evokes and departs from, which are dedicated to the articulation of publicly recognized standards and to the celebration of their own powers of utterance. Collins's poem is reticent not only about its topic but about itself, about the capacity of "*Fancy*" to articulate "unseen" and silent mysteries. It is a reflection *on* more than *of* its kind, which depends on its special situation in it. In this way the title "Ode, Written in the beginning of the Year 1746" finds its own quietly powerful expressiveness.

These two odes—in Collins's 1746 volume separated by position, form, and title gloss—were reprinted in Robert Dodsley's *A Collection of Poems by Several Hands* in 1748. The date May 1745 is added to the ode commemorating "the Action of Fontenoy," and the other poem is closely bound to it by its adjacent position and new title, "Ode, Written in the same year." Whether it was the editor or the poet who changed this presentation, the effect of the revision is to identify the topic with a specific event (the defeat of the English forces by the French in 1745).[18] The reasons for the revision are less clear than their effect. It may be that as time passed, whatever event was originally hinted by dating the poem early in 1746 became confused or overlaid in public memory with other happenings. Especially if this were so, it may be that the unusual withholding of any more information in the title that would identify the topic of the ode was a source of uneasiness for the poet, the editor, or the audience. That is, the revision seems to be an attempt to make the title less mysterious, to bring the poem more fully in line with clearly articulated conventions of its kind, the public commemorative ode, than its original presentation allows or than the text of the poem sustains.

New terms

The marked preference for classical naming of kinds in titles of later-seventeenth- and eighteenth-century poems gives special weight to the one prominent exception, the choice of the modern term *essay* for many even of the most prestigious poems in this period. Often cited is the triad praised by Joseph Addison in *The Spectator* in 1711 as English poems (by the Earls of Roscommon and Mulgrave and by Pope) worthy of comparison with Horace and Nicolas Boileau: "we have three Poems in our Tongue, which are of the same Nature, and each of them a Master-piece in its kind; the Essay on Translated Verse, the Essay on the Art of Poetry, and the Essay upon Criticism."[19]

Poems assigned to this modern kind include many that could have appropriated classical authority by using the traditional term *epistle* in the title: for instance, Benjamin Stillingfleet's *An Essay on Conversation*, published in 1737, and William Whitehead's *An Essay on Ridicule* of 1743. Each is in the form of an address to a friend, a requisite in most definitions of the epistle, for instance Ralph Johnson's of 1665: "a Discourse wherein we talk with an absent friend, as if we were with him."[20] Sometimes, in fact, the same poem is assigned to both these kinds, as in the 1734 version of Pope's title *An Essay on Man, In Epistles to a Friend*. It could be argued that the pairing of these alternatives was a device for dignifying the modern term by making it a synonym for a kind with a history stretching back to Rome, and there is likely to be some truth in this. Sir Francis Bacon had earlier defended his title *Essayes* saying: "The word is late, but the thing is ancient; for *Senecaes* Epistles to *Lucilius*, yf youe marke them well, are but *Essaies*."[21] Still, it is surprising that there seem to be virtually no hostile comments, in this period of heightened sensitivity to generic hierarchies, about the arriviste status of the nonclassical term *essay*, no apologies for its recent birth or defenses of its legitimacy. Among titling practices of the period, it must have had some compelling cultural appeal of its own to account for its exceptional prominence.

To seventeenth- and eighteenth-century writers and readers the word *essay* had built-in meanings as well as social implications now largely submerged. They were more attentive than we are to its root in the verb *to assay, to try*, prominent in dictionary definitions like those cited by Samuel Johnson, who gives among synonyms for the noun *attempt, endeavour, trial, experiment*. This is the meaning it has in what seems to be its first appearance in English in 1584 in the title of a volume consisting mainly of verse translations by the amateur poet who became King James I, *The Essayes of a Prentise in the Divine Art of Poesie*. The term stayed close to its roots in the seventeenth century when used for translations in particular, as in the prefatory epistle to John Hayward's *Davids teares* of 1623: "I did put forth two of these psalmes at the first, for an assay." Used this way it refers to the attempt *of* someone, a "Prentise" like James Stuart or someone making a new experiment or testing it out, which seems to be Drayton's meaning in the prefatory letter to *Poly-Olbion* of 1612 where he defends himself for "publishing this Essay of my Poeme."[22] When the preposition changes in presentations of translations, for instance in Sir John Denham's *The Destruction of Troy, An Essay upon the Second Book of Virgils AEneis* of 1636, the term still seems to retain the suggestion of modest tentativeness built into its root sense, *to make an essay on*.

By the second half of the seventeenth century a new generic meaning for the term crops up in titles for poems, for instance one published in 1657 in a volume ascribed to Henry King. Although *essay* is not among the kinds listed in the book's title, *Poems, Elegies, Paradoxes, and Sonnets*, it seems to have the status of a generic term in the presentation of one of the poems that manuscript evidence proves was chosen by King, "An Essay on Death and a Prison." Here "on" makes sense as a synonym for "about" the way it is used in Ralph Johnson's definition of 1665: "An Essay is a short discourse about any vertue, vice, or other common-place."[23] This use of *essay* as a formal term gained favor after the publication in 1668 of Abraham Cowley's *Works*, which included "Several Discourses by way of Essays, in Verse

and Prose"; by the early 1680's, with the publication of the Earl of Mulgrave's "An Essay upon Poetry" and the Earl of Roscommon's "An Essay
on Translated Verse," presentations of poems in titles combining this generic term with a topic or "common-place" claimed an esteemed rank in
the hierarchy of poetic kinds.

The publishers of the volume that includes "An Essay on Death and a
Prison" justify their piracy of King's poems in a prefatory letter to the author by quoting Bacon's defense of self-presentation prefixed to the first
edition of his *Essayes* in 1597: "The Lord *Verulam* comparing ingenious
Authors to those who had Orchards ill neighboured, advised them to publish their own labours, lest others might steal the fruit: Had you followed
his example, or liked the advice, we had not thus trespassed against your
consent."[24] The popularity and prestige of Bacon's often reprinted essays
made them a valuable precedent in a period when many poets no longer
wanted to preserve the reputation of writing only for a private circle of
friends. At the same time these poets were intent on presenting themselves
as respected members of a society of cultivated persons, holding conversation in their published verse with readers belonging to the same society. A
special kind of balance was required of poets to maintain this polite posture
while setting themselves apart from earlier amateur "*Versifiers*," scorned
by Pope for writing "like a Gentleman, that is, at leisure hours, and more
to keep out of idleness, than to establish a reputation."[25]

Even in the earlier period no stigma attached to publication by learned
writers of prose like the "Lord *Verulam*," whose own social title lent status
to the kind associated with his name. His self-presentations in prefatory
letters also helped to guard the essay from the charge of professionalism by
carrying over into its definition as a literary form its root meaning of a
tentative trial or attempt. Bacon describes his own essays as "fragments of
my conceites," "breif notes," "dispersed Meditacions."[26] Far from being
derogatory—in his lordly "Epistle Dedicatorie" to the Duke of Bucking-
ham in the final expanded version of 1625 he calls the essays his "best
Fruits"—these descriptive phrases make serious though modest-seeming
claims.[27] They associate the essay with an easy, unstudied manner by implied contrast with a more formal and pedantic style suited to discourse
among professional scholars but not between persons of shared social
standing who are at least potentially friends.

In the later period, John Locke's choice of the generic title for *An Essay
Concerning Humane Understanding* of 1690, influential on the titling of
poems in the generation after Dryden, reflects these continuing associations. In "The Epistle to the Reader" Locke describes his *Essay* as "hasty
and undigested Thoughts . . . written by incoherent parcels" in a "discon-
tinued way of writing" before being put into "order" in a style free from

pedantry to make them "plain and familiar."[28] Locke's authorship of the
Essay is announced on the title page starting with the second edition of
1694, and it confirms the special appeal of the generic title for the adjustment of social attitudes toward self-presentation that this was his only major work published with his name on it during his lifetime.[29]

Locke's own comment on this issue points to the connection between
the essay as a literary form and the growing acceptance of self-publication
in the later seventeenth and eighteenth centuries:

I have so little Affection to be in Print, that if I were not flattered, this Essay might
be of some use to others, as I think, it has been to me, I should have confined it to
the view of some Friends, who gave the first Occasion to it. My appearing therefore
in Print, being on purpose to be as useful as I may, I think it necessary to make,
what I have to say, as easie and intelligible to all sorts of Readers as I can.[30]

An "easie and intelligible" style such as one might address to friends suits
the meaning of the term *essay*, which, like some of Dryden's generic titles,
has an air of making no pretentious claims for itself. Dryden acknowledges
this device in "To the Earl of Roscomon, on his Excellent Essay on Translated Verse" in 1684: "Yet modestly he does his Work survey, / And calls a
finish'd Poem an ESSAY."[31]

To title a poem an *essay*, then, was to present it as a work intended for
publication, written by a poet in conversation with other members of society whose assumed familiarity with the literature of Greece and Rome
makes them fit readers to appreciate modern English models like Bacon
and Locke in prose, Cowley in verse. By encoding an interpretive characterization of the poem in the seemingly neutral definition of its form, *essay*,
the title defines the tone of the poem. That is to say, it sets up a relationship
between the poet and the reader even though they are kept out of the title,
allowing an element of drama without blurring the focus on the status of
the poem as an independent entity or on its membership in a recognized
and respected kind occupying a privileged position in the authoritative hierarchy.

The ode survived the Romantic realignment of formal kinds while the
neoclassical specialty, the essay, virtually disappeared in the nineteenth century—exceptions being Elizabeth Barrett Browning's "An Essay on Mind"
and Oliver Wendell Holmes's "Poetry: A Metrical Essay"—to be revived in
a few twentieth-century titles, some of them pointed allusions to Pope:
Louis Untermeyer's "Essay on Man"; Randall Jarrell's "An Essay on the
Human Will"; Karl Shapiro's "Essay on Rime"; Frank O'Hara's "Essay
on Style"; Robert Pinsky's "Essay on Psychiatrists"; Robert Duncan's "An
Essay at War." The different histories of the two kinds were shaped by the
perception of them as polar opposites. An early paradigmatic statement of

this view is Joseph Warton's "Advertisement" to his volume of *Odes on Various Subjects*, first published in the same month of the same year as Collins's *Odes*. There Warton predicts that the preference for "didactic Poetry alone, and Essays on moral Subjects" will be displaced by renewed interest in the ode as the vehicle for the "chief faculties of a Poet," which are "Invention and Imagination."[32] Generic revolutions like this, which seem to be fought in virtually every period, are temptingly describable in generalizations, but they are of course made to happen only through detailed changes in particular poems, sometimes brought into sharpest focus in their titles.

Generalizations about Romantic reinterpretations tend to take as their starting point the volume of *Lyrical Ballads* published in 1798, also a likely place to look at some fine details in titling that signal these larger transformations. Geoffrey Hartman has given us an excellent model for this kind of exploration in his essay "Inscriptions and Romantic Nature Poetry." He begins it by observing that Wordsworth's "Lines left upon a Seat in a Yew-tree, which stands near the Lake of Esthwaite, on a desolate part of the shore, yet commanding a beautiful prospect" is a generic invention that "challenges the same apparent freedom of designation" as Coleridge's description of "The Nightingale" as a "conversation poem." About Wordsworth's "Lines left upon a Seat . . . ," ". . . Tintern Abbey," and other poems in *Lyrical Ballads*, Hartman writes, "There is a pleasure in not knowing, or not being able to discern, the traditional form; the lack becomes a positive virtue, and we begin to seek, not quite earnestly, for the proper formal description."[33] His article then goes on earnestly and convincingly to show the way Wordsworth transformed the "nature-inscription" into a freestanding poem. The detail he ignores, because it is beside that point, is that Wordsworth does in fact give not a "traditional" but a "proper formal description" in a number of their titles, including the one for the poem Hartman, like the rest of us, refers to as "Tintern Abbey." Wordsworth describes them by the formal term "Lines."

Among the nineteen poems by Wordsworth in the 1798 volume, five have titles that present them as "Lines." This feature is quietly emphasized by the absence from the titles of his other poems except "Anecdote for Fathers" of any formal terms. Wordsworth's repetition of "Lines" seems a still more pointed choice when we learn, as we can from Robert Mayo's indispensable article "The Contemporaneity of the *Lyrical Ballads*," that it excludes alternative titles for stanzaic and blank verse poems similar in topics and structures to Wordsworth's that were popular in magazine verse of this decade.[34] From Mayo's survey we discover that while titles like "Lines, (Written at Old Sarum, in Wiltshire, in 1790)" do appear in these magazines, the commoner formal terms for presenting such poems are "Verses" and "Stanzas," both in the neoclassical vocabulary for titling by kind. Examples are Pope's "Verses to the Memory of an Unfortunate Lady," later promoted to "Elegy," and Gray's first title in manuscript, "Stanza's Wrote in a Country Church-Yard," which, at the suggestion of his editor, was also elevated to "An Elegy."[35] Other generic alternatives for titling magazine poems of the same types are also common: "Inscription," "Sonnet," "Ode." Although the evidence supports Mayo's argument that none of Wordsworth's titles in the *Lyrical Ballads* is itself an original "experiment" (his own description of the poems in the "Advertisement") that would set it at odds with contemporaneous practice of titling poems similar in topics and forms, still what is in fact out of the ordinary is their cumulative emphasis.

The exclusive repetition of "Lines" in the presentations of poems in the volume leads up to the longer poem reserved for the privileged last place (occupied in *Poems* of 1807 by Wordsworth's only poem originally titled simply "Ode"). As the title for this poem first appeared on the page, the formal term looms large:

L I N E S

Written A Few Miles Above

TINTERN ABBEY

On Revisiting the Banks of the WYE During

A Tour,

July 13, 1798.[36]

The importance Wordsworth gave to this title for this poem is shown in a note about his choice of formal term added in the 1800 edition of *Lyrical Ballads* (where the poem keeps its privileged position by coming at the end of the first volume): "I have not ventured to call this Poem an Ode; but it was written with a hope that in the transitions, and the impassioned music of the versification would be found the principal requisites of that species of composition."[37]

Not to venture "Ode" as its presentational signal is a limited accommodation to conventional expectations, since poems of that kind are traditionally in stanzas, not in blank verse. It is also a gesture of seeming modesty, the substituted term "Lines" having no recognized status in the generic hierarchy while, as Wordsworth's comment acknowledges, the ode occupied the highest or greatest rank in the usual grading of shorter kinds. Still, the choice of "Lines" to present a poem of such scope and power, placed as the climactic last entry in the volume, is at the same time an act of self-assertion, staking out a position at odds with established notions of poetic kinds. These "Lines," the presentation of the poem implies and Wordsworth's later comment on it states, are a worthy match for the ode. They embody the "principal requisites" that constitute its greatness, making these "Lines" deserving of equal valuation with the grandest of shorter forms. In saying that he has refrained from titling the poem an "Ode," he virtually says that it is to be read not exactly as a new form of ode but as a poem freely existing in its own right outside the hierarchy of kinds and commanding greatness independent of that authority.

The choice of verse form for the poem supports the quiet self-assertion of its title, since both the term "Lines" and the nature of blank verse grant what Hartman calls "apparent freedom of designation." Although *lines* could be applied to rhymed verses or even to stanzaic poems (and Wordsworth does so use it for other poems in the volume), it has a different emphasis. That is, the term *stanzas* in a title contains the poem it presents within grouped divisions of lines. Even the Pindaric ode, though it allows the stanzaic units to be shaped, as it were, by the spontaneous overflow of emotions into irregular groupings, imposes more structural restraints than *lines*. Similarly the term *verses*, though it could properly be used to describe a poem not in stanzas and unrhymed, may have been associated with more formal restrictions, more determining precedents than *lines*, even though the terms were then literally synonymous.

Verses has a much longer history than *lines*, which according to the *OED* entered the English vocabulary of versification only in the sixteenth century. The Latin word *versus*, active in English centuries before Chaucer used it, had ancient roots referring to the regular linear furrows and turnings of a plow. This original sense was still much closer to the surface of its English translation in the eighteenth century than it has become since. For instance, the root meaning of *versus* is present in a couplet of Pope's "Spring, The First Pastoral, or Damon," which implies a comparison so familiar to his contemporaries that they did not need to have it explained, namely between the oxen's measured plowing and the poet's rhymed and end-stopped lines: "Sing then, and *Damon* shall attend the Strain, / While yon slow Oxen turn the furrow'd Plain."[38]

Carrying this metaphorical sense, the term *verses* gives more emphasis than *lines* to the predetermined movements of lineation, and especially to line endings. Working toward the same effect is the historical tendency to associate *verses* with rhyme. As the term *blank verse*—also introduced in the sixteenth century—tells us, unrhymed lines were defined as deviations from the norm by what they leave out: like sounds in their final words, which inevitably tend toward closure. Blanking out those rhymed endings opens other possibilities.

Wordsworth's preference for the presentational term "Lines" may then be bound up with his claims for the last poem in *Lyrical Ballads* that it achieves the power and grandeur of an ode. Christopher Ricks has shown that the word *line:lines* figures richly in many lines of Wordsworth's poems (Ricks does not consider titles), and naturally so as an expression of his passionate attention to transitions from line to line.[39] Other, more visually striking transitions in this poem are marked by the spaces between verse paragraphs that, like the stanzas in a Pindaric or *irregular* ode (the accepted alternative term sometimes used by Wordsworth), are relatively free in meter and unpredictable in length. These spaces often divide the later part of a line from the earlier, which happens also in transitions within paragraphs, so that the metrical pattern is respected while the line is otherwise freed from its predetermined form. The transitions from line to line, such as Ricks describes, and from one larger structural or grammatical unit to another create the "impassioned music of the versification." This description of Wordsworth's is apt because the lines and larger units appear to be shaped by movements of thought and feeling rather than by the outward forms of stanzas or verses.

Transitions from line to line are explored in finely observed detail in Ricks's essay. Those between verse paragraphs or even within a paragraph depend less on subtle nuances than on larger shifts that are more obviously striking. One such transition in the second verse paragraph can therefore suffice here as an example. The middle of its three sentences builds to a final affirmation of visionary power absolutely declared. Then the movement of sentences begins again by questioning that affirmation (the 1798 edition marking the transition by wider spacing than is used in later editions):

> While with an eye made quiet by the power
> Of harmony, and the deep power of joy,
> We see into the life of things.
>   If this
> Be but a vain belief, yet, oh!

To borrow a device from Ricks, if we consider the effect of the lines differently spaced, we can see and hear what would be their loss of expressive "power":

> We see into the life of things. If this
> Be but a vain belief, yet, oh!

or worse still:

> Of joy, we see into the life of things.
> If this be but a vain belief, yet, oh!

The grammatical break is intensified by dropping the final iamb of the transitional line to its lower position, but that device does not actually disrupt the metrical regularity. Instead it creates a visible space and heard pause marking a spontaneous crisis of realization, and it is this inward motion, it seems, rather than the predetermined metrical pattern of the lines or grammatical division of the paragraph into sentences, that expresses this "impassioned" transitional moment in the poet's experience.

"Lines" in this title, like spaces in the poem, expresses what it does not say. In its quiet way it announces a new kind of poem that the title must direct us how to read because, its presentation implies, it occupies an independent place outside the authority of traditional classification. As a key to reading the poem it is very precise: it tells us to focus on the lineation, which means following its transitions and listening to the music of its versification. The literalness of the formal term "Lines"—that is after all what the poem is made of—and its self-effacing modesty seem not to direct attention to this poet's performance in a kind practiced by many. At the same time "Lines," by contrast with other formal terms, does hint at the poet's individuality. It grants the freedom to follow natural, inner motions rather than the constraining dictates of man-made conventions, what Wordsworth in the "Advertisement" calls "pre-established codes of decision." Some lines early in the poem elaborate on this suggestion of the title by echoing it in describing "lines" made by natural process in the scene before the poet's eyes:

> Once again I see
> These hedge-rows, hardly hedge-rows, little lines
> Of sportive wood run wild.

This is a metaphor for the poet's natural freedom in his "Lines," written as he wanders along the banks of the Wye, itself a "wanderer through the woods."

The implied contrast between a title presenting "Lines" and titles invoking traditional kinds is subtly drawn here when measured by a more aggressive declaration of independence from the authority of traditional classification in a heading in Wordsworth's *Poems* of 1807, "Moods Of My Own Mind." The group under this heading includes "To the Cuckoo" and both poems titled "To a Butterfly," along with others regularly attacked in reviews as "odes" on what one critic calls "objects which poetry has from the first been permitted to disdain."[40] The insistence of hostile reviewers on imposing an established generic term where Wordsworth resolutely avoids it is a response to the defiance in his titling. "Moods" are inward motions rather than outward forms; not publicly recognized norms but intensely personal experiences, a claim underlined in "Of My Own Mind." The form and measure of a poem presented as a *mood* in Wordsworth's sense must come from within, resisting generic ranking, as the choice of topics for these poems disdains a hierarchical ranking of natural "objects."

A shift in the same direction is visible beginning also in the very late eighteenth century in other newly common terms for formal kinds: "Musings," "Thoughts," "Effusion," with their claims to inward sources; "Sketch," "Impromptu," "Extemporary Verses," and again "Effusion," suggesting spontaneous expression and experimentation. Wordsworth in a letter of 1816 defends the looseness of the term "Effusions rather than Compositions" when the poem's "occasion is so great as to justify an aspiration after a state of freedom beyond what a succession of regular Stanzas will allow."[41] Coleridge uses a number of these terms, sometimes defying traditional titling by calling attention to substitutions like "Effusion," a term of abuse in neoclassical criticism, for "Sonnet."[42] In other titles he makes a gesture wholly dismissive of conventions, for instance "Something Childish, but very natural." The addition of the subtitle "A Desultory Poem" for Coleridge's title "Religious Musings" is a device for exaggerating its suggestion of impulsive motions.

Calling a poem a *fragment* or *unfinished* makes similar signals. Whether it might be a decision about design or a way of dealing with the fact of incompleteness, the willingness to publish verses under such a title declares their new freedom. "A Fragment" appeared as the original title, later made the subtitle for Wordsworth's poem renamed "The Danish Boy," and in numerous other subtitles. Examples are: Coleridge's "The Foster-Mother's Tale. A Dramatic Fragment"; "Kubla Kahn; Or, A Vision in a Dream. A Fragment"; Lord Byron's "The Giaour: A Fragment of a Turkish Tale"; Keats's "Calidore: A Fragment"; Leigh Hunt's "Ariadne Waking. A Fragment"; an entry in Thomas Percy's collection of *Reliques Of Ancient English Poetry*, "King Arthur's Death. A Fragment." Subtitles in this period were often used as a device for loosening the restrictions of generic titling, in contrast with neoclassical subtitles typically given the work of legitimizing the poem by invoking the authority of traditional generic standards.[43]

Recent extensions of traditional classification

As the range of formal terms has continued to expand in the titling of twentieth-century poems, their distance from traditional classification has widened in varying measures. In generic titles at one end of the spectrum the shift in vocabulary is deliberately shocking, extending into regions outside the wall built up by the hierarchy of kinds to divide the conventions of poetry from those of other vocabularies we use in very different areas of experience, even some we tend to think of as hostile to poetry. Among them, newspapers, business correspondence, legal documents, political papers, scientific or philosophical treatises, and other still more specialized sources provide new formal terms in the titles of many twentieth-century poems. Examples can show something of their remarkable variety among resemblances: Laura Riding's "Advertisement"; Robert Lowell's "Obit"; D. H. Lawrence's "Manifesto"; Claribel Alegría's "Documentary"; May Swenson's "Question"; Derek Walcott's "Codicil"; Josephine Miles's "Statute"; Philip Booth's "Chart 1203"; Eamon Grennan's "Compass Reading"; Etheridge Knight's "Memo #32"; Tony Towle's "Scrap Paper"; Carolyn Forché's "Message"; Frank Home's "Toast"; Charles Wright's "March Journal"; Charles Simic's "Progress Report"; Edward Dorn's "Thesis"; Langston Hughes's "Theme for English B"; Anthony Hecht's "Curriculum Vitae"; Thomas Kinsella's "Wyncote, Pennsylvania: a gloss"; Roy Fuller's "Notebook"; W. S. Merwin's "Cover Note"; Christopher Logue's "Footnote"; Lawrence Ferlinghetti's "A Note After Reading the Diaries of Paul Klee"; Amy Clampitt's "Notes on the State of Virginia"; William Empson's "Note on Local Flora."[44]

The title of Stevens's "Note on Moonlight" from *The Rock*, the final volume in *Collected Poems* of 1955, announces a distinctively twentieth-century poem by borrowing from the vocabulary of treatises, especially scientific ones since its topic is a phenomenon of the physical universe. It says that what follows will record some observation on this topic, but not be a full treatment of it or a whole body of recordings preparatory to a finished treatise, like the much longer earlier poem, "Notes toward a Supreme Fiction." The later title "Note on Moonlight" classifies the poem as an annotation or brief appendix to a larger work: possibly the volume, where it is placed fourth from the end; the long earlier poem; the entirety of Stevens's previous work; more particularly, his many treatments of "Moonlight" in response to a strand of the Romantic tradition in nineteenth-century poetry.

The first stanza in its most insistent features lives up to the title's prediction that the imagined model for the poem is a scientific note. Observation, like notation in the title unattached to anyone observing, is focused on "The one" phenomenon of the moon lighting up "the mere objectiveness of things," not some composite image loosely evoked by the word "moonlight" and its associations.[45] The uninflected, impersonal mode of the poem set here centers it in the category of "Note" named in the title. Human presence is excluded except in comparisons and in the hidden self behind the pronoun "one." This suppression of the first person recalls other poems by Stevens discussed in earlier chapters, but here it is associated with the grammar of scientific reports, also imitated in passive constructions like "the purpose to be seen."

The dominant impression of seemingly scientific "objectiveness" in the opening lines distracts from the way they pick up the hint of the title's interest in "Moonlight." That is, the topic of study here, "The one moonlight," may light up "the mere objectiveness of things," but the poem says that it more glamorously "Shines," and compares it to a poet contemplating "The sameness of his various universe." This is a modernized version of Matthew Arnold's deceiving, moonlit "world" in "Dover Beach," which only seems "So various, so beautiful, so new." These first hints of "a" poet's presence and responsiveness grow steadily stronger in Stevens's poem until the last two stanzas, where, "In spite of the mere objectiveness of things," there is "A change of color in the plain poet's mind." Now what is "to be seen" is no longer "the sameness of his various universe" but "the various universe," charged with "a purpose"—however "empty" or "absurd"—existing outside the poet's own mind. A now personal voice in the last line (sounding unlike Arnold, still less like a scientific "Note") tentatively "at least" affirms this various, new, and beautifully "intended" world: "Certain and ever more fresh! Ah, Certain, for sure . . ." The trailing dots unsettle what another exclamation point or even a period would conclude. Toward the end, though, there has been a quietly prepared for change of perspective, "Like a cloud-cap in the corner of a looking-glass," turning the poem into an appended "Note" on the Romantic tradition that skeptically allows its affirmations. The title, paradoxically by virtue of the impersonal, static term chosen to describe the poem, comes to play an active part in its dramatic movement.

Earlier generic terms are extended in a different way by titles that revise them in a distinctively modern idiom without crossing the boundary into vocabularies wholly alien to previous poetry. For example, the verse epistle is the more or less distantly recognizable ancestor of recent poems with such modernized titles as: Stevens's "A Postcard from the Volcano"; Derek Mahon's "A Postcard from Berlin"; Marge Piercy's "Postcard from the Garden"; Karl Shapiro's "V-Letter"; Owen Dodson's "Open Letter"; Charles Wright's "Nightletter"; May Swenson's "A Thank-You Letter"; Frank O'Hara's "A Note to John Ashbery."

The title of a two-part poem in Seamus Heaney's *The Haw Lantern* of 1987 claims just such a distant generic connection with the epistle, but it is phrased as if it were spoken by a modern voice: "Two Quick Notes." The idiom is familiar. We recognize the phrase as a casual, unserious apology from a person in a hurry, taking a couple of minutes on a too-full day to write to someone familiarly, someone probably not far away who is likely to get and answer scraps of correspondence from an understandably busy writer, and without much delay.

The first lines following the title, though they confirm the impression that the "Notes" are written to a "friend," in other ways jolt our expectations: "My old hard friend, how you sought / Occasions of justified anger!"[46] There is something too studied about the address, too summarizing about the description, and too charged about the exclamation to suit a few hurried lines to a friend. Among these disturbing details, the act of starting off in the past tense after the immediacy of the title already seems ominous, growing more so as the grammar relentlessly repeats it up to the last stanza, and with terrible meaning behind the familiar idiom "when you turned on yourself." Then the grammar changes to the apostrophic present in the closing stanza, where the writer again addresses the friend, but now as an object that cannot hear or answer. The utterly final line repeats the salutation of Catullus to the silent ashes of his brother:

> O upright self-wounding prie-dieu
> In shattered free fall:
> Hail and farewell.

Now we know not only the formal unsuitability of the title to this poem, which is not "Notes," not even an epistle, but an obsequy. In knowing this we also discover its devastating expressiveness. These so-called "Notes" are the work of a person caught up in daily experiences, conscious of time and energetically using it, remembering and looking forward since the act of writing to someone expects a response. Above all, because the title describes these "Notes" not as *brief* or *short* but "Quick," it reminds us that they are the words of someone fully living, driven to utter them in defiance of the knowledge that they must fail to be heard or answered across the gulf separating the quick and the dead. The absoluteness of the failure is measured by the vivid contemporaneity of the title.

Recent treatments of traditional terms

At the other end of the spectrum from titles that invade territories earlier thought to be inimical to poetry are twentieth-century titles that discover new expressive possibilities in using traditional names for formal kinds: *pastoral, rhapsody, sestina, sonnet* will serve as examples here. These long-established terms can of course encode new meanings in the presentations of more recent poems because they appear in the cultural situation of poetry when poets have shown themselves generally skeptical of attitudes previously associated with them, and so have tended to avoid or revise them in presenting their poems. More particularly, such traditional generic titles raise our suspicions when we meet them in the immediate context of other work by the same writer from whom we expect poems presented in titles more at odds with older generic conventions, more hostile to their authority.

Williams in a letter to Marianne Moore translates as "To him who wants it" the idiosyncratic dedicatory phrasing on the title page of his volume published in 1917: *A Book of Poems*, with below it in larger, bolder type *Al Que Quiere!* The order and typographical form of this presentation itself—fooling around with traditional relationships among title, subtitle, and dedicatory subscription—is a gesture of defiance made more humorous by the choice of Spanish instead of fashionable French, and more aggressive by supporting claims for the book on its dust jacket: to be "brutally powerful and scornfully crude," and to "outweigh . . . a dozen volumes of pretty lyrics."[47] This presentation raises the expectation that titles in the book describing poems by formal terms would borrow them from vocabularies outside or hostile to traditional generic classification, as do "Metric Figure," "Tract," "Dedication for a Plot of Ground." We are not prepared to find three poems with the title "Pastoral." Of all generic terms, this is likeliest to make us think of "pretty lyrics," ideally graceful, elegantly polite. Compared to another title for a poem in the volume, "Smell!" so obviously calculated to rub our noses in its comical crudeness, "Pastoral" seems, though hardly brutal, still meant to fill us with the shock of a milder surprise. Besides the joke of its discordant title in this context, the "Pastoral" beginning "When I was younger" is teasingly placed in the volume just after its Whitman-like opening manifesto, "Sub Terra," in which the poet asks where he can find "you my grotesque fellows," like-minded members of an underground movement subversive to traditional poetic authority, "to make up my band?"

The second poem, working with its incongruous title, seems to do everything it can to make us read it as an anti-pastoral; that is, as a modernist criticism of falsely idealizing prettiness in traditional pastoral. The long middle sentence takes up sixteen of the poem's twenty-two lines with a version of a convention dear to earlier poems in this kind, the catalogue of pleasures yielded by willing nature. Williams transports his poem to urban streets where the poet walks, "admiring the houses / of the very poor." Nature survives only grotesquely here in "chicken wire" littering backyards that display an assortment of discarded objects as ramshackle as the houses themselves,

>   all,
> if I am fortunate,
> smeared a bluish green

> that properly weathered
> pleases me best[48]

The poem seems to conduct an argument against pretty enhancements of nature in earlier pastoral, opposing them with scrupulously exact description of unglamorous objects that make up the modern city. The observer omits connectives and comparisons that might betray the poet arranging things, and avoids the ordering features of predictable metrical patterns or rhyme. Until the last lines of the catalogue the observer leaves out adjectives that would paint objects in evocative colors, implying that if the scene "pleases," it is not the poet's doing except insofar as the description is truthful, letting the shapes and surfaces of city dwelling show themselves to the attentive but unsentimental observer.

The last lines of the catalogue, without raising its voice, turn on the anti-pastoral argument implicit in it earlier by superimposing Williams's description of urban objects on Wordsworth's catalogue of natural things in the scene near Tintern Abbey. The decaying houses "all . . . smeared a bluish green" are versions of Wordsworth's "plots of cottage-ground, these orchard-tufts," remainders of former human dwellings now "with their green and simple hue," later revised to "clad in one green hue." In Williams's catalogue the past participle "smeared," as much as Wordsworth's "clad," hints at some agency working on the visible scene. It points forward to "weathered" in the next line with its broader hint of the cooperation between nature and the poet in making and perceiving order. Now the poem seems not to be an anti-pastoral, but a recasting of Wordsworthian pastoral.

Directions for reading the poem are then further complicated when we get to its last sentence, which works with the opening to make what seems to be a poorly fitted frame for the catalogue: "No one / will believe this / of vast import to the nation." In the familiar idiom we hear the poet defiantly claim that the poem is politically important no matter what anybody thinks, or—since "of vast import" is self-mocking—it is at least meant to be. In the end, then, there is still another possible reading embedded in the claim for the poem's political importance. It focuses attention on the fact that the catalogue describes what makes up the lives of "the very poor," looked at by someone more "fortunate" who can walk these mean streets admiring forms abstracted from their meanings, savoring what "pleases me best." It might be that the importance of the poem to the conscience of "the nation" is that it both participates in this aesthetic and exposes it as political in what is to be read as a new, distinctively modernist "Pastoral."

The transaction taking place between poet and reader in the title, instead of giving directions for us to follow, requires us or challenges us to figure out the clues it does give us. That would not be Pope's design in titling a poem "Pastoral," even though such a seemingly uncharged traditional term can encode complex signals expressing more than the title purports to tell us. Williams engages his readers in a more playful but a trickier game, because generic conventions no longer work in ways agreed on by both poet and audience, with the result that we are made to play the game without being sure we know the rules.

This tendency in modernist titling shows up in somewhat different ways in Eliot's "Rhapsody on a Windy Night," appearing in a volume published the same year as *Al Que Quiere!* A brief comment in Chapter 3 on Eliot's title touches on the way it raises false expectations, to be expanded on here. Most obviously it makes connections with nineteenth-century presentations of poems using the term *rhapsody* at once in its general sense, the sublime expression of rapture or ecstasy, and in its more special application to a new kind of free-ranging, enthusiastic musical composition. An instance is Elizabeth Browning's "Rhapsody of Life's Progress," with its epigraph "Fill all the stops of life with tuneful breath." Placing his "Rhapsody" just after another poem with a musical title, "Preludes," Eliot exploits these associations to make one move in his game with the reader.

A title presenting a poem as a "Rhapsody" in the nineteenth-century musical sense, which is derived from its more general meaning, is in the climate of earlier twentieth-century poetry as suspect in its intentions as Williams's "Pastoral." Williams himself uses the adjective *rhapsodic*—in a letter to Marianne Moore dated 1931—as a derogatory term for what he wants work of his not to be: "Rhapsodic? Not at all. I mean every word of it in the strictest sense of which I am capable."[49] The incongruity in Eliot's choice of kind is brought more directly to bear on the reader's experience of the poem by the context of the volume it appears in, described in its title as *Observations*. That term better suits the mean and unmellifluous style of the poem itself, which plays off against further expectations raised by a "Rhapsody" echoing what is heard "on a Windy Night." That title prepares us misleadingly for a poem that will sound like Shelley's "Ode to the West Wind." Recognizing this clash early in our experience of the poem (but not warned of it in the title, as we would be if it were in a cruder form like Richard Aldington's "Rhapsody in a Third-Class Carriage" or David Wright's "Rhapsody of a Middle-aged Man"), we follow the opening move in the game set up by the title.

Eliot's interest in tradition and the place of individual poems in it guarantees his knowing the ancient origins and pre-nineteenth-century history of the generic term *rhapsody*. Less certain but likely is his knowing that all but a very few of his readers would not know this tradition. *Rhapsody* (from the Greek combining the verb *to stitch* with *song*) derives from the task of the singer, the rhapsodist, who gathered together and memorized for recitation the parts of oral poems like Homer's. In English critical vocabulary before the nineteenth century—when many formal terms began to be loosened from their roots—*rhapsody* started out as a neutral term to describe a collection of poetic pieces gathered together, as it is used in the title of the miscellany *A Poetical Rapsody*. In the seventeenth century it crops up somewhat more often in titles for single poems like Henry Vaughan's "A Rhapsodis. Occasionally written upon a meeting with some of his friends at the Globe Taverne . . . ," published in 1646. This is a long poem stitched together in irregular verse paragraphs of couplets often with comically undercutting rhymes: "disclose"/"Nose," "wine"/"divine," "we shall all / have dreams Poeticall."⁵⁰ Unsurprisingly, earlier eighteenth-century writers stress the ancient root meaning, which they find useful to sanction critical attacks like those of John Dennis on Pope: "*Windsor-Forest* is a wretched Rhapsody"; the *Dunciad* a "whimsical Rhapsody."⁵¹ The abusive sense of the term in these attacks is as Elisha Coles's dictionary of 1717 succinctly defines it: "a confused Collection."⁵² It does not yet have to do with meanings accumulated around the term in the nineteenth century, although Ephraim Chambers's *Cyclopedia* of 1728 signals changes to come by cross-referencing *rapture*, which has an altogether different root in *rapere* (*to seize*), to *rhapsody*.⁵³

This long and mixed history stands behind the generic term in Eliot's title. Although it gives no clues to help readers recognize less familiar associations than those with nineteenth-century rhapsodies, in its connections with the poem the title seems to draw from more of its rich inheritance, perhaps specially from its affinities with Swift's "On Poetry: A Rapsody," first published in 1733. Eliot's appreciation of Swift's work guarantees that he knew this poem. In 1916 when he offered to write about Swift for Harriet Monroe, he grouped him among "a few poets whom the age neglects," suggesting that he would not count on any but a select or even imagined few readers of his own "Rhapsody" to know Swift's.⁵⁴

Swift's poem is a satire on London literary life as it collects in Will's and Grub Street, where it is carried on by those "*blasted* with poetick Fire" and their readers, who are the "Criticks."⁵⁵ His condemnation of these makers and judgers of poetry is carried out in sarcastic appropriations and applications of their critical vocabulary. The process begins in the title with his choice of their abusive term "Rapsody" to present his poem in its proper kind. It is structured in unequal stanzas loosely connected and made up of tetrameter couplets satirically rhymed: "far gone" / "Jargon," "*Dryden*" / "confide in," "bite 'em" / "*ad infinitum*," "*Longinus*" / "outshine us,"

"dupes us" / "*Peri Houpsous*" (the title of Longinus's treatise on the sublime). By appropriating the language of the current literary scene he makes
it serve his exposure of it in his own poem.

Eliot's title, it seems, may have in it an obscure allusion to parallels between "On Poetry: A Rapsody" and his own loosely shaped poem of irregu-
larly grouped lines that are sometimes in four-stressed couplets, sometimes
rhymed in undercutting combinations that sometimes use words untranslated from other languages: "comes"/"geraniums," "Cologne"/"alone,"
"moon" / "aucune rancune."[56] Beginning with his title, he makes the discordant sounds of his own "Rhapsody" out of the quintessential Romantic
vocabulary: "Whispering," "incantations," the "secret," the "memory," the
"moon," the "beach," a "rose," a "child." This vocabulary is eerily comic
in its distorted applications to the nightmarish modern streetscape revealed
by a lamp shining on a whore, a "paper rose," "dry geraniums," "dust in
crevices." These dislocations have effects comparable to the grotesqueries
of literary jargon in Swift's savagely polite satire. Eliot's poem is in the tradition of nineteenth-century rhapsodies transformed or informed by being
incorporated with earlier history of their kind. It uses its inheritance without letting on to its readers except by an obscure hint in the title that it is
also in the tradition of "On Poetry: A Rhapsody," in turn transformed or
informed by incorporation with later poems.

In his essay "John Dryden" of 1922, Eliot recommends reading late-
seventeenth- and eighteenth-century poetry to "those whose taste is formed
entirely upon the English poetry of the nineteenth century," that is, "to the
majority" of readers. The reasons he gives are that "the twentieth century
is still the nineteenth, although it may in time acquire its own character,"
and that learning to appreciate neoclassical verse, which means the perception of other values than "sublimity" in poetry, is a way "to pass beyond
the limitations of the nineteenth century into a new freedom."[57]

Hugh Kenner argues persuasively that Dryden and other Augustan poets became "part of the rich amalgam that gathered in Eliot's mind" in preparing for *The Waste Land*, and shows how the decorums of their verse
shape the poem in its earlier stages along the lines of an urban satire.[58] Perhaps Swift's "On Poetry: A Rapsody" plays something like that role in the
formation of "Rhapsody on a Windy Night," but in those years Eliot was
apparently not ready to give "the majority" of his readers the kind of interpretive guidance Kenner finds in the later published remarks on neoclassical poetry. The title of the earlier poem plays a game with "the majority"
of readers, who know only some of the rules because they are still trapped
in the nineteenth century. It does not give them directions they can recognize for escaping into the "new freedom" the poet has found by making a

place for the poem in the richer "amalgam" of tradition encoded in the generic term *rhapsody*.

Williams's and Eliot's titles using traditional generic terms work as presentations only in special and deliberately restricted ways. They refuse to give the audience at large readable guidance for what to make of the poem, but they do present it unmistakably to all its readers as an expression of its time that is about being a poem of its time. This does not seem to be true, or not true in the same insistent or polemical way, of Elizabeth Bishop's titles presenting poems by formal kind. A simple contrast can be made if we look again at expressive possibilities in the broadest and most neutral-seeming generic term, *poem*.

Williams uses it for an entry among others by him grouped under the timely heading "Interests of 1926," printed in *The Little Review* that year. This one, a prose poem, is placed between an untitled poem and a letter in prose. The juxtaposition of the text and title of "Poem" is first meant to be funny, and shocking, and pugnacious. Part of the joke depends on the contrast between this bland, traditional title and earlier titles by the same poet that are antitraditional and attention-getting in various ways, like "Shoot It Jimmy!," "The Eyeglasses," "Spring and All." Still, the joking title "Poem" for a passage of prose works in a more seriously contentious way in the still wider context of contemporaneous critical discussions. It uses the broadest of formal terms to break down the broadest of formal classifications, the distinction between poetry and prose, which was an impassioned cause championed by Pound and supported by other poets. Besides signaling that allegiance, Williams's use of "Poem" to present what consists entirely of a catalogue naming quintessentially American heroes is contentious in its more particular challenge to the Europeanism of Eliot's poems. Here the term "Poem" is a manifesto announcing the poet's stance against notions about poetry that he dismisses as unmodern and un-American.

A half century later in her last volume, *Geography III*, Elizabeth Bishop includes close to its center a poem titled "Poem." There is no other entry with that or a similar title, and in her earlier books only one poem, "Sestina," is titled by a noun naming its traditional kind. While this late poem particularly looks back to one in her first book, "Large Bad Picture," their very close connection only points out the difference that the later poem is not called "Little Painting" but "Poem," even though no poem is mentioned in the text. Yet its title, though uncharacteristic of Bishop's work, is not polemical: we see nothing in its form to challenge its title, and this point seems to be emphasized because "Poem" comes just after an entry titled "12 O'Clock News," which is arranged in passages of prose.

Then as we read the text, "Poem" becomes an appropriate title because this one is utterly characteristic of this poet in being a careful description of an object, an artifact, turned contemplation in the very act of looking. What it looks at is a painting dimly representing an actual remembered landscape, "but how live, how touching in detail." What it touches in the poet is recognition of the ways "Life and the memory of it" have empowered the painting and her writing—"our looks, two looks"—with glimpses "the size of our abidance" that lift "art" out of personal and historical time.[59] The title tells us that the poem called "Poem" is about what enduring essential makes a poem; it is a retrospective reflection and a quiet manifesto. Its difference from Bishop's other titles points to its specially charged expressiveness without making it contentious.

The title "Sestina" in Bishop's *Questions of Travel* of 1965 has the same unqualified noun form, by contrast with generic titles announcing the contemporaneity of the poem, like Donald Justice's "Sestina on Six Words by Weldon Kees," Diane Wakoski's "Sestina from the Home Gardener," Barbara Lefcowitz's "Emily Dickinson's Sestina for Molly Bloom." These suggest some sense of distance if not incongruity between the intricate Italian verse form, which we tend to associate with richly elaborated Renaissance poems like Sidney's "Yee Gote-heard Gods," and our concerns voiced in our idioms. Bishop's title simply purports to identify the poem by the traditional term for its specially complex form, which, in her use of it, is not at odds with the everyday matters of the poem. They are summarized in the six simple end words—"house," "grandmother," "child," "stove," "almanac," "tears"—made by cyclical repetition to sound all the more like words in a child's book such as might be illustrated by pictures of a house with a winding path and a carefully placed flower bed. The title does not seem incongruous, but it also does not seem to give guidance beyond calling attention to the form of the poem, by contrast with a loaded interpretive title like her previous choice of "Early Sorrow" (which in a letter of 1960 she claims not to remember), or even simply a key noun from the poem like "The House," which would sound like the caption under an illustration in a child's book.[60]

Instead the poet has chosen a still more reticent name, even an unreadable, neutral-seeming title for the poem. Then that very quality of inscrutability becomes an interpretive signal because it points to the way "Sestina"—at once the title and the poem—resembles the "inscrutable house" named in the last words, which is both the actual house and the house in the child's drawing. "Sestina" is like the actual house in being a containing structure. It is like the house in the drawing in being an image in art form of the actual house. Both these images—drawing and poem—represent the house as inscrutable, keeping secrets by denying the tears popping up everywhere to belie the grandmother's forced cheeriness. The drawing awkwardly reveals the child's unspoken response to what is not said in the

house. "Sestina" gives expression to the poet's awareness of the same unspoken grief in the escaping tears, and opens it to the reader. The poem can
do what neither the actual house nor the drawing can, by creating a form to
contain and express the tears. Because the title calls attention to the poem's
specially prominent form, it makes claims for the power of art, which by
its traditional means can express what is unutterable, and in doing so can
make it endurable and enduring. The title, which purports merely to name
the poem's kind, becomes a metaphor in the poem and for the poem.

Bishop's poem dated the year of her death, 1979, is an uncannily fitting
retrospective. Its apparently neutral title, "Sonnet," is an invitation to look
for its appropriateness to the poem and to its maker's craft.[61] The question
about the title's fitness is raised by the very look of the poem on the page,
where its lines—made of from one to four words—do not make the box-
like design that immediately identifies a sonnet. Even though we find by
counting the lines—move one in decoding this riddle-poem—that there are
fourteen, they make a shape more like an anti-sonnet. The too-short lines
are too unevenly strung in a narrow strip of print, and without visual
rhymes to catch the eye in patterned connections. What we do see instead
is the uneven division of the lines, coming not conventionally after the
eighth but the sixth, marked by a period dividing what turn out to be two
nonsentences. They begin with the words "Caught—" and "Freed—,"
made to look freestanding by the only capital letters and dashes in the
poem. Their prominence invites us to take them as terms of contrast around
which the poem is built.

Our first impression, particularly after reading some earlier twentieth-
century poets, might then be that the title points to the constraining authority of generic tradition in the strict demands of the "Sonnet," which the
poem seems by its looser looking shape to have burst, having "broken" the
box-like form imposed by conventional constraints: grammar, lineation,
meter, rhyme. Williams's well-documented hostility to the sonnet might
encourage this reading, for example. Still, experience of other poems by
Bishop like "Sestina" would make us uneasy about reading this one as an
anti-sonnet, and a more careful look at its formal features soon teaches
another way of reading it and its title, which purports only to name its kind.

When we listen to the uneven looking lines we hear that they are regularly two-stressed and built around four end-rhymes—"bubble"/"level"/
"needle"/"bevel," "divided"/"undecided," "mirror"/"whatever," "away"/
"gay"—and an internal rhyme—"wobbling"/"wavering"/"running"/"flying." The second nonsentence, though longer, only seems to be "running
away" when in fact it keeps to the same strict pattern of stresses and the
same number of five rhymed endings, completing the opening end sound
and closing the poem with its most emphatic rhyme, "away"/"gay," the only

one falling on the stressed last syllable, which is experienced by both eye and ear. The apparently "Freed" second nonsentence is a fulfillment of rather than an escape from form.

The intricately ordered way of putting words together in the form of the poem is an interpretive signal for how to take its title. So are the meanings of the words. They describe the things that make up its catalogue—the "spirit-level," the "compass," the "thermometer," the "mirror"—all small-scale, man-made objects. Inside each is something moving—the "bubble," the "needle," the "mercury," the "rainbow-bird" spectrum—each a "creature" seeming by its motions to have life and purpose. Together they are tools of a craft, made to measure or represent everyday things like this poem, which is itself in turn a small-scale, made measure or representation of everyday things.

The signifying function of the words in the poem, then, is another interpretive direction for reading its title. That is, the tools described in the catalogue are analogues for poetic forms that both contain and express the mysterious life of meanings, "spirit-" or "bird"-like embodiments "flying" free in timeless motion. The title is a metaphor for the enduring power of poetic forms and their meanings as measures or reflections of things. Its stripped, unqualified noun form represents the poem's existence as a freestanding object; the meaning of the noun "Sonnet" signifies its ties to tradition. Together they reflect a transformed understanding of the possibilities in generic titling for poets who have found new freedom to redefine its authority on their own terms.

CHAPTER SIX

What the poem is "about"

Tⁱᵗˡᵉˢ that purport to tell the reader what the poem is about make up what is probably the commonest category in the history of titling in English. The vague idiom "is about" is deliberately chosen to start off discussion of presentations in this category because it can include what are usually described by such terms as *occasion, situation, topic, theme, central image*, a vocabulary we tend to think of as making more precise distinctions than it often does in actual use. The intentional vagueness of the phrasing "what the poem is about" seems not only practical here for allowing this inclusiveness, but appropriate in its own right as a reminder of the obvious fact that no features singled out by a title are commensurate with the poem it is chosen to present; that a poem is almost literally "about" all dimensions of language that contribute to its total expression.

It can of course be said that titles in all the categories previously explored in some way or other convey a sense of what the poem is about. That could be argued using Keats's "Ode to a Nightingale" as a model. It entered the discussion of generic titles in Chapter 5; it could also have been included beside Wordsworth's "To the Cuckoo" in Chapter 4 among titles that present the poem as an address *to* some listener. Or it could be fitted into Chapter 7 among title quotations because, being addressed to the most literary of birds, it has predecessors among the presentations of earlier poems. "Ode to a Nightingale" could also on several grounds be included here among titles that let the reader know what the poem is about. For Keats's title names the central image of the ode and uses it to signal that its topic is poetry because the nightingale is traditionally associated with poetic inspiration. It also predicts a poem having to do with the possibility of using a natural creature as a poetic symbol because it is closely linked with other poems addressed to birds like "To the Cuckoo," where this question is at issue. It even works more particularly like some titles discussed in this chapter because only the title calls by name what the poem is "about." Admittedly, then, divisions of titles into categories will be overlapping. Still, even titles built on the broadest presentational formula *this is a poem about* can legitimately be considered as a distinct category because they can work in certain ways effectively different from titles that prepare the reader to focus on other dimensions of the poem.

One way a title can answer the question *what is this poem about?* is to tell the reader something of the poem not knowable from the text itself. This function was fulfilled by many early editorial titles that worked something like marginal glosses bringing information to bear from outside the poem: who wrote it, to whom, when or where, on what occasion. There is another and much more common way a title can answer this question. That is to simplify the reader's act of interpretation by telling ahead of time in summary form what would otherwise be found out from the poem with varying degrees of effort: its occasion, situation, topic, theme, central image. Poets, as they assumed the authority to be their own titlers, soon discovered unique opportunities in the apparent directness, the seemingly straightforward claims of both glossing titles and especially summarizing titles simply to answer the reader's most basic question about the poem.

The preposition *on*

Poet-titlers in the seventeenth century appropriated the authority of traditional title forms but early learned to shape them to their own expressive designs. Beginning again with Jonson, his *Epigrammes* is the first volume of short poems in English where we find nearly absolute regularity in the formation of titles that focus on what the poem is about, which take up roughly a quarter of the collection. He makes these titles by following the common practice of translating one of the Latin forms used in humanist editions of classical epigrams: *on* (for *de*) preceding the noun or name for what the poem is about. Besides its classical sanction, there is also something suggesting authority in the actual formation *on* followed by noun or name, which Jonson seems to have recognized and exploited to enforce his controlling presence in the volume.

To see this, suppose Jonson's scathing four-line *Epigrammes* 15 beginning "All men are wormes: But this no man" were titled only by the name—or noun—"Covrt-worme." While the creature's name is of course the creation of the poet, it is treated in both title and text as if it were not. The satire in fact depends on the fiction that this figure exists independently in the actual world outside the poem. Still, in the true title, "On Covrt-worme," the preposition "On" formally brings the creature from the beginning under the control, and here the condemnation, of the poet, because the prepositional phrase presupposes an unspoken nominative, something—or more specifically the poem—acting *on* the object: "[Epigram] On Covrt-worme." It brings into the title an explicit acknowledgment of the poet's performance in an established kind. In the context of the whole collection, the title seems even to evoke the presence of Jonson himself— "[Jonson's Epigram] On Covrt-worme"—because of the plentiful references to him in the verses, the frequent first-person pronouns in their titles, and because many of the poems are addressed *to* persons known to Jonson, evoking an actual world where he finds what to censure or celebrate in his epigrams. Since there are many poems in the collection, most of them very short, the continual repetition of the same title form accumulates its own kind of expressiveness, emphasizing the poet's authority to pronounce judgments *on* what he chooses to write about. Jonson seems to have discovered for himself that this formula for presenting the poem can also have local effects to be illustrated here by two of his best and best-known epigrams.

Epigrammes 76, "On Lvcy Covntesse of Bedford," is presented in one of the two grammatical forms repeated throughout the collection, though with a pointed difference. It is the only title in the volume naming as its topic a living person worthy to be praised that is not directly addressed *to* that figure. The point is emphasized by the immediate proximity of *Epigrammes* 84, "To Lvcy Covntesse of Bedford," beginning "Madame, I told you late," which by its joking social manner contrasts with the formal distancing of the title for the epigram "On" the same person printed shortly before it. The variant choice of "On" allows the title to take part in the witty trick the poem plays *on* the poet who tells his story in the verses, a game that Jonson meanwhile plays *with* his audience, which of course must include his patroness, the Countess of Bedford.

In the first framing lines the poet tells how he sat down that very morning in a well-timed poetic fit to form a "kinde of creature" in his verses.[1] The poem he "meant to make" then unfolds in lines 5 to 18 as a sonnet: three quatrains followed by a couplet intruded on by another voice (in imitation of Sidney's sonnet opening *Astrophil and Stella*). Until he is instructed in this last line, Jonson's sonneteer has not known that what he desired "To honor, serue, and loue" was not a "creature" of his own making but the living Countess of Bedford, whom he did not recognize in his description of her. He is even unaware that he has in spite of himself written a blazon truly praising her. This naively conventional and hapless sonneteer is not

Jonson, who knows the Countess of Bedford well enough to address her directly and playfully on the opposite page in *Epigrammes* 84; who writes no love poems and no blazoning sonnets even in her praise. What he does write are epigrams properly presented *to* her. Jonson as titler assigns the presentation "On Lvcy Covntesse of Bedford" to the love sonnet made, it seems inadvertently, by the sonneteer. Meanwhile Jonson demonstrates his own authority by the game he plays in making an unsuspiciously traditional title form play a trick "On" conventional expectations. It is part of his witty compliment to the Countess that he assumes she will recognize and enjoy the play.[2]

Jonson copies the traditional title form for *Epigrammes* 22, "On My First Davghter," using it to create another altogether original dramatic interchange between the title and the poem. We hear it as soon as we begin to read the verses: "Here lyes to each her parents ruth, / Mary, the davghter of their youth."[3] The title tells us that it has been chosen by the poet for a poem about his own daughter, which would not be known from the verses alone where the poet speaks but not in the first person, as if he were telling of some other man's loss. He uses the third person: "her parents" in "their youth," "her mother," and, with bleakest impersonality, "the father." If Jonson had broken his self-made rule always to refer to himself in titles by the first person, substituting the editorial third person "On [His] First Davghter," the verses would not shock us with their terrible suppression of *I* or with the avoidance of personal pronouns altogether in the nonsentence of the last line—"Which couer lightly, gentle earth"—where the poet speaks as "the father" imagining a blanket being drawn not by him over his sleeping child. The grammatical shift from the first person in the title to the third person in the opening, building to the final broken sentence that suppresses all persons, dramatizes the inward division of the poet, who can write a poem *on* what as father he cannot bear to feel.

For this poem the preposition *on* in the title has the meaning it also has in Jonson's satirical epigrams: *on the subject of, about*. At the same time it means *on* in the more particular sense of *inscribed upon* because the poem begins with the formula traditionally carved on gravestones, "Here lyes," identifying it as belonging to a species of epigram, the epitaph. In the Greek Anthology the preposition *epi* in titles has this literal meaning, while perhaps already slipping toward the sense of *peri* (*about*).

The same preposition is also traditionally attached to titles for the variety of poetry that has come to be called *occasional*. According to the standard definition in recent handbooks, occasional verse celebrates or memorializes "a specific occasion, such as a birthday, a marriage, a death, a military engagement or victory, the dedication of a public building, or the opening performance of a play."[4] From the original root meaning of the Latin *occasion* (*falling* [of things] *toward* [each other]), the term *occasional* also extends to include the falling out of anything, something happening. In an essay on Jonson, Thom Gunn expands the term so far as to argue that "all poetry is occasional: whether the occasion is an external event . . . whether it is an occasion of the imagination, or whether it is in some sort of combination of the two."[5] Poets ever since the seventeenth century have discovered various ways to make this title form work with the poem to define the specialness—which may be publicly recognized or privately discovered—of the occasion declared in the title to be what the poem is *on*.

The title of the poem placed first in Milton's collection of 1645, "On the morning of Christs Nativity. Compos'd 1629," serves the design of the volume to show his growth as a poet by the gloss giving the date, which tells readers that this dazzling poem was written early. More particularly, the dating calls attention to a double time scheme compressed in the title but worked out in the poem in its larger structural divisions and its grammar. That is, the gloss "Compos'd 1629" makes possible two readings of the preposition in the title. The conventional sense of *on* says the poem is *about* the morning when Christ was born. This predicted poem, beginning "It was the Winter wilde," tells the story of that first Christmas in what seems to be an interweaving—traditional to narrative poetry—of the past tense with imitation of the Latin historical present.[6] An example is the fluidity of time in the eleventh stanza, which describes the sunrise: "At last surrounds," "array'd," "Are seen." The poem *about* that morning has its own separate title, "The Hymn," printed above the stanza where the storytelling begins, which then unfolds in stanzas of eight lines numbered from I to XXVII. These presentational devices support the storybook opening line to distinguish "The Hymn" as a poem in its own right from the frame made for it by the different stanzas of seven lines coming before it, numbered I to IV. By contrast with "It was the Winter wilde," these framing stanzas begin in the present. "This is the month, and this the happy morn" of the different day identified in the title gloss as the date the poem was written, which gives the preposition *on* its second meaning, *at the time of* December 25, 1629. This is the morning when, Milton tells Diodati in "Elegia sexta" (also in *Poems* of 1645), dawn had brought him the inspiration to make the poem as a birthday gift to the Christ child.

The unusual structural division and the contrast of tense in the different opening lines of frame and hymn seem to separate the two readings of the title, so that the stanzas composed *at the time of* Christmas morning, 1629, introduce "The Hymn" *about* the dawning of the first Christmas. Then what happens is that without obliterating this division, the two parts of the poem working together magically transcend it. This is made to happen first midway through the opening stanzas when the youthful poet invokes the "Heav'nly Muse" to inspire a "hymn" that will welcome the Christ child "Now," before the dawn of Christmas day, 1629. In answer he is granted the power of the poet-prophet to enter a visionary present and to enact it in his poem:

> See how from far upon the Eastern rode
> The Star-led Wisards hast with odours sweet:
> O run, prevent them with thy humble ode,
> And lay it lowly at his blessed feet;
> Have thou the honour first, thy Lord to greet,
>   And joyn thy voice unto the Angel Quire,
> From out his secret Altar toucht with hallow'd fire.

At once "The Hymn" inspired by the Muse begins, first in the past tense but by the third line merging it with a tense that though in the form of the Latin historical present, here becomes the timeless present of prophetic vision. The closing stanza of the inserted hymn responds to and completes the movement begun in the last of the introductory stanzas, transcending the original division between the poem's two parts: "But see the Virgin blest, / Hath laid her Babe to rest." The author of "The Hymn" returns to the actual time when he writes the poem, Christmas morning of 1629, smiling now at his own youthful eagerness to be first to lay a gift, his "humble ode," before the Christ child: "Time is our tedious Song should here have ending."

Milton, characteristically, finds a wholly original use for a traditional form in this title. Although specially fitted as the cornerstone in the carefully made structure of this poem, the title may have come to serve a different purpose as a model adapted by Wordsworth for his glossing title "Compos'd Upon Westminster Bridge, September 3, 1802," another presentation grounding the visionary moment of the poem in the day-by-day existence of the poet. Here the title locates that particular experience in the past, while the poem is in the present tense, enacting the inspiring power of memory to transcend the limits of human time. His passionate preoccupation with this process may be a reason for Wordsworth's attraction to titles formed in past participles: *composed, written, occasioned.* They add another layer to the temporality allowed by *on, upon.* That dimension is not present in the other prepositions conventionally used in titles that purport to state the poem's topic or occasion—*at, in, by*—unless they are modified by a temporal term like *once,* as in Frost's "Once by the Pacific."

Present participles

As they expanded the conventions of titling in other ways, poets in the nineteenth century began to experiment with new grammatical constructions. Keats gives his own direction to the traditional title form that tells what occasion the poem is *on* in "On first looking into Chapman's Homer," published in *Poems* of 1817. What makes the grammar of this title significantly different from Jonson's or Milton's is Keats's use—and it is his preferred choice for titling occasional poems—of a present participle acting as the noun naming what the poem is about. In titles formed this way the gerund presupposes an unnamed doer of the action, who can be general or representative, as in Keats's "On [one's] Visiting the Tomb of Burns" or "On [someone's, anyone's] seeing the Elgin Marbles." If the rest of the title attaches the verbal noun to a unique or unrepeatable performance, then its action must imply a personal pronoun—"On [his, my] receiving a curious Shell, and a Copy of Verses, from the same Ladies"—referring to the *I* in the poem. Or an unmistakably autobiographical gloss—"On receiving a laurel crown from Leigh Hunt"—identifies the personal pronoun more specifically with John Keats. Still, because the first person is left out of such a title, it keeps the gerundive force of continual action in an undetermined present that generalizes the performance. Even in this autobiographical glossing title the omission of the personal pronoun works with the formal and distancing "On" to make the troubled act of reflecting on poetic immortality in the sonnet itself an expression of all poets' fears and ambitions. By contrast, the past participle "Composed" in the traditionally formed glossing title of Wordsworth's sonnet juxtaposes the time-bound particularity of the occasion with the present memory of it rising in the poem to a mythic timelessness. For Keats the present participle does the work of memory in preserving the immediacy of the occasion while generalizing its particularity.

"On first looking into Chapman's Homer" weaves these grammatical possibilities into a rich fabric of connections with the sonnet. Although "first" particularizes the verbal noun and places it in a time scheme, "looking" still keeps its generality and sense of continuousness (which are weaker in the clumsy manuscript version of the title, "On the first looking into Chapman's Homer"). Because the grammar can do this, it works with the formal pronouncement "On" the poem's occasion to make a great public event out of what Charles Cowden Clark in his *Recollections* describes as an intensely personal occasion when he and Keats read aloud all night from Chapman's translation. Keats composed his sonnet on the way home in the morning.[7]

The authority of this title to pronounce judgment "On" the occasion matches the assurance we hear in the opening lines. The "I" of the sonnet speaks there as a man of the world so well "travell'd" that he has come to know, and to be known throughout, the civilized world and can justly take its measure.[8] Because the title has prepared us for what is not told in the poem, that it is about an act of reading, the famous discoveries and explorations described by the traveler are from the beginning recognizable as metaphors attaching their glamor and excitement to the experience of beginning to read Chapman's translation. Since the title teaches this literal interpretation of the poem's occasion, it seems to simplify the reader's interpretive work, but then the poem retrospectively superimposes on the title its own metaphorical understanding of the great event. That is, the wholly metaphorical language of the sonnet, at first seeming to belong to a different order of apprehending from the literal terms in which the title interprets it, actually makes a figurative design that pulls the title into it.

Coming before the poem in the title space, the familiar idiom "looking into" escapes close attention; it is easily accepted as synonymous with opening a book and beginning to read in it. But the title of another sonnet by Keats, "On sitting down to read King Lear once again," uses a more direct verb, while a truly literal account of the actual occasion would have more faithfully presented it as "On first hearing Chapman's Homer," which is said in the sonnet to "speak out loud and bold." These plausible alternatives—*read*, *hearing*—suggest some special point to the idiom "looking into."

As we read on, the metaphors in the poem of the "watcher of the skies" who sees an undiscovered planet appearing, or the explorer "with eagle eyes" who "star'd at the Pacific" reflect back on the action of "looking into," making the phrase more charged. It takes its place as the first in this sequence of intensifying metaphors for acts of seeing. Then the "demesne" of "deep-brow'd Homer" ("deep" revised from "low" in manuscript) becomes a "wide expanse" of nature like the sky or the sea, and the act of "looking into" it becomes itself a metaphor for having sight that penetrates far into the "deep" mystery that is the focus of yearning in so many nineteenth-century poems. What first seems to be a literally stated interpretation of the sonnet in the title in retrospect offers a metaphorical reading that plays a part in the poem's design. That is to embody what it is to read great poetry that no statement *on* the experience can be adequate to express.

Because a present participle can be a verbal noun or a pure nominative, its double status allows it to name simultaneously the occasion and the topic of the poem. If the participle stands alone in the title space, it takes fullest advantage of that special feature. This grammatical possibility began to be tried out in titles for a few nineteenth-century poems, among which Wordsworth's "Nutting," first published in the 1800 edition of *Lyrical Ballads*, may be the earliest model.[9] By its simple construction it can diagram the primary ways a present participle alone can be made to work in a title that purports only to tell what the poem is about.

"Nutting" has the same nominal status as would a hypothetical title in the form, say, of "Hazelnuts," but with the difference that the participle has an awareness of time built into its verbal continuous present. This gives it a special immediacy among other nominal forms when it is not arrested by *on* (a quality prized in some later-nineteenth-century participial titles like Gerard Manley Hopkins's "Hurrahing in Harvest" and Whitman's "Crossing Brooklyn Ferry"). It calls up an ongoing experience that we might expect to unfold in the poem. The lines start out in the present tense, which seems to be both the present of the poem's occasion—"Nutting"— and of the poet now saying the verses: "It seems a day / One of those heavenly days that cannot die."[10] Then in the next line the time scheme is split in two when the poet shifts to the past tense to tell about a particular day in his childhood, but the force of the participle is still felt as he relives the occasion in memory—"unless I now / Confound my present feelings with the past." That layering depends not only on the timeless present of the defining participle, but on another of its dimensions: its traces of an unspecified doer performing the ongoing action of gathering nuts, whose presence would not be engaged if the title were in a different noun form, for instance "A Harvest of Hazelnuts." It is the doer's memory of the doing that the present participle of "Nutting" acts out grammatically.

Along with its sense of continuous present activity, the participle in the title simultaneously treats the poem's occasion as a topic, because the noun is not modified by terms that would tie it to a particular experience—as if it read "Nutting [in Lorton Vale]," "Nutting [in My Childhood]"—so that its grammar expresses its universality. Again the verses support this claim for the title. First the story-telling form itself conveys some sense of the exemplary. Then the poet describes himself boyishly costumed as a typical "Figure" in an adventure story, striding forth "Towards the distant woods." This childish myth turns portentous when the boy's actions in the hazel nook begin to be described in language thick with Miltonic allusions as the violation of "A virgin scene" by an intruder succumbing to the tempting fruit of trees standing "Tall and erect" until "dragg'd to earth." The moral the poet delivers in the last lines, stepping out of his concluded story to urge reverence for nature, reinforces the title's claim that the poem is about a topic of universal application: "Nutting" represents the violation of nonhuman nature by fallen human beings.

One of the possibilities suggested by the title "Nutting," which is perhaps made of a rustic idiom, is that it stakes out ordinary rural labors as worthy topics for a new pastoral poetry. This seems to have had special appeal for John Clare, who devised parallels in "Haymaking" and "Black-berrying," poems describing the actions of "the swain and maid" or "He . . . the schoolboy." In another poem for which Clare also uses the title "Nutting," the poet includes himself with the pronoun "we" in the remembered childhood activity.[11] Ralph Waldo Emerson's similar title "Berrying" declares the topic for a twelve-line poem framed in past-tense verbs—"Said I," "I said"—but the occasion of the poem is reenacted in the present participles of the middle lines: "strolling through the pastures . . . Feeding on the Ethiops sweet, / Pleasant fancies overtook me."[12] Here Emerson's choice of a present participle for the title seems to go beyond interest in its capacity to generalize and dignify the poem's rustic topic. He makes it a device for expressing the immediacy of its occasion: an experience reenacted in the author's memory of nature's ongoing power to nourish human feelings; to take hold of poets' "fancies" with "dreams thus beautiful."

Frost, perhaps encouraged by his reading of Wordsworth and Emerson, early discovered titling by present participles as a compression of effects he specially valued in the poems of his first four volumes. There he chose to use such titles often and for poems he considered among his best, poems that have since become best known to his readers. There are four in *A Boy's Will*, including "Mowing," of which he wrote, "I come so near what I long to get that I almost despair of coming nearer."[13] Of the two in *North of Boston*, "Mending Wall" has pride of place in opening the volume. There are three such titles for poems in *Mountain Interval*; three also in *New Hampshire*, among them "Stopping by Woods on a Snowy Evening," the poem Frost called "my best bid for remembrance."[14] In later volumes, which tend more toward epigrams, six of the eight titles naming what the poem is about in a present participle precede it with *on* in agreement with tradition, while none is worded that way in the first four volumes.

By its grammatical form Frost's title "Mowing," like "Nutting" or "Berrying," succinctly summarizes what the poem is about by naming what is both its occasion and its topic. The present participle implies a doer whose ongoing activity is more strongly stressed here because its stem is itself not a noun but a verb, and this is true also of all Frost's other titles in this form: *gather*ing, *wait*ing, *going*, *mend*ing, *put*ting, *find*ing, *stop*ping, *look*ing, *sit*ting. At the same time "Mowing" can act as a simple noun with the status of the nominative in a sentence like *Mowing reaps a harvest*; instead of an ongoing effort engaging someone's energy, the noun names something that is whole, freestanding. In this way the title works effects, some of which are not only different from but seemingly at odds with the sense of immediacy and process acted out in the mower's voice.

The difference can be diagramed by paraphrasing what is implied in the two ways of reading the title that are legitimized by its grammar: "[I] Mowing," which names the occasion; "Mowing [Is Labor]," which states the topic. The title is at once immediate and distanced. Its immediacy is in preparing for the voice talking in the poem. Its distancing is in the separation between the mowing and the making of the poem: a poem is not synonymous with whatever talking can be done while someone mows, as Frost's naming of the sonnet a "talk-song" implies. In the distanced reading the poem is not a process like mowing but something made, like the hay. Both possibilities, though theoretically in contradiction, are predicted at once in the pure present participle of the title and fully earned in the thirteenth line: "The fact is the sweetest dream that labor knows."[15] The strangeness of this sentence is in the way it unites mowing and versing, poem and harvest by suspending the nouns that name them all—"fact," "dream," "labor"—in the ongoing present of "is" and "knows." The still stranger effect of ending the poem in the infinitive—"My long scythe whispered and left the hay to make"—is a refusal to tip the balance between the two readings of "Mowing," by contrast with the way Wordsworth weights "Nutting" toward interpretive closure.

Present participles in spoken idioms

Frost's most innovative and most influential discovery in participial titling begins with "Mending Wall," where he joins the grammatical possibilities built into the present participle to the dramatic potential of a title that itself suggests a voice.[16] Along with his other uses of spoken idioms in titles, this invention seems to have charted the direction for titling experiments by many more recent poets.

The maker of this title is a sophisticated chooser of words who plays with the rules of grammar—which would dictate *mending walls, the wall,* or *a wall*—and the conventions of common speech—where colloquial idiom would predict *mending fences.* The titler sounds very like the "mischief"-maker we hear in the poem, who plays a "kind of out-door game" of mending "the wall" that divides his farm from his neighbor's, and a parallel game of emending the other's platitude "Good fences make good neighbours." Whether "Mending Wall" is his invention or his appropriation of a local idiom, this title phrase is mischievously formed as an oblique but grand claim that the poem is about something as fundamental, as universal as the dimensions of human existence we name by such age-old formulas as *keeping house* or *baking bread.*

If it is clear that we are to associate the titler with the "I" in the poem, this farmer is not a conventional figure for the poet like the mower, and his voice is farther removed from song than the rhythms of the sonnet. The degree to which he is like Robert Frost, sometime farmer living north of Boston, is blandly ignored in title and poem, but it must be intended to work subversively against any clear separation between the poet and what we are asked to think of as a freestanding figure in a dramatic monologue, among others in the volume that Frost had first considered giving such titles as *Farm Servants and Other People* and *New England Hill Folk*.[17] Also by indirection the title itself works with the poem to draw speaker and poet together. "Mending" is a process of remaking, "Wall" something made, and forms of the verb *to make* show up in prominent places seven times in the poem. Frost's mention of "my innate mischievousness" in a letter commenting on "Mending Wall" more than a dozen years after its publication in *North of Boston* mischievously tips his hand in a way that title and poem refuse to do, likening the voice we hear in the poem to the poet's, which is a circuitous way of telling us what the poem is about.[18]

The title "Stopping by Woods on a Snowy Evening" is still more evasive in its uses of grammar and voice to complicate the way it works with the poem. "Stopping" carries the sense of someone involved in a present occasion, supported by the voice of the "I" in this poem, who uses only the simple present tense. Simultaneously, since "Stopping" is "by Woods," the title suggests something beyond the occasion, because "Woods" names a category of landscape more than a place like "these" woods; and "a Snowy Evening" can be both singular and representative: *I was outside on a snowy evening in December* and *I like being out on a snowy evening.*

More gradually than it supports the immediacy of the title, the poem hints of its vaster or deeper reach, beginning at the point where the "I" perceives "these" familiar woods weirdly suspended by the enjambment of "near/Between." The "frozen lake" turns mythical, like the "frozen seas" of "To a Butterfly"; "The darkest evening of the year" is apocalyptic. We are prepared for the dangerously hypnotic last stanza, which picks up the "sound" of "sweep" made by unlocated wind and snow in the closing rhymes of "deep," "keep," "sleep," "sleep."[19]

The point here, though, is that the title itself does not prepare for such a threatened response to the occasion. On the contrary, the phrase "Stopping by" has, as Richard Poirier says, "a sort of pleasant neighborliness," as if the person were paying a friendly call on nature;[20] "a Snowy Evening" sounds invitingly pretty and comfortable, even snug, especially measured by "The darkest evening of the year" (though in retrospect "Snowy" might hint at the temptation to oblivious sleep in "downy flake"). What all this means is that the title, unlike the pure present participle "Mowing," suggests a voice. It sounds, still more than "Mending Wall," like someone talking because it is nearer to a whole sentence, and one in a familiar idiom.

This gives it the potential for drama in itself, and creates a dramatic play between it and the verses, where the voice acquires a different sound.

The title gives a commonplace, commonsense account of the occasion that in the poem threatens with the "dark and deep" loveliness of extinction, the giving up of self. Has the "I" of the poem, if it is he who says the title, forgotten the sense of danger in what he experienced when he presents the occasion in a title sounding like a gallery label for a New England landscape by a local painter? Has he simply recovered his ordinary balance? Is he trying to suppress the fear he felt of threats to himself as a person connected to life? Or perhaps the discrepancy between the imaginings of the occasion in title and poem is a signal that the voice in the title belongs to the poet distanced from the first person in the poem, who is no traditional pastoral figure like the mower, nor a Wordsworthian solitary who represents the poet gazing into a wide expanse of nature. He is characterized in some detail as a man of business working in and out of a country village, tied to everyday responsibilities.[21] Yet again the resemblance to Robert Frost is evoked even as it is ignored. Are the different versions of the experience in title and poem a way of trying to suppress the poet's sense of threat to his poetry from its too "easy" sounds, too "lovely" mysteries? Or are they a way of declaring that the poet has overcome those threats by dramatizing the occasion in the voice of a fictional "I"; by making the poem and giving it a title telling the reader, however obliquely, what it is about?

Most oblique, and in its evasiveness possibly most revealing about Frost's interest in idiomatic participial titles, is "The Most of It" as it was published in *A Witness Tree*, emended from its original form, "Making the Most of It." The truncated idiom in the revised title is unsettling, as is "Mending Wall," in that we hear the dislocation of the common phrase, but its effect is more disturbing here. While the familiar phrases evoked by the earlier title—like *keeping house* or *baking bread*—enlarge and celebrate the new idiom, the parallel phrases whose presences are called up by "The Most of It" are demeaning: *the least of it, the worst of it,* even *the best of it,* which always seems to go with *a bad situation.*

In another way this title works more like "Stopping by Woods on a Snowy Evening," because it raises the question of whose comment on the occasion in the poem it is. Is the title in the words of the solitary described in the poem, who seems to be distanced from the poet-narrator by the opening line, "He thought he kept the universe alone"; whose self-centered demands "on life" are kept at arm's length by the poet's six uses of third-person pronouns in the first nine lines?[22] If the title is "his" response to what merely "appeared" to be a "buck" in the later lines of the poet's story, then "The Most of It" is meant to reverberate with such belittling echoes as *the least of it, the worst of it.* In these effects the title matches the closing words,

"and that was all," by expressing "his" disappointment with "all" that
came. In "his" understanding "all" is reduced merely to "it" (used five times
in lines 10 to 20), that is, to nothing but the indifferent "buck."

The question whose comment the title is might be asked another way
here because the detached, critical, or even hostile sounding third-person
pronouns all but disappear after the first nine lines, weakening if not obliterating the division between poet-narrator and self-centered subject. Is the
solitary egoist then to be taken as a lesser self or former self (as allusions
to Wordsworth's "There Was a Boy" might hint) of the poet who in the
course of the poem becomes an immediate witness rather than the narrator
of someone else's story?[23] If this is so, then the title is the poet's comment,
not the utterance of a separate "he," matching in mood the way "it" looks
forward to the "embodiment" that "appeared" in the unfathomable vision
of lines 10 to 20, and to "all" of the last line. In the poet's understanding,
"all" encompasses a vast and awful mystery, of which the "buck" may be
the "embodiment." This reading suggests why "Making" of the original
title is suppressed: that it could have seemed a too clear reference to the
poet, too decisively resolving the ambiguity of selves. In the revised title,
"Making" can be sensed only as a ghostly player in the enigmatic dramas
acted out between the poet-narrator and the solitary witness, between the
title and the text of the poem.

More recent participial idioms

Like Frost's manipulations of personal pronouns in titles and glosses
for poems in his first volume and his avoidance of them after, his ways of
using and suppressing present participles in idiomatic titles act like doors
not fully opened to admit the presence of the author. More recent poets, it
seems under his influence directly or indirectly, have seen their own opportunities in titles formed on that model for different ways of suggesting what
the poem is about. To try out a generalization, later-twentieth-century poets seem to be less interested in such titles as refusals to satisfy the curiosity
they raise about the poet's implication in the participial action, or to settle
the question whose voice we hear in the idiom of the title. Their versions
allow the reader to begin by taking for granted that the title is said by the
author. This in turn frees the poet to point more openly toward the way
the title purporting to *tell* what the poem is about uses its own idiom and
grammar to *represent* what it is about.

Philip Larkin's title "Church Going" has the sound of a familiar spoken
phrase, making it a representation of the poet's language and voice. Although it is not actually common in speech, it fits without jarring into our
language because of its closeness to existing idiomatic phrases, and that

easy fit is itself expressive. Unlike "Mending Wall," which manipulates grammar to make a purposely idiosyncratic idiom, "Church Going" copies the form of ordinary phrases in common use—*theater going* comes to mind—so closely that it can be accepted without surprise. And that is to the point. The unemphatic form of the title assumes that readers in 1955, when the poem appeared in *The Less Deceived*, and since would not be likely to be taken aback by this new idiom, just as they would not be shocked when the person church going says in the poem "God knows how long," not meaning it any more than we usually do, or repeats "Wondering" and "I wonder," which have little to do with wonders.[24]

The poem's title fits into that familiar language because it too is an emptying phrase. "Church Going," by its closeness to *theater going*, takes the traditional meaning out of *going to church*, which—like *church goer*—is an idiom not heard nearly as often as it once was (witnessed by the fact that the slang phrase *see you in church* means anything but what it says). Even the present participle seems emptied of its sense of ongoing action, in the title because it comes after the unqualified noun "Church"; in the poem because the act of "going" is not continuous and immediate but repetitive, obsessive, boring: "Another church" with "nothing going on." Repeated church going always leaves the "I" of the poem "at a loss," another idiom representing the sense of emptying or diminishment in the language of title and poem, which is itself a representation of the way we speak now. In this respect the "I" is one "representative" of our place in the cultural movement when "wonder" is "at a loss" but before "disbelief has gone." "Church Going" locates itself following earlier poems expressing their authors' sense of their different places in this history: for instance, Arnold's "Stanzas from the Grande Chartreuse" and Hardy's "A Cathedral Façade at Midnight." These titles are not spoken phrases; they do not do the work of "Church Going" to represent the poet's language and voice, which in turn represent our cultural emptying.

James Merrill's title "Losing the Marbles" from *The Inner Room* of 1988 also sounds very close to a common idiom rewritten, but plays the changed version off against the original with joking effects, as Frost does in "Mending Wall." Displacing the personal pronoun we always use in this idiom—"Losing [My] Marbles" (or [Yours] or [Hers])—the new idiom announces a generalized topic—one like "Losing the [Elgin] Marbles." This form could predict a poem about a historical, cultural loss analogous to the emptying of meanings from the modern idiom of "Church Going." Indeed, precisely this suggestion is carried on by the "I" of the poem in suspiciously romantic sounding phrases likening "the gathering dusk," "'the dying of the light'" to the looting of the sculptures from the Parthenon.[25] By leaving out the personal pronoun from what is usually a wryly comical confessional formula, *losing my marbles*, the title turns into a serious or, as we sense from the start, mock-serious presentation announcing a public topic. The revised idiom also seems by its pretend generality to joke about the evasiveness of earlier titling forms like Frost's that might be its models, where the participant implied by the ongoing action of the participle is not admitted to be the poet. In contrast, this is a mock-confessional poem, wittily figuring what Merrill says in an interview of 1967 about "confessional poetry" in general: that it "is a literary convention like any other," that a poet working in it "can, of course, tell the truth, but I shouldn't think that would be necessary to give the illusion of a True Confession."[26]

The "my" of the first line is the pronoun missing from the title, and that of course is its ultimate joke: a representation of what the poem is about, the "aphasia" of age creeping up on the poet's memory: "And what were we talking about at lunch? Another / Marble gone." This is the ongoing process of "Losing," and the poem is studded with typographical representations of its erosions: [ ], . . . , —, above all the blanks in the lines of part 3, like the "tracts of raw, uncharted canvas" of the Cézanne sketch described in part 4. Parallel to these are grammatical representations. The poem is "Brimming" with present participles echoing the movement of "Losing," but much as the "sorry spaces" in part 3 are beautifully filled in the poem of part 5 with words that "Return to the tongue's tip, / . . . Invigorated," so the present participles are continually "exchanging the wrong words" for "the right ones," "Feverishly restoring the papyrus." In the closing section the marbles are not finally *gone* but "missing."

The restorative energy—the poem calls it "grace"—is focused in the likeness of words to marbles. They are small, solid, shaped things, each with a distinct identity or name—"targets and strikers, / Aggies and rainbows"— and you can play games with them. The moves in the poet's game begin, we have seen, in the title. In the poem they are carried on by "hard play of wit" with puns ("into thyme, / *Out* of time"), outrageous rhymes ("few"/ "QE2"), word cut-ups ("stained"/"sustained"), meter ("Deducing from one dactyl / The handmaiden, the ode"), and other verbal feats. Together they fill what seems "featureless" with "pattern and intent," as in part 7 the marbles "embedded at random" by the poet in the deck around the pool have a "sparkle" that "Repeats the garden lights or moon- or starlight." The design they make "as though the very / Here and now were becoming a kind of heaven" is the "counterfeit/Heaven" that "Art"—the Parthenon sculptor's, or Cézanne's, or the poet's—can offer. Like being "the acrobat in Athens," which the poet tells us is his personal idea of "heaven," playing with the word marbles of the poem is a kind of balancing act on "this high wire / Between the elegiac and the haywire." Unlike earlier poets' games of hide-and-seek with the reader, which Merrill's title seems to joke about, "Losing the Marbles" creates the illusion that we are watching the poet performing the poem's moves up there on the tightrope for all to see. What we do see on the page is a series of magic tricks played with the representational power of words in their every dimension.

The title poem of Seamus Heaney's volume of 1991, "Seeing Things," accepts words in both their literal and idiomatic senses simultaneously, indivisibly. In doing so it surprises us into recognition of their mysterious power to force contradictions into intelligibility (as does another of Heaney's titles for a poem of 1993, "Keeping Going"). In "Seeing Things," grammar and idiom represent simultaneously the experiences of taking in the appearances of objects and believing in apparitions, and so above all they represent a phenomenon of seeing double. The title phrase uses the same words to name at the same time two distinct orders of experience. Absolutely fused in the title, they represent a third order in which "Seeing" and "Things" are mysteriously united.

A similar, slightly eerie effect is created by another title form in the volume, spotlighted by its oddness and its repeated use: "Markings" followed by "Three Drawings" early in part 1; in part 2 the closing group of "Lightnings," "Settings," "Crossings," "Squarings," followed by "The Crossing." These titles are plural nouns made out of present participles with stems that are themselves both verbs and nouns, all of which have meanings to do with the workings of the artist. The special character of these titles is highlighted in another way by their pointed contrast with a different title form also used repeatedly. This one is made of a single noun (or compound of two nouns) naming a familiar physical object modified by the definite article: examples are "The Pitchfork," "The Ashplant," "The Schoolbag." The grammar of this title form stresses the solid, tangible thingness of the object.

The other form consisting of a participial plural noun names phenomena that are visible but neither solid nor tangible, like the words in which the poet writes the title and lines of the poem, or like the lines carved by the sculptor on the cathedral façade described in the middle section of the poem "Seeing Things":

> Lines
> Hard and thin and sinuous represent
> The flowing river. Down between the lines
> Little antic fish are all go. Nothing else.
> And yet in that utter visibility
> The stone's alive with what's invisible.[27]

Both kinds of "lines" are seeable in the same way as the things they are made of, ink or stone, but as representations they can make us see things that are not there: the "handsewn leather schoolbag"; the "squarings" in the "game of marbles"; the "ghosthood immanent" of the poet's father; "Larkin's shade."

Charles Tomlinson's "Saving the Appearances" also repeats a familiar idiom, but returns it to the unidiomatic meanings of the words that make it up. In common speech the title phrase has the falsely genteel overtones of malicious gossip, so we might expect a satirical poem about a social occasion or topic. Instead we get a description virtually free of emotionally charged language unfolding in the present tense as a horse "appears" in "light," "distance," "space" from the perspective attached only late in the poem to some "one."[28] The word that comes closest to attributing feeling appears in the closing lines: "on this / November unsombre day / where what appears, is." Still, "unsombre" escapes personifying by its closeness in position, lettering, rhyme sound to impersonal "November." Its recovered root meaning—*without shadows*—works with the relatively objectified grammar as another representation of what "Saving the Appearances" is about.

This poem, published in Tomlinson's *American Scenes and Other Poems* of 1966, could with its title serve as a manifesto for a kind of art, and is in fact very close to the early poem placed to do that work by introducing Tomlinson's *Collected Poems* of 1985. About the choice of that archetypally titled "Poem" he writes in the preface:

"Poem" stands in the present volume as a kind of prelude to what follows. I realized, when I wrote it, that I was approaching the sort of thing I wanted to do, where space represented possibility and where self would have to embrace that possibility somewhat self-forgetfully, putting aside the more possessive and violent claims of personality. The embrace was, all the same, a passionate one, or so it seemed to me.[29]

Stripping from the poem the "claims of personality" is no more a means of evasion than "Saving the Appearances," which strives for an impassioned kind of grammar and diction, of seeing in poetry, that clears away the obscuring shadows of personally charged interpretation. Title and poem are representations of that "possibility"; their language is the acting force implied by the present participle "Saving," which is the poet's work of freeing words to mean what they say.

The title of A. R. Ammons's "Becoming Become Of" from *Sumerian Vistas* of 1987 calls attention to its comically odd formation so insistently that its grammar becomes as much a part of what the poem is about as the processes of nature that the poem but not the title explicitly refers to. The first line below the title even identifies grammatical and natural formations as parallel instances of some general phenomenon, because the unexplained opening statement "It's a clear case with rivers" must refer to something just said above.[30] This would make the other, less "clear case" the title's grammar. It is an invented combination of the verbal noun "Becoming" (used often in common speech—*that's a becoming hat*—as an adjective) with "Become of," a phrase cut out of the typically humorous question

"[What's] Become Of [So-and-So]?" or its more quizzical or querulous version, "[What's Ever] Become Of [So-and-So]?" It follows then that the general "case" of line 1 and the pronoun "they" in line 2 may be taken to include the title as well as "rivers," together exemplifying a process that is both natural and grammatical:

> they're going to go on with the ongoing;
> otherwise, darters headed upstream
>
> would have no currency to keep true-still in.

The parallel between rivers and grammar depends on another process set in motion by the title: stripping words of their idiomatic "currency" in order to give them the natural "curren[t]cy to keep true-still." This cut-up of the common imperative *keep still—shut up and don't wiggle*—frees "still" to mean *always, in an ongoing process* and at the same time *motionless*, that is, like rivers. Adjectives, another human imposition on nature in the "currency" of poetic language, are excluded from the title and in the poem are pared down to verb and noun forms, the essential elements of grammar that correspond to process and thing in nature: "stuck fronds," "unshucked coconuts," "wharf legs," "riverweeds."

   This playing with words strives to make them represent nonhuman nature in its own most elemental terms. While Ammons may have recognized similar directions in the work of Williams, for instance in his title "Spring Strains," Ammons's own more extreme grammatical manipulations suggest words "riddling free," to borrow a phrase from another poem in the same volume also about rivers "becoming motion," which has another grammatically arresting title, "Motion's Holdings."[31] The illusion of no human presence in the processes of these poems has nothing to do with Frost's efforts to evade the involvement of the poet in them, and not much more in common with purging the claims of personality implied by the interaction of title and poem in "Saving the Appearances." There is no dramatic play between title and poem, as there is none between the poet and the nonexistent *I* of the poem. By the process of cutting up idioms and rearranging grammatical units and sequences, which begins in the wording of the title, "Becoming Become Of," Ammons carries to its extreme limits the capacity of the title to *represent* what the poem is about, until it can almost be said to *become* what it is about.

Unqualified nouns

   Dictionaries define a noun as a "word that is the name of a subject of discourse, as a person, place, thing, quality, idea, action." Then it follows that any title purporting to tell what a poem is about, what is its subject of discourse, acts formally as a nominative, from the Latin *nominativus, of a noun*. This is most obviously true of titles themselves formed with nouns, which make up the most usual type in this most common of categories.

A noun by itself in the title space is inherently the least expressive grammatical form for a presentation. In what it purports to do it comes closest to a label stating what is in a container or to a sign on a door saying what is in the space beyond it. It seems to invite no interpretation, claiming only to identify by naming. It has no voice and implicates no performer other than someone anonymous who sticks on the label or sign, unless it is the name of a literary kind or device, like Bishop's "Sestina" or "Anaphora," which then distantly acknowledges the poet who works in or with it. Even so, as this book has argued all along, poets at least since the seventeenth century have recognized that a title can be made to do more than it purports; that any title form can be charged with expressiveness not only by the ways it is made to work with the poem, but even to some degree by virtue of its own inherent features, as participial titles have just illustrated. The argument holds even for unqualified noun titles that, poets have seen, can be exploited precisely because of their impersonality or neutrality. Frost apparently took advantage of this feature when he dropped the participle "Swinging," which puts the focus on performer and performance, from the original title of "Birches."

Paradoxically, the expressive power of noun titles most often depends on their inexpressiveness. The earliest poet to discover this was George Herbert, a true believer in paradox. Like Jonson, whose *Epigrammes* he seems to have studied, Herbert gave sustained attention to titling, choosing and sometimes revising the titles for every poem in the manuscript of the "little Book" he bequeathed to Nicholas Ferrar that became *The Temple* when it was printed after Herbert's death in 1633. Besides the importance of titles, he may have learned from Jonson the value of formulating them according to regular patterns that work together in the design of the volume. For like Jonson in *Epigrammes*, he consistently limited his choices for titles of individual poems—in both surviving manuscripts but even more strictly in the later expanded and revised collection—according to a few principles, but very different ones from those Jonson invented or copied from generic titling traditions.

Herbert's titles are all made out of nouns. They absolutely exclude pronouns, both Jonson's *I* and *my* and the editorial third persons they replace. His titles also strictly avoid prepositions, either evoking a listener *to* the poem or identifying it as *on* a topic or occasion that would classify it as an epigram, epitaph, or any other classical kind (although Herbert regularly uses *ad*, *in*, and *de* in titling his Latin verses). Among nominatives, he excludes nouns or names that would identify the *I* in the poem. These decisions and his consistency in applying them are themselves remarkable for a collection of short poems of mixed kinds in this period, but still more radical is his preference among his noun title forms.

Herbert gave by far the largest number of his poems a title consisting almost unvaryingly of a single noun referring to an abstraction purported to be the topic of the poem, unqualified by a pronoun, a preposition, an adjective, or even an article. Not only did he favor this grammatical form by using it for close to seventy poems, but he most often repeated particular titles made from unqualified nouns for two or more poems: "Affliction," "Employment," "Justice," "Love," "Praise," "Sinne," "Vanitie." Before 1633 only a few titles were printed in this form in a very small number of English collections of mainly secular epigrams and emblems. Herbert's models, I have suggested elsewhere, seem to have been the endlessly repeated places, topics, or heads grouping entries in what were called commonplace books.[32] The adjective *common* granted their universal application as well as their anonymous origins. Herbert's extraordinary preference for this grammatically least expressive title form has been largely ignored in critical discussions of his titles, which are attracted to more obviously attention-getting devices. By contrast, his own greatest interest seems to have been in the character of the unqualified noun: its neutrality, which is to say its freedom from personality, performance, voice; and, it will be argued here, its abstraction from particularity, which gives it a specially charged simplicity.

Whoever retitled Herbert's "Life" as "The Poesie" when it was reprinted in a miscellany of 1650 tamed the poem by giving an apparently less neutral but ultimately much less radical name to what the verses are about.[33] Most obviously they do seem to be about the central image of the flowers tied together by the "I" of the poem into a "posie," spelled in the revised title so that the second meaning of *poesy* is more explicit.[34] The noun of Herbert's chosen title seems to play a much less prominent part, appearing in the text itself only in line 3 and there modified as "My life," where the pronoun seems almost to change the meaning of the noun: when we say *my life* we are not thinking precisely of what "Life" is the name for. The difference is driven home by the insistent repetitions of the qualifying pronoun in only eighteen lines—"my remnant," "my hand," "My hand," "my heart," "my minde," "my fatall day," "my sent"—and the five instances of "I" beginning with the opening phrase, "I made a posie." The human figure in the poem, unlike the flowers he persists to the end in personifying, is tied by the first-person pronouns attaching him to the parts of his body, his senses, his days, the poetry he makes, including this "posie," out of all those particulars. What the innocently self-centered "I" who tells his version of everyman's story can never fully attain in his "life," what the later editor misses, what all readers of the poem lack, is the power to envision "Life" wholly abstracted from the particularizing personal possessive that measures the limits of our timebound existence. This vision is figured in the purely anonymous, voiceless, timeless, unqualified noun in the title space, which is language working in a different dimension from the poem's.

The title word of Herbert's "Vertue" does not appear until the last stanza, and there in adjective form characterizing "Onely a sweet and vertuous soul."[35] The adjective is not purely abstract as is the unqualified noun naming what the poem is about, since as an adjective it must be attached to something. Still, it is nearer to that absolute state than the sensuous adjectives in earlier stanzas describing the too much loved particulars of poetic tradition. The quality of being "vertuous" cannot be seen, heard, tasted, or smelled, nor can the "soul," which is a different order of being from the "sweets" of the "day," the "rose," the "spring." The point is emphasized by the indefinite article, which makes "Onely a sweet and vertuous soul" an ideal here unattached to any loved person, by allusive contrast to Jonson's line flatteringly ascribing "Onely a learned, and a manly soule" to his patroness in "On Lvcy Covntesse of Bedford." The appearance in Herbert's last stanza of a new kind of adjective signals the emergence of a new kind of poem ascending toward the pure abstracted vision figured in the unspoken noun of the title, which no human language can absolutely attain.

The title noun "Redemption" appears nowhere in Herbert's sonnet, which is quite often the case in *The Temple*. Here that is only one of the reasons the conjunction of this poem with its title comes as a shock. The sonnet itself is a story told by a poor and simple-sounding narrator about his hapless search for his "Lord" to ask for a lease he can "afford." After looking in all the wrong places, the narrator accidentally comes upon the one he seeks, "Who straight"—before being asked—"*Your suit is granted*, said, & died."[36] This closing line is shocking in its abruptness. Its unconnected and unexplained sequence clashes with the insistent logic of the tenant: "I resolved," "I him sought," "I straight return'd." The original version continued "and knowing his great birth, / Sought him in Citties." Herbert revised that line to "Sought him accordingly," which puts extra stress on the right-seeming deductions the narrator depends on to explain his actions. This revision cooperates with Herbert's change of title from "The Passion" to "Redemption." The revised title clashes the legal or financial meaning of the term for the reciprocal transaction the tenant wants his lord to make—*redemption of a lease*—with the theological meaning of the term for the mystery, unexplained and unexplainable, in the last line. Our surprise at the end of the sonnet implicates us the way a biblical parable would, as representative human beings constrained by the same logic of reciprocity, of cause and effect, as the tenant's, and that means it implicates the poet as well. Narrator, reader, and poet are left wordless at the end of the verses, incapable of supplying the title reference to a mystery beyond worldly understanding of redemption. This leaves the voiceless noun title outside the story to preside over the poem with an authority that seems not to have a human source.

William Blake chose for what seems to be the earliest nightmare vision of a city in English poetry an unqualified noun title that is not abstracted from human conditions but has its different kind of detachment, as voicelessly neutral as a sign in a railroad station: "London."[37] Although the volume that included it, *Songs Of Innocence and Of Experience*, is subtitled *Shewing the Two Contrary States of the Human Soul*, the poem's title seems to be soulless, impersonal, unfeeling, unlike such emotionally loaded later titles as: Letitia Elizabeth Landon's (L.E.L.'s) "The City of the Dead"; Christina Rossetti's "The Dead City"; Poe's "The Doomed City"; James Thompson's "The City of Dreadful Night"; Frances Cornford's "London Despair." Blake's title is empowered by its relative inexpressiveness. "London" is the official designation of an actual place. It is a proper name, not a charged noun characterizing it metaphorically, like *death, doom,* or *night*, and not an epithet like Eliot's "Unreal city" expressing a specially colored view of it. Our capacity to accept Blake's title matter-of-factly is itself then drawn into the nightmare of the verses that turn the proper name "London" into a synonym for "woe," the word that fills "every cry" reverberating in the lines. Because we are capable of taking the title for granted, we are implicated in the cruel indifference that makes possible the acceptance, the allowance of what happens to "every Man," woman, and child in the modern city. The prophet whose denunciation is the poem has the authority to judge us for this indifference by virtue of his absolute vision, which penetrates the true meaning in the modern world of the emotionless noun "London."

Robert Pinsky pays tribute to Herbert, the virtual inventor of unqualified noun titles, in a poem in *The Want Bone* of 1990 titled simply "Shirt":

> George Herbert, your descendant is a Black
> Lady in South Carolina, her name is Irma
> And she inspected my shirt.[38]

Though "Shirt" is not the kind of abstract noun Herbert chooses to let stand by itself in the title space, it is identical in form to his preferred type, working grammatically in the same way, unlike other titles identical in the topic they name, like Thomas Hood's "The Song of the Shirt" or Jon Silkin's "The Shirt." The special grammatical form of "Shirt," like the grammar of other titles in this discussion, itself figures what the poem is about.

Pinsky's lines move from the start by cataloguing details—"The back, the yoke, the yardage. Lapped seams, / The nearly invisible stitches along the collar." The title form subsumes this attention to particulars in the act or process of what dictionaries define as *abstraction*, which "separates the parts or qualities of things wholly for the sake of considering them in themselves, or in relation to like parts or qualities in other things." The detailed descriptions of how the parts or qualities of the thing, "my shirt," are made generate delighted recognition of their likeness to other made things: "Wonderful how the pattern matches perfectly / . . . like a strict rhyme / Or a major chord," particulars abstracted from poem or musical composition. The accuracy of naming in the catalogues—"Prints, plaids, checks, / Houndstooth, Tattersall, Madras"—and the care that goes into describing precisely how the pattern is made to match "Across the placket and over the twin bar-tacked / Corners of both pockets" represent the acts of making things and of inspecting them. Smilingly abstracted from the vast differences between "Irma" and the poet—"George Herbert," Robert Pinsky— these acts of naming and describing liken them. They are united in the emblem of "my shirt," which by "Its color and fit," its "feel and its clean smell have satisfied / Both her and me. We have culled its cost and quality." In this poem the process of abstraction, of culling, which is controlled by the form of the title, transcends particulars by loving inspection of them. The result is that the "cost" of making and the "quality" of the thing made in "Shirt" are not as different in kind from what "Vertue" figures in Herbert's title as might be predicted by the different ontological orders the nouns refer to.

Like Pinsky, Thom Gunn shapes the features of the unqualified noun to contemporary language in a title in *The Man with Night Sweats* of 1992, which names what the poem is about by a starkly unmodified noun now become a terrifying adjective, "Terminal."[39] Part of the horror of the title is that the word was used before mainly as a genuinely neutral noun—for instance when referring to train stations—but in 1992 and after most readers can be expected to take the title as the common adjective used impersonally by what we impersonally call the medical profession to blunt the terror of fatal disease. It is said now especially often of AIDS, itself named by a hideously indifferent acronym that we have come to accept without thinking that it stands for a horror there are no aids for: the affliction that makes the poet, looking at a dying friend not many years older than his lover, "Think of Oedipus, old, led by a boy."

The poem that should have the last word in this part of the discussion is the only one I have found with a title that is an exception to everything so far said about the inherent features of impersonality or inexpressiveness in unqualified noun titles, their exclusion of voice, personality, or performance. This powerful exception is Sylvia Plath's "Daddy" in *Ariel* of 1965. Even standing alone in the space above the poem, the title reverberates with the sound of a voice because "Daddy" is always experienced as a spoken word. It is something a parent teaches a child to say, a substitute for *father* (which could be used as a voiceless noun title) formed out of the babble sounds an infant is capable of. It makes claims of love and dependence; it pleads for attention, comfort, protection; it protests in anger, fear, disappointment, grief. The noun expresses the full range of these tones of voice, and because it is spoken alone in the title space, it raises them to a horrifying pitch. The reason it has this effect is that, given its status as a presentation purporting to instruct the reader on what the poem is about, it does not evoke the fiction that the titler is a child. It must then be understood as spoken by someone trapped in the feelings attached to an infantile name. It is the voice of the "I" in the poem who says other babble sounds like "Achoo" and "gobbledygoo" and chants the nursery rhyme of the opening lines—"You do not do, you do not do / Any more, black shoe"—that the first stanza tells us is recited by someone "thirty years" old.[40]

In the poem the title noun is said repeatedly—"Daddy," "daddy," "So daddy," "Daddy, daddy"—to "you." If this personal pronoun were used in the title space in place of the noun, its effects would be very different. It would be relatively inexpressive, without the charged sounds of an exclamation, a plea, a scream, or a curse. Since the actual title makes "Daddy" synonymous with "you" in the text of the poem, there the pronoun becomes charged with the same range of tones as the title, especially as "you" is repeated even more obsessively than "Daddy": once italicized; once apostrophized "O You"; once translated "Ach, du"; maddeningly paired as an end rhyme with a wild assortment of verbs, nouns, adjectives, nonsense sounds: "do" (twice), "shoe," "toe," "Achoo," "blue" (twice), "two," "Jew" (four times), "true," "gobbledygoo," "Through" (five times). While repetitions of "Daddy" and "you" in the poem insist on the inescapable presence of the absent father, in the title space the unqualified noun is said to no one, which adds to its horror and redirects its statement of what the poem is about. It is not about "Daddy." It is about the thirty-year-old child who calls out the infantile syllables to nobody, which is to say that the title itself, as much as the poem, embraces performance.

Nouns modified by articles

Herbert's second preference among his strictly nominal titles is for a noun that does not name an abstraction, preceded by an article, regularly *the*. This combination, which he used for close to forty poems, is a choice consistent with his most preferred form, even though it does not have the specially charged simplicity of unqualified abstract nouns, because of its own inherent neutrality, its impersonality. It is also free of performance because, although grammatically it fits more easily into a wider range of sentences—for instance, we would say *the collar* in more contexts than simply *collar*—it does not sound like a phrase that would imply much about a speaker and a listener. Like unqualified noun titles, a title made of a noun modified by an article formally comes close to doing only the work it purports to do, to name what the poem is about: "The Altar," "The Banquet," "The Call," "The World" (those coming closest being the titles of pattern-poems like "The Altar" that give the name of the object depicted below). This impersonality, it will be argued here, is the feature Herbert characteristically exploits in his most written-about title, "The Collar."

Discussions of it usually assume its dramatic expressiveness on the grounds that it represents the tensions in the situation of the narrator in the poem by its combined senses of *collar*, *choler*, and *caller*. They are taken to be present and at work in the title because Herbert often draws on multiple meanings for expressive purposes in both poems and their titles. Almost all the other instances in *The Temple* so far identified by critics, along with some not yet annotated, regularly coincide in sound and often in spelling with only occasional slight variations, usually in vowels pronounced alike.[41] Typical is the title "The Sonne" for a poem built on the traditional analogy of *son* and *sun*, where Herbert praises such layerings of meanings for "How neatly" they "give one onely name" to all elements of the pun (a term introduced into English in the later seventeenth century and used since without distinctions for a variety of devices that were divided in separate rhetorical categories in Herbert's time). Since the very different spellings of *collar* and *choler* and probably different pronunciation of *caller* do not work "neatly," it may be unsafe to assume their simultaneous presence.

In the light of Herbert's most common titling practice, it seems possible that "The Collar" has its effect on the poem not by embodying the tensions in it but by standing aloof from them. No *collar* appears in the verses, although variously related nouns abound there: like "bayes to crown," "garlands," "cage," above all "suit." And although we might use *collar* in the same contexts, its authority as the key noun telling what the poem is about is, even in retrospect, mysterious in its origin and application, as "Choler" or "The Caller" would not be.

The absence of the title noun from the text of the poem can be read to signal that the narrator who tells his story is not given, even at the end of it, the key to its meaning offered the reader outside the story, which would liken this narrator's situation to the tenant's in "Redemption." Both hear a voice that speaks mysteriously, changing them in an instant. The worldly logic of the tenant in the sonnet is silenced; the choleric "I" of "The Collar" answers in a newly simple and acquiescent voice. It is not the title noun but "*Childe*," which he does hear, that resolves his angry confusions. This noun is a personal appeal to his particular neediness and foolishness, recognizing his smallness and helplessness, meeting his human situation. By contrast, "The Collar" embodies a perspective abstracted from personality and performance, which fill the narrator's speech. It tells us what the story is about, but it is not a key that any reader would be likelier to find unaided than would the narrator either in his choler or in his state of childlike acquiescence. For these reasons it seems possible that the article-noun title standing apart in its own space sealed off grammatically from the text of the poem may not include the unlike nouns *choler* and *caller*, which belong to the human drama in the verses.

The particular kind of neutrality in Blake's combined article and compound-noun title "The Chimney Sweeper" can be partly defined even before we begin to read the verses by its placing in *Songs Of Innocence*, where it is immediately surrounded by less featureless titles. In them the noun is modified by adjectives—"The Little Boy lost," "The Little Boy found," and "The Little Black Boy"—implying the poem's sympathy for its subject and evoking the reader's. The inexpressive noun title "The Chimney Sweeper" purports to tell only that the poem is about a particular figure, or else a category of them who all do the same work. Beyond that, it implies a perspective on the sweeper that views him from outside because it is in the grammatical form used for third-person reference. In the poem we hear a single "I" who belongs to a group, but we learn from him what the title does not tell, what it can simply assume that readers in late-eighteenth-century London did not need to be told: that of course all chimney sweepers were young boys. It would have been redundant to title the poem "The Little Chimney Sweeper."

The boy speaking the verses calls the others by their names: "thousands of sweepers Dick, Joe Ned and Jack."[42] He shows sympathy for them— "There's little Tom Dacre"—like that predicted from readers of surrounding poems by their titles but pointedly withheld in this one. The implacably impersonal category by which the title names the boy raises terrible possibilities: that he is not called by his name, or worse, that the boy himself does not use his name. When he matter-of-factly says "So your chimneys I sweep," he conjures up a scene of the child knocking at our doors saying "The Chimney Sweeper," or if he is too young to pronounce that, lisping "weep weep." Worst of all is the suggestion that, since his mother died and his father sold him when he "was very young," perhaps as little as the still younger sweep seems to him now, this boy may not know his own name. Following these suggestions, what emerges is that the cate-

gorizing authority exercised over him by the title that denies him his identity, his childhood, and his name is the authority of the social forces that
teach the children to speak of themselves as anonymous. We hear it at its
deadly work when the boy repeats the lesson they have been taught: "So if
all do their duty, they need not fear harm." While we can shudder at the
title's implications, we are still complicit in them by virtue of the ease with
which we can let the title get away with cruelty that passes as neutrality.
The simply declarative article-noun title clashes with the little boy's speech,
intensifying the force of the moral judgment in his innocently accusing "So
your chimneys I sweep."

While Richard Wilbur's title "The Writer" in *The Mind-Reader* of 1976
is like "The Chimney Sweeper" in its inherent neutrality or inexpressiveness, the words are silently charged with feeling that we sense even in the
title itself, though its depth can only be gauged by reading the poem. The
reason the title works this way in spite of its neutral form is that we read
it and others to be discussed in the context of recently changed situations
of poetry. Since it has long been possible to take for granted that the poet
is also the titler, readers now understand a title like "The Writer" to signal
that the poem is either about the author of it or about someone also a writer
for whom the poet must therefore have some personal feeling of kinship,
must recognize in some special bond. Wilbur makes beautiful use of this
possibility, juxtaposing private feeling and impersonal formality in his
choice of "The Writer" for the title of a poem about a young girl who in
the first stanza he refers to as "My daughter," in the last speaks to as
"my darling."

The poem is a story the poet tells in the present tense about his daughter,
who "is writing a story." Listening outside the closed door of her room "at
the prow of the house" to the sounds and silences of her typing, he imagines
her on a hard and dangerous voyage, and wishes her "a lucky passage."
Now he remembers the starling once trapped in the same room, battering
itself in the struggle to be free until finally "Beating a smooth course" out
the open window "And clearing the sill of the world." Moved by this memory, in the last stanza the poet shifts from the third person of the story he
has been telling the reader to say to "The Writer":

> It is always a matter, my dàrling,
> Of life and death, as I had forgotten. I wish
> What I wished you before, but harder.[43]

The feeling silent in the title has found its full voice, which in retrospect
paradoxically enhances the impersonal formality of the title's form. To
call his daughter "The Writer" is the fullest expression of the poet's imaginative sympathy and loving respect for her, "Young as she is," carrying the

"great cargo" of "her life" on a voyage as necessary and perilous as "life or death."

The fact that poets have long been known to be their own titlers has encouraged readers to take references in titles to writer, author, or poet as in some degree self-referential. At least by the nineteenth century that way of reading had extended to include titles referring to other kinds of artists, especially painters and musicians. Examples discussed in Chapter 3 are titles for poems by Browning, later imitated by Pound. More recent examples are Heaney's frankly generalizing title "An Artist" for a poem describing but not naming Cézanne, and Stevens's evasively particular title "Peter Quince at the Clavier," which claims the poem to be about a musical performer with the name of a play actor who is—in the fictional reality of *A Midsummer Night's Dream*—a carpenter. Stevens's layering of identities for the figure named in this title may obliquely refer to the further extension in the twentieth century of self-referential interpretation to include titles naming makers who would not now be called artists but artisans, like Quince the carpenter. The same association has been made with laborers like Frost's mender of walls and, still more recently, with factory workers like the maker and inspector of Pinsky's "Shirt."

Gwendolyn Brooks seems to have had this mini-history of self-referential interpretation humorously in mind in choosing the title of a sonnet in strict Shakespearean form, "The Egg Boiler," from *The Bean Eaters* of 1960. The work—labor, artisanship, art—has moved into the kitchen, as it has in other poems by women such as Adrienne Rich's "Peeling Onions," but that kind of domestic task is not finally what Brooks's formally neutral and impersonal but—in its effect—funny title says the poem is about. It is about someone for whom, the poet goes on to explain, "The boiling of an egg is heavy art."[44] This artist mocks the sonnet writer for being one among poets who make their poems out of weightless, airy sights and sounds. By contrast, the author seems with deadpan politeness to approve her critic's recipe for making a poem:

> The egg, spooned gently to the avid pan,
> And left the strict three minutes, or the four,
> Is your Enough and art for any man.

Here the sonnet writer echoes the other's manly scorn in the last of these lines (where, as in the rest of the sonnet, iambic pentameter is as strictly counted as the egg boiler's minutes), playfully hinting a criticism of her mocker's assumption that the opposite of "heavy art" is lightweight, even a hint that "heavy" might mean wooden. In silent defiance the sonneteer goes on writing in the manner of the scorned poets still "Shaping a gorgeous Nothingness from cloud" (a line with echoes that might include Shakespeare and Donne among those poets), while "You watch us, eat your egg, and laugh aloud." Although the sonnet's good manners leave unsaid who really gets the last laugh, they allow no doubt that it is the sonnet maker. She is also the maker of its title in the politely neutral form of "The Egg Boiler," which in retrospect turns jokingly self-referential: there are more ways than one to boil an egg, or write a poem.

While it would be unlikely for readers now, any more than in the late eighteenth or the nineteenth century, to take "The Chimney Sweeper" or Wordsworth's "The Waggoner" as a stand-in for the author or a figure in some personal bond of connection with the writer of the poem as a type of the poet, we are trained to recognize such identifications in the signals of twentieth-century titles naming an artist, an artisan, a laborer, or other kind of maker. A less obviously traceable but parallel cultural shift makes it quite likely that we would take Adrienne Rich's neutral seeming title "The Roofwalker," dated 1961 in *Snapshots of a Daughter-in-Law*, as a reference to the poet even though the way the figure is named there does not suggest association with some form of making. This title encodes other metaphorical suggestions with familiar psychological implications open to the kind of self-referential reading we are used to giving titles of twentieth-century poems: we expect Stevens's "The Man on the Dump" or Yeats's "A Crazed Girl" to be somehow about the poet.

The relation of Rich's title to the poem not only assumes this way of reading but makes it the focus of the poem, what it is about: a poet who rejects being figured as a maker, first implicitly in the title and more explicitly in the poem. The opening lines describe men who are in fact there called "builders," but it is pointedly not in that role that they are presented. The poet pictures them as "roofwalkers, / on a listing deck," having laid down their tools because "the wave / of darkness" is "about to break / on their heads."[45] These are the grounds for the poet's identification with them:

> I feel like them up there:
> exposed, larger than life,
> and due to break my neck.

And "even / my tools are the wrong ones / for what I have to do." The closing lines extend the self-referential interpretation of the title. The poet does not feel kinship with "The Roofwalker" considered as a builder, a maker, but as "a naked man fleeing / across the roofs." This is a desperate fugitive escaping capture by leaving everything behind, and especially by abandoning well-made poems (as Rich's are described by her praisers on the dust jacket of this volume) to be read "sitting in the lamplight / against the cream wallpaper / . . . about a naked man / fleeing across the roofs." "The Roofwalker" is a figure of another kind of poet who does not work with tools but by dangerous self-exposure. The position of the poem last in the collection, and its dedication to Denise Levertov, presumably another roofwalker, support its own interpretation of its title as a declaration of a new poetics. Yet even before we read the poem we are able to recognize "The Roofwalker" as a self-referential title because we have been trained to respond to twentieth-century titles of this kind in ways that are not invited by earlier titling. This means that their expressive power depends on more than the inherent features of their grammatical form and the meaning of the noun that states what the poem is about.

Nouns paired with adjectives

When joined to nouns in titles, adjectives might be supposed to do what they usually do, which is to give some more particular cast to the noun by announcing a perspective on it. Expressive adjectives have always been a rich resource in poetry, a history that might predict their parallel usefulness in telling what the poem is about. In fact adjective-noun pairings have been relatively rare in titling poems in English compared to the much greater number of titles where the noun is modified only by an article, and among those that poets have used, the adjectives have been typically limited to types that are not likely to be highly colored. These tendencies can suggest ways to think about not only the work of adjective-noun combinations in the presentation of poems but about all noun titles.

Not many adjectives appear in noun titles expressing feelings as intense or explicit as Thompson's "The City of Dreadful Night," or so special a perception as Hopkins's "The Handsome Heart: at a Gracious Answer," or a perspective as sharply defined by personality as Stevens's "A High-Toned Old Christian Woman." Much more common are adjectives that name some clearly apparent, often ordinary attribute of the subject as an indirect way of reflecting the attitude that finds its focus in that attribute. An example is "The Little Black Boy." The adjectives *little* and *black* in themselves do not inevitably associate a particular feeling with any noun they modify, but in Blake's title they predict a poem about a small child perceived as tender and vulnerable to mistreatment, demanding sympathy. The relatively uncharged adjective in Williams's "The Young Housewife" prepares for a poem that will view the woman from a perspective distanced by age, which brings an awareness the young woman does not have of her subjection to time. The colorless adjective in Claude McKay's "The White City" does not itself tell what a reader knowing his work would predict, that it will be darkened by bitterness in the sonnet. Larkin's "High Windows," largely because of the expectations we have been taught to bring to poems in a volume published in 1974, makes a neutral pairing of adjective

204 AUTHORITATIVE HIERARCHIES

with noun into a hint of a poem opening onto some austere vacancy "that shows / Nothing, and is nowhere, and is endless."[46] These adjectives, relatively impersonal in themselves, are of the sort most often attached to nouns in titles. Without violating the voiceless impersonality of the noun title, they tilt it in a direction that gives a fuller prediction of what the poem is about.

Almost as common are titles like Arnold's "The Forsaken Merman" and Sarah Orne Jewett's "The Caged Bird," which combine nouns with adjectives formed of past participles. The highly formulaic character of such titles shows not only in their grammar but often even in the same choice of adjective: Oliver Goldsmith's "The Deserted Village"; Dorothy Wellesley's "Deserted House"; Poe's "The Haunted Palace"; Robinson Jeffers's "Haunted Country"; Paul Lawrence Dunbar's "The Haunted Oak"; Felicia Hemans's "The Ruined Castle"; Reginald Gibbons's "The Ruined Motel"; Hart Crane's "The Broken Tower"; James Percival's "The Broken Heart"; Seba Smith's "The Drowned Mariner"; Louise Glück's "The Drowned Children"; Rosanna Warren's "Drowned Son." Each adjective colors the noun but by means special to the past participle. "The . . . Merman" who is "Forsaken" will call on the reader's sympathy in the poem about him because something has been done or has happened to him that moves the reader to pity, and this is true of all the other subjects described in these titles by past participles. They purport not to invite a responsive feeling in the reader because some perspective or attitude has been imposed on them in the title, as would be in "The [Pitiful] Merman," but because of something done by an agent not identified in the title and acting independently of its authority, which is merely to report the action. These adjectives made from past participles have their own way of respecting the impersonality of the noun title while expanding it to include the response the poem will evoke.

The corollary to the neutrality inherent in the noun title still to be tested here is that to some degree its neutrality can even extend to adjectives that would ordinarily express an attitude toward what the noun names. Blake's "London" and "The Chimney Sweeper" have already worked as models of how the unqualified noun and article-noun forms can be at once neutral and expressive, or more precisely, how they can be made expressive in their neutrality. Something like the same effect can be argued using an adjective-noun title from *Songs Of Experience* as a paradigm: "The SICK ROSE."

In Reuben Brower's discussion of the poem, he invites readers to set beside it his rephrasing of it as a hypothetical statement by a gardener to an assistant: "This rose is diseased. The petals have been eaten by a flying worm, which is killing it."[47] The contrast serves Brower's purpose, "to distinguish between degrees of imaginative organization," but his detailed discussion of the poem leaves its title out of consideration, as do most readings of most poems, another example relevant here being Jonathan Culler's minute scrutiny of all but the title of "London."[48] The title "The SICK ROSE" should be taken into account as part of the poem's design, and in particular because of its form, which brings it closer to the gardener's sentence about the rose than it is to the language of the poem, which is wholly addressed *to* the rose.

Blake's title is predicated on roughly the same meaning as the gardener's statement—"This rose is diseased"—but its grammar makes it even more impersonal because, not being in sentence form, it is more like the label on the shelf of the garden shed than like something spoken, which would evoke the kind of situation, speaker, and listener implied in Brower's paraphrase. The abstraction of the title phrase from these imagined particulars also makes it more general than the gardener's sentence, just as the article "The" is susceptible of generalization while Brower's substituted demonstrative "This" is not.

To show the special force of Blake's title, let us set beside it Herrick's "To Blossoms." There the preposition creates a fictional situation, though an admittedly generalized or unlocated one unlike Robert Burns's "To a Mountain-Daisy, On turning one down, with the Plough, in April — 1786." Even generalized, the fiction of an address to flowers implies a figure speaking out of some personal need to imagine that such inanimate things can listen and respond, though in the absence of adjectives Herrick's title does not reveal as much about the feeling that prompts the personification as does John Clare's "To an Insignificant Flower Obscurely Blooming in a Lonely Wild." Herrick's title does give a subtler generic prediction of the poem's tone because the prepositional form signals an epigram while the personification of "Blossoms," fragile and fugitive natural beauties, is conventional to the elegiac epigram. By contrast, "The SICK ROSE" is a phrase from an unlocated source. It does not bring into the title a human being impelled by feeling to speak *to* the flower as if it were a responsive fellow being, and so diminishes the personifying possibilities in calling a rose "sick."

Coming after Blake's relatively toneless title rather than one in the form of "[To] The Sick Rose," the poem's opening apostrophe—"O Rose thou art sick"—brings the implications muted in the title to shocking life.[49] The visionary whose voice admonishes in the poem can see "The invisible worm / That flies in the night" and has penetrated the "secret" of the rose, knowledge that charges the apostrophe with strong feeling while at the same time the title's anonymity and generality give impersonal authority to the impassioned vision in the poem. The title does not present it as one human being's feelings expressed by personifying the flower, or as the author's personification of a traditional image chosen for the expressive design of the poem. It is a vision of fallen nature that transcends the personal and the particular, which are excluded from the title by its stripped form, even though the elements that make it up are the same article, adjective, and noun as would be in "[To] The Sick Rose." The more impersonal grammar of Blake's title makes it a freestanding symbol that controls the design of the poem and charges it with visionary power.

Nouns paired with nouns

Frost in his early volumes seems to have discovered the value of another kind of adjective-noun combination that allows his titles to reveal still less of the poem's perspective: they consist of adjectives that are inherently stripped of perspective because they are nouns. Among them "A Line-Storm Song" may trace its lineage in a traditional type of grammatical pairing: a noun joined directly with another that is a term for the poem, substituting for a combination joined by *of* (*belonging to, composed of, about*) or *on*. A familiar example is the title of a poem by Wordsworth, "A Night-piece," used by poets at least as early as Waller; in the twentieth century by James Joyce, John Hall Wheelock, Siegfried Sassoon, C. Day Lewis; appearing in many related pairings such as Wordsworth's "A Night Thought," Linton's and Larkin's "Night-Music," George Meredith's "Twilight Music," Felicia Hemans's "Sea Piece." In these traditional pairings the adjectival function of the first noun tends to give it slightly more coloring than it would inherently have in the nominative—*night* hinting at depth and mystery, for example—whereas Frost's "Line-Storm" is for most readers neutral, free of associations, implying no emotional shading.

Frost's other titles modifying noun with noun are peculiar to him in their frequency and their variety within the double noun form. From his first four books, where they are most prominent, examples are: "Home Burial," "Ghost House," "House Fear," "Storm Fear," "Pea Brush," "The Oven Bird," "The Kitchen Chimney," "The Cow in Apple Time," "The Hill Wife," "The Star-Splitter," "The Wood-Pile," "The Gum-Gatherer," "The Axe-Helve," "A Dream Pang," "A Hillside Thaw." A title in this form hides its interpretive function under the mask of its inherent grammatical inexpressiveness, but because these purportedly neutral double nouns are clustered so thickly among the titles in Frost's early volumes, they convey an unacknowledged perspective. They accumulate a sense of the homely solid-ity and integrity, the inviolable thingness of things, and they attach to dis-embodiments like "Ghost," "Fear," "Pang" the objective status of the things they are bound to.

The remaining two chapters will concentrate on treatments of the title space, some of them touched on in earlier discussions, that are more extreme attempts to undermine or destroy the title's interpretive authority.

Part IV

UNDERMINING TITLES

CHAPTER SEVEN

Quotations in the title space

T HE TITLE of a poem acts visually something like a frame around
a painting, which plays a part in the viewer's experience of it while not
actually being on the canvas. Typically the picture frame is even made of
different material, of another color and texture from the painting it sets off.
Though this is not true of a poem's title, which is in the same medium of
language as the text, its different shape and position—and when printed
often its typeface—set it apart, while the poem on the page can only be
seen as it is framed by the title. This effect is of course most visible in the
presentation of shorter poems. The frame marks the boundaries of the
painting or poem and holds it up to be looked at in a certain way, which
means that it has presentational authority. Someone has exercised the right
to put the work in a frame before we see it.

Grammatically the title of a poem acts as a statement, comment, observation, or signal about the poem that is inseparable from the reader's experience of the whole without being contained in the text. Even though we
now understand the title to be chosen by the poet as a feature of the poem's
design, we make a perfectly ordinary distinction between words *about* the
poem and the words *of* the poem. Most concretely, the grammar of the title
embodies that difference, as examples of titles in all the categories so far
discussed have shown.

Self-referential quotations

It should follow from this distinction between words about the poem
and the words of the poem that when the title space is filled with a quotation

repeating a line or phrase from the text, then the quoted words would not have the status of a title. Actually the one exception that seems to fit this rule is the practice, conventionally accepted now but virtually unknown in English before the nineteenth century, of quoting the poem's opening line or phrase in the title space just as the reader experiences it on beginning to read the poem. These exactly repeated opening quotations will be reserved for the next chapter because they belong to its discussion of treatments of the title space formally designed as evasions of its authority. Otherwise quotations from elsewhere in the text when they precede the poem at least seem to say something about it in answer to the kinds of questions anticipated by titles in the categories previously explored.

While the next chapter will propose that exact repetitions of the poem's opening line or phrase in the space above the text are not formally titles, discussion here will begin with examples showing how the slightest change in such a quotation can transform it from a reference claiming to tell only which the poem is—*this is the poem beginning*—into what purports to be an interpretive suggestion about how to read it. This effect can be seen as if under a microscope in the minute change in the beginning clause of a poem by Philip Larkin, "If my darling were once to decide / Not to stop at my eyes," when it is repeated where we read it before the poem.[1] The addition of a comma to the quotation in the title space, "If, My Darling," turns words said about the woman into something said to her, though presumably (we learn from the poem) only in a scene acted out in the embittered lover's fantasy. His intonation, changed by the comma, expresses his soured feelings as he reflects on what he has said about the woman in the poem and on what he would like to say to her. The change makes the quoted phrase into a title framing the poem from a more explicitly skeptical perspective than we would hear in the opening words of the poem if they were exactly repeated in the title space. Such sleight of hand may have been suggested by Hardy, Larkin's admitted first master, who seems to have invented another and more subtle way of using punctuation to turn a self-referential opening quotation into an unobtrusive frame shaping the reader's response to the poem. The fact that he uses this typically unobvious device often throughout his volumes makes its effect especially telling.

Hardy's intense interest in titling is shown by the fact that even in manuscript he seems to have carefully assigned and often revised titles for all his poems. This means that any consistent practices we find in them result from considered choices; they are reliable reflections of his designs. One such pattern is his remarkable preference for self-referential opening quotations in the title space. He uses them perhaps more often than any other poet writing in English except Whitman, and unlike Whitman's, Hardy's self-referential quotations are not additions to poems originally left untitled.

Another pattern, observable in his way of handling these titles, is his virtually invariable practice both in manuscript and in collections printed in his
lifetime (all but the latest wholly supervised by him with meticulous attention to detail) of enclosing his self-referential opening quotations in quotation marks when they appear on the page above the poems, as well as in
the tables of contents for printed volumes.

These quotation marks are a visual representation of the framing power
of a title; verbally they signal that the quoted words are a repetition of what
has been said before in the poem. Here, then, they reinforce the conventional assumption that the title has been assigned after the poem has been
completed, by someone privileged by prior knowledge of it to present it to
readers who have not yet encountered it. It is the titler's decision that the
opening line or phrase is worth quoting to the reader in advance as a direction about how to read the poem. This mediating function seems to be the
value for Hardy of quotation marks around self-referential opening quotations preceding the poems. They are a useful means, like many of his titles
in other forms, for protecting his poems from autobiographical readings.

A representative instance of how Hardy makes them work is a song-like
poem in *Poems of the Past and the Present*:

"I Need Not Go"

I need not go
Through sleet and snow
To where I know
She waits for me.[2]

The "I" through four stanzas flaunts his power over a woman who will
never "upbraid" him, until in the last stanza "Ah, no!" returns the song in
its closing words to its opening rhyme sound: "She will not blame me, /
But suffer it so." So "I Need Not Go"? The circular rhyme scheme takes us back
to the opening line framed by quotation marks in the title space. Now it
reads like a sardonic repetition of the speaker's boast, echoed by someone
who with distanced amusement hints in advance of the jauntiness we hear
as we read the poem.

The quotation marks around the self-referential quotation signal that it
is being repeated to make a point about how the first sayer of it sounds to
the titler; that what the titler who quotes "I Need Not Go" playfully calls
attention to is the self-centeredness of the "I" in the poem, who is not to
be identified with the maker or titler of it.

These plentiful opening quotations have a cumulative effect in Hardy's
volumes that might at first glance seem curiously at odds with his characteristically distancing ways of framing his poems. In contrast with his editorial
third-person forms of *he* and *his* referring to the first person in the poem,

his titles made from opening quotations typically include and even begin with *I*, but the quotation marks enclosing them tend to circumscribe this egoism with varying degrees of skepticism matching the detached perspective of Hardy's other titles. Often the distancing effect of the quotation marks is underlined by a subscription to the title reinforcing the detachment of the titler, understood to be the poet, from the first person in the poem. For instance, "I Said and Sang Her Excellence" is subscribed "(Fickle Lover's Song)," explicitly defining the dramatic impersonation in the poem. Paradoxically, then, what happens to the words of the *I* when they are framed in the title space by quotation marks is actually something like the effect brought about by use of the editorial *he*.

Browning seems to have been among the earliest poets to discover that modifications in a self-referential quotation of the first line or phrase can change its status from a reference to a title. How this is so can be seen in the interchange between Browning's most famous dramatic monologue, with the abrupt opening line "That's my last Duchess painted on the wall," and its title, "My Last Duchess," as it appeared in *Dramatic Lyrics and Romances* of 1849. The immediacy of the title contrasts with the poem's earlier generalized presentation in *Dramatic Lyrics* of 1842 as "Italy," which was paired with "France" (titling what became "Count Gismond") to frame portraits of different national characters. "My Last Duchess" also contrasts with the third-person forms of reference to the speaker used in titles of Browning's other dramatic monologues. On their model the poem might have been titled something like "The Duke of Ferrara Displays the Portrait of His Last Duchess," which would separate the author who makes the framing title from the *I* in the verses. Instead Browning achieves this end, but with more dramatic effect, by plucking a first-person phrase out of the opening line. In the title space it both calls attention to itself as a defining example of the way the figure in the poem speaks and implies that way of speaking to be what the poem is about.

Although by itself in the space above the poem "My Last Duchess" sounds almost like a conventional form of reference to a deceased lady of title, "Last" rather than *late* makes her an item in a series, while "My" locates that item in the sequence of phrases in the poem enumerating the duke's entitlements: "my last Duchess," "my favour," "My gift," finally "my object," with its double meaning of aim and owned thing.[3] The whole title phrase in its interchange with the poem therefore hints at what the strange wording of the line it is taken from expresses about the duke's twisted possessiveness toward both the woman and the painting of her. To him she was in life a possession, a work of art to display in his gallery like the Neptune cast in bronze "for me" (the final words in the poem). Conversely, in the strangely phrased opening line the duke speaks of the portrait as if it were its subject—"That's my last Duchess"—but more human, so that now she is dead, painted, framed to decorate the wall, she appears to her husband "Looking as if she were alive," revealing in "that pictured countenance / The depth and passion of its earnest glance," whereas on her living face he only saw "that spot / Of joy" as if painted on her cheek.

The choice of quotation for the title therefore alerts us to this interpretation of the duke's language; his words in the title space are characteristic of him. They are ones he likes to say, taking complacent pleasure in repeatedly referring to "My Last Duchess" without uneasiness about how he sounds to his listener. This creates the illusion that we are listening to someone speak without the mediation of a titler, and that independence gives the speaker a more fully dramatic identity separate from the poet than is conferred by a title in the distanced third person, which can make the *I* in the poem seem to be the author's creature.

Frost's exploration of the expressive possibilities in new title forms extends to radically original uses of self-referential quotations. An example is his poem with the abbreviated first-line quotation "Acquainted with the Night" in the title space. This poem has seemed to critics atypical, both formally and expressively, because the *I* who speaks it "ends where he began." This has encouraged the judgment that "the poem establishes no progression," leading William Pritchard to conclude with some puzzlement that it "is—for one of Frost's—extraordinarily undramatic."[4] Frank Lentricchia argues a similar view that this poem "is an especially passive moment for the self consistently dramatized in Frost's poetry" because by ending with its opening line, it leaves us with "an image of frozen will, of feet stopped, with darkness all around and no constructive act forthcoming."[5]

While admittedly the structure and lineation of "Acquainted with the Night" are remarkable in Frost's work, the poem can strike us somewhat differently if we pay attention to the truncated title quotation as part of its design, which Frost's well-documented interest—and dazzling inventiveness—in choosing his titles should encourage us to do. What the kind of critical reading just cited leaves out of account is that Frost does not precisely repeat in the title space the line that opens and closes the poem, a choice that would have reinforced its seemingly undramatic structure. Instead he quotes only part of that line, disrupting its obsessive rhythm and changing its tone, pointedly inviting us to ask what is important about the omissions from "[I have been one] Acquainted with the Night."

Most obviously, and least surprisingly for Frost, the title leaves out the first person, a cut that could scarcely be made more emphatic since six of the first seven lines below the truncated title begin "I have."[6] This pattern makes us see the pronoun prominently repeated in a line down the page, and hear it all the more loudly because the lines it opens are the only metrically disrupted lines in the poem. Also left out of the title is the un-Frostlike impersonal pronoun "one," which in its hint of pomposity matches the stilted syntax of "I have been one."

The origin of these idiosyncracies may be suggested in Frost's report to Elizabeth Sergeant that "This poem came to me after a visit from A.E. [George Edward Russell] the Irish mystic, who subtly murmured: 'The Time is not right.' "[7] The repeated phrase "I have been one" seems almost comically out of keeping with the manner of other poems in the same volume, *West-Running Brook* of 1928, or belonging to roughly the same period of Frost's work. By contrast, the sentence fragment chosen to precede the poem seems characteristically modest and casual, so much so that it lessens the solemnity of "acquainted with." Its social meaning takes over in the title, suppressing the archaic sense and sound of the faint echo in the poem's first and last lines of Isaiah 53:3—"a man of sorrows, and acquainted with grief."

The altered quotation in this self-referential title can be read as a reflection on the poem that allows the kind of dramatic effect otherwise denied by the circular repetition of its opening and closing lines. If we accept the possibility that the title is said by the same voice we hear in the poem echoing itself, then a considerable change takes place in it. The title suggests some stepping back from the posture of the first person who makes himself an archetype—"I have been one"—or some recognition that his repeated declarations could sound melodramatic. The quoted fragment preceding the poem has a slightly deflating or tamping down, calming or quieting effect, like the last lines of other poems in the same volume, for instance "Spring Pools," which is placed first, and "Once by the Pacific," which opens the section headed "Fiat Nox" that closes with "Acquainted with the Night." Most of all this works like another quoted title for a poem in *New Hampshire* of 1923, previously titled with the self-referential quotation "Wrong to the Light," for which Frost substituted the poem's modest and casual closing words, said in an unmelodramatic, quieting tone: "For Once, Then, Something." What is suggested by this way of reading "Acquainted With the Night" as part of the poem's design is that the abbreviated title quotation dramatizes something like the kind of self-recognition expressed in the endings of other poems by Frost. It is reflected in the change of tone, more marked than any of the variations in the sound of the voice reciting the lines of the text, that would be disallowed without the contrast between the sentence beginning and ending the poem and the fragment of it quoted by the same speaker who has listened to his own voice with some tentative self-awareness.

What has been said about altered quotations from the opening phrase or line holds true also for exact quotations from elsewhere in the poem because (unlike the conventional use of precisely repeated openings to be discussed in the next chapter) both these types of self-referential titles reflect a selective interpretation. They choose to alert the reader ahead of time to some word, phrase, or line that has recognized importance to the privileged reader with prior knowledge of it. This means that they purport to do more than tell which poem the reader is about to begin. Sometimes these quotations can seem to act rather like a label saying what is the chief ingredient in the container if they repeat wording that has obvious prominence in the poem due to its position, for instance as the last line or phrase, or due to its repetition within the poem, as in a refrain. Quite often the quotation chosen to present the poem has both kinds of prominence, as an early example, Wordsworth's "We Are Seven" from the first edition of *Lyrical Ballads*, illustrates. What more it exemplifies is that even an innocently obvious choice of self-referential quotation can have more subtly expressive effects than simply giving advance notice of an important ingredient in the poem.

Wordsworth's title phrase repeats the final words of the poem, which are themselves a version of other phrases recurring throughout, until in the last two stanzas they constitute a kind of refrain. They are spoken by the child in the poem about her sisters and brothers—"seven in all"; "Seven are we"; "Seven boys and girls are we"; "Oh Master! we are seven!"; "Nay, we are seven!"—to correct the poet's insistence that since two have died, "Then ye are only five."[8] The choice for the title quotation, though unsurprising, has expressive effects that go well beyond its function of pointing to what anyone having read the poem would pick out as its interpretive focus.

Because, by Wordsworth's time and ever since, readers have accepted titles as the poet's choice, this one can do more than call our attention to the child's unshakable faith, unassailable by adult logic. That is, since the child's words in the title space are quoted there by the poet who in the poem speaks a different language, his granting her statement that position of authority reveals more about him than could be known from the poem alone or from the alternative choice to use its opening phrase, "A simple child," in the title space. His quotation of the child's words to frame the completed poem shows that he has not only continued to reflect on them after meeting her—he tells the incident in the past tense by contrast with the child's habitual use of the present—but still feels their power. He repeats her last words either with respectful tenderness for her "simple" ignorance of death or because that simplicity has triumphed over adult knowing, converting the poet to her understanding. If the poem does not clearly settle on either of these alternatives, it clearly raises them, and most pointedly by the juxtaposition of the child's words above the poem with its opening phrase. "A simple child" is a metrical fragment using a third-person form of reference conventional for a title framing the poem from the poet's perspective (as in

Wordsworth's "A Poet's Epitaph," "A Jewish Family"). The choice, instead, of the unconventional title "We Are Seven" seems to be a way of expressing the greater power of the child's language over the poet than his own.

When the self-referential quotation used to present the poem is not an obvious choice, when it is wording from a less prominent position or is not otherwise emphasized, for instance by insistent repetition, it still keeps its purely visual aspect as a frame, but its status as a signal about the poem is less clear. That is, any reader of "We Are Seven" would recognize those repeated words as the catalyst for the poet's feelings and would to some degree share the surprise, or bafflement, or troubled sense of difference they raise in him. By contrast, it seems unlikely that a reader of Coleridge's poem beginning "Well, they are gone, and here I must remain" would, if it were untitled, choose as its interpretive focus a fragment from what in *Sibylline Leaves* of 1817 is its second line, "This Lime-Tree Bower my Prison" (originally the third line in the manuscript of 1797).[9]

The choice is quite unpredictable, so that it seems more private. We are not expected to share the idiosyncratic feeling of being imprisoned in a "Bower," in pastoral tradition protected as a sacred or amorous retreat, that prompts it. It also sounds spontaneous, even without the exclamation point that follows it in line 2, because it is fragmentary, an appositional phrase. "This" seems to burst in on something with an immediacy matched in the opening line, and the ending of the title phrase in the middle of an iambic foot makes it casual and unsettled. It does not have the grammatical structure of a conventional title—"The Lime-Tree Bower," "In a Lime-Tree Bower," "Meditation on a Lime-Tree Bower"—or the cadence of a title quoting a metrical line—"This Lime-Tree Bower My Prison Is." What is more, the quotation does not recur, where it might be expected, in the opening line, and the setting, which is what we take the "Bower" to be, disappears the minute these words are said, not to return for more than forty lines. When it surfaces again as "This little lime-tree bower," although the change in wording is significant, the distance between the two instances tends to dim the reader's first awareness of the shift and of its weight. Besides, the position of the second appearance in the text of "bower" as an appositional phrase in the fourth line of the closing verse paragraph is not specially prominent, and its cadence is not unsettled, like the title quotation, because it does not break off in the middle of an iamb. In other words, its harking back to the title is not emphasized, so that although careful reading discovers the process of the poet's mind reflected in the highly charged change from "This . . . Bower my Prison" to "This little . . . bower," the movement still seems inward and unwilled. This process starts with the title, an extemporaneous *effusion* (a term Coleridge uses as a generic title for many entries in *Poems on Various Subjects*, published the year before this poem was written). It is the seemingly spontaneous expression of a mood that unfolds as an unforced movement of private reflection for which its easy, unrhymed pentameter lines in irregular paragraphs are the fit medium.

As Reeve Parker suggests in his different argument about the poem, Coleridge's heading "Meditative Poems in Blank Verse" for the group that included this poem in *Sibylline Leaves* is a more appropriate description than the recently preferred category of "Conversation Poems."[10] Even though a line like "For thee, my gentle-hearted Charles" calls up the presence of Coleridge's friend Lamb, it is a literary evocation more than a direct address spoken to a friend, leaving the inwardness and privacy of the poet's movement of thought more meditative than conversational.[11] Looking back, we are able to recognize the title quotation as a catalyst for the evolution of the mood we can retrospectively trace to that outburst, while at the same time we only sense its internal source. Even with hindsight, the importance of the title phrase lies, as it were, beneath the surface. It is not what anyone but the poet whose inward process it sets in motion would have chosen as the focus of the feelings unfolding in the poem. This means that our presence is not acknowledged by the title or the poem, as it is by Wordsworth's choice of a title with obvious significance to readers of "We Are Seven," where we are also admitted as the audience by its didactic opening and story-telling manner. The more surprising choice of the title quotation "This Lime-Tree Bower my Prison," by its pretense of spontaneity and offhandedness, supports the poem's inward and seemingly unplanned meditative movement.

Just as surprising is Frost's choice to quote as the title for a sonnet in *A Witness Tree* of 1942 its thirteenth line, "Never Again Would Birds' Song Be the Same," but this unconventional selection has a very different effect from Coleridge's.[12] Here the self-referential quotation in the title space is not formally modified in any detail from its occurrence late in the poem, so it does not point to a change in the voice we hear in the sonnet. If anything happens, then, between the title and the penultimate line, it can best be measured by their effects on the reader in their different positions.

Reading the title before we begin the poem, it does not strike us as unconventional. It sounds like the kind of self-referential opening quotation commonly used in the title space or for identification, as we use the first line of Shakespeare's sonnets (and Frost here uncharacteristically follows the Shakespearean rhyme scheme). It sounds this way because it scans as the pentameter line of sonnet tradition, a feature that is emphasized since the line is grammatically and logically complete (unlike the actual first line of the sonnet, "He would declare and could himself believe"). Both features give it the sureness and emphasis, suited to the authority of a title, that come with closure. It is also unsurprising in another way because it seems like a generic signal associating the poem with traditional laments for the fallen world of pastoral, where Ralegh's "*Philomell* becommeth dombe"; where the "Willows" and "Hazle Copses" "Shall now no more be seen, / Fanning their joyous Leaves" to the "soft layes" once sung by Lycidas.[13] Like Milton's "now no more," Frost's "Never Again" expresses the poet's mortal consciousness of endings that, he seems to hint, is darkening even the singing of birds and so all the more his own human song.

In keeping with the generic signal of the title, the first two lines of the poem take us back into the prefallen natural world, as yet undarkened and unconstrained by limits. We expect it will be celebrated in the untrammeled singing of the "birds there in all the garden round," then lamented in the poet's elegiac song. Instead that unfallen world, the singing of the birds, and the sonnet itself beginning with line 3 are filled with "the daylong voice of Eve," which carries "aloft," as if it had winged power, her loving exchanges with Adam (the "He" of line 1 who is given to declaring her supremacy). Her "eloquence," the poet admits, inevitably "had an influence on birds"—a smiling allusion to Eve's role in legend—filling their song with the "tone of meaning" that made her voice distinctively human: joyful in its "laughter"; communicative, beckoning in its "call"; willful or stubborn in having "persisted." That change in birds' song is the fall of the natural world into mortality in this poem, reflected in the time-bound vocabulary that enters in line 11. There "the garden" has become "the woods" where "now," "so long," "never" return us to the title line, but it too has an added "tone of meaning." Now it is more than the lament for the loss of the unfallen world that it sounded before the beginning of the poem; it is a loving tribute to Eve's human voice that "added" an "oversound" to birds' song, giving it the enduring power of poetry that "never would be lost."

The sonnet itself acts out that power in the unconventional way it uses its self-referential title quotation. By deferring its original until almost the end of the sonnet instead of repeating it in the opening line, Frost allows the poem's rich "tone of meaning" to add an "oversound" to the title. By the time we hear the line again, the poet's voice has guided us to recognize it as a celebration, which is then not allowed to end the poem. Although in itself "Never again would birds' song be the same" has the definitiveness and closure of a final line, Frost characteristically unsettles it in the fourteenth line by the human mixture in the tone of the poet's voice—skeptical, loving, funny, sad: "And to do that to birds was why she came." The conventional third-person "He" of line 1 now includes—with Adam, everyman—the generic poet of sonnets who "would declare" their elegiac strain and the disguised first-person poet who "could him self believe" the tones he has "added" to it. This dramatic interchange between the title and

the sonnet also adds an "oversound" to poetic tradition by its transformations of conventions. In them there is a hint that because of this sonnet, the
songs of poets and the ways readers hear them would never be quite the
same again.

That claim would hardly seem too large for Frost's even more startlingly
original use of a self-referential title for another poem in *A Witness Tree*,
"Come In." Since the title repeats words said twice by the "I" in the poem,
common sense and convention would lead us to assume that the speaker
is the same in both title space and text, repeating his own words. But they
sound very different in the body of the poem, because they do not stand
alone as they do in the space above it, where they have to be heard as a
spoken imperative. Still more unsettling to our assumption of a single voice
is that the story told in the poem does not easily support it. There the narrator tells how, walking near the woods at night, he heard the song of a
thrush, "Almost like a call to come in / To the dark and lament," but that "I
would not come in."[14] The title does not repeat the phrase with the original
grammatical status it has in either of these two instances in the text, and
that creates differences in cadence as well. In stanza 4, "come in" is part of
an anapest, in the fifth ambiguously anapestic or iambic—"Ĭ woúld nŏt
cŏme iń" or "Ĭ woŭld nót cŏme iń"—while the stresses in the title words
are undetermined. Reuben Brower suggests for them the iambic cadence
of a neighborly invitation, "Cŏme Iń," combined with the Romantic seduc-
tiveness of a trochaic "cóme iń to the garden," but even an uninflected pyr-
rhic or an imperious spondee might be allowable (suggestions not far-
fetched for the title of a poem that plays games with meter as sophisticated
and complicated as Frost's here).[15] Though we recognize "Come In" to be
a spoken idiom, we cannot settle on how it is said, with what tone of meaning, or even who says it, since when the narrator twice uses the same words
in the poem they cannot be read as a friendly invitation, a seductive call, a
neutral imperative, or a command.

The logic of the story only allows the title voice to be the narrator's if
he is giving an imitation of what the bird's song "Almost" sounded like, a
tempting call to enter the darkling mysteries of nature, or if he is warding
off the threat of its seductions by domesticating it, making it sound familiar
and homely. At the same time the story may invite us to imagine that the
title is an echo of what the speaker first called out, which would predict the
situation in the poem (though not in its title) placed shortly after in the
volume, "The Most Of It": the human being cries out to nature the response
he wants from it, but receives only "the mocking echo of his own" words.
Still another identity for the voice in the title is allowed because the poem
is built on a paradigm of the Romantic lyric, most particularly "Ode to a
Nightingale" (with traces of Hardy's "The Darkling Thrush"). The voice

we hear before we start the poem may belong to poetic tradition, or to Keats's bird, beckoning the later poet "into the forest dim." In this script, the question of tone is still skeptically and playfully left open. Does Romantic poetry invite a successor seductively; or as if to a friendly neighbor; or indifferently; or imperiously, impatiently, because whoever is at the door is refusing to "come in"?

Quoted titles

When the title space is filled with a quotation from some source outside the poem, its likeness to a frame is stronger because it is, as it were, of another material or has a different color and texture. It can even act as a kind of double frame sometimes visually represented by quotation marks setting off the quoted words, a form of punctuation introduced into English late in the seventeenth century. Both the words in their prior context and their repetition are present in the title space. Though not contained in the text like self-referential quotations, together in the framing position they can both enter into the reader's experience of the poem. The contribution of the original, external context as it is brought to bear by its repetition can of course vary enormously: depending on whether the borrowed words are from the title or the text of the prior work; whether they are quoted exactly as they originally appeared or are changed in being repeated; whether they are taken from another poem or from a source of some different kind, written or spoken.

The commonest form of what might be called quotation is a formula belonging to a tradition of titling: "Ode," "Thyrsis," "To the Reader," the suffix of *The Dunciad*, "Self-Portrait," "Preludes."[16] To call these titles a form of quotation is most simply a way of saying that they are *conventional*, a word rooted in the Latin *conventio* (*a coming together or meeting*). Although the term was apparently not applied in English to literature until the nineteenth century, poets since they became titlers have understood the workings of conventions in their titles. The title quotation "Ode" hypothetically convenes all its prior uses, bringing them together in the title space as a statement about what kind the new poem is, what other poems with the same title meet in it to make it that kind. If the title quotes a more specialized formal term like "Monody," which appears fairly often above eighteenth- and nineteenth-century poems, then it convenes a narrower range of sources, in this instance Milton's "Lycidas" and such descendants as: William Mason's "Musæus: a monody to the memory of Mr. Pope, in imitation of Milton's 'Lycidas' "; William Bowles's "Monody on the Death of Dr. Warton"; Coleridge's "Monody on the Death of Chatterton"; Herman Melville's "Monody" (generally thought to be about the death of

Hawthorne). These titles are a form of quotation, beyond the fact of their conventionality, because by explicitly naming a particular formal kind they insist that recognition of the name and its implications must be an important feature of the reader's response to the poem, and such recognition in turn depends on knowing that the name has appeared above other, earlier poems. Though they act in this sense as quotations, they work differently from the types of quoted titles to be discussed here, which point to the coming together of the new poem with some particular prior source or combination of sources. Among these, the title precisely copying the title of another poem is less common than a title borrowed from a work of some different type or medium—a play, a novel, a painting—and very much less common than titles taken from some place in the text of another piece of writing.

Although prior titles of poems might seem a promising source for later poets to borrow from, they have turned to it surprisingly seldom in the history of titling in English (once we discount quotations like "Ode"). The reason poets have very rarely been attracted to this form of borrowing may be that it tends to narrow its expressive possibilities, because the source and the quotation of it have the same status. Since both are titles, words about the poem, the way the original title frames its text is a specially determining force in the framing of the later poem. This means that the double frame focuses the meeting between the source and its quotation on relatively few well-defined features.

A brief history can outline the different meeting grounds between a title for a poem borrowed from the title of an unlike work or from the title of another poem. Spenser chose to present his "Æglogues" in 1579 under the title *The Shepheardes Calender*, described in the prefatory epistle as "an olde name to a new worke." The borrowed title needed no further identification because it was taken from a popular book, *Le Compost et Kalendrier des bergiers*, first published in 1493 and reprinted in seven editions by the time Spenser translated what he wanted of its title.[17] He could count on his readers knowing that the "olde name" was the title of this typical medieval collection of mixed verse and prose pieces with assorted forms and topics but distinctly Catholic interest, loosely associated by its title with illuminated manuscript conventions. By translating and applying it to his altogether unlike volume of eclogues carefully ordered by the months and sung by the shepherd-poet of classical tradition, Spenser could free the borrowed title to be a manifesto for his distinct contribution to humanist, Protestant verse in English, presenting him as "this our new Poete" of a "new worke." Because his title previously framed a very different kind of work, his repetition of it need not be circumscribed by what it originally said about the prior text, so that Spenser is licensed to choose its framing perspective. It could even be said that this freedom itself constitutes the focus of Spenser's borrowed title: on how it has shed its "olde" skin.

By contrast, the reframing effect of *The Shepherd's Calendar* as the title for a group of poems by John Clare published in 1827 is more narrowly focused by the perspective Spenser's earlier title imposes on this volume of the same kind. The suggestion for borrowing the "Name which Spenser took for a poem or rather collection of Poems of his" came to Clare from his publisher, John Taylor, whose aim was most likely entrepreneurial: to promote a salable volume imitating Spenser's unified plan—"like his divided into Months, & under each might be given a descriptive Poem & a Narrative Poem"—and with a fashionably Spenserian title (also recalling John Gay's *The Shepherd's Week* of a century before).[18] The presence of the original title is strongly felt in the presentation of the later volume, signaling that these are poems in the English pastoral tradition. Because the title is repeated for verse by Clare, already known to readers as an actual rustic whose version of the shepherd's yearly round would be rooted in having lived it and not in reading the Greek, Latin, and Italian poets listed in the epistle to Spenser's volume, the quotation allows an added perspective in the title space. It is the meeting ground of two English shepherd-poets, a learned Elizabethan author and a modern rural muse.

When an earlier poem's title is repeated for a later poem, its presence can be felt in other, more complex ways than as a generic signal. Still, it is true that the grounds of meeting between source and quotation are more determined than in other types of title quotations because what the original title says about the poem is said again. To illustrate, Matthew Arnold borrows the title of Thomas Gray's poem "The Progress of Poesy," first presented this way in 1768, but changes Gray's subtitle "A Pindaric Ode" to "A Variation," seemingly to call attention to his own title as a quotation with a layered relation to its original. Arnold's subtitle says about his "Progress" that it is both a variation on the topic announced for the poem and a variation of its form: it is not an ode. These differences imply that his poem will present its own later perspective on poetry's progress, and that the differences between its form and Gray's Pindaric ode will embody the progress of poetry as it appears from that changed perspective.

In Gray's poem the history of poetry is a majestic "progress" of a "Sovreign" power moving forward from Greece and then Rome to England.[19] There her "awful face" is unveiled to Shakespeare and Milton, who are followed onto "the fields of Glory" by Dryden's "less presumptuous car." This note of diminishment turns elegiac in the closing stanza:

> But ah! tis heard no more—
> Oh! Lyre divine, what daring Spirit
> Wakes thee now?

In answer Gray offers himself, no "Theban Eagle" but an imitator carried aloft on Pindar's wings. His emulation of elevated diction and luxuriant sound in his poem, its form strictly modeled on the Pindaric ode, is the end point of that "Progress" from the empowering source to its imitation, inevitably diminished as an echo is weaker than its originating sound.

In Arnold's poem the movement is not charted through poetry's history but confined to the poet's own dessicating process from young manhood to old age, making "Progress" a satirical or self-mocking reflection. Because "Youth," the "man," the "old man" labors alone "on life's arid mount," his search for the vein of inspiration is unsustained by its source, unenriched by tradition, and unacknowledged by history.[20] His isolation and negation are embodied in the meager diction of the poem's three minimal stanzas and their bitter rhymes—"chops"/"drops," "nigh"/"dry," finally "stones"/"bones." The "Variation" in the form of the poem expresses its changed perspective from Gray's. "Progress" ends here not in the figure of an imitator carried aloft by borrowed power but in the poet as "the old man" who "feebly rakes among the stones" for "water from the fount" in a wasteland where "The mount is mute, the channel dry." The poem reads, like Gray's closing stanza in its own way, as a personal statement.

The context of the volume it was first published in, *New Poems Of Matthew Arnold* of 1867, extends that reading beyond the personal to include a perspective on poetry in the later nineteenth century, parallel to Gray's vision of his ode's situation in eighteenth-century poetry. The volume opens with an untitled prefatory poem (in 1877 given its present title, "Persistency in Poetry"):

> *Though the Muse be gone away,*
> *Though she move not earth to-day,*
> *Souls, erewhile who caught her word,*
> *Ah! still harp on what they heard.*[21]

To this poet, as to his eighteenth-century predecessor, the strains of poetry heard in his time are the sounds of imitators, who by now are heard to "harp on" echoes of the past in weaker songs further diminished in form and more bitter in tone. Read in this context, the double frame of Arnold's title quoted from Gray's generalizes personal statement as literary history, placing the later poem in the perspective of poetry's decline prophesied by Gray a hundred years before.

Charles Tomlinson's "Crossing Brooklyn Ferry," published in 1984 in *Notes From New York and Other Poems*, stakes out common ground with Whitman's poem by repeating its title, but here there is no subtitle admitting to what is obviously its radical variation in form.[22] Yet the very spare if not meager look of the printed poem makes its borrowed frame seem almost comically ill-fitting. Besides the title quotation, it consists of nine pentameter lines that barely fill the top quarter of the page, a space scarcely seeming in scale with the dimensions framed by the original title for Whitman's poem of nine expansive and exclamatory, loose and irregular verse paragraphs. The grammar of Tomlinson's poem is equally un-Whitmanlike in its constrictions. The lines make up a single sentence beginning with an infinitive phrase, "To cross a ferry," which has as its subject "The eye," not Whitman's exuberant "I" overflowing into "me," "myself," "we," "us." The only personal pronoun allowed in Tomlinson's sentence-poem is distanced and generalized—"the stakes that you can see"—by contrast with Whitman's incantatory repetitions of direct address—"I see you face to face!" "Closer yet I approach you"—so that there seems no meeting ground between the two poems except that, incongruously, the second is reframed by the title of the first.

Yet what "you see" in Tomlinson's poem are "the ghosts of Whitman's ferry," what "is no longer there," meaning that the "eye" piloting "you" has visionary powers: "It travels the distance instantaneously / And time also." This is a seeing empowered by the invisible presence of Whitman's "I," silently exclaiming, "It avails not, time nor place—distance avails not, / I am with you," "Who knows, for all the distance, but I am as good as looking at you now, for all you cannot see me?" Such ghostly echoes of Whitman's poem inhabit Tomlinson's, fulfilling the claim of the title quotation to a meeting between them. Whitman's "images/Crowding" what seems to be the spareness of the later poem bear witness that even its restrained impersonality is impassioned by the inescapable vitality and generosity of Whitman's presence. Here, then, the meeting of the two poems in the title quotation, their "Crossing," is a visionary experience, its potency intensified by the unlikely way a seemingly ill-fitting title quotation encloses the matter-of-fact meaning of the words in a mythic perspective. The double frame of Tomlinson's borrowed title turns his poem into an improbable but nonetheless powerfully inevitable fulfillment of Whitman's vision prophesied in his poem a century before: "Others will enter the gates of the ferry and cross from shore to shore."

When the title of a poem borrows another poem's title but changes some detail of it, the new version naturally stands in a different relation to the original than when the later title quotes its source exactly. Its framing features have been adjusted, and the adjustment itself then decides the perspective in which the changed quotation leads the reader to view the poem it frames. A perfectly adjusted example is *The Rape of the Lock*. Behind Pope's title is the partially quoted title of Shakespeare's *The Rape of Lucrece*, changed by a substitution borrowed from Catullus's translation of Callimachus, known as *The Lock of Berenice* (an English translation from a French version had appeared in 1707). Since Shakespeare's poem is a tragic narrative of heroic female virtue and Catullus's translation a parodic celebration of female piety, the combination of their titles quoted in Pope's is absurd, almost a paradigm for the art of sinking. The deflating substitution of *the Lock* for *Lucrece*, by purporting to erase the sexual meaning of *Rape*, pretends that what is at stake in the poem is not a woman's virtue, or honor, or body, but her hairdo. Yet because the ludicrous substitution does not wholly blot out the tragic original, Pope's altered title quotation is, as Reuben Brower writes about the cutting of the lock itself, "absurd, but also much more than absurd."[23] It hints at cruel and ugly violence hidden under its amused and amusing surface, giving a more finely adjusted signal about how to read the poem than the subtitle, used for both the 1712 and expanded 1714 versions of the poem, characterizing it by a bathetic combination of generic categories as *An Heroi-Comical Poem.*

Eliot's title "Whispers of Immortality" in *Poems* of 1919 sets itself up against Wordsworth's "Intimations," but as usual with Eliot, what seems to be a contrast between sensibility or belief now lost and the diminished way "our lot" thinks and feels turns out to be more than or other than a contrast.[24] The substituted noun "Whispers" in his title quotation does add suggestions of the clandestine or furtive, of intrigue, which it has as Eliot uses it in "Gerontion" where a "depraved" ritual is performed "Among whispers, by Mr. Silvero / With caressing hands." It is also traditionally associated with seductions of all sorts, as a concordance to Shakespeare's plays shows at a glance, which is the way Eliot uses it again in "Gerontion," to describe how "History . . . deceives with whispering ambitions." Wordsworth's latinate noun "Intimations" does not have these sexual and political connotations, but it does suggest secrets hinted rather than revealed and caught only in *glimpses*, to use another Wordsworthian word for visionary experiences of hidden mysteries momentarily or partially unveiled. While Eliot's substitution of "Whispers" introduces these other associations, it at the same time acknowledges its roots in Romantic poetry, as had the earlier title "Rhapsody on a Windy Night." There "Whispering lunar incantations" evoke such passages as the charged moment in Wordsworth's sonnet "Composed by the Side of Grasmere Lake" when the poet hears "Great Pan himself low-whispering through the reeds," or the mesmerized opening of Keats's sonnet "On the Sea," echoing nature's "eternal whisperings."

Eliot's altered title quotation both distances itself from its Wordsworthian original and draws that into his poem, complicating the contrast in it—sharply marked by a row of dots—between the first four stanzas about John Webster and John Donne and the second four stanzas about modern poets and readers. At first the title seems to be exclusively associated with the later stanzas describing the dessicated state of "our lot" crawling "between dry ribs," an association that could be supported by Eliot's later descriptions of our representatives, "The Hollow Men," whose "dried voices . . . whisper together." Yet the sound of whispering in "Whispers of Immortality" is heard not only in the second part but in the title and throughout the poem. For instance, the sibilance of "Grishkin is nice," "her Russian eye," "for emphasis," "Gives promise of pneumatic bliss" has already sounded in the first stanza: "Webster was much possessed," "And saw the skull beneath the skin," "And breastless creatures," "with a lipless grin." The "Whispers" substituted in Eliot's altered title characterize the whole of the poem, written by a modern poet who, despite his affinity for Webster and Donne, cannot escape his inheritance of nineteenth-century poetic language.

Stevie Smith makes a much simpler change in her borrowing from Wordsworth's presentation of his "Ode," using it to frame her poem—comically short to treat its grandiose topic—from a satirically single-minded perspective. The grammatical shift from plural to singular in her title makes its point with humorous directness. One "Intimation of Immortality" is enough, or more than enough:

> Never for ever, for ever never, oh
> Say not aeonial I must for ever go
> Sib to eternity, to confraternity
> Of Time's commensurate multiples a foe.[25]

The abstract diction of the title is relentlessly carried through the poem. Only the comically jarring lapse into the slangy vocabulary of live speech, "Sib," points up the threat to this poet of even one deadeningly impersonal "Intimation of Immortality." The title quotation makes this jibe again by another contrast. The inhuman abstractness it imposes on the poet's language is at variance with the insouciantly lowercased title of the 1937 volume that is its context, *a good time was had by all*. This cheerful, sociable idiom understands by *time* something like *party*, whereas in the poem its most preposterous word, "aeonial," so dead any reader must look it up, is not an intimation that in the timeless future a good time will be had by any.

Elizabeth Bishop's quoted title "The Fish" makes an even more minute alteration, even an invisible one, in its probable model, the title of Marianne Moore's "The Fish." Only when we read beyond the title of the later poem can we recognize that it has changed the collective noun into the singular. The near imperceptibility of this change may itself be a tribute to Moore, Bishop's mentor and friend, whom she called (in an article published two years after Bishop's "The Fish" appeared in *North & South*) "The World's Greatest Living Observer."[26] Implied in the allusion of the title is that Moore, with her powers of microscopic observation, will take note of the shift invisible to the naked eye.

The altered title also signals a change in the perspective with which it frames the new poem. Moore's places "Fish" in their natural habitat, accumulating observations that lead to a general statement based on what "Repeated / evidence has proved."[27] An imagined model for it is, characteristically for Moore, the encyclopedia article, which derives its authority from patiently objective gathering of material and tested conclusions. Bishop's models include Moore's poem, which furnishes some details in it as well as its title, but also Wordsworth, Hopkins, poems in the Romantic tradition where the poet has "looked into" the nature of some particular nonhuman creature, as Bishop's narrator, having caught "a tremendous fish," patiently "looked into his eyes," that careful plural telling us she held it close to and facing her.[28] There what she sees, though "shallower" than what Hopkins in "God's Grandeur" sees "deep down things," is finally, triumphantly beyond the limits of ordinary human sight, not because of the poem's objective, microscopic scrutiny, but because it is, for all its reticence, passionately engaged in looking. What the narrator perceives, and makes us see, is the separateness of the creature's indomitable, individual thingness, its being singularly "The Fish."

When the title of a poem borrows the title of a work that is not a poem, the involvement of the prior text in the act of framing is weaker. Such borrowings have most often been taken from fiction and drama, and those only quite recently, since Shakespeare's plays and Victorian novels became familiar enough to many readers that their titles have entered ordinary language. D. H. Lawrence's poem "A Winter's Tale" is a stark recounting of a woman's rejection by her lover, set in a grimly darkened snow scene. Dylan Thomas's poem "A Winter's Tale" is an incantatory recital of a myth about a man "In his firelit island ringed by the winged snow." In their wholly different ways each uses the title quotation to suggest a poem telling a story as elemental and universal as the seasons, without asking the reader to find much more detailed connections between it and Shakespeare's play. Rudyard Kipling's title "A Tale of Two Cities" for a poem satirizing the greediness on which empires are built seems not to make more than a loose connection with Charles Dickens's political "Tale" as a way of generalizing the poem's satirical point. Patrick Kavanagh's "Tale of Two Cities" draws a modernist parallel between the streets of London and Dublin, both "paved with failures." Auden uses "Through the Looking Glass" as a title framing in its perspective a pattern of metaphors in the poem itself: "The earth turns over"; "The painter's gifts can make its flatness round"; "That mirror world where Logic is reversed."

Each of these title quotations, without taking detailed account of the original text, makes a contribution to the new poem both by its own verbal suggestiveness and by its status as a quotation. That is, because the title is borrowed, it defines the new poem as something retold, something that has the special weight of the familiar, the remembered, something that belongs to age-old experience. To make this kind of frame for his poem evoking another common image or archetypal memory, Edwin Markham adds the subtitle "Written after seeing Millet's World-Famous Painting" to the borrowed title for his poem "The Man with a Hoe," by which the painting is known.[29]

These titles do not act in quite the same ways as titles copied from poems. As their original text in a different form or medium is not much felt to be a presence in the poem, so the text of the poem does not reflect on the play, novel, or painting that provided the title, does not enlarge or remake its context. We do not read Shakespeare's play or title from an altered perspective because Lawrence and Thomas repeat its title for their poems, since it is the suggestive wording of the original title itself and the fact that it has been said before and has been often resaid that are its framing features.

Quoted texts

While the practice of borrowing titles from Shakespeare's plays and from Victorian novels coincides with their absorption into the common language of the reading public in the later nineteenth and twentieth centuries, it is only one instance of a larger cultural shift. Quotations of all sorts, both self-referential and borrowed, are a relatively recent phenomenon in the history of titling in English, probably constituting another dimension of the still larger movement, already illustrated in earlier chapters, toward a wider and freer range of title forms. Even quotations from Scripture are rarely if ever used in earlier periods except as a way of identifying which biblical passage the poem takes as its text, as if it were the daily lesson, for instance in the title space above Edward Taylor's "Meditation. Cant. 2.1. I am the Rose of Sharon."

Christina Rossetti seems to be among the first poets in English, and one of few, to explore extensively the framing possibilities of biblical quotations. Most often, as might be predicted, she finds them to be a means of generalizing, allowing the *I* in the poem to speak in a personal voice out of a timeless human condition. An example is a poem dated 1862 with a title repeating one of the most familiar verses in the Psalter, David's cry in the opening of Psalm 130: "Out of the Deep." The poem itself does not quote, paraphrase, or closely imitate other wording in the psalm, but recasts its situation in a more modern idiom: "I can hardly bear life day by day. / Be I here or there, I fret myself away"; "I pray for grace: but then my sins unpray / My prayer."[30]

Elsewhere she finds more surprising and individual ways of internalizing the biblical wording quoted in the title space. For instance, in a poem dated 1853 she borrows an equally familiar verse from the Sermon on the Mount, "Consider the Lilies of the Field" (Matthew 6:28). Here the poet repeats to her readers the original imperative when she quotes it before the poem, but then rewrites the sermon in a series of new lessons. The rose, favorite flower of poetic tradition, speaks first, warning of beauty bound to a thorn; the poppy and the violet also teach us virtues, and so do the lilies, but what they preach does not repeat the original lesson the biblical verse asks us to consider. Here the lilies speak for themselves, saying "Behold how we / Preach without words of purity."[31] Even more unexpectedly, a break between verse paragraphs moves the poem still farther away from the biblical passage that follows the imperative quoted in the title: "Wherefore, if God so clothe the grass of the field, which today is, and to morrow is cast into the oven, shall he not much more clothe you, O ye of little faith" (Matthew 6:30). Here is the end of the lesson as Rossetti rewrites it:

> But not alone the fairest flowers:
> The merest grass
> Along the roadside where we pass,
> Lichen and moss and sturdy weed
> Tell of His love who sends the dew,
> The rain and sunshine too,
> To nourish one small seed.

The meeting of the original imperative with its resaying in the title acts out the inward experience of the poet who never uses *I* about herself in the poem but has an identifiably personal voice. She has heard and considered the biblical imperative, reflecting on its truth to experience as she goes "Along the roadside," repeating it until she has made it her own. By doing so she has earned her quiet authority to preach her own distinctive understanding of it in this poem. In another dated ten years later she retells the same biblical passage, repeating its lesson more closely though still in her reticent, slightly awkward modern manner. Here by cutting down the quoted imperative in the title space to a more abrupt "Consider," then repeated as the first line, she gives it too the sound of her own quietly urgent speech. Her presence is more immediate in the quotation, expressing the need in this voice, speaking in the first-person plural, to tell us directly how "Much more our Father seeks / To do us good."[32]

Unless the poet can somehow internalize the authority that belongs specially to a biblical quotation, its unassailability can jeopardize the double framing made possible by the presence of the resaying together with the original wording in the title space. This may be a reason why more recent poets have not followed Christina Rossetti's exploration of biblical quotations in their titles, even when skepticism or disbelief have not stood in the way of some internal appropriation. More often they seem drawn to the much older tradition of titling religious poems by quoting liturgical formulas, perhaps encouraged by the example of Eliot in "The Burial of the Dead" and "Ash-Wednesday," and by the interest he helped to revive in seventeenth-century religious poetry where such titles are common. Auden's group of poems with titles naming *Horae Canonicae* may be another influential model for poets as various as John Berryman, Geoffrey Hill, James McMichael, and Paul Muldoon. This kind of title quotation is less threatening to the authority of the poet who repeats it as a framing device than a biblical quotation that, originally carrying the force of the divine Word, involves a risk of self-effacement not many poets have taken. Hardy, surely a reader of Christina Rossetti, appropriates the authoritative perspective of biblical phrasing enclosed in quotation marks for " 'And There Was a Great Calm' (On the Signing of the Armistice, 11 Nov. 1918)" (Mark 4:39) and "In Time of 'The Breaking of Nations' " (Jeremiah 51:20), where both God and the poet who is His mouthpiece pronounce devastating judgments on the stupidity of human wars. Frost in the title "A Servant to Servants" quotes the judgment pronounced on Cain (Genesis 9:25) as a devastating recognition that the afflicted woman in the poem is one of the eternally cursed.

Less threatening than biblical quotations, and at least partly for that reason more common, are borrowings for titles from within literary texts, especially from other poems. This again is a practice emerging, it seems, in the nineteenth century, but it had roots in much older presentational devices. On the title page of earlier-seventeenth-century collections of verse by a single author there is often a quotation printed under the title and author's name; later in the century it became common practice to print a quotation under the title of a single poem. The close relation between these presentational devices is reflected in the fact that historically the terms *motto* and *epigraph* have been used more or less indiscriminately for both. They will be separated here for convenience—*motto* referring to a quotation on a title page, *epigraph* to borrowed wording under the title of a poem—but on some historical grounds.

The slightly older term in English, *motto* (first cited in the *OED* for 1589 while 1633 is given for the relevant meaning of *epigraph*), originally referred to words explaining the significance of an emblem. Related is the use of *motto* for a proverb or pithy phrase adopted, for instance, by a nobleman as a ruling sentiment worn on his arms. A motto was also useful to a poet as a coded signature added at the end of a poem printed anonymously, where it served as an actual or pretended way of disguising his identity from the uninitiated. This now lost meaning points to an early connection between such personal insignia and the quotation on the title page of a volume, where it introduces the author by his poetic motto. Milton's *Poems* of 1645 bears a carefully chosen motto serving this purpose, with its source, Virgil's seventh eclogue, identified: "*Baccare frontem / Cingite, ne vati noceat mala lingua futuro.*" Louis Martz, in his indispensable discussion of the multiple devices for self-presentation in this first volume, teaches the importance of reading the quotation in its context, where the shepherd-singer describes himself as "your rising poet, shepherds of Arcady," "your predestined bard."[33] The use of mottoes continued in the eighteenth and on through the nineteenth century—Shelley's *Queen Mab* of 1813 has on the title page quotations in their own languages from Voltaire, Lucretius, and Archimedes—along with epigraphs for separate poems within a volume.

As the practice of borrowing from another, at first almost inevitably a classical source, extended to the quotation under the title of a single poem, its explicit focus shifted from the poet to the poem. The earliest example of such an epigraph among Dryden's published poems can illustrate the shift, and his prestige was a powerful encouragement to imitators. *Astraea Redux A Poem On the Happy Restoration & Return Of His Majesty Charles the Second* was printed in 1660 with an epigraph from Virgil's fourth eclogue linking the myth of the Virgin Goddess of Justice alluded to in the title to the topic of the poem named in its subtitle: "*Jam redit et Virgo, reduent Saturnia regna*" ("Now too the Virgin returns, and the reign of Saturn returns"). The italics (the formal way of setting off quoted words before quotation marks came into common use) underline the mutual exchange that takes place in the meeting between the original and its repetition. The source enriches the borrowing, here with the authority, glamor, and generalizing power of such classical references, while the quotation incorporates the original into a larger, living context, conferring immortality on it. In a general sense, this is the meeting of prophesy and hindsight, each with its own kind of privileged knowledge, that we have seen taking place in later title quotations, but as it happens here in the epigraph for this poem, it has particular bearing on its topic. The return of Charles to the English throne is the living fulfillment in history of the ancient Roman myth, and the reign of the Virgin Goddess of Justice is restored. In the presentation of the poem, this is accomplished by the conjunction of title, subtitle, and epigraph.

These classical epigraphs are very common in poetry in the period after Dryden (and even in prose works like the *Spectator* essays, which also drew especially on Virgil and Horace). They are a means of supporting neoclassical ideals of affinity between the Roman and English Augustan ages, and perhaps a way of extending presentational devices for poems at a time when the range of title forms was itself narrower than it became in the nineteenth century. Wordsworth uses epigraphs only sparingly, and then typically in English, but in the exceptional instance where he originally restricted himself to the purely generic title "Ode," he follows neoclassical practice by extending the presentation with an epigraph, and true to tradition it is from Virgil. His choice, the opening of the prophetic fourth eclogue—"*Paulò majora canamus*" ("Let us sing a greater song")—explicitly focuses on the poem, its loftier generic status implying a grander theme. It may also hint of uneasiness that his uncharacteristic use of a neoclassical title might need the supporting authority of an epigraph, that his repetition of Virgil's claims for the eclogue might strengthen his own credentials for writing an ode.

Epigraphs continue to appear under the titles of early-nineteenth-century poems. Byron's first volume, *Hours of Idleness* of 1807, includes quotations in Latin, Greek, and English (two of them from Ossian). Shelley borrows from Latin, Greek, and Italian authors for epigraphs, and once from Byron. Also in the first half of the century, new forms of titles for poems began to evoke classical associations by other means than epigraphs. Tennyson's interest in "Ulysses" and "Tithonus," his introduction into English titling of the term *idyl* and Browning's borrowing of it from him are other gestures toward renewed classicizing. In 1850 W. M. Rossetti observes this having taken place in Arnold's writings, where his partiality "for antiquity and classical association" is shown in "such poems as 'Mycerinus,'" and elsewhere, "rather in the framing than in the ground work, as in the titles 'A Modern Sappho,' 'The New Sirens,' 'Stagyrus,' and '*In utrumque paratus*,'" the last with its quotation from the *Aeneid* lending authority as title rather than epigraph.[34] Examples of the same sort can be found in the titling preferences of many poets in the course of the century, among them: Robert Bridges, Arthur Hugh Clough, Aubrey DeVere, Ernest Dowson, Walter Savage Landor, Francis Palgrave, Coventry Patmore, Algernon Swinburne, John Aldington Symonds.

The interest of nineteenth-century poets in using quotations for the presentation of their own poems assumes a new shape in the evolution from epigraphs—gradually borrowed more and more from English texts for poems and for prose such as the chapters of novels—to quoted titles. It is almost possible to watch this happening. In 1830 Tennyson's "Mariana" appeared in his *Poems, Chiefly Lyrical* with its epigraph quoting from *Measure for Measure*: "Mariana in the moated grange." In 1849 a collection of poems by Arthur Hugh Clough was included in *Ambarvalia. Poems*. In Clough's part of the volume many poems beginning with the first have no title, some when in sequence are numbered but untitled, others have wording in Latin or Greek in the title space, and one is preceded by a biblical phrase. Among these assorted uses of the title space is an instance where above the poem is a quotation from Wordsworth's "Ode": " 'Blank Misgivings of a Creature moving about in Worlds not realised.' " Because this is the only instance in the collection where the wording in the title space is framed in quotation marks, and because the norm established in the first entry and often repeated in the collection is of untitled poems, this exceptional presentation seems to be suspended in its status somewhere between an epigraph for an untitled poem and a quotation used as a title. Such ambiguity has disappeared by 1855, when Browning published in *Men and Women* his poem with the subscription "(See Edgar's song in 'Lear')" to what is clearly its title, with its status as a quotation so marked, " 'Childe Roland to the Dark Tower Came.' " It is certainly among the first titles of its kind in English.

When the title of a poem is taken from wording in another text, such as a play by Shakespeare, it works in some ways like a title copied from another title, for instance "A Winter's Tale," in that it brings to bear on the poem its own verbal suggestiveness along with the resonance of something often repeated, belonging to our language and our history. At the same time there are important differences in the way borrowed wording from another text rather than from its title can frame a new poem. One such difference is that traditionally titles tend to follow certain conventional forms because as titles they purport to say something explicit about one or more features of the work. This means that their range of grammatical constructions is limited and that those allowed are declarative in function, purporting to tell something about the poem's kind or topic, or about who makes it or says it and to whom. By contrast, titles both self-referential or borrowing language from within another text can be freer in form; as Browning's quoted sentence illustrates, they are not limited to the grammatical constructions conventional in titling. They can therefore, as is also allowable for epigraphs borrowing from another text, be more loosely or freely suggestive, more wide-ranging in the ways they bear on the poems they are chosen to frame.

Tennyson's epigraph and Browning's title quotation seem to take advantage of this more fluid suggestiveness, as critics of their generation noticed. In 1856 David Masson wrote of Browning's borrowed title: "The notion of the poem, as in Tennyson's *Mariana*, is that of expanding one of those snatches of old ballad and allusion which have such a mystic effect in Shakespeare. 'Childe Roland to the Dark Tower came' is one such snatch of old song quoted by Edgar in *Lear*; and Mr. Browning offers us *his* imaginative rendering of these gloomy hieroglyphic words."[35] Tennyson himself attributes the same "mystic" or Orphic power to his epigraph when he insists that his "*moated grange* was no particular grange, but one which rose to the music of Shakespeare's words."[36] His way of describing it implies that it does not ask to be taken as a declaration about some feature of the poem but more as an evocation of mood and atmosphere.

There is another vital difference between a title or epigraph quoting from the body of a work and one copying its title, which is that the phrase from within a text calls up its more particular original context—"Mariana in the moated grange" is a more focused allusion than *Measure for Measure* would be—making that context's presence felt along with the evocative wording of the quotation itself. It might be supposed that such greater particularity would inevitably restrict the suggestiveness of the quoted title or epigraph, narrowing it to framing the poem in a more defined perspective, but Christopher Ricks has shown persuasively that Tennyson's epigraph escapes such an effect of closure. When in his poem the repeated phrase "He cometh not" still reappears in the last stanza as "He will not come," it promises no relief, while the epigraph brings to bear the different fate of Shakespeare's "dejected Mariana," whose long waiting at "the moated grange" is in the end relieved by Angelo's return to her and their marriage.[37] The presence of the original context, Ricks writes, makes the outcome of the poem "profoundly equivocal—optimistic and a cause for hope, in that Mariana is *not* to pine forever," but at the same time "pessimistic," since the world of Shakespeare's play, where a benevolent Providence intercedes, "is patently not the real vulnerable world, whereas the world of 'Mariana' may be."[38]

A still more equivocal relationship between Browning's title quotation and his poem has been noticed by critics since the mid–nineteenth century, one reviewer in 1856 complaining that "from beginning to end we can discover no hint as to what the allegory means, and find only description preparatory to some adventure which is to disclose the symbol of the 'dark tower' and its terrible neighborhood—but the adventure never comes off in the poem."[39] Casting the same baffled response in sympathetic terms, Ian Jack fills an entire page with the questions of more recent critics about the poem, beginning and ending with "What is the point of the initial reference to *King Lear*?"[40] In its original context the line is what Masson calls "hieroglyphic," a prelude inscrutable in itself to a mad song recited by someone not mad. It brings the hero of its medieval or Spenserian romance (with an additional model suggested by Byron's title *Childe Harold's Pilgrimage. A Romaunt*) up to the moment when the outcome of his quest hangs in the balance and leaves him there, as does the poem. It is open-ended, like Tennyson's "Mariana," defying interpretive closure because of, rather than in spite of, the presence in the title quotation of its particular context in the original.

The workings of Tennyson's epigraph and Browning's title, influential examples of their kind, suggest that quotations from other literary texts used to frame a poem were for poets of their generation a valued source of strongly evocative language that is at the same time enigmatic in its allusiveness. The most compressed instance of this nineteenth-century interest is, fittingly, the title of Hardy's "The Darkling Thrush," a reflection on the century's poetry dated "*December* 1900."[41] John Hollander has traced the layered allusiveness of the word *darkling* in its prior contexts, as it is quoted from Milton by Keats, from both by Arnold, and from all three by Hardy.[42] While these earlier borrowings are from text to text, Hardy's is from text to title, giving new prominence and new implications to the accumulated weight of the original and its resayings. Now the quoted word is in a title purporting to tell the reader that this poem is about a "Thrush," while signaling that it is also about the word "Darkling," which in its prior contexts has been associated with nightingales and poets and for Arnold with the "world" of nineteenth-century poetry. The title asks us to notice what happens to the word *darkling* when Hardy's title attaches it to the bird in his poem.

We might begin by imagining the poem without this title, which now, with hindsight, seems brilliantly inevitable but was in fact substituted by Hardy for the original, unfortunate title "By the Century's Deathbed." That frame would have imposed a more explicitly defined perspective on the poem by classifying it as a funeral dirge. The "growing gloom" of the nineteenth century would then seem bound to overtake the poet, making louder the hints that the hopeful sounds he "could think" he heard in the thrush's song were wishful thinking or were rationalizations he "could think" but could not feel. The "aged thrush, frail, gaunt, and small" would more unequivocally represent a diminishment of the mythical nightingale glamorized by poetic tradition, which inspired Milton and teased Keats out of thought. Hardy's mortal bird would be wholly consigned to Arnold's nineteenth-century "world."

The revised title does not rule out this reading; it actually adds some support to it by linking Arnold's "darkling plain" to Hardy's landscape and the deception of Keats as he listens "Darkling" to the nightingale with what Hardy's wishful poet "could think" he heard in the thrush's song. It even allows the possibility that "Darkling" describes the thrush itself as self-deluded, in the dark, its "happy" carols belied by all the visible signs of its dying world. At the same time the revised title encourages another way of reading the poem that the original title would have excluded or submerged. For "Darkling" also evokes Milton's figure of inspiration, newly empowering in the context of a poem with a distinctively modern bird announced as its topic. The thrush is a common English variety that can be seen every day in nature but not in poems, and the fact that it is visible, not shrouded in Keatsian "verdurous glooms," makes it an available image for a new poetry belonging to a new century: the poem is not dated 1899. While the poems of Milton and Keats contain only the song of the unseen nightingale, Hardy gets the thrush bodily into the later part of his poem, where it is described in a new poetic diction: "aged," "frail," "gaunt," "small" are a different kind of adjective from *darkling*, if it is an adjective, which in Hardy's title juxtaposes its archaic literariness to the homely word "Thrush." The past contexts of "Darkling" meet with its attachment to a new kind of bird at a threshold that readers following the suggestiveness of Hardy's revised title "could think" his poem has or has not crossed. By using a borrowed word with multiple contexts in the title, Hardy frames the poem in a layered perspective that unsettles it, opening it to more equivocal readings than would have been suggested by its original title.

In the proposed title for what became *The Waste Land*, Eliot reflected on his own poetic practice by borrowing from Dickens the sentence "He do the Police in Different Voices." In its original context in *Our Mutual Friend*, the sentence describes someone reading aloud from a newspaper in various voices, and in the poem we hear many more, as we do typically in the presentations of Eliot's poems. Often the title is a partial quotation from another poem's title—"Whispers of Immortality," "Sweeney Agonistes"—or it is in a foreign language that is itself a form of quotation—"Conversation Gallante," "Gerontion"—and still more often the title is followed by one or more epigraphs in one or more other languages. "La Figlia che Piange," sounding like a quotation of the title for an Italian painting, is followed by an epigraph, unidentified, from Virgil. The cumulative effect is what another of Eliot's untranslated titles, quoting a line from Tristan Corbière's poem "Epitaphe," calls "Mélange Adultère de Tout." These presentational devices seem to extend or elaborate on the equivocating effect of Tennyson's epigraph and Browning's quoted title, which are originally spoken in the voices of figures who are themselves otherwise unconnected to the poem. While Tennyson's and Browning's borrowings bring to bear a context that prevents the title from framing the poem in a defined perspective, Eliot's titles quoting foreign voices and epigraphs from eclectic sources seem designed to do in the very idea of an authoritative perspective. That would be a version of doing the police in several voices. Far from directing the reader toward or even away from interpretive closure, these titles and epigraphs exclude most if not all of the audience, which is often not told the source of the quotation, and when that is given cannot be counted on or even expected to read its language or to know its context in detail that could be brought to bear on the poem.

Quotations from other literary texts preceding the poem, both as titles and as epigraphs, are for some reason scarcer in later-twentieth-century poetry. A few examples of recent title quotations—for example Robert Lowell's "'To Speak of the Woe That Is in Marriage,'" Frank Bidart's "Guilty of Dust," Seamus Heaney's "A Waking Dream"—gain power besides their suggestive allusiveness from the very fact of their rarity in the poet's work, which makes the unusual choice seem earned by a compelling decision. Where there appear to be no longer powerfully felt needs for title quotations, a poet's frequent borrowing from other texts for titles nowadays runs the risk of seeming a too easy or external evocativeness. This is the cumulative impression made by quoted titles of Anne Sexton's, which seem more like window dressing than like frames made to the dimensions of the poem.

Another titling practice emerging in the nineteenth century is the quotation from a written source outside of literature and even hostile to it, beginning in English perhaps again with a poem by Browning, this one published in 1864 in *Dramatis Personae*. Here the "I" of the poem, like the "He" in Eliot's proposed title borrowed from Dickens, is a reader of newspapers. He quotes a phrase from one in the title, "Apparent Failure," giving its context in the epigraph "'We shall soon lose a celebrated building.' *Paris Newspaper*."[43] The title phrase is unmistakable in its disengaged tone but ambiguous in its application. The epigraph directs attention to the one building in the poem, "Only the Doric little Morgue!" which may be a failure for not keeping the promises of its classical façade or its temple shape, or may fail for not keeping its claim on a piece of Paris real estate. Certainly the three suicides now "enthroned / Each on his copper couch" are included in the title's reference. Perhaps also implicated is the newspaper that calls their deaths "Apparent Failure," when their escape from their abhorred lives may not make them failures, or may make them not apparent but real failures. Finally, the poet's self-mockery in the poem makes him a likely target for the title phrase, for pitting himself against the newspaper's prediction that the building will be lost: in the first line he boasts, "No, for I'll save it!" The poem, then, may be a failed attempt in the eternizing tradition of Shakespeare's "Not marble, nor the guilded monument." Or its appearance of failure may be part of its expressive design, making out of the meanness of its late-nineteenth-century resources—the newspaper's language, the city, the morgue, the suicides—a new contribution to poetic tradition. These equivocal possibilities allow the journalese of the title quotation to enter into the dramatic design of the poem, which would not happen if Browning had chosen in its place to quote the opening line of Shakespeare's sonnet.

"A Poet's Epitaph" or simply "Elegy" could have been a fitting title quotation for a poem in Stevens's *Ideas of Order* of 1935, for which he chose to quote in a foreign language what sounds like a headline from another

Paris newspaper, "Anglais Mort à Florence." Like many of Stevens's stylish titles, it reflects self-mockingly on its own stylishness: in that it is a
quotation from a newspaper, that it is in French, that it multiplies distances among the maker of poem and title, the voice in the title, the narrator of the poem, and the "he" in it who is an alien like Wallace Stevens,
the American poet who quotes a French newspaper about an Englishman
who died in Italy, another "Mélange Adultère de Tout." The parallels here
with Browning's title clipped from a newspaper suggest again that this
kind of quotation, like titles borrowed from literary texts, has the general
attraction of its potential for multiple framing that can make the reader's
interpretive work more difficult. Besides, the particular attractions of newspaper quotations in these titles are their modernity, their escape from generic classification and from other literary associations, their explosion of
earlier ideals of decorum in levels of diction and other authoritative hierarchies.

These quotations from newspapers are early instances of the interest in
widening the range of language appropriated for titles, which has since expanded to include still more untraditional written sources. A few examples
can point to more ways of thinking about their appeal for poets in this
century. Advertisements and other commercial brochures are such a source
of quoted titles: Yvor Winters's "See Los Angeles First"; Howard Nemerov's "Instructions for Use of This Toy"; D. J. Enright's "Buy One Now";
Elizabeth Bishop's "Over 2,000 Illustrations and a Complete Concordance"; James Merrill's "Family Week At Oracle Ranch." Other titles
quote writing one might see on the street: on a marquee, like Merrill's "Hô-
tel de l'Univers et Portugal"; on a storefront sign, like Rita Dove's "The
Satisfaction Coal Company"; on a building, like Auden's "Musée des
Beaux Arts"; on a monument, like Larkin's "MCMXIV"; on a sidewalk, like
Stevens's "Red Loves Kit." Paul Muldoon's "7, Middagh Street" seems to
copy the address on an envelope; Etheridge Knight's "Boston 5:00 A.M.—
10/74" mimics a memorandum on a telephone pad. Yeats's "Nineteen Hundred and Nineteen" is in the form given to dates in history books. Stephen
Spender's "Hamburg, 1929" could be a caption for a documentary. Alfred
Kreymborg's "$17+4 \times 3-0$" looks like a problem in an arithmetic work-
book; Kenneth Rexroth's "GIC to HAR" is the familiar binding on an encyclopedia volume; John Ashbery's "Le livre est sur la table" is from everyone's first French phrase book; Merrill's "Vol. XLIV, No. 3" is a biblio-
graphical reference.

Like newspaper quotations, these titles are borrowed from sources
available to an audience wider than writers or readers of poetry. They ignore separations between literary and other kinds of language and dissolve
distinctions between private and public poetry, both of which are generally

observed in earlier traditions of titling. They also point toward evasions of the title's authority by seeming to loosen it. They have that effect because they have a found quality, as Howard Nemerov points out in the title "Found Poem" with the subscription *after information received in* The Saint Louis Post-Dispatch, 4 *v* 86," and Donald Davie in "Well-found Poem," which takes off from a military bulletin. The poet seems to have come on the title by chance, in the randomness of daily experience; to have seized on it as a suggestion for writing a poem or as a chance way to frame a poem already written.

Quoted familiar speech

Suspended in some intermediate space between borrowings from written sources and from spoken language are proverbial quotations, which are common in the early period of titling in English, when poems were closer to oral compositions than they have since become. Some Elizabethan and early-seventeenth-century examples are: "The pore estate to be holden for best" from Tottel's miscellany; "No woordes, but deedes" from the *Paradise of Daintie Deuises*; Robert Southwell's "Times goe by turnes" and "Lewd Love is Losse"; Richard Sylvester's "*Simile Non Est Idem*: Seeming is not the Same, Or All's not Gold that glisters." As the distinctions between oral and written, literary and nonliterary sources sharpened in the later seventeenth and eighteenth centuries, proverbial titles tended to disappear from printed volumes of verse except for some satirical poems such as "There's no Tomorrow," subtitled "A Fable imitated from Sir Roger L'Estrange," by Anne Finch, Countess of Winchelsea.

When titles sounding proverbial reappear occasionally in the nineteenth century, it may be with the encouragement of the Elizabethan and especially Shakespearean revival. Coleridge's "Duty surviving Self-Love" and its subtitle, "The only sure Friend of declining Life," or his more philosophical title "Constancy to an Ideal Object" seem to be in the vein of titles assigned by editors to Elizabethan verse, above all to Shakespeare's sonnets. This practice begins with *Poems: Written By Wil. Shakes-peare, Gent.* of 1640 (the second edition, which passed itself off as the first). Some in that volume are: "A Lovers affection though his Love prove unconstant"; "The benefit of Friendship"; "Happinesse in content"; "Familiaritie breeds contempt"; "Fast and loose." Tennyson continues in this tradition with the titles for his poems "Why to Blush is Better than to Paint" (a sonnet in an Elizabethan manner), "Nothing Will Die," and "All Things Will Die" (in the manner of Herrick's "All things decay and die"). So do later anthologists in the titles they inflict on Shakespeare's sonnets, such as: Francis Palgrave's "The Life Without Passion"; Samuel Waddington's "Hope against Hope"; worse

still, in an anthology edited by Leigh Hunt and S. Adams Lee, "True Love
Not at the Mercy of Time and Circumstance" or "The Consciousness of
Being Loved by a Noble Nature a Triumph Over All Troubles."

Frost's "Nothing Gold Can Stay" is a graceful little postscript to proverbial titling, not common in his work or in twentieth-century poetry. Instead, Frost's influence is strongly shown elsewhere by the pervasiveness in
recent poetry of titles quoting spoken phrases of another sort, bits of everyday modern speech, what he calls "sentence-sounds." Titles of this variety
have already entered the histories traced in this book at a number of points:
in Chapter 1 with discussion of Frost's use of the truncated idiomatic title
"Into My Own" for the opening poem of his first volume; in Chapters 2
and 4 with consideration of what Auden in particular may have learned
about such titles from Frost, and more recent poets from both; in Chapter
6 where titling by present participles in spoken phrases (including Frost's
title truncated from its original version "Making the Most of It") is explored, one strand among many twentieth-century title forms using bits of
speech to create dramatic play between title and poem.

While it is likely that Frost and Auden are the immediate models from
whom many British and American poets since have learned most directly
the possibilities in such titles, there are scattered examples of them in nine-
teenth- and earlier-twentieth-century poetry that may have attracted the
interest of Frost himself. Some examples are: Browning's "The Worst Of
It"; Coventry Patmore's "The Worst"; Francis Thompson's "The End Of
It"; Browning's—and Arnold's—"Too Late"; William Cullen Bryant's
"Not Yet"; Ella Wheeler Wilcox's "Nothing New"; John Greenleaf Whit-
tier's "At Last"; Christina Rossetti's "At Last" and "Better So"; D. G. Rossetti's "Even So"; Hardy's "Welcome Home."

It remains in this chapter to look at spoken idioms in titles of a different
kind from those so far considered. While they are made out of speech fragments that qualify them as a subset under Frost's category of sentence-
sounds, because of the more specialized areas of speech they are quoted
from, they work somewhat differently from the common idioms in his titles
and those of other poets in the same vein. This different kind of title quotes
idiomatic phrases that are familiar to us but at the same time deeply alien.

There is something jarring from the start about the grammar of "No
Second Troy," the title of a poem in Yeats's *The Green Helmet and Other
Poems* of 1910. One reason is that it does not sound like the title of a poem,
especially one that has classical associations, because although titles are
traditionally phrases rather than complete sentences, this one is not in an
established declarative form such as "The Disappearance of Troy," which
would exercise the presentational authority of the title to tell what the poem
is about. For another reason, the slangy form of the phrase sounds like pop-

ular speech; it has the familiar ring of political slogans (copied more literally in James Kirkup's title "No More Hiroshimas"). As we read on the title
seems even more inappropriate, in an alien language from the poem. The
lines themselves are entirely made of questions, first asked out of bitter personal involvement, then enlarged to include contemporary history, which
is finally seen in the context of disinterested philosophical issues. There are
no pauses in the poem for answers to be chosen from the alternatives implied, not even for the last question, which is left the most equivocal by its
metrical ambiguity: "Wăs thére another Troy for her to burn?" or "Wăs
thĕre"?[44] In the end the blunt negation in the title seems to be the only answer given to the poem, but its crude language is not the poet's and besides,
it is said before the poem, with resounding indifference to its increasingly
subtle and complex questioning. Having listened to the poet, we do not
imagine him or ourselves saying the title phrase.

"No Second Troy" repeats the street shout of the "ignorant men" whose
violent singlemindedness the poet disdains. Their chanting quoted in the
title loudly asserts itself as the one and only answer, shouting down all questions, but the poem subverts that authority by is own open-endedness. Here
the title figures the threat to the poet of modern slogans belonging to partisan areas of speech that are alien, even hostile to poetry. It is not the kind
of spoken language Frost quotes in his titles, which typically embrace the
vitality and richness of tonal possibilities in idiomatic speech. This means
that although the spoken fragment "No Second Troy" is unequivocally not
in the poet's words, which can rarely be said with assurance of Frost's titles,
even so in its own way it involves the title in the drama of the poem.

Auden in *The Collected Poetry* of 1945, we have seen, gave calculatedly
startling titles to many of the poems, which shock because they are phrases
we know well but only outside of poetry. Many we have said ourselves,
while others are familiar but personally foreign to us: for instance the fragment of speech from the academic bureaucracy, "Not All the Candidates
Pass," which we expect will be exposed in the text of the poem so that its
smug authority is undermined. That seems to happen as the title quotation,
the examining board's coldly self-satisfied pronouncement of standards,
expands in the lines that follow to include among those who do not "Pass"
not only schoolboys but the absent young men "With guns beneath your
arms" who guard "Our peace to us with a perpetual threat."[45] The heart-
lessness of the title quotation is exposed by the fear and sympathy in the
voice we hear in the poem, but the effect is not like that of Kipling's "The
White Man's Burden," where the poem satirically undermines the authority
of the title that frames it in another familiar but hatefully alien quotation.
Auden's juxtaposition of title and poem is absurd, but neither cancels out
the other. Ultimately the poem makes us see that the familiar but unsympa-

thetic speech quoted in the title is not untrue to the realities contemplated in the poem. It makes us recognize that there is a funny and appalling way that the British system of school examinations is a paradigm for life, death, and final judgment, however far its officialese is from expressing how we feel about them. This recognition is not provoked by any interaction between the voices in the title and the poem, so that—unlike "No Second Troy"—it is essentially undramatic.

The most adept student of Auden's titling in this manner seems to be Philip Larkin, for example in "Naturally the Foundation will Bear Your Expenses," "Send No Money," and "Next, Please." Again the titles are funny in themselves because they sound so familiar and so unlike the titles of poems, as do many of Ogden Nash's titles Larkin is on record as admiring.[46] We can call up precisely the original situations they are quoted from and recognize the participants in them as spokesmen with the authority of the bureaucratic institutions and commercial enterprises behind them. In this sense these titles of Larkin's are like Auden's "Not All the Candidates Pass" and unlike Frost's idiomatic titles in being made out of familiar expressions that are not our own. We hear them addressed to us but do not imagine ourselves saying them. While their double status as recognizable but alien language makes them initially the butt of the poet's humor and ours, as in Auden's poem they become more than that. "Next, Please" (originally titled "Always too eager") from *The Less Deceived* can illustrate how Larkin, seemingly following Auden's moves, finds his own way of juxtaposing the voices we hear in title and poem.

"Next, Please" is a phrase we know all too well from waiting our turn outside an office door or in line in front of a window. The person who says it is someone whose power over us we are helpless to influence. We have waited with varying degrees of impatience and anxiety to hear it, but it is always said indifferently, with the same intonation to everyone, by someone who is merely a spokesman with no stake in summoning us. For these reasons the voice is familiar but not ours; we do not cast ourselves as the one who says "Next, Please." By contrast, the voice in the first line of the poem says "we," and speaks our language—"every day / *Till then* we say"—but only to warn that we have picked up "bad habits of expectancy."[47] This representative tells "us" that instead of the "Sparkling armada of promises" we wait for, only a black and empty ship "unfamiliar" to our hopes will come for us, towing "A huge and birdless silence." This is the poet's beautiful and terrible representation of what we will experience when it is at last our turn to be told "Next, Please." That familiar and alien phrase meanly expresses in bureaucratic speech the poet's vision of what is waiting for us. As is true of "Not All the Candidates Pass," in a funny and terrible way title and poem confirm each other's authority, working together to leave the reader the less deceived.

Another student of Auden, John Ashbery, imitates this kind of title with a difference that cancels both its dramatic possibilities and its framing authority: "Thank You for Not Cooperating," from *A Wave*. Because the familiar bureaucratic formula is recast in the negative, the title makes it impossible for us to imagine a situation where we would hear it, or who would say it and to whom. We look then to the poem for a signal about how to read the title, already a reversal of the purported relation between the wording in the space above the poem and what follows it. As the teasing title quotation might warn, though, the poem is no help. In it an observer, a voyeur perhaps, explicitly identified only as one among the category of "Person-objects," introduces a long quotation sung "Separately" in one voice by "Two lovers."[48] The second section of the poem then reflects on their singing, turning the lovers into some version of the imagined mermaids who will most probably not sing to J. Alfred Prufrock, here "communicating each to each in the tedium / Of self-expression." The poem does not fit the title, which in turn refuses to frame it. Together, or rather apart, they leave the reader bemused, but also amused at the unlikely possibility that title and poem are being thanked by some higher bureaucratic power—perhaps the compound ghost of Eliot and Auden?—for not cooperating with each other, with the conventions of titling, or with the reader. The altered quotation in "Thank You for Not Cooperating" is more than a variation on the recent practice of borrowing spoken formulas from familiar but alien speech to redefine the authority associated with wording in the title space. Ultimately it is a device for evading that authority by giving the reader what a parodic catalogue of hypothetical titles in Ashbery's poem of 1994, "Title Search," lists as "Hocus Focus." It can therefore introduce the discussion in the next chapter about other such forms of evasion practiced by poets in the nineteenth and twentieth centuries.

CHAPTER EIGHT

Evasions of the title space

WHILE poets writing now have a very much wider range of possibilities than in earlier periods for how to treat the space above the poem, one choice is not available to them: they cannot ignore it. By the later seventeenth century, the authority of tradition seems to have fixed the expectation that published poems—perhaps with the one exception of sonnets or poems of other kinds in a sequence—be given a title. Milton, in his *Poems, &c. Upon Several Occasions* of 1673, gives a title to every poem except those in the section headed "Sonnets." There, following a practice established for English poets by Petrarch, all the Italian and eleven of the fourteen English sonnets are untitled. The titles for the dedicatory sonnet "To Mr. H. Lawes, on his Aires" and for the occasional "On the late Massacher in *Piemont*" are predictable exceptions. His choices of titles, his revisions of some, and his careful omissions all show consistent attentiveness to titling that scarcely any English poets besides Jonson, Herbert, and Herrick had given to it earlier.

Absent titles

Since the end of the eighteenth century the very process of expanding and eventually evading or escaping earlier conventions of titling has made the act of choosing how to use the title space still more self-conscious, the effect of the choice more loaded. Though it is suspiciously neat to point to 1800 as a pivotal moment, in the expanded edition of *Lyrical Ballads* of that year the second volume includes six poems that are the first of Wordsworth's to be printed with no wording in the space above them. While the persisting practice of leaving sonnets untitled may have been an encouraging model, none of the untitled poems here is a sonnet. Four are love poems (two naming the beloved "Lucy"), which perhaps loosely associates them with the sonnet tradition, but since they are all in stanzas, they might have been presented under the conventionally vague generic term *song*. That title is in fact given in the same volume (but dropped in 1820) both in the table of contents and in the title space to another poem also naming "Lucy," which is now commonly printed under the quotation of its first line, "She dwelt among th' untrodden ways." In later collections Wordsworth continued to enlarge the number of untitled entries: for instance, *Poems in Two Volumes* of 1807 includes three love poems without titles in the first volume and one more in the second, along with seven untitled poems of other kinds. Two of them are given titles—"The Emigrant Mother" and "Personal Talk"—in later volumes, but the one now quite often printed with its first line quoted in the title space, "I wandered lonely as a Cloud," was printed with no wording above it in all editions published during Wordsworth's lifetime.

These and other varied treatments over time point to considered choices. So does the appearance in the collection of 1800 of two poems on facing pages in the same four-line stanza form—one of three stanzas and one of two—each on the death of a young woman. On the left-hand page is the one titled "Song," beginning "She dwelt among th' untrodden ways"; on the right, untitled with only parallel lines printed horizontally in the space above the text, is the poem that opens "A slumber did my spirit seal." That presentation remained unchanged in all printings of the poem before Wordsworth's death. The fact that he mentions in a letter this conventional typographical device for setting off a poem, calling it "the Title Lines," is another clear sign of his detailed attention to the way the space above the poem is treated.[1] Absent titles, then, are unlikely to have been the result of inconsistency or oversight.

Beginning with the first edition of *Lyrical Ballads* in 1798, Wordsworth worked to expand or loosen titling conventions. There the precedence of "Lines" over other generic terms and the self-referential title quotation "We Are Seven," giving the child in the poem a voice in presenting it, are examples of this design discussed in earlier chapters. The related argument here is that Wordsworth's withholding of titles in subsequent volumes, beginning in 1800, is part of the same effort to give poems greater freedom of expression. The wordless space preceding "A slumber did my spirit seal" matches the silence in the space between its two stanzas, allowing full force to what is terribly left unsaid in this poem: that "she" died. In this particular instance, any title, even the innocuously conventional "Song" given to the adjacent ballad-like poem on the same topic, would intrude with its focus on utterance. In a different way, the unfilled space above "I wandered lonely as a Cloud" is peculiarly suited to allow the unpremeditated flow of experience in that poem, which a title like the one habitually given by hostile reviewers categorizing it an "ode" on daffodils would interfere with. That would call attention to the poet's predetermining choice of form and would predict the reader's response appropriate to it.

This is the speculation of hindsight about Wordsworth's decisions, to be sure, like all critical readings. Still, what seems clear is the deliberateness of choice in his varied treatments of the title space, among them the decision (regularly obscured in editions printed after his death) to leave some of them unfilled. Like his earlier preferred formal term "Lines," the absence of a title tends to promote the impression of spontaneity or inwardness of movement. For Wordsworth it also encourages a sense of privacy because it escapes the formal acknowledgment of an audience to whom the titler, who is also the poet, presents it. At the same time, his avoidances of titles do not shut out the reader from the private space in the poem. Instead the absence of a title addressing the reader from outside that space encourages the fiction of its unviolated intimacy. In it we are allowed to hear the poet's unmediated voice.

Withholding words from the title space became, among other formal omissions, a more public or attention-getting gesture for poets in the earlier twentieth century, who seem to have found less distant models than Wordsworth among contemporary visual artists working explicitly against traditional framing and labeling devices. In an entry dated 1913 in Williams's *Autobiography* he speaks for the contemporaries he will represent here when he recalls "arguments over cubism" linked to discussions of new structures for poems: "It seemed daring to omit capitals at the head of each poetic line. Rhyme went by the board. We were, in short, 'rebels,' and were so treated."[2] In the same year in a letter to Harriet Monroe Williams makes the connection of this formal rebellion with new evasiveness in titling poems: "To directly denote the content of a piece is, to my mind, to put an obstacle of words in the way of the picture" that is the poem.[3] Acting on this ideal of leaving "the way clear for a distinct imaginative picture," he chose to withhold titles altogether from the poems included among the prose passages in *Spring and All* as it was first published in 1923. The proximity of that date to the time when *The Waste Land* appeared suggests that Williams's omission of titles may have been partly prompted by antipathy to Eliot's elaborate presentational machinery in this and others of his poems surrounding it in time, which often borrow their titles and sometimes multiple epigraphs from ancient or contemporary foreign sources, in Williams's view an unforgivably unmodern and un-American practice.

Williams's book is clearly a manifesto—imitating even the typography then associated with such documents in headings like "THE BEGINNING," "SPRING," "THE TRADITIONALISTS OF PLAGIARISM"—but what it manifests is not clearly explained. Some of this lack of clarity may be due to the philosophical naïveté of what Hugh Kenner calls Williams's "homemade" theories, but there is also deliberateness in his obscurity.[4] It derives in part from his posture toward the reader—"who cares for anything I do? And what do I care?"—but more importantly from acting on his conviction, articulated in the letter of 1913, that to "denote" is to put an "obstacle" between the work and the experience of it.[5] In *Spring and All* the "obstacle" becomes more formidable, more hostile, and Williams's forms of opposition to it more extreme: "There is a constant barrier between the reader and his consciousness of immediate contact with the world. . . . nearly all writing, up to the present, if not all art, has been especially designed to keep up the barrier between sense and the vaporous fringe which distracts the attention from its agonized approaches to the moment."[6] It follows that scaling the "barrier" or knocking it down cannot be accomplished by denotative explanations, but by "escape" and "annihilation": "an escape from crude symbolism, the annihilation of strained associations, complicated ritualistic forms . . . such as rhyme, meter as meter and not as the essential of the work," the omission of capitals at the beginnings of lines, of periods at the ends of poems, and—to the point here—the withholding of titles.[7]

Imagine meeting without the mediation of titles poems beginning: "By the road to the contagious hospital"; "No that is not it"; "The rose is obsolete"; "What about all this writing?"; "Somebody dies every four minutes"; and—with not even a capital letter to mark off the beginning of the poem— "so much depends." The immediate approach to what Williams calls "the moment," "the picture" is not arrested by a frame. The absence of words above the poem leaves its own space free, not with the effect of unviolated privacy encouraged by Wordsworth's omissions of the title, but "detached" from ordinary seeing, which is mimetic.[8] That at least seems to be the intended effect, worked out most literally in the poem beginning "The rose is obsolete," which imitates Juan Gris's cubist composition of 1914, *Roses*: "each petal ends in / an edge," "so that to engage roses / becomes a geometry."[9] Cubist designs, geometric figures, and machines are layered analogies for Williams's ideal of an untitled poem.

Why Williams later gave titles to the poems in *Spring and All* when some of them were included in *Collected Poems* of 1934, and to more of them still later, is puzzling. Possibly he felt that without their original prose context they needed some other form of presentation, preferably one equally indirect, free of explanation (although to add to the puzzle, *The Complete Collected Poems* of 1938 omits both titles and prose). With some exceptions the titles he added still reflect that preference for indirection. They are as oddly angled or as rebellious against convention as those from *A Book of Poems: Al Que Quiere!* of 1917 discussed in Chapter 5. Some examples are: "Spring and All"; "At the Faucet of June"; "The Right of Way"; "Rapid Transit"; "Rigamarole"; "Shoot It Jimmy!"

This preference for untraditional titling raises further questions about other titles added at the same times that seem at least at first glance to "directly denote the content of the piece," working against the effects of Williams's other formal omissions: of rhyme, traditional meters and structures, capitalization, punctuation. The most obvious example is "The Rose," which is an archetypally conventional title in form and topic. By contrast, in Williams's earlier volumes many titles name flowers that, unlike the rose, do not grow in every period of poetry: "Chicory and Daisies," "Healall," "Butterandeggs," "Thistle," "Blueflags," and the group of "Daisy," "Primrose," "Queen Anne's Lace," and "Great Mullen," which Williams says he thought of as "still lifes."[10] These titles name their less traditionally poetic flowers by unqualified nouns, a form that has some models in nineteenth-century titles like Emerson's "Blight" or Henry David Thoreau's "Mist," "Haze," "Smoke," but in the earlier twentieth century this form is associated mainly with the titles of paintings, photographs, and sculptures. Like Williams's (and Constantin Brancusi's and Max Ernst's) "Bird," they are designed not to denote or describe but to lay bare the essential form of the object in matchingly stripped grammatical form.

Williams uses this kind of title often in his earlier volumes not only for poems with flowers: "Gulls," "Trees," "Spouts," "Blizzard," "Dawn," "Hero" are examples. He seems, then, to be making a point in the uncharacteristic choice of a quintessentially traditional and therefore to him an "obsolete" title form for "The Rose," instead of "Rose" or "Roses." Or he could have used a still more abstract title like "Composition," which he in fact did assign to the originally untitled poem beginning "The red paper box." Another possibility would have been to avoid direct denotation by quoting the first line in the title space, as he does in a poem of 1922, "My luv," which substitutes for Robert Burns's "is like a red, red rose" a comparison to an "insulator," calling to mind similar mechanisms in paintings by Charles Demuth and Charles Sheeler. "The Rose" is a less blatantly inappropriate title than "The Nightingales" is for a poem from *Sour Grapes* of

1921 that is not about the poetic bird often found among roses but about "shoes." Even so, in its more quietly playful way "The Rose" through indirection may also represent an "obstacle" or "barrier" that is here undermined by the cubist design of the poem.

If "The Rose" can work this way, then what about "The Red Wheelbarrow"? Why is "so much depends" not given as nonrepresentational a title as "Composition," chosen for "The red paper box" in the same volume of 1934? It may be that the title was assigned to make a rebellious claim for unconventional topics in poetry, like "The Eyeglasses" for a poem about seeing things as they are "related to mathematics." Still, since "The Red Wheelbarrow" differs in so many details from the rendering of "a red wheel / barrow" in the text of the poem, there may be more points being made in the title.

It follows titling conventions in its grammar and capitalization and imitates unexamined speech in making a compound out of what the text carefully separates: "wheel" from "barrow." All these conventions work in opposition to essential verbal patterns in the poem. That is, its formal design is to enjamb grammatical elements so that, to borrow from John Hollander's discussion of the poem, in "the vision of a moment" its "phenomenological constituents"—"wheel," "barrow," "rain," "water," "white," "chickens"—are set free from their "compounded properties" by the rainwashed light.[11] Then the title "The Red Wheelbarrow" may work in the same way suggested for "The Rose," as a joke about the kind of "obstacle" or "barrier" set up by traditional forms of titling between the "moment" or "picture" that is the poem and the immediate experience of it. These readings seem likely possibilities in the clear light of Williams's commitment in this period to allowing poems not to be framed by formal conventions, including titles that "directly denote" what the poem is about.[12]

What all this self-consciousness shows is that once the presentation of poems grew to be expected, the absence of a title became inescapably expressive, which has also come to be true of the frame when it is omitted from a painting, for instance by Piet Mondrian. The expressive effects of the wordless title spaces on Wordsworth's untitled poems are quiet, contributing to their reticence, while in *Spring and All* the omissions are much louder. In that volume the absent titles make what amounts to a polemical statement that then imposes an unspoken perspective on the poem. That is what the wordless space purports not to do.

Labels

Something like the same paradox seems almost as inevitably built into related efforts, part of the larger movement away from traditional literary classification, to apply to poems presentations originally describing visual works. The earliest type, which appears toward the end of the nineteenth century and increasingly in the twentieth, borrows generic terms: Arthur Symons's "Pastel"; Oscar Wilde's "Impression" (as in the French for *print*); Kipling's "Study of an Elevation, In Indian Ink"; Austin Clarke's "Japanese Print"; Amy Lowell's "Miniature"; Jon Stallworthy's "Still Life"; Alfred Kreymborg's "Calligraphy"; Wilbert Snow's "Etching"; Louise Guiney's "Monochrome"; Sarah Webster Fabio's "Chromo"; George Oppen's "Drawing"; Denise Levertov's "Ink Drawing"; Robert Hass's "Spring Drawing II"; June Jordan's "Cameo No. II." In comparison with generic terms borrowed from music for poem titles—*rhapsody, prelude, serenade, melody,* and the most common, *nocturne*—these names for visual kinds are relatively dissociated from mood or feeling (an exception being Larkin's punning "Dry-Point," which seems to undercut the neutrality of such borrowed terms). In these generic titles the difficulty of avoiding a framing perspective is less obvious than in later borrowings of more radically unconventional generic terms, where again Williams is representative of his generation. These exaggerated types attempt more vehemently and therefore work more paradoxically to free poems from titles that impose their interpretive authority.

Williams's attention to untraditional titling makes inevitable his interest in the practice among earlier twentieth-century visual artists of proclaiming their works "Untitled," or merely numbering them, or identifying them by some almost equally uninterpretive label taken from vocabularies applied to visual arts, mathematics, or machinery: for instance, Fernand Léger's *Contrast of Forms*, Mondrian's *Composition*, Joan Miró's *Four Figures*, Pierre Roy's *Metric System* (all in the collection of Williams's friend and fellow poet Walter Arensberg). This interest is reflected in such titles for Williams's poems as: "Composition," "Metric Figure," "Construction," "A Formal Design," "Exercise No. 2." For abstract artists the intention in this kind of labeling seems to have been, as Hazard Adams says, "to evade the domination of language over plastic forms."[13]

That is clearly not even an imaginary possibility in the titling of poems (or in the attempts of poets more recent than Williams's generation to make idiograms of the words and letters in what are called *concrete poems*). W. J. T. Mitchell argues that it was also a self-defeating paradox for the abstract painters who were Williams's models, because the fewer the narrative or denotative clues in the title, "the more demand for the spectator to fill the void with language." That is, "the wall erected against language and literature by the grid of abstraction only kept out a certain kind of verbal contamination, but it absolutely depended, at the same time, on the collaboration of painting with another kind of discourse . . . the discourse of theory."[14] The argument seems to hold also for Williams's abstract labels, which call attention even more aggressively than his absent titles to what is not said, and in doing so impose a theoretical frame on the poem. Ultimately they point to what is explicitly stated in Stevens's title "Thirteen Ways of Looking at a Blackbird": that the poem is about ways of seeing.

It is not clear how fully Williams recognized this paradox, but other poets have made poems out of it, Hardy unsurprisingly being one and perhaps the first. His characteristic detachment seems to have given him a sardonic perspective on such would-be neutral labeling, which he expresses in a poem dated 1867 in *Wessex Poems*. Typically the title itself is implicated in the paradox: "Neutral Tones." In the poem the first-person speaker, who may or may not be the maker of the pronounless title, paints a remembered scene in "white," "gray," and "grayish" tones that increasingly expose the bitterness, self-righteousness, and self-pity in what he likes to think are the "Neutral Tones" of his voice. The title indirectly exposes the self-contradiction inherent from its beginnings in this tradition of purportedly neutral labeling by titles borrowed from the visual arts.

Ashbery makes a more jokingly sardonic comment on this kind of evasion of the title's interpretive authority in a poem from *Shadow Train* of 1981 with the title "Untilted" (*sic*). Like its abstract model, this *un*tilted label purports not to let on what the poem is about, what its slant is, and in any ordinary sense it lives up to that claim. Still, it tilts "Untitled," which is the label making the most extreme claim, and the most paradoxical, not to tilt toward any interpretation of the work. This makes Ashbery's "Untilted" a comment, like "Neutral Tones" but a more playful one, on would-be neutrality. The "I" in the poem professes balanced maturity of perspective in the matter-of-factness of "but then this is not a win or lose / Situation" or "Why not just / . . . Forget," by contrast with his youthful glamorizing in "the tilt of the wine in the cavalier's tilted glass," but the hilarious pseudo-label preceding the poem laughs at this claim.[15] Or so it seems. What is at least clear is the extreme indirection of "Untilted," exemplifying the "aim" Ashbery sees himself sharing with abstract painters "to give the meaning free play and the fullest possible range" by not framing the poem with a title that tilts toward an authoritative reading of the poem.[16] His way of approaching this ideal differs from Williams's attempts at neutral labeling in that Ashbery's poem exploits the paradox Williams seems to ignore: that titles designed to escape the effects of conventional framing tend to do to the poem what they purport to free it from, by imposing a perspective on it.

Mystifiers

Frank O'Hara's "Why I Am Not a Painter" of 1956 tells a disarmingly confiding story about how one of his earlier poems, "Oranges," came to have its title: "One day I am thinking of / a color: orange. I write a line / about orange."[17] This is just how a reader might imagine the genesis of a poem ultimately titled "Oranges," but when the poem is finally "finished," the poet finds he has not "mentioned / orange yet." So, the later poem blandly continues, "It's twelve poems, I call / it ORANGES." The inside story this mock-confessional narrative tells about another poem's title actually turns out to deny the possibility of clarifying either the title or the poem, or the title and the painting "SARDINES" that is its visual counterpart, because titles are not presentational but secretive. No reader could fathom what the poem is about from the title "Oranges," even after having read the pseudo-explanation of it in "Why I Am Not a Painter."

Although that poem's details and sense of immediacy place it in its actual environment of the New York art world in the 1950's, its roots are in the work and some of the theorizing about it by the generation of visual artists who had interested Williams. O'Hara's little fable about how a title happens does not idealize neutral labeling, though elsewhere he seems to approach that evasive technique in giving more than fifty poems the title "Poem," a gesture most likely meant to suggest casual indifference to the whole question of presentation. Instead the story of "Oranges" in O'Hara's poem sounds like a playful version of the platform for erasing "any vestige of representation either concrete or symbolic" from the titling of abstract paintings, for instance as announced in "Modern Art and the Public" of 1913 by Gabriele Buffet, wife of Francis Picabia:

The mistake on the part of the public is in desiring to find that a particular subject has aroused the emotion (as was the case in old-fashioned painting) and in frantically trying to find some objective point of contact between the title of a picture and the picture itself. This point of contact doesn't exist; and the title represents only the state of mind, the emotion, which influenced the artist to desire and express a certain artistic equilibrium.[18]

Such a platform is in the background of O'Hara's slyly disguised manifesto "Why I Am Not a Painter." More immediately, its chief representative among poets beginning to write around 1913 is Wallace Stevens, who later made revealing admissions about his titling: "Titles with me are, of course, of the highest importance"; "Very often the title occurs to me before anything else"; "Possibly the relation" between the title and the poem "is not as direct and as literal as it ought to be."[19] Presumably he means not as clearly explanatory as it should be in the eyes of the same readers who would expect a poem titled "Oranges" to be about oranges, or to viewers who would look for content in Picabia's watercolors *New York* or *Negro Songs*, titles he gave them "only because he did them when stimulated by his impression of the city or by the bizarre rhythms of ragtime."[20]

Here is Stevens's account of how one of his titles happened, from a letter of 1949: "Now that I have had the new picture [Pierre Tal Coat's *Still Life*] at home for a few days, it seems almost domesticated. . . . I have even given it a title of my own: *Angel Surrounded By Peasants*. The angel is the Venetian glass bowl on the left with the little spray of leaves in it. The peasants are the terrines, bottles and the glasses that surround it."[21] The relation of the title to the visual image here has its parallels in titles like Demuth's *Aucassin and Nicolette* for a view of a smokestack and a water tower, or *End of the Parade* for a group of factory chimneys.[22]

The poem inspired by the painting and by the title Stevens gave it is placed last in *Auroras of Autumn* of 1950 (with the slightly modified title "Angel Surrounded by Paysans"). "*The angel*" who is identified as saying most of the lines is greeted in the opening by "*One of the countrymen,*" but otherwise the painting is scarcely present.[23] The bowl, leaves, terrines, bottles, and glasses have been erased, and there is virtually nothing else given the reader to look at in the poem except the details that are said to have been stripped away: "I have neither ashen wing nor wear of ore / And live without a tepid aureole." Nothing in the text suggests that it describes a painting, although the title raises the expectation that it will, by its visual description of an arranged religious scene and by the unqualified noun naming its grammatical subject. The result is that the title reveals more about its own secrecy than it tells about the text, obscuring that this is a poem *about* a painting *about* a bowl of leaves surrounded by bottles and glasses.

In another letter Stevens responds to questions about the title of a poem in *Parts of A World* of 1942, "On an Old Horn." Its traditional form predicts a poem *on* the topic of an old horn or a song such as might be played *on* one, or most likely both, since layered meanings are characteristic of twentieth-century poems and titles and since the instrument is a recognizably modernist version of the lyre, harp, or pipe traditional to the poet. Those signals, it turns out, do very little to make the relation of this title to this poem "direct," as Stevens seems to acknowledge in the letter defending the "difficulty" that "On an Old Horn" poses to the reader. He writes, "If you understand the body of the poem, of course you understand the title."[24] Although the casual "of course" in this remark takes it lightly, it is a statement of assumptions at the center of Stevens's ideas about titles that constitute a radical revision of traditional thinking. His *if . . . then* proposition denies the precedence associated with the title's position above the poem, which strips it of its presentational function, its interpretive authority. This amounts to an admission that the title "On an Old Horn" mystifies instead of clarifying, as it purports to do; that its signals will not guide us toward an understanding of the poem. When we then follow those signals, what they lead to is the re-creation at the end of the poem of a hilariously latinized noise declined as an adjective: "Pipperoo, pippera, pipperum . . . The rest is rot." Stevens himself acknowledges the difficulty, if not the impossibility, of recognizing the poem in his explication of what it "means" when he adds that the letter "is not just an explanation" but more a memory of "the sort of thing that produced the poem," something mysterious in the prior consciousness of the poet that is not revealed in the seemingly explanatory title. He writes: "To a person not accustomed to the vagaries of poetic thinking the explanation may seem to be a very strange affair, but there you are; its strangeness is what gives it poetic value."[25]

Other titles by Stevens seem designed to distract the reader from their relation to the poem by the wild contrast of their style to the poem's, which may deliberately simulate the difference in medium between any wording and the painting or sculpture it titles. More particularly, these exaggeratedly inapposite-seeming titles by Stevens bear a resemblance to some Dadaist presentations, for instance *Why Not Sneeze* for one of Marcel Duchamp's readymades, where the relation of title to object is made into a puzzle by the title's quotation of a recognizable spoken phrase belonging to a style that seems ludicrously inapposite to the work it attaches to. An example among Stevens's titles is the singsong minstrel routine "No Possum, No Sop, No Taters" for a somber description of a frozen landscape in a catalogue of very different negatives: "not," "absent," "without," "away," "emptiness." Another is a pat sounding prescription "How to Live. What to Do" for a mythic tale of "The man and his companion" confronting a "great height" and hearing a "heroic sound." While these titles can, if reduced to paraphrase, be found to have points of connection with what the poems have to do with—barren negation, the majestic sublime—the contrast between their exaggerated stylization and the very different rhetorical manner of the poems tends to puzzle more than help the work of interpretation.

Others of Stevens's titles evade their presentational function in the manner of titles for surrealist paintings, like Arshile Gorky's *The Leaf of an Artichoke Is an Owl*, or like those of Yves Tanguy, which Ashbery, comparing them to Stevens's titles, describes as having "the arbitrary but invincible

logic of the *cadavre exquis*, the poetic game of chance which Tanguy used
to participate in with his Surrealist friends in the 1920s."[26] Among Stevens's
non-sense titles are: "The Poem That Took the Place of a Mountain";
"Mountains Covered with Cats"; "Saturday Night at the Chiropodist's";
"The Woman Who Blamed Life on a Spaniard," about which Hugh Kenner
writes that there "is no procedure for thinking of a title like that. You find
it by turning over stones."[27] That is to say, we are not supposed to understand what it *means*, what its "direct" or "literal" value as a presentation
of the poem is, because it is a mystifier rather than a signifier. This makes
it an appropriate element in the evasive design of the poem, and conse-
quently not an authoritative interpreter of it. Stevens admits to such an aim
when he complains about the search for the kind of guidance he withholds
in such titles and poems in a letter of 1952 where he backs away from questions about "Angel Surrounded by Paysans": "recently I have been fitted
into too many philosophic frames."[28] This is what his mystifying titles seem
designed to prevent, but which, paradoxically, their very evasiveness encourages because the position of the title in the space above the text has
traditionally raised the expectation that it is put there to help us read the
poem.

   John Berryman pays a kind of tribute to the "Mutter," the puzzle of
"wits" in Stevens's "flourishing art," in a poem in *Dream Songs* of 1969
with the quizzical title "So Long? Stevens." The question mark may suggest that goodbyes are not called for, that Stevens's presence is still felt,
as indeed it seems to be in Berryman's own exaggeratedly preposterous or
enigmatic titles: "April Fool's Day, or St. Mary of Egypt" for a poem beginning "—Thass a funny title, Mr Bones"; "or Amy Vladeck or Riva Freifeld,"
which may or may not be a postscript to the poem but is clearly not a presentation of it; "The Following Gulls" for a poem with no gulls in it. Equally
baffling in their relation to the poem are some of Charles Olson's titles, like
the exotic sentence "A Fish is the Flower of Water" and the folk song–like
chorus "Only the Red Fox, Only the Crow" for poems giving advice—"For-
bear to drive life into a corner," "make most of love"—to future generations. Stevens's titles may be the model for these of the next generation—
"So Long? Stevens" calls itself a "counter-mutter" to Stevens's—but
Olson's and sometimes Berryman's titles in this style seem relatively peripheral because their mystifications tend to remain eccentric to the poem rather
than mysteriously opening onto or reaching into its enigmatic center.

First-line identifiers

   Readers now tend to refer to poems by opening line or phrase if they
are not printed with wording in the title space—Shakespeare's sonnets are
the most familiar example—but by title when they are. Like Shakespeare's

sonnets, many of Wordsworth's poems, including some of his best-known non-sonnets, are now referred to by their opening lines, but for a somewhat different reason: we are used to seeing them with those self-referential opening quotations above the text. By now our presuppositions about wording in that space encourage us to respond to first lines there as titles, as presentations that are part of the design of the poem, whereas there is evidence, including references by Wordsworth and his circle, that the author did not originally grant that status to the openings of his poems. One of them now often printed with its first line above the text, "I wandered lonely as a Cloud," is not referred to that way by Wordsworth or his sister, who instead refer to it by its central image, "The daffodils."[29] Coleridge names "A slumber did my spirit seal" according to its kind as an ' Epitaph," calls "She was a Phantom of delight" Wordsworth's "*apparition* poem," and gives "Three years she grew" the name of "Nature's Lady."[30] Although these and other opening lines commonly appear above many of Wordsworth's poems in modern editions and anthologies, they got to where they are by a kind of accident of history, which will be traced briefly here because it bears on the status of self-referential opening quotations in the framing position.

The use of such quotations in the place of a title is a very old practice, likely to derive from the *incipit* preceding the poem in manuscript. In the earliest printing of the English prayer book of 1549, following pre-Reformation tradition, the first words are quoted in the space above the psalm assigned to be read on a particular day. Each psalm is specified before the verses by its opening words in Latin as well as by number. Beginning with the reading for the first Sunday in Advent, "*Beatus vir.* Psalm i" is printed above the opening verse: "Blessed is that manne that hath not walked in the counsalye of the ungodly." This practice has been a continuing tradition of the English Church. Along with occasional presentations of hymns by first words, it may have encouraged later uses of them in reference to poems, but there is clear evidence that the Latin quotations above the verses of psalms did not have the status of titles.

English writings about the Psalter in this early period do give a great deal of attention to what they everywhere refer to as "the titles of the Psalmes"—what each is "intitled," "named," or "caled"—by which the writers do not mean the quotation of opening words but other formulas with a very long tradition of use in Latin Psalters that were regularly printed above the verses in early English bibles. These were argued, for instance by Donne, to be "Canonicall" aids, each "the key" (the metaphor is cited as St. Jerome's) to "get into the understanding of the Psalm."[31] Some examples from the authorized translation of 1611 are: "A prayer of Dauid"; "A Psalme, and song at the dedication of the house of Dauid"; "To the chiefe Musician. A

Psalme of Dauid"; "A Psalme for Solomon"; "A Psalme of praise." These "Titles" or "Inscriptions" are typically described in the terms George Wither uses about them in *A Preparation to the Psalter* of 1619. He categorizes them according to the questions they answer, much as titles are grouped in these chapters: "what persons are introduced speaking . . . and when the Author speaketh himselfe . . . whether it declare somewhat touching the matter . . . or the Instrument wherewith it was played . . . or the quality of the *Dittie*, or the *Tune*, or the occasion . . . or the vse of it, or the time in which it was principally to be sung . . . or whatsoeuer other circumstances."[32] Such descriptions would not fit the way opening words of psalms work in the space above the text; accordingly those self-referential quotations were never called titles.

Opening words were also a common form of reference to distinguish among the many entries in collections of classical authors, for instance Horace's odes, where in Renaissance editions more than one poem is often given the same title, such as "*Ad Maecenatem.*" William Drummond relies on this convention in his conversations with Ben Jonson of 1619 when, as recorded in a late-seventeenth-century manuscript, he remembers that Jonson "read his translation of that ode of Horace Beautus ille qui procul negotiis etc.," but there is no reason to think these opening fragments were considered to be titles any more than were the parallel references to particular psalms.[33] The translation Drummond mentions is actually presented in Jonson's posthumous volume *The Vnder-Wood* (correctly numbered Epode 2), with the space above the text filled by a traditionally formed title announcing the poem's kind and topic: "The praises of a Countrie life."

In the same period self-referential opening quotations were not a common way of distinguishing English poems. A reason why this was so may be suggested by Drummond's way of phrasing his reference to "that ode of Horace Beatus ille" rather than to *an ode of Horace that begins Beatus ille.* He seems to take for granted an audience familiar with Horace's poems, even knowing them the way congregations would know the psalms from hearing them regularly, who would therefore be able to identify "that ode" by opening phrase or line. By contrast, English poems, not being part of the educational curriculum, would not then have had the same predictable currency. Yet by the end of the sixteenth century references to poems began to be institutionalized in tables of contents for some collections of untitled poems where, as cross-references within the volume, they would not assume the reader's prior familiarity with the poems. Barnabe Barnes's *Parthenophil and Parthenophe. Sonnettes, Madrigals, Elegies and Odes* of 1593 merely numbers its entries in the text but lists them alphabetically by opening words in a table. Henry Lok's *Svndry Affectionate Sonets Of A Feeling Conscience* of 1597 is presented the same way. Thomas Campion's lyrics for his songs are only numbered in the text but listed sequentially by first line in the tables to his books of airs published between 1601 and 1617. As such listings of contents became a more expected feature, first lines began to appear in them even for some poems that have titles: in Edmund Waller's *Poems, &c* of 1645, a number of entries are titled simply "Song" in the text but the table adds the opening phrase—"A Song. Say lovely dreame"—identifying which song.

In the eighteenth century tables of contents became still more common in volumes of poetry even when they had relatively few entries, all of them titled, as in *Lyrical Ballads, with A Few Other Poems* of 1798, which lists its twenty-three poems in the table by number and by title. None is referred to by opening phrase or line. The same pattern holds for the somewhat enlarged first volume of *Lyrical Ballads, with Other Poems* of 1800, but in the table of contents for the second volume half a dozen poems are listed by opening line—"A slumber did my spirit seal, &c."—while in the text these poems have no wording in the space above the verses. There they are preceded only by what Wordsworth in the letter cited earlier calls "the Title Lines." In the table of contents for *Poems, in Two Volumes* of 1807, some untitled entries are listed by opening line or phrase—"I am not One, &c."—while others—for instance "I wandered lonely as a Cloud"—are acknowledged only by a row of dots. The table in *Poems* of 1815 uses only self-referential opening quotations for untitled poems, but in more abbreviated form—"A slumber"—as does the list of contents for *The Miscellaneous Poems of William Wordsworth* of 1820, where the even more awkwardly abbreviated wording—"I travelled among," "She dwelt among"—makes it specially clear that designations of poems by opening quotations were still not being considered as titles. They were shorthand references increasingly useful as the volumes included more poems and as readers came to know more of Wordsworth's work. Only in editions later than 1849–50, the last printed in his lifetime, did self-referential quotations of the opening line begin to be printed in the title space where, in the cultural situations of later-nineteenth- and twentieth-century poetry, they encourage readers to take them for granted as titles given by the poet and therefore to weight them with presentational authority.

The special features of this kind of quotation used in place of a title can be seen in outline by looking back at the early paradigm "*Beatus vir.* Psalm i." It is not a presentation of the verses by the titler giving some directions for reading them, because the words are not *about* the text but *of* the text. The quotation does not even purport to be a neutral label. Instead it is a mode of reference with the same status as the number of the psalm. Both are intended to answer the question *which psalm is this?* which can imply that the reader is already familiar with these verses, and indeed the quotation above them provides no special knowledge of the text the way a glossing title would, nor does it purport to simplify the reader's interpretive task, like a summarizing title.

What this paradigm shows, then, is that opening quotations do not formally claim the status of a presentation by someone who knows the poem to someone who does not. Because they are words of rather than about the poem, they do not impose a perspective on it by acting like a frame setting it off in a different medium by shape, position, grammatical form, or in many instances by metrical pattern. In anticipating the question *which poem is this?* with the answer *this is the poem beginning*, quotations of opening lines tell us at most only what we learn as soon as we start to read; "Not marble, nor the guilded monument" in the title space has the same status as would "Sonnet 55."

Among substitutions for the title above the poem, first-line quotations tend to attract less attention, to be less assertive than any of the other forms of evasion discussed in this chapter. A reason may be that although we now assume this kind of substitution to be the author's choice, as we do the others, it still seems less like self-presentation than like a simple form of reference, the way any of us might identify the poem we are talking about if we do not remember its title (or number). This tendency to unassertiveness may be what makes such opening quotations in place of a title attractive to certain poets. An example would be Edward Thomas, whose other treatments of the title space are also quiet and modest, at the opposite pole from Williams's polemical or Stevens's idiosyncratic titles or evasions of titling. Although the titles Thomas himself seems to have assigned to poems do perform their presentational function, almost always by naming the topic of the poem—"The Barn," "Snow," "Aspens," "Parting"—they do so by such simple means that they almost match his first-line quotations in self-effacement, in seeming to escape self-presentation, much as they avoid personal pronouns. The one poet whose use of self-referential quotations in place of titles seems to be the gigantic exception to this generalization about their relative unassertiveness is Walt Whitman. He precedes his poems with them so often and in such assertive patterns that he makes them a means of self-expression and a powerful instrument for voicing the poet's authority.

The first edition of Whitman's *Leaves of Grass* of 1855 had only that title, without separate presentations for shorter groups of lines or even for longer poems such as the one later titled "Song of Myself." Presumably a reason they were omitted is that frames setting off the poems might seem to interrupt the organic unfolding of the *Leaves*, which are presented not as bound pages but as a growing body of lines for which the living body of the poet is a metaphor. The final, much revised and vastly enlarged authorized edition of 1891–92, with the same volume title, groups under fourteen headings well over three hundred poems, each with wording above it in the title space. The larger number of entries makes some way of referring to the individual poems an obvious practical necessity, but one that could have been met by a table of contents distinguishing poems by number and first line, allowing the text of the poem to appear on the page with no wording above it. Instead, in the final edition of *Leaves of Grass* Whitman fills all the title spaces. Sometimes he uses traditional forms of presentation, as in "Song of Myself" and "To the Sun-set Breeze." Much more often he fills the title space with words then repeated exactly in the first line of the poem. As he makes them work, these opening quotations are another and more insistent way of enhancing the sense of the poet's unmediated presence.

Like the first-person pronouns in his otherwise conventionally framed titles, the self-referential opening quotations are grammatically continuous with the poem. More importantly, they are not set off by saying something *about* it. What they do say is *of* the poem, not only in the same grammatical person but in the very same distinctive cadence of their identical wording: "Scented Herbage of My Breast"; "Whoever You Are Holding Me Now in Hand"; "These I Singing in Spring"; "Not Heaving from My Ribb'd Breast Only." Also working toward this effect, Whitman's self-referential quotes preceding the poem are not framed by quotation marks like Hardy's, which would set them apart as something said again after the poem, except in two instances. " 'Going Somewhere' " is in quotation marks signaling that it is quoted from lines also framed that way in the text because they are spoken by someone the poet calls "my noblest woman-friend." The title " 'The Rounded Catalogue Divine Complete' " is also identified as a quotation from someone not the poet by quotation marks and by a note below it saying that the phrase is quoted from a sermon the poem is written to answer. These careful exceptions confirm that the otherwise perfectly consistent practice of leaving the quotation from the poem unframed in the space above it is part of a design making it continuous with the poem, an organic element of the whole. By these ways of treating the words in the title space that are then repeated in the first line, Whitman makes them act less like a frame made to set off a completed work than like the beginning of a chant continuing in uninterrupted rhythm through the poem and even beyond it in the growing body of the *Leaves*.

The words coming before the opening poem under the first heading in the volume are "One's Self I Sing." They are repeated in the first line of the text; modified in a succession of other lines ending in "I sing," culminating in the final line, "The Modern Man I sing"; then varied in title spaces later: "For Him I Sing"; "Still Though the One I Sing"; "I Sing the Body Electric." Rather than arresting the organic unfolding of the *Leaves*, the lines above the poems in this final edition nourish it. Because they are in an even more prominent position than the opening lines that repeat them, the rhythm they set in motion and its repetitions in the verses are especially pronounced, enhancing the claims of these initiating phrases to the power of bardic song. Their unmediated force is also enlarged because very many of the self-referential quotations that open the chantings include first-person pronouns, and not only in the conventional possessive form but in the more assertive nominative and objective: "I Hear America Singing"; "I Am He that Aches with Love"; "Me Imperturbe"; "Spontaneous Me." While these opening quotations do not act like titles in that they do not exercise their authority to say something *about* the poem, they have their special power over it. They are its originating source. They initiate the chanting of the bard whose living or, as it were, bodily presence and force of personality empower the opening line and reiterations of it that follow, and from poem to poem, with energy and passion. Whitman's use of repeated first lines might then be said not so much to evade the function of a title as to supplant it with a different kind of authority.

Grammatical run-ons

The treatments of the title space already described in this chapter are efforts not to let words printed above the text intrude on its internal space; to keep them from violating the integrity of the poem imagined as a moment or as a picture, a geometric figure, a machine, an organism, or some other autonomous entity. Except for Whitman, the poets discussed so far try to achieve this effect by omitting the title, by neutralizing it, or by widening its separation from the poem to sever or at least cover up their connections. The device sometimes called a *run-on* is another move toward the same ideal: to draw the wording above the text into the poem's internal space in such a way that it does not impose a perspective on it from outside. Whitman seems to attempt this by making the words in the title space the source of the line that follows them, with the effect that what is traditionally the beginning of the poem acts like a refrain echoing a prior sound. In this mythic design the words in the title space are made conceptually inseparable from the rest of the poem since it could not exist without its source.

A more extreme way to prevent the intrusion of a framing title is to substitute, in the space traditionally occupied by something said about the poem, the opening words of the grammatical sequence continuing then without interruption in the line that comes after it. This makes title and poem inseparable parts of a whole not, as in Whitman's poems, by imagining a mythic echo but by the ordinary logic of grammar. The result is that what is said in the title space gains in importance. Paradoxically it becomes essential, even irreplaceable to the poem in its very avoidance of the authority traditionally attached to the title as presentation.

Williams and Marianne Moore are among the first poets writing in English to experiment with treating the title space this way. Although Williams's rejection of titles in *Spring and All* may have readied him for such experiments, which he began to try out by 1927, he had already met poems where such an occupation of the space traditionally reserved for the title had taken place, in Marianne Moore's volume *Poems*, published in 1921. His study of her work, he announces in *Spring and All*, led him to the position that she "is of all American writers most constantly a poet" because she most effectively "escapes" the same formal barriers he struggles against, which would include conventional titles that frame the poem in an interpretive perspective.[34]

The interest of both Moore and Williams in this untraditional use of the title space seems to reflect the criteria for being "constantly a poet" for which Pound was seen by their generation to be the chief spokesman. Moore in her own critical writings often states these ideals by quoting Pound's: "Like Ezra Pound, I prefer the straightforward order of words, 'subject, predicate, object'"; "'straight talk, straight as the Greeks!'"; "'A coherent paragraph in plain English'"; "'the problem of style. Effect your meaning. Then stop.'"[35] The paradigm for what makes a poem that these formulas imply is not abstract painting but ordinary prose, as Pound articulates in two other often quoted pronouncements: "Poetry to be good poetry should be at least as well written as prose," and, speaking for his generation of poets, "We desire the words of poetry to follow the natural order. We would write nothing that we might not say actually in life—under emotion."[36] This paradoxical elevation of prose as the ideal model for poetry is the extreme expression of the need to escape generic and other boundaries that is embodied in compressed form in modernist experiments with the title space.

The argument proposed here is that respect for the particular models these prerequisites of a good poem point to—for Moore especially the diagram of a sentence, for Williams the order of prose—may have encouraged the device of starting the grammatical sequence of the poem where there would otherwise either be wording in a separate but nearly always incomplete grammatical unit or a space signifying its absence. The title of Pound's most famous poem, "In a Station of the Metro," itself moves toward this escape from traditional titling. Here a diagram of how it does so can perhaps show some ways that the later, more extreme invasions of the space above the poem carried out by Moore and Williams can satisfy the criteria for good poetry they shared with Pound.

As his poem first appeared in *Poetry* in April 1913, last in a group of twelve poems headed "Contemporania," and again in *Lustra of Ezra Pound* in 1916, "In a Station of the Metro" is centered in the space above the two lines of the poem and printed in a different typeface used also for preceding titles.[37] That visual appearance and its traditional form—compare Longfellow's "In the Churchyard at Cambridge," Hardy's "In a London Flat"—identify it as a presentation of the poem saying something specific about it that, it turns out, we would not know from reading the lines following it. Wordsworth's "Composed Upon Westminster Bridge, September 3, 1802" is a more detailed glossing title that, like Pound's, grounds the vision of the poem—Pound calls it "The apparition"—in actual experience.

What is untraditional, though, is the grammatical relation of Pound's title to what follows it. In the three examples just cited for comparison, title and text are sealed off from each other in separate and unlike grammatical units. Wordsworth's way of further isolating the title is to add a past participle to the prepositional phrase and to follow it with a date so that the words above the poem are in a temporal scheme, by contrast with the timeless, visionary present-tense sentences inside the private room of the sonnet. Pound, to the contrary, sets up no grammatical barriers between the title and the text, so that they can be read as three continuous lines belonging to a single sentence with subject, verb, and connective understood: "In a station of the metro [I see] the apparition of these faces in the crowd, [like] petals on a wet, black bough."

Pound himself in his account of how the poem came into being calls it a "*hokku*-like sentence" and gives a lesson in this way of reading it that includes an explanation of its formal kind. He quotes in translation an example of the Japanese *hokku*: "The footsteps of the cat upon the snow: / (are like) plum-blossoms."[38] Then he adds, "The words 'are like' would not occur in the original, but I add them for clarity," implying precisely the understanding of the reader's interpretive role that Moore attributes to him: "As for comprehension of what is set forth, the poet has a right to expect the reader, at least in some measure, to be able to complete the poetic statement; and Ezra Pound never spoils his effects by over-exposition."[39] Her phrase "the poetic statement" can summarize the argument here: that Pound's title and text are in the form of a statement (not overexposed); that together they are understood to belong to a single sentence that begins in the space traditionally occupied by the separate grammatical unit of a title made out of words about rather than of the poem. Read this way, "In a Station of the Metro" is a prediction of the still more radical treatments of the title space in poems by Moore and Williams.

Williams himself may take a first partial step in the same direction in *Spring and All* with the untitled poem opening "so much depends." Although this first line does not actually take over the space above the text, it makes something like the same claim as poems where that does happen. The reason is that what a poem starting in the traditional title space "depends" on, what it hangs down from or is sustained from above by, is the beginning of its own grammatical sequence, which is what also happens to this untitled poem. The difference is that its absent title presents it as an unframed object, while in instances where the title space is filled with the first words of the sentence continuing in the text, the poem is not imagined as an object—framed or unframed—but as a grammatical sequence. While these two understandings of what a poem is may seem incompatible, they share features making it conceivable that a poet with Williams's convictions might pledge allegiance to them simultaneously. Both an object and a unit of grammar have a distinctive and appropriate structure or design that is untranslatable in other terms. Then each is analogous to what Williams thinks a poem is because in his view a poem excludes the interpretation imposed by a title that, being words said about the text, must be external to the poem's structure or design.

Moore earlier than Williams takes the full step of filling the title space with words that begin the sentence continuing without interruption in the text. Eight of the poems in the volume of 1921 begin this way, among others that differently defy titling conventions by the form of the titles themselves—"Diligence Is to Magic as Progress Is to Flight," "Roses Only," "Is Your Town Nineveh?"—or by announcements of untraditional topics—"Dock Rats," "To a Steam Roller." Among the eight poems that escape titling, some give visible signals from the start that the words nearest the top of the page are bound, for instance by a conjunction or a comma, to what is printed below them—"In This Age of Hard Trying Nonchalance Is Good, And" or "Feed Me, Also, River God,"—while another creates the same effect by grammatical reference to what follows: "He Made This Screen."

Two others have what look like conventional titles sealed off in grammatical units: "The Fish," in the most common article-noun title form; "England," using the unqualified noun preferred in this period. We are taken in by their likeness to familiar titles telling what the poem is about, so that what comes next—"wade/" and "with its baby rivers"—surprises us into recognizing that our habits of reading are being revised. We are not asked to focus on "The Fish" as some thing or things represented in the text, which in fact observes only their habitat, but as the grammatical subject of the poem. This is a milder version of the radical revision in our reading habits that takes place in Moore's "An Octopus" from her next volume, *Observations* of 1924. What appears to be a conventional title we then learn in the line below, from the phrase "Of ice," is an article-noun combination joined to a prepositional phrase acting as a metaphor for the actual topic of the poem, not an octopus but a glacier. This could well be an illustration of what Williams means by calling Moore's poems "diagrammatically informative."[40]

A different kind of revision happens as we read the opening of another poem in her earlier volume, "When I Buy Pictures," which continues with the line "or what is closer to the truth, when I look at." What might have been a title announcing the poem's topic (like Hardy's "When Oats Were Reaped") is taken back by the rest of the sentence so that the first words are exposed as having no interpretive authority. That is to say, they are stripped of the status traditionally associated with their precedence over the rest of the poem, while they acquire a new importance because what follows depends on them grammatically.

These first examples predict Moore's work with this kind of evasion of the title space in her later volumes; they also act in essentially the same ways as Williams's parallel experiments. Another type of substitution, apparently of his own contriving, is to place where we would expect a title a word that grammatically makes little or no sense by itself: "Sluggishly," "Middle," "These." This radical device was not much taken up by other poets, it seems, until quite recently, as in: Bruce Andrews's "While"; Ted Greenwald's "And, Hinges"; Jackson MacLaw's "Recommend"; James Sherry's ":About"; Diane Ward's "Approximately."

Elsewhere Williams elaborates more than Moore on the process, perhaps suggested to him by her, of revising the way we experience what at first appears to be a conventional title. An example, from *An Early Martyr and Other Poems* of 1935, is "To a Poor Old Woman." It imitates the form of a title stating who the poem is formally addressed to. At the same time, by calling her "Poor" and "Old" it tells us that the woman will not be imagined as actually listening—it would be unkind to call her that to her face—but that the poet is paying her a tribute designed only for the reader to hear. In this sense the title prepares for a poem dedicated "To" her.

We know how to interpret this complex but familiar signal because we accept automatically that words in the title space are put there to address the reader about the poem. The fact that they are by convention sealed off from it grammatically and formally (by being excluded from its structure) allows them to signal something to the reader as if out of earshot of any imagined listener in the poem. What Williams jokingly does is to expose this highly artificial fiction built into a conventional title form so familiar we tend to accept it unthinkingly. That is to say, he tears down the barrier it would set up in front of the poem by running it into both the grammar and the structure of the stanzas below it. The way he does this grammatically is to run "To a Poor Old Woman" into a colloquial sequence we might "say actually in life—under emotion":

To a Poor Old Woman

munching a plum on
the street a paper bag
of them in her hand

They taste good to her[41]

—this last line-sentence then being said three more times in various patterns of lineation. The way he forces the entry of the wording above the
text into its formal structure is by manipulation of its stanza form. As the
lines just quoted show, the poem seems to begin with a three-line stanza
below the title space. Reading on through the following stanzas, all in four
lines, we come to recognize that the first stanza also has four lines, the first
being "To a Poor Old Woman." Paradoxically, these grammatical and structural evasions of the title space, like others discussed here, can of course
only work by evoking the presence of the conventional title they simultaneously dismantle.

Williams's most richly original and, perhaps partly for that reason, most
famous treatment of the title space is "This Is Just to Say" in *Collected
Poems* of 1934.[42] If these starting words were printed as the first line under
a traditional title like "To Flossie" or "Apology" (actual titles of other
poems by Williams), under the unqualified noun "Plums," or even under a
wordless space, they would be presented to the reader as being really the
opening of a poem only pretending (without the expectation of being believed) to be a note. The way these first words actually appear on the page,
they ignore the reader and avoid identifying what follows by saying something about it as a poem belonging to a formal kind, or on a topic. "This"
points only to the rest of what is being said, the statement it belongs to,
not to something outside the poem represented in it. While "This" has an
identifiable reference on the page, it does not distinguish what it points
to as either a poem or a note. Williams again seems to avoid making this
distinction in a playful answer he gives to questions asked in an interview
about what makes "This Is Just to Say" a poem: "It's curious how a thing
of this sort, which was really just a passing gesture, actually took place just
as it says here. My wife being out, I left a note for her, just that way, and
she replied very beautifully."[43]

Here "This" is called "just a passing gesture" or "a note," but since he
says he left it for his wife "just that way," he teasingly leaves open the possibility that because he is a poet, and one known for scribbling his poems on
odd bits of paper in the course of a busy day, the "note" he taped to the
refrigerator door or left on the kitchen table was one such scribble in "just"
the form we know it by. The repeated word "just" here, as in "This Is Just
to Say," defines it as a "thing" made *only* and made *precisely* of words. The

definition, "just" as true of a note as of a poem, obliterates the distinction between them.

Other poets of the same generation worked in some of the same directions to escape titling their poems—among them Witter Bynner, e. e. cummings, Gene Toomer, and Louis Zukofsky with "Poem beginning 'The.'" This intense interest in the enterprise seems not to have been sustained by many more recent poets. A few start a grammatical sequence in the title space, but the device seems to be peripheral rather than to be a defining feature of the poem's essential design or an expression of strongly felt convictions about what a poem should be or do. Examples are: Plath's "You're," and "I Am Vertical"; Anne Stevenson's "And even then," and "It came as a sign"; Ted Hughes's "You Drive in a Circle"; Robert Bly's "When the Dumb Speak"; Peter Armstrong's "I See Myself in the Womb." Other poets have found a way of undermining what interpretive authority might still attach to beginning the poem's sentence in the title space, because they make a grammatical prediction in an unfinished phrase that is not continued in what follows, like Olson's "The Ring of" and Gavin Ewart's "Going to."

Ashbery in *As We Know* of 1979 shows once again his characteristic interest in experiments with titling conventions that expose their paradoxical tendency to undo their own claims when pushed to extremity. The volume includes a group of four poems, each consisting of a main clause like "I HAD THOUGHT THINGS WERE GOING ALONG WELL" or a sentence fragment like "THE CATHEDRAL IS" printed in the capital letters of the typeface used for all titles of poems in this volume (which may have been the choice of the book's designer but is likely to have been shown to the author for approval). Below is a space such as traditionally separates the title from the text, and below that comes the rest of the sentence in a single line of much smaller letters, all but the first in lowercase. Each of the four is printed by itself on the page where the large, blank spaces all around it heighten attention to its unconventional proportions. These are most absurdly obvious where the title takes up two lines, twice as many as the text:

OUT OVER THE BAY
THE RATTLE OF FIRECRACKERS

And in the adjacent waters, calm.[44]

If we can shift our attention from the pyrotechnic visual display to what the words mean, we realize that the title makes all the noise.

The oddities here exaggerate the invasion of the title space by the grammatical beginning of the poem beyond any of Moore's quiet occupations of it or Williams's louder assaults, to the point where the starting words seem to exploit their position above the poem. They exercise their own kind of tyranny over it, intruding on or at least crowding or overshadowing its space as much as words about it might do in a conventional title. If this is one of the games Ashbery is playing, he is once again pushing earlier experiments in evasive treatments of the title space to their limits here. These little poems seem to be another expression of amused awareness that such unconventional experiments make their own conventions, which have a tendency to behave like the ones they were designed to replace. The paradoxical treatment of the title space in these poems is a very small aperture into what Vernon Shetley describes as Ashbery's suspicion of "an avant-garde that has become an establishment."[45]

Questions

All these various treatments of the title space try to diminish the control exercised in advance over the reader's responses to the poem by predicting as little as possible about it. Another recent title form redefines the transaction that goes on in the title space by filling it with a question asked of the poet in place of an answer (given, implied, pretended, withheld, or suppressed) that anticipates a question the reader might ask about the poem before first looking into it.

In the past questions have rarely been asked in the title space, and then not asked of the poet. Traditionally when they do appear they are most likely to repeat a question said in the first line of the poem, for instance in Ebenezer Elliott's "What Is Bad Government?" and Clare's "What Is Life?" As self-referential opening quotations these identify which poem will follow without saying more about it, although being questions they tend to have more urgency than quotations that give no sign of grammatical mood. The emotional temper of the question can be further adjusted if the form of it is altered from the way it is said in the text, either in the first line or elsewhere, as Christina Rossetti's "What to Do?" generalizes the more personally troubled "What shall I do?" in the verses. Later poets have made larger adjustments of self-referential quotations that frame the poem with more loudly expressive effects. Langston Hughes's "What?" preceding the text jokingly insists on getting an answer to the question the poet asks less abruptly in the last line, "So what would you do?" Larkin's "Whatever Happened?" makes a question out of an indicative phrase said by the poet in the first line, unmasking its bewilderment and fear, its status as an exclamation rather than in interrogative. Lawrence's title "What Are the Wild Waves Saying?" quotes from the first line of the poem, which in turn quotes from the title and first line of a sentimentally pious poem by Joseph Edward

Carpenter, changing its context so radically that the question must have some new, satirically quizzical stress on "Are."

Sometimes the poet repeats in the title space a question asked by some figure in the poem, as in Christopher Smart's "Where's the Poker?" which is what the distraught kitchen maid would like to know. Howard Nemerov's "What Kind of Guy Was He?" repeats what the first line tells us someone inside the poem has asked outside it: "Just so you shouldn't have to ask again." In other instances the title is the poet's question asked of *you* in the text: intimately and immediately in Ginsberg's " 'What You Up To?' "; Hamish Brown's "What Are You Thinking About?"; Robert Penn Warren's "So You Agree with What I Say? Well, What Did I Say?"; more publicly in Lawrence's "What Would You Fight For?" and Amiri Baraka's "What Are You Waiting For?" The pronoun in Yeats's "Are You Content?" includes readers among "those" it refers to explicitly, the poet's ancestors and heirs. C. Day Lewis's "Where Are the War Poets?" seems to be addressed to a generation of writers and readers. Marianne Moore's "What Are Years?" is the first in a sequence of rhetorical questions following the title. So is Ashbery's "What Is Poetry," the absent question mark perhaps hinting at skeptical detachment from the pretense of interest shown up by the title's conventional and rhetorical manner.

Another form of question appearing in twentieth-century titling is the quotation of a familiar spoken idiom, again an instance of interest in what Frost calls sentence-sounds, which express a recognizable bundle of feelings associated with a typical situation in a phrase we have all said or could say. Auden may have set the most influential examples, as in "Are You There?" and "What's the Matter?" Other instances are: Lawrence's "What's To Be Done?"; Carl Sandburg's "Again?"; Alfred Kreymborg's "What For?" Ruth Stone's "Who's Out?" is a familiar grammatical formula for expressing skepticism or sarcastic incredulity, asked in response to "It was Chatauqua / Got the woman out of the kitchen." Denise Levertov's "Why Me?" may be asked both by the poet-lover who says the poem and the poet-lover who hears it, expressing their mutual wonder. Lloyd Schwartz's "Who's on First?" combines an idiomatic question originally about baseball with quotation of its most famous context, an Abbott and Costello routine. David Ferry's unpunctuated "What's Playing Tonight" is phrased in the familiar non-sense of the sort of unanswerable non-question we want to ask about the madness in the poem.

These idiomatic questions have their own ways of fulfilling the title's function: to answer some question about the poem in advance of the reader's experience of it. For instance, many of the examples just given illustrate how such questions can be used for their comical or satirical effects, letting the reader in on the humor as a way of signaling what kind of poem will follow, what attitude it will take toward its topic, speaker, or listener. The rest of this discussion will look at uses of questions that seem to evade rather than to fulfill the role of a title, because they are asked of the poet. Examples of this still very rare treatment of the title space can trace how far efforts to escape the traditional authority of the title have so far extended.

The tentativeness of the question asked above a poem in John Hollander's *In Time & Place* of 1986 calls attention to it as an experiment in the relation between wording in that traditionally authoritative position and the text. The elegantly rhymed four-line stanzas that follow compose a love poem in the Elizabethan eternizing mode, explicitly associated here with Shakespeare's "Not marble, nor the guilded monument" and Spenser's "One day I wrote her name vpon the strand." The poem—"these few leaves of the late mail"—sent to the beloved situates itself in the twentieth century as a revision of the tradition. It is "Not graven to eternize you / In the bright adamant of myth," "But written in the speaking tongue / The neck, the breast, the legs apart," yet the sophistication of the poem guarantees its awareness that such revisions are themselves part of the tradition.[46] So are the plea of the closing stanza and the last line's qualifying "if" and ambiguously placed "only":

> Guard these few leaves of the late mail
> That they may live as long as you,
> Their whisperings forever new,
> Blown abroad only if they fail.

"They Failed. (But To Do What?)" is the comment in the title space preceding these stanzas, shockingly juxtaposed to them by its radically different style and antitraditional form. The past tense of the verb signals that it is to be thought of as made after the verses, making the statement "They Failed." a gloss on them telling what happened after they were written and mailed. If those were the only words said in the title space, we could read the comment simply as the poet's self-mockery, perhaps an allusion to Shakespeare's self-mocking sonnets. Following our training as readers to trace its direct link with the last line, we would be guided toward types of ambiguity familiar at least since Shakespeare: did the verses fail because they could not sustain "the speaking tongue"? because the beloved did not tenderly "Guard" them but let them be indifferently "Blown abroad" like dead leaves? because the closing plea turns them into the "high protesting monolith / Ever to wail and plead and sue" of sonnet tradition that the twentieth-century poet had tried to escape?

We could accept these multiple possibilities as a recognizable form of unsettled interpretation if it were not for the parenthetical question "(But to Do What?)" in the title space, which is asked of whoever says "They Failed." Here the ambiguities are of an unfamiliar kind because the wording above the text has abandoned the rules for titling so that we cannot read the signals. If the poet makes the statement and then asks himself the question, both strip him of the authority to impose an interpretive title on the text. If the poet makes the statement but the reader asks the question (as the parentheses might signal), or more emphatically, if both are said by the reader, then our baffled response is the authoritative last word on the stanzas of the poem: we decide if "They Failed," but do not know at what.

This speculation cannot lead to conclusions, even to unsettled interpretations, precisely because the words preceding the stanzas depart so radically from their role as the presentation of them to the reader by the poet who makes the title. All that can perhaps be said with any degree of assurance is that this juxtaposition of traditionally centered stanzas with an extravagantly antitraditional substitute for a title is an experiment in heterogeneously yoking them by violence together. It does this by moving the disruptions of interpretive closure into the title space, which traditionally has supplied or at least purported to supply answers to questions about the poem rather than to impose new ones.

The question asked of the poet in the space above a poem in John Berryman's last volume, *Delusions, Etc.* of 1972, takes part in a kind of vaudeville act that pulls the rug out from under many of the conventions of titling discussed in this history of them: the fiction originating in the actual circumstances of early titling, and imitated later in unlike cultural situations, that the poet is not the presenter of his own poems; the presumptions that the title is assigned after the poem is complete by someone who knows it, and put in place to answer in advance a question the reader who does not know it might ask about it; the premise that the differences in grammatical form, and often in metrical stress and typeface, between the title and the text are verbal and visual representations of what the empty space between them also signifies, their different status as words about the poem and of the poem. It is by turning these conventions upside down or inside out that the question to the poet makes its comically theatrical appearance in the space above Berryman's poem: "'How Do You Do, Dr Berryman, Sir?'"

Here the form of the question supports the fiction that the poet is not his own titler, but not by making the traditional third-person references that in early titles acknowledge the separate identities of the poet and the editor and later attempt to distance the author of the poem from the fictional first person in it. By directly addressing this poet, calling him to his face by his actual name, the question to "Dr Berryman" collapses the convention of third-person titling, which is in turn a way of unmasking the notion of a persona. In the new fiction created here, the "I" speaking in the text—"I know it sounds incredible"—is the actual John Berryman.[47] Because the question is asked him in an exaggeratedly different voice, it must be said by someone else or by the poet pretending to be someone else, that is, a persona. To readers of earlier volumes by Berryman, the voice belongs recognizably to "Henry," mentioned by name also in this poem, who like his maker is a middle-aged white American male given to sounding like an actor in blackface.

The relation of the lines that follow to the question asked the poet reverses the order of composition presumed in traditional titles. Here it implies that the text is prompted by the ridiculously formal question, answering it in an abrupt, fragmentary, spontaneous-seeming form, beginning with the first line—"Edgy, perhaps. *Not* on the point of bursting-forth"— and punctuated by spaces, dashes, and an absent final period. The contrast in styles between title and text, rather than representing the different status of words imposed on the poem and words belonging to it, instead seems to act out the difference in *personality*, in all its philosophical and colloquial senses, between "Berryman" and the exaggeratedly polite figure "Henry" is pretending to be. The question makes an elaborately stagey show of following the rules for what is conventionally understood to be a formulaic greeting, not a personal question looking for an answer. The answer refuses to play by the rules, ignoring the convention by giving a detailed, intimate, convoluted but self-exposing account of how "Berryman" does actually "Do."

The exchange can then be read to act out in its own hilarious terms the "supposition" that Martin Dodsworth suggests Berryman's "*superfluous oddity*" is predicated on, "that what is superfluous to the conventional demands of literature may establish a means of personal expression and communication with the reader, something that cannot . . . be contaminated by the . . . desire to incorporate all literature into some vast and inoffensive system of conventions."[48] It seems that in this poem such a system is associated especially with conventional titling. The wording above the poem parodies what titles are traditionally expected to do by purporting to be a question while being conventionally understood as something else. The answer purports to ignore the convention while paradoxically calling it into play.

Here, in closing, is a poem from Alan Shapiro's volume of 1983, *The Courtesy*:

What Makes You Think It's Fear

Each morning from the house he sees the cat
who won't come near him, entering the garden.
It moves along the fencetop, through the ivy,

making the sounds of someone keeping quiet,
making him listen.
                            He wonders what it fears:
what makes it leap away when he goes out—
to perch on the far corner of the fence,
its paws drawn under it, the tail pulled round
like a moat?
                   In time the cat will stay, he thinks,
in time learn how mistaken its fears are.
He brings an offering to prove he's kind,
holding out to it a bowl of food,
shaking the bowl to prove that it is full
and not a trap,
                        calling out sweet names.
But far into the leaves the cat retreats
before it disappears; its green eyes glaring
and yet with no alarm, as he approaches,
holding the bowl and, almost fearful,
                                       calling,
calling out as if he asks for alms.[49]

   The startling effect of the words we read before the poem does not here
involve a clash of style with the lines that follow, since they are said in
a similarly thoughtful, searching, quietly urgent manner. Nor is their surprise heightened by any eccentricity in the wording of the question, which
is phrased just as we would ordinarily ask it. The shock of what precedes
the text depends simply on its originality in expanding the possibilities of
what can happen in the title space, but the simplicity is a multilayered
achievement.
   The asker, who has clearly read and thought about the poem, focuses
the question on the interpretation of a nonhuman being's behavior as described in it. In the poet's account, the creature is called "the cat" three
times, nine times "it," but once "who" (not *which*) and compared to
"someone" (not *something*) whose motives and feelings are susceptible of
interpretation. The reader's question must therefore be asked of the poet,
probing the uneasy movement of the language in and out of personification.
This can be traced in the confused grammatical references to the creature
and more strongly in the apparent contradiction between the observation
of "its green eyes glaring / and yet with no alarm" and the speculation about
"what it fears." The anxiety may even be sensed in the poet's omission of
a title that would claim to tell something authoritative about the poem:
suggestions might be "The Cat," "A Morning Ritual," "In the Garden,"
"Personification." "What Makes You Think It's Fear" is asked of the poet
by a reader who may also know versions of the question we have met often

before in nineteenth- and twentieth-century poems, beginning with Words-worth's "To the Cuckoo." There it is directed by the poet to the bird whose mysterious being is the provocation for the asking of it. Here the reader who raises the question in the space outside the poem seems to sense that the poet suppresses it.

The pronoun "You" in the reader's question, since it can be either singular or plural, may be asked both of the poet who narrates the lines and of "he" whose daily ritual they describe throughout in the third person. It is "he" whose garden the cat enters quietly, "making him listen"; who approaches the cat "calling out sweet names" as if it could understand; "calling out as if he asks for alms," with a "fearful" need to be trusted, not to be rebuffed or feared, to "prove" kinship with nonhuman nature, like the poet in Wordsworth's "To a Butterfly" who also suppresses uneasiness about his own wishful personifying. By this conflation of the poet and "he" in "You," the question preceding the poem suggests that the reader who asks it sympathetically recognizes phrases like "He wonders," "he thinks" as a device of the poet's for distancing himself from the would-be tamer of the cat, who, for instance, wishfully imagines that it will "in time learn how mistaken its fears are." How would the poet know of this wish if "he" were not a version of himself? It follows, then, that it may also be the poet who asks "What Makes You Think It's Fear" of his third-person representative, that is, of himself, making a common bond of perception between the poet and the reader who asks the same question.

How does placing the poet's question outside the space of the poem differ in effect from asking it explicitly in the text, where the poet asks his version of it in "To the Cuckoo"? As it appears in the title space in its own self-enclosed grammatical unit, it is sealed off from the text, not part of its fiction. The separation here creates the possibility of a different fiction, that the poet who chooses the words for the title space separates himself from the poet who says the lines referring to himself evasively as "he." This distinction in turn allows the suggestion that what is said outside the poem is more direct, more forthright, more knowing about the actual poet than what is said obliquely by the fictional poet inside its space. In this light the poet who asks himself "What Makes You Think It's Fear" reveals what is suppressed in the poem. He not only calls in question the act of personifying, but he does so in a self-exposing form. That is, he does not ask himself *what makes you think it feels anything?* or *think that you can interpret what it feels?* which would probe his own need to impose human nature on the cat. Instead the question he asks himself exposes the origin of that need: it is rooted in his own instinct that difference is "fearful"; in his sense of the other outside the human space of his fenced-in garden as something to be wooed and tamed, something he must prove the worth of his humanity to. Read as the poet's self-knowing and self-exposing question to him-self, the words in the title space can act as something authoritative said about the poem, which may be why the phrase is not punctuated with a question mark. At the same time, since the words may be asked sympatheti-cally by the reader together with the poet, making a common bond of per-ception between them, the question "What Makes You Think It's Fear" turns this evasion of the title space into a wholly original redefinition of what can happen in it.

THIS book can have no last words calling themselves a conclusion, because it looks at an unfolding process that is far from having exhausted itself in these last years of the twentieth century. Tracing the history of short poems in English since the beginning of printing has shown that titles belong to a rich and flexible tradition. What gives it these dimensions is that titles always look back to their past—imitating, modifying, questioning, rebelling against it—at the same time that they vividly reflect and energetically respond to the cultural situations that constitute their present. This double awareness or engagement would seem to promise their own ongoing vitality.

REFERENCE MATTER

Notes

Introduction

1. These are titles of poems by: Henry Vaughan; Anne Finch, Countess of Winchelsea; William Blake; Walter Savage Landor; Samuel Johnson; and William Wordsworth.

2. John Ashbery, *The Poet's Craft*, ed. William Packard (New York: Paragon House, 1987), 79.

3. George Lensing, *Wallace Stevens: A Poet's Growth* (Baton Rouge: Louisiana State University Press, 1986), 166–200.

4. Mary Ellen Rickey, *Utmost Art* (Lexington: University Press of Kentucky, 1966), 92–102, 116–19.

5. G. K. Hunter, "Drab and Golden Lyrics," *Forms of Lyric*, ed. Reuben Brower (New York: Columbia University Press, 1970), 1–18; Helen Gardner, "The Titles of Donne's Poems," *Friendship's Garland*, ed. Vittorio Gabriele (Rome: Edizione di Storia e Letteratura, 1966), 1: 187–207; John Shawcross, "But Is It Donne's? The Problem of Titles on His Poems," *John Donne Journal* 7 (1988): 141–49; Geoffrey Hartman, "Inscriptions and Romantic Nature Poetry," *The Unremarkable Wordsworth* (Minneapolis: University of Minnesota Press, 1987), 31–46; Marjorie Levinson, *Wordsworth's Great Period Poems* (Cambridge: Cambridge University Press, 1986), 14–57; Alastair Fowler, *Kinds of Literature* (Cambridge, Mass.: Harvard University Press, 1982), especially 92–98, 130–48. Mixed categories of titles, such as "layered," "ironic," "visual," "reader-Oriented," "self-negating" are illustrated almost exclusively by contemporary poems in the article on titles in *The Longman Dictionary of Poetic Terms*, ed. Jack Myers and Michael Simms (New York: Longman, 1989), 308–20.

6. Gérard Genette, "Structure and Functions of the Title in Literature," trans.

Bernard Crampé, *Critical Inquiry* 14 (1988): 692–93n1. The essays on the list that give some attention to titles of poems in English are Harry Levin, "The Title as a Literary Genre," *Modern Language Review* 72 (1977): xxiii–xxxvi; E. A. Levenston, "The Significance of the Title in Lyric Poetry," *Hebrew University Studies in Literature* 6 (1978): 63–87.

7. Jacques Derrida, "Title (to be specified)," trans. Tom Conley, *Sub-Stance* 31 (1981): 5–22; Hazard Adams, "Titles, Titling, and Entitlement To," *Journal of Aesthetics and Art Criticism* 46 (1987): 7–21; John Fisher, "Entitling," *Critical Inquiry* 11 (1984): 286–98; Steven Kellman, "Dropping Names: The Poetics of Titling," *Criticism* 17 (1975): 152–67; Jerrold Levinson, "Titles," *Journal of Aesthetics and Art Criticism* 44 (1985): 29–39.

8. John Hollander, "'Haddocks' Eyes': A Note on the Theory of Titles," *Vision and Resonance*, 2nd ed. (New Haven, Conn.: Yale University Press, 1985), 219–20.

Chapter 1

1. H. S. Bennett, *English Books and Readers, 1475–1557*, 2nd ed. (Cambridge: Cambridge University Press, 1969), 212.

2. For a parallel discussion of these issues as reflected in the titles assigned in Tottel's miscellany, see Anne Ferry, *The "Inward" Language* (Chicago: University of Chicago Press, 1983), 16–22.

3. Robert Herrick, *Hesperides: Or, The Works Both Humane & Divine of Robert Herrick, Esq.* (London, 1648), 398.

4. See the editor's note in Robert Herrick, *The Poetical Works of Robert Herrick*, ed. L. C. Martin (Oxford: Clarendon Press, 1956), 487–88n.

5. Paula Loscocco has pointed out to me similar claims on the title pages of printed volumes of poems by Edmund Waller (1645), Abraham Cowley (1647), Sir John Suckling (1648), but none earlier. From Stephen Orgel I have learned that this kind of claim is sometimes made earlier on the printed title pages of plays.

6. John Milton, *The Poetical Works of John Milton*, ed. Thomas Newton (London, 1761), 3:531; Dayton Haskin, *Milton's Burden of Interpretation* (Philadelphia: University of Pennsylvania Press, 1994), 98.

7. W. B. Yeats, *The Poetical Works of William B. Yeats* (New York: Macmillan, 1906).

8. W. B. Yeats, *The Wind Among the Reeds* (London: Elkin Matthews, 1899), 73–74.

9. Ibid., 94–95; William Blake, *The Writings of William Blake*, ed. Geoffrey Keynes (London: Nonesuch Press, 1925), 2:246.

10. Yeats, *The Wind Among the Reeds*, 101–2.

11. W. B. Yeats, *The Autobiography of William Butler Yeats* (New York: Macmillan, 1953), 52–53.

12. Ibid., 53.

13. W. B. Yeats, *The Letters of W. B. Yeats*, ed. Allan Wade (London: Rupert Hart-Davis, 1954), 583.

14. Elizabeth Sergeant, *Robert Frost: The Trial by Existence* (New York: Holt, Rinehart and Winston, 1960), 97.

15. Robert Frost, *Selected Letters of Robert Frost*, ed. Lawrance Thompson (New York: Holt, Rinehart and Winston, 1964), 85.

16. Louis Mertins, *Robert Frost: Life and Talks-Walking* (Norman: University of Oklahoma Press, 1965), 106; William Evans, *Robert Frost and Sidney Cox* (Hanover, N.H.: University Press of New England, 1981), 56.

17. Robert Frost, *A Boy's Will* (London: David Nutt, 1913).

18. Sergeant, *Robert Frost*, 97.

19. Lawrance Thompson, *Robert Frost: The Early Years, 1874–1915* (New York: Holt, Rinehart and Winston, 1966), 409–10.

20. Mertins, *Robert Frost*, 106–7.

21. Thompson, *Robert Frost*, 397.

22. Richard Poirier, *Robert Frost: The Work of Knowing* (New York: Oxford University Press, 1977), 33.

23. Henry Wadsworth Longfellow, *The Complete Poetical Works of Henry Wadsworth Longfellow*, ed. H. E. Scudder (Boston: Houghton Mifflin, 1893), 194.

24. Edmund Spenser, *The Minor Poems*, ed. Charles Osgood and Henry Lotspeich, in *The Works of Edmund Spenser*, ed. Edwin Greenlaw et al. (Baltimore, Md.: Johns Hopkins University Press, 1943), 1: 5, 7, 15, 17; John Milton, *Poems of John Milton*, type-facsimile (Oxford: Clarendon Press, 1924), 102, 65.

25. Frost, *Selected Letters*, 73; Sergeant, *Robert Frost*, 97; Mertins, *Robert Frost*, 106.

26. Frost, *Selected Letters*, 94.

27. Sergeant, *Robert Frost*, 423; Evans, *Robert Frost*, 56.

28. Sergeant, *Robert Frost*, 118.   29. Frost, *Selected Letters*, 111.

30. Evans, *Robert Frost*, 103.   31. Frost, *Selected Letters*, 89.

32. Thompson, *Robert Frost*, 561n19; Sergeant, *Robert Frost*, 126.

33. Robert Frost, *North of Boston* (London: David Nutt, 1914), 10.

34. Evans, *Robert Frost*, 11; Milton, *Poems*, 65.

35. Milton's uses of Virgil's *pascua* and *pascentis*, shown to me by Marlene Gast, are discussed in her unpublished dissertation, "Wordsworth and Milton: Varieties of Connection" (Boston College Department of English, 1985), 86–87. We had many talks about "Lycidas" in which we taught each other to see Milton's transformations of pastoral in the language of the closing lines.

36. Florence Emily Hardy, *The Later Years of Thomas Hardy, 1892–1928* (New York: Macmillan, 1930), 196.

37. Thomas Hardy, "Preface," *Poems of the Past and the Present* (London: Macmillan, 1912), ix.

38. Thomas Hardy, "Preface," *Time's Laughingstocks and Other Verses* (London: Macmillan, 1909), v.

39. Thomas Hardy, *Thomas Hardy's Personal Writings*, ed. Harold Orel (Lawrence: University of Kansas Press, 1966), 245–46n22.

40. Dennis Taylor, *Hardy's Poetry, 1860–1928* (London: Macmillan, 1981), xiv.

41. Thomas Hardy, "Apology," *Late Lyrics and Earlier with Many Other Verses* (London: Macmillan, 1922), xiii.

42. Robert Pinsky, *The Situation of Poetry* (Princeton, N.J.: Princeton University Press, 1976), 30.

43. Thomas Hardy, *Human Shows, Far Phantasies, Songs, and Trifles* (London: Macmillan, 1925), 207.

44. T. Hardy, *Time's Laughingstocks*, 87–88.

45. F. Hardy, *Later Years of Thomas Hardy*, 218.

46. Ibid., 26.

47. Thomas Hardy, *Moments of Vision and Miscellaneous Verses* (London: Macmillan, 1917), 167; Pinsky, *Situation of Poetry*, 30.

48. T. Hardy, *Late Lyrics and Earlier*, 177.

49. T. Hardy, *Moments of Vision*, 139.

50. Thomas Hardy, *The Variorum Edition of the Complete Poems of Thomas Hardy*, ed. James Gibson (New York: Macmillan, 1979), 886n.

51. Thomas Hardy, *Winter Words in Various Moods and Metres* (London: Macmillan, 1928), 113–14.

52. F. Hardy, *Later Years of Thomas Hardy*, 209.

53. Ezra Pound, *A Lume Spento and Other Poems* (New York: New Directions, 1965), 53.

54. Frank Bidart, *Golden State* (New York: George Braziller, 1973), 8.

55. Frank Bidart, "An Interview—With Mark Haliday (1983)," *In the Western Night: Collected Poems 1965–90* (New York: Farrar, Straus and Giroux, 1990), 238.

56. Ibid., 236.

57. Robert Lowell, *Imitations* (New York: Farrar, Straus and Cudahy, 1961), 99.

58. David Kalstone, *Five Temperaments* (New York: Oxford University Press, 1977), 175.

59. John Ashbery, *Self-Portrait in a Convex Mirror* (New York: Viking Press, 1975), 68–83.

60. John Ashbery, *Reported Sightings*, ed. David Berman (Cambridge, Mass.: Harvard University Press, 1991), 32.

61. John Bayley, "Richly Flows Contingency," *New York Review of Books* 38 (Aug. 15, 1991): 3.

Chapter 2

1. Richard Helgerson, *Self-Crowned Laureates* (Berkeley: University of California Press, 1983).

2. Ben Jonson, *Epigrammes*, in *Epigrams, The Forest, Underwoods* (New York: Facsimile Text Society, 1936), 769. All quotations from Jonson's poems are from this facsimile edition.

3. Martial uses the term in the introduction to the first book of his epigrams.

4. Jonson, *Epigrammes*, 771.

5. Jonson, *The Forrest*, 819. Consideration of the title led to a somewhat different perspective on this poem than in an earlier discussion in Anne Ferry, *All in War with Time* (Cambridge, Mass.: Harvard University Press, 1975), 63–68.

6. Helgerson, *Self-Crowned Laureates*, 110.

7. William Habington, *The Poems of William Habington*, ed. Kenneth Allott (Liverpool: University of Liverpool Press, 1948), 5.

8. Patrick Kavanagh, *The Complete Poems of Patrick Kavanagh*, ed. Peter Kavanagh (New York: Peter Kavanagh Hand Press, 1972), 8; Christina Rossetti, *The Poetical Works of Christina Rossetti*, ed. William Michael Rossetti (London: Macmillan, 1906), 251.

9. John Haffenden, ed., *W. H. Auden: The Critical Heritage* (London: Routledge and Kegan Paul, 1983), 167.

10. Edward Mendelson, "Editor's Preface," W. H. Auden, *Collected Poems* (New York: Random House, 1976), 14.

11. Auden, "Foreword (1965)," ibid., 15–16.

12. W. H. Auden, *The Dyer's Hand* (New York: Random House, 1962), 38.

13. W. H. Auden, *The Collected Poetry of W. H. Auden* (New York: Random House, 1945), 135–36.

14. Auden, *Dyer's Hand*, 342–43.

15. Haffenden, *Auden: The Critical Heritage*, 167, 113.

16. Auden, *Collected Poetry*, 39–41. The original title does something like the work of the parodic context in which the poem was originally published, a scene from *The Dog Beneath the Skin* where the Vicar of Pressan Ambo directs Alan Norman on a quest invoked by a chorus that recites the poem.

17. Auden, *Collected Poetry*, 136–40.

18. Edward Mendelson, *Early Auden* (New York: Viking Press, 1981), 115n.

19. Richard Poirier, "Robert Frost," *Poets at Work*, ed. George Plimpton (New York: Viking Press, 1989), 67.

20. Auden, *Collected Poetry*, 72.

21. Christopher Isherwood, *Goodbye to Berlin* (Harmondsworth: Penguin Books, 1958), 1. Auden and Isherwood collaborated on *The Dog Beneath the Skin*.

22. Auden, *Collected Poems*, 630–31.

23. John Berryman, *Love & Fame* (New York: Farrar, Straus and Giroux, 1970), 77, 7.

24. Peter Stilt, "John Ashbery," *Poets at Work*, ed. George Plimpton (New York: Viking Press, 1989), 393.

25. John Ashbery, "The Poetic Medium of W. H. Auden" (unpublished Harvard College honors thesis, 1949), 21, 31, 32.

26. Ibid., 20.

27. John Ashbery, *April Galleons* (New York: Viking Press, 1987), 20–21.

28. John Ashbery, "Introduction," Frank O'Hara, *The Collected Poems of Frank O'Hara*, ed. Donald Allen (New York: Alfred Knopf, 1971), viii; O'Hara, "Larry Rivers: A Memoir," ibid., 512.

29. O'Hara, *Collected Poems*, 481–82.

30. Ibid., 499.

31. Ibid.

32. Ashbery, "Introduction," ibid., vii.

33. O'Hara, *Collected Poems*, 261–62.

34. Barry Miles, *Ginsberg: A Biography* (New York: Simon and Schuster, 1989), 391.

35. Allen Ginsberg, *Composed on the Tongue* (Bolinas, Calif.: Grey Fox Press, 1980), 76.

36. Ibid., 112.

37. Ibid., 111.

38. Ibid., 147.

39. Allen Ginsberg, *White Shroud: Poems 1980–1985* (New York: Harper and Row, 1986), 40.

40. Ibid., 84–85.

41. Ginsberg, *Composed on the Tongue*, 112–13.

42. A description of how "this poet" spends his lunch hours is given on the back cover of Frank O'Hara, *Lunch Poems* (San Francisco: City Lights Books, 1964).

Chapter 3

1. Sir Philip Sidney, "An Apologie for Poetrie," *Elizabethan Critical Essays*, ed. G. G. Smith (Oxford: Clarendon Press, 1904), 1: 166.

2. Alfred Tennyson, *Poems, Chiefly Lyrical* (London, 1830), 31–42.

3. Christopher Ricks, *Tennyson* (New York: Collier Books, 1972), 40.

4. Richard Crashaw, *Steps to the Temple. Sacred Poems, With other Delights of the Muses* (London, 1646), 43–47.

5. John Jump, ed., *Tennyson: The Critical Heritage* (London: Routledge and Kegan Paul, 1967), 46.

6. Alfred Tennyson, *The Poetic and Dramatic Works of Alfred Lord Tennyson*, ed. W. J. Rolfe (Boston: Houghton Mifflin, 1898), 4n.

7. William Cartwright, *Poems* [1651], *The Plays and Poems of William Cartwright*, ed. G. Blakemore Evans (Madison: University of Wisconsin Press, 1951), 461–62.

8. T. S. Eliot, *Prufrock and Other Observations* (London: The Egoist, 1917), 27–30.

9. Christopher Ricks, *T. S. Eliot and Prejudice* (Berkeley: University of California Press, 1988), 2. The discussion here is clearly indebted to Ricks's in many respects.

10. Ibid., 4; Hugh Kenner, *The Invisible Poet: T. S. Eliot* (New York: McDowell, Obolensky, 1959), 3.

11. A direct connection between Tennyson's choice of "Waterproof" and a description of "Mr. Bumble" in *Oliver Twist* has been pointed out by Paul Turner, cited by Christopher Ricks, ed., in Alfred Tennyson, *The Poems of Tennyson* (Berkeley: University of California Press, 1987), 2: 96n.

12. Another contribution might be the name of "Will Honeycomb" for the man-about-town in the club created by Joseph Addison and Richard Steele in *The Spectator*.

13. Pound makes this distinction in a letter of 1913. See T. S. Eliot, *The Letters of T. S. Eliot*, ed. Valerie Eliot (London: Harcourt Brace Jovanovich, 1988), 1: 101.

14. Samuel French Morse, "Wallace Stevens, Bergson, Pater" and Robert

Buttel, "Wallace Stevens at Harvard: Some Origins of His Theme and Style," in *The Act of the Mind*, ed. Roy Harvey Pearce and J. Hillis Miller (Baltimore, Md.: Johns Hopkins University Press, 1965), 58n2, 31n1.

15. Alexander Pope, "A Discourse on Pastoral Poetry," *Pastoral Poetry and an Essay on Criticism*, ed. E. Audra and Aubrey Williams (London: Methuen, 1961), 29.

16. Ambrose Philips, "Preface," *Pastorals* (Menston: Scolar Press, 1973).

17. *Englands Helicon*, ed. Hyder Rollins (Cambridge, Mass.: Harvard University Press, 1935), 1: 184–85.

18. Andrew Marvell, *The Poems and Letters of Andrew Marvell*, ed. H. M. Margoliouth, 3rd ed., rev. Pierre Legouis and E. E. Duncan-Jones (Oxford: Clarendon Press, 1971), 1: 44–47.

19. I have also not found any precedents among titles for Italian poems.

20. John Milton, *Poems of John Milton*, type-facsimile (Oxford: Clarendon Press, 1924), 30–36.

21. The title phrase "A Poem Nearly Anonymous" was invented for an essay, "Lycidas," by John Crowe Ransom. See *The World's Body* (New York: Charles Scribner's, 1938), 1–28.

22. Milton, *Poems*, 37–44.

23. William Wordsworth, *The Poetical Works of William Wordsworth* (London, 1849), 1: 282.

24. W. B. Yeats, *Words For Music Perhaps and Other Poems* (Dublin: Cuala Press, 1932), 24.

25. Hallam Tennyson, *Alfred Lord Tennyson: A Memoir* (London: Macmillan, 1906), 696; George Marshall, *A Tennyson Handbook* (New York: Twayne, 1963), 95.

26. Robert Browning, *Dramatic Lyrics* (London, 1842), 3: 2.

27. Robert Browning, *Men and Women* (Boston, 1856), 343–51.

28. Robert Langbaum, *The Poetry of Experience* (New York: W. W. Norton, 1957), 91.

29. H. Tennyson, *A Memoir*, 427.

30. Browning, *Men and Women*, 29.

31. Boyd Litzinger and Donald Smalley, eds., *Browning: The Critical Heritage* (London: Routledge and Kegan Paul, 1970), 177.

32. Ezra Pound, *The Letters of Ezra Pound*, ed. D. D. Paige (London: Faber and Faber, 1951), 36.

33. Ezra Pound, *A Lume Spento and Other Poems* (New York: New Directions, 1965), 28.

34. Pound, *Letters*, 294.

35. Donald Davie, *Ezra Pound* (London: Routledge and Kegan Paul, 1965), 23.

36. Eric Homberger, ed., *Ezra Pound: The Critical Heritage* (London: Routledge and Kegan Paul, 1972), 228.

37. Pound, *A Lume Spento*, 52.   38. Ibid., 38–40.

39. Ibid., 17–19.   40. Ibid., 56.

41. Ezra Pound, *Personae of Ezra Pound* (New York: New Directions, 1971), 32.

42. Pound, *Letters*, 36.

43. George Starbuck, "'The Work!' A Conversation with Elizabeth Bishop," *Elizabeth Bishop and Her Art*, ed. Lloyd Schwartz and Sybil Estess (Ann Arbor: University of Michigan Press, 1983), 319.

44. Richard Steele, "Steele's Account of Selkirk," in Daniel Defoe, *Romances and Narratives*, ed. George Aitken (New York: AMS Press, 1974), 3: 324.

45. John Howell, "Introduction," *The Life and Adventures of Alexander Selkirk* (Edinburgh, 1829), 8; letter dated Feb. 6, 1787, printed in *Gentlemans Magazine* 58 (1788): 206.

46. Steele, "Account of Selkirk," 328.

47. Daniel Defoe, *Robinson Crusoe and Other Writings*, ed. James Sutherland (New York: New York University Press, 1977), 5. All quotations of this work are taken from this edition.

48. Elizabeth Bishop, *Geography III* (New York: Farrar, Straus and Giroux, 1976), 36–39. A different point about "Crusoe in England" is made by Robert Hemenway, "Afterword" to David Kalstone, *Becoming a Poet* (New York: Farrar, Straus and Giroux, 1989), 255, by citing the second and third of these lines from "Poem" but omitting the question "Which is which?"

49. Bishop, *Geography III*, 9–18.

50. Defoe, *Robinson Crusoe*, 59.

51. William Cowper, *Poems* (London, 1782), 305–8.

52. Defoe, *Robinson Crusoe*, 134, 120, 83.

53. Quoted by Bonnie Costello, *Elizabeth Bishop: Questions of Mastery* (Cambridge, Mass.: Harvard University Press, 1991), 208.

54. D. H. Lawrence, *Look! We Have Come Through! The Complete Poems of D. H. Lawrence*, ed. Vivian de Sola Pinto and Warren Roberts (Harmondsworth: Penguin Books, 1978), 250.

55. Thomas Hardy, *Moments of Vision and Miscellaneous Verses* (London: Macmillan, 1917), 164–65.

56. Ibid., 217–18.

57. Joan Richardson, *Wallace Stevens: The Early Years, 1879–1923* (New York: William Morrow, 1986), 235. Elizabeth Bishop recognizes the affinity among the differences between Hardy and Stevens in a letter of 1965: "Re-reading Hardy I was struck by his titles—just looking them over in the index—and thought what wonderful titles a lot of them would have made for Wallace Stevens, too." Titles such as "'Voices from Things Growing in a Churchyard' or 'On One Who Lived & Died Where He Was Born' could perfectly well be Wallace Stevens titles—and what would *he* have done with them?" Elizabeth Bishop, *One Art*, ed. Robert Giroux (New York: Farrar, Straus and Giroux, 1994), 442.

58. Thomas Hardy, *Time's Laughingstocks and Other Verses* (London: Macmillan, 1922), 45–46.

59. Wallace Stevens, *Harmonium* (New York: Alfred Knopf, 1931), 128.

60. The other two poems are "Banal Sojourn" in *Harmonium* and "Poems of Our Climate" in *Parts of a World* (New York: Alfred Knopf, 1945), 8–9.

61. Otto Jespersen, *Essentials of English Grammar* (London: George Allen and Unwin, 1933), 150–51.

62. Stevens, *Harmonium*, 12.
63. Stevens, *Parts of a World*, 74–75, 22–24.
64. Wallace Stevens, *Transport to Summer* (New York: Alfred Knopf, 1947), 87.
65. John Ashbery, *Self-Portrait in a Convex Mirror* (New York: Viking Press, 1975), 8.

Chapter 4

1. Ben Jonson, *Epigrammes*, in *Epigrams, The Forest, Underwoods* (New York: Facsimile Text Society, 1936), 769.
2. Both these tendencies in criticism at large and with respect to Jonson in particular are exhibited and discussed in representative ways in *Lyric Poetry: Beyond New Criticism*, ed. Chaviva Hošek and Patricia Parker (Ithaca, N.Y.: Cornell University Press, 1985).
3. Jonson, *Epigrammes*, 773–74.
4. Robert Herrick, *Hesperides: Or, The Works Both Humane & Divine of Robert Herrick, Esq.* (London, 1648), 3, 32, 33.
5. Percy Bysshe Shelley, *The Complete Works of Percy Bysshe Shelley*, ed. Thomas Hutchinson (London: Oxford University Press, 1948), 550.
6. Ibid., 625.
7. Raymond Williams, *Culture and Society* (New York: Harper and Row, 1958), 33–34.
8. John Gould Fletcher, *Fire and Wine* (London: Grant Richards, 1913), 56; Louis MacNeice, *The Collected Poems of Louis MacNeice*, ed. E. R. Dodds (London: Faber and Faber, 1966), 443.
9. MacNeice, *Collected Poems*, 443.
10. Robert Graves, *New Collected Poems* (New York: Doubleday, 1977), 43.
11. John Ashbery, *A Wave* (New York: Penguin Books, 1985), 13.
12. Walt Whitman, *Leaves of Grass* (Philadelphia, Pa., 1891–92), 426.
13. Ibid., 17–18.
14. Ibid., 427.
15. Ibid., 186.
16. Cited by Randall Jarrell, *Poetry and the Age* (New York: Octagon Press, 1982), 114.
17. Frank O'Hara, "Personism: A Manifesto," *The Collected Poems of Frank O'Hara*, ed. Donald Allen (New York: Alfred Knopf, 1971), 498.
18. W. H. Auden, *The Collected Poetry of W. H. Auden* (New York: Random House, 1945), 42–43.
19. Mark Strand, *The Late Hour* (New York: Atheneum, 1978), 23.
20. O'Hara, *Collected Poems*, 545.
21. Roman Jakobson, "Shifters, Verbal Categories, and the Russian Verb," *Russian Language Project* (Cambridge, Mass.: Harvard University Press, 1957), 2.
22. O'Hara, *Collected Poems*, 342–43.
23. Richard Helgerson, *Self-Crowned Laureates* (Berkeley: University of California Press, 1983), 101–84.

24. John Stuart Mill, "Thoughts On Poetry and Its Varieties," *Dissertations and Discussions* (London, 1859), 1: 71.

25. Northrop Frye, *Anatomy of Criticism* (Princeton, N.J.: Princeton University Press, 1957), 249–50.

26. Alexander Pope, *Minor Poems*, ed. Norman Ault and John Butt (London: Methuen, 1954), 244n.

27. William Wordsworth, *The Poetical Works of William Wordsworth* (London, 1849), 1: 221.

28. Ibid., 1: 217.

29. Ibid., 2: 305.

30. J. B. Leishman, *The Art of Marvell's Poetry*, 2nd ed. (n.p.: Minerva Press, 1968), 70.

31. For evidence of the circulation of Marvell's poems, see the catalogue of manuscripts compiled by Hilton Kelliher, *Andrew Marvell, Poet & Politician* (London: British Library, 1978). Mary Marvell, "To the Reader," in Andrew Marvell, *Miscellaneous Poems*, 1681.

32. The OED cites uses of the adjective by Spenser and by Shakespeare in his narrative poems; a poem of Drayton's is titled "To His Coy Love, A Canzonet"; *Witts Recreation* of 1640 includes "On a coy woman"; Marvell's poem alludes to the line "Then be not coy, but use your time" in Herrick's persuasion "To the Virgins, to make much of Time."

33. Park Honan, *Matthew Arnold* (New York: McGraw-Hill, 1981), 153, 164.

34. Matthew Arnold, *Empedocles on Etna and Other Poems* (London, 1852), 96–97.

35. Donald Davie, "On Sincerity from Wordsworth to Ginsberg," *Encounter* 31 (1968): 62.

36. Robert Lowell, "A Conversation with Ian Hamilton," *Collected Prose*, ed. Robert Giroux (New York: Farrar, Straus and Giroux, 1987), 286.

37. Robert Lowell, "An Interview with Frederick Seidel, 1961," ibid., 235–66.

38. Ian Hamilton, *Robert Lowell: A Biography* (New York: Random House, 1982), 240–49.

39. Robert Lowell, *History* (New York: Farrar, Straus and Giroux, 1973), 138.

40. Lowell, "Interview with Seidel," 246–47.

41. Jonathan Culler, *The Pursuit of Signs* (Ithaca, N.Y.: Cornell University Press, 1981), 135–38.

42. Ibid., 143.

43. John Milton, "Of Education. To Master Samuel Hartlib," ed. Donald Dorian, in *Complete Prose Works of John Milton*, ed. Douglas Bush et al. (New Haven, Conn.: Yale University Press, 1959), 2: 404.

44. Roy Fuller, *New and Collected Poems, 1934–84* (London: Secker and Warburg, 1985), 133.

45. O'Hara, *Collected Poems*, 175.

46. Herrick, *Hesperides*, 204.

47. William Wordsworth, *The Letters of William and Dorothy Wordsworth*, ed. Ernest de Selincourt, 2nd ed., rev. Mary Moorman (Oxford: Clarendon Press, 1969), 2: 194.

48. This and all subsequent dictionary definitions, unless otherwise specified, are taken from *Webster's New International Dictionary of the English Language,* 2nd ed.

49. William Wordsworth, *Poems, in Two Volumes* (London, 1807), 2: 57–59.

50. Ibid., 2: 60–61.

51. David Ferry, *The Limits of Mortality* (Middletown, Conn.: Wesleyan University Press, 1959), 17–19, 33–36.

52. William Carlos Williams, *Pictures from Brueghel and Other Poems* (Norfolk, Conn.: New Directions, 1962), 41.

53. Marianne Moore, *Tell Me, Tell Me: Granite, Steel, and Other Topics* (New York: Viking Press, 1966), 17.

54. Ibid., 43–44.

55. Wallace Stevens, *Opus Posthumous* (New York: Alfred Knopf, 1957), 165; O'Hara, *Collected Poems,* 545.

56. Louis Martz, "Manuscripts of Wallace Stevens," *Yale University Library Gazette* 54 (1979): 53–54.

57. Wallace Stevens, *Harmonium* (New York: Alfred Knopf, 1931), 117.

Chapter 5

1. John Hollander, *Vision and Resonance,* 2nd ed. (New Haven, Conn.: Yale University Press, 1985), 218–20.

2. Wordsworth's changes in the presentation of the "Ode" are discussed by: Stuart Curran, "Multum in Parvo: Wordsworth's *Poems, in Two Volumes* of 1807," *Poems in Their Place,* ed. Neil Fraistat (Chapel Hill: University of North Carolina Press, 1986), 235–36; Peter Manning, "Wordsworth's Intimations Ode and His Epigraphs," *JEGP* 82 (1983): 526–40.

3. Donald Reiman, ed., *The Romantics Reviewed,* part A (New York: Garland Press, 1972), 2: 845.

4. Hollander, *Vision and Resonance,* 213, 218.

5. John Dryden, "Discourse concerning the Original and Progress of Satire," ed. A. B. Chambers and William Frost, in *The Works of John Dryden,* ed. H. T. Swedenberg et al. (Berkeley: University of California Press, 1974), 4: 88.

6. John Dryden, "Annus Mirabilis," *Works of John Dryden,* ed. Edward Hooker and H. T. Swedenberg (1956), 1: 50.

7. Michael Drayton, *The Works of Michael Drayton,* ed. William Hebel (Oxford: Basil Blackwell, 1932), 2: 130, 382, 346.

8. Ibid., 2: 346.

9. John Dryden, "Absalom and Achitophel," *Works of John Dryden,* ed. H. T. Swedenberg (1977), 2: 3–5.

10. John Dryden, "Religio Laici," ibid., 2: 98.

11. These substituted titles are cited by Helen Vendler, *The Poetry of George Herbert* (Cambridge, Mass.: Harvard University Press, 1975), 126–28.

12. Alexander Pope, *Minor Poems,* ed. Norman Ault and John Butt (London: Methuen, 1954), 376. This epitaph and its title are discussed by Joshua Scodel, "'Your Distance Keep': Pope's Epitaphic Stance," *ELH* 55 (1988): 615–41. For

discussion of its historical context, see Howard Weinbrot, *Augustus Caesar in "Augustan England"* (Princeton, N.J.: Princeton University Press, 1978), pp. 120–49.

13. Samuel Johnson, "The Criticism upon Pope's *Epitaphs*," *Lives of the English Poets* (London: Oxford University Press, 1961), 333.

14. Alexander Pope, *The Correspondence of Alexander Pope*, ed. George Sherburn (Oxford: Clarendon Press, 1956), 4: 13.

15. Samuel Johnson, "An Essay on Epitaphs," *The Gentleman's Magazine: And Historical Chronicle* 10 (1740): 593.

16. William Collins, *Odes on several Descriptive and Allegoric Subjects* (London, 1747, but in fact published Dec. 1746), 19.

17. Ibid., 32–35. The title of the volume pointedly announces that the *Odes* in it are *on . . . Subjects*, not *occasions*.

18. Richard Wendorf and Charles Ryskamp, "Commentary," in William Collins, *The Works of William Collins* (Oxford: Clarendon Press, 1979), 136.

19. Joseph Addison, *The Spectator*, ed. Donald Bond (Oxford: Clarendon Press, 1965), 2: 485–86.

20. Ralph Johnson, *The Scholars Guide From the Accidence to the University* (London, 1665), 16.

21. Sir Francis Bacon, ms. dedication to the Prince of Wales, *The Essayes or Counsels, Civill and Morall*, ed. Michael Kiernan (Cambridge, Mass.: Harvard University Press, 1985), 317.

22. Drayton, *Works*, 4: v.

23. Johnson, *Scholars Guide*, 13.

24. "The Publishers to the Author," *Poems, Elegies, Paradoxes, and Sonnets* (London, 1657), where Henry King is identified as the author of the contents although no name appears on the the title page of the volume.

25. Pope, *Correspondence*, 1: 109–10.

26. Sir Francis Bacon, "To M. Anthony Bacon his deare Brother," *Essayes* (London, 1597); ms. dedication to the Prince of Wales, *Essayes or Counsels*, 317.

27. Sir Francis Bacon, *The Essayes or Covnsels, Civill and Morall*, newly enlarged (London, 1625).

28. John Locke, "The Epistle to the Reader," *An Essay Concerning Humane Understanding* (London, 1790). There is no author's name on the title page but "The Epistle Dedicatory" is signed JOHN LOCKE.

29. Steven Zwicker, "Politics and Literary Practice in the Restoration," *Renaissance Genres*, ed. Barbara Lewalski (Cambridge, Mass.: Harvard University Press, 1986), 270.

30. Locke, "Epistle to the Reader."

31. Dryden, *Works of John Dryden*, 2: 173.

32. Joseph Warton, *Odes on Various Subjects*, 2nd ed. (London, 1747).

33. Geoffrey Hartman, "Inscriptions and Romantic Nature Poetry," *The Unremarkable Wordsworth* (Minneapolis: University of Minnesota Press), 31.

34. Robert Mayo, "The Contemporaneity of the *Lyrical Ballads*," *PMLA* 69 (1954): 486–522.

35. Thomas Gray, *The Poems of Mr. Gray*, ed. W. Mason (York, 1775), 108.

36. William Wordsworth, *Lyrical Ballads with a Few Other Poems* (London, 1798), 201–10.

37. William Wordsworth, *Lyrical Ballads with Other Poems* (London, 1800), 1: notes.

38. Alexander Pope, *Pastoral Poetry and an Essay on Criticism*, ed. E. Audra and Aubrey Williams (London: Methuen, 1961), 63.

39. Christopher Ricks, "William Wordsworth 1: 'A Pure Organic Pleasure From the Lines,'" *The Force of Poetry* (Oxford: Clarendon Press, 1984), 89–116.

40. Reiman, *Romantics Reviewed*, 2:656.

41. William Wordsworth, *The Letters of William and Dorothy Wordsworth*, ed. Ernest de Selincourt, 2nd ed., rev. Mary Moorman (Oxford: Clarendon Press, 1969), 3:284.

42. Samuel Taylor Coleridge, "Preface," *Poems on Various Subjects* (London, 1796), ix: "Of the following Poems a considerable number are styled 'Effusions,' in defiance of Churchill's line 'Effusion on Effusion *pour* away.'"

43. On the subjects of subtitles and in particular the generic title *fragment*, see: Stuart Curran, *Poetic Form and British Romanticism* (New York: Oxford University Press, 1986); Marjorie Levinson, *The Romantic Fragment Poem* (Chapel Hill: University of North Carolina Press, 1986). Also relevant is the more general discussion of fragmentation in Thomas McFarland, *Romanticism and the Forms of Ruin* (Princeton, N.J.: Princeton University Press, 1981).

44. Titles reflecting the notion of the "poem-as-notebook" are discussed by Michael Davidson, "Postmodern Poetry and the Material Text," *Genre* 20 (1987): 307–27.

45. Wallace Stevens, *The Collected Poems of Wallace Stevens* (New York: Alfred Knopf, 1955), 531–32.

46. Seamus Heaney, *The Haw Lantern* (New York: Farrar, Straus and Giroux, 1987), 16.

47. William Carlos Williams, *The Selected Letters of William Carlos Williams*, ed. John Thirwall (New York: McDowell, Obolensky, 1957), 40, and *Collected Poems of William Carlos Williams*, ed. A. Walton Litz and Christopher MacGowan (New York: New Directions, 1986), 1:480. Williams said his friend Alfred Kreymborg's "surmise" that the Spanish words were a coded dedication of the volume to him, "Al K.," was "a proper one." See *The Autobiography of William Carlos Williams* (New York: Random House, 1951), 157.

48. William Carlos Williams, *A Book of Poems: Al Que Quiere!* (Boston: Four Seas Company, 1917), 14–15.

49. Williams, *Selected Letters*, 116.

50. Henry Vaughan, *The Works of Henry Vaughan*, ed. L. C. Martin, 2nd ed. (Oxford: Clarendon Press, 1957), 10–12.

51. John Dennis, *The Critical Works of John Dennis*, ed. Edward Hooker (Baltimore, Md.: Johns Hopkins University Press, 1943), 2: 135, 361.

52. Elisha Coles, *An English Dictionary* (London, 1717).

53. Ephraim Chambers, *Cyclopedia: Or, An Universal Dictionary of Arts and Sciences* (London, 1728), 2:958.

54. T.S. Eliot, *The Letters of T.S. Eliot,* ed. Valerie Eliot (London: Harcourt Brace Jovanovich, 1988), 1: 141.

55. Jonathan Swift, *The Poems of Jonathan Swift,* ed. Harold Williams, 2nd ed. (Oxford: Clarendon Press, 1958), 2: 639–59.

56. T.S. Eliot, *Prufrock and Other Observations* (London: The Egoist, 1917), 27–30.

57. T.S. Eliot, *Selected Essays* (New York: Harcourt, Brace, 1932), 264–65.

58. Hugh Kenner, "The Urban Apocalypse," *Eliot in His Time,* ed. A. Walton Litz (Princeton, N.J.: Princeton University Press, 1973), 27.

59. Elizabeth Bishop, *Geography III* (New York: Farrar, Straus and Giroux, 1976), 38.

60. Elizabeth Bishop, *Questions of Travel* (New York: Farrar, Straus and Giroux, 1965), 80–81, and *One Art,* ed. Robert Giroux (New York: Farrar, Straus and Giroux, 1994), 380.

61. Elizabeth Bishop, *The Complete Poems, 1927–1979* (New York: Farrar, Straus and Giroux, 1983), 192.

Chapter 6

1. Ben Jonson, *Epigrammes,* in *Epigrams, The Forest, Underwoods* (New York: Facsimile Text Society, 1936), 789–90.

2. Different arguments are made about this epigram and its title, and also about the title of 22, by Mary Crane, "'His Owne Style': Voice and Writing in Jonson's Poems," *Criticism* 32 (1990): 41–43, 33–34. For an earlier discussion, see Anne Ferry, *All in War With Time* (Cambridge, Mass.: Harvard University Press, 1975), 142–48.

3. Jonson, *Epigrammes,* 774.

4. M.H. Abrams, *A Glossary of Literary Terms,* 5th ed. (New York: Holt, Rinehart and Winston, 1988), 123. For a wide-ranging discussion of prepositions, including *on,* see John Hollander, "Of 'of': The Romance of a Preposition," *Addressing Frank Kermode,* ed. Margaret Tudeau-Clayton and Martin Warner (Urbana: University of Illinois Press, 1991), 184–204.

5. Thom Gunn, *The Occasions of Poetry,* ed. Clive Wilmer (San Francisco: North Point Press, 1985), 106.

6. John Milton, *Poems of John Milton* [1645], type-facsimile (Oxford: Clarendon Press, 1924), 1–12.

7. Walter Jackson Bate, *John Keats* (Cambridge, Mass.: Harvard University Press, 1963), 84–86.

8. John Keats, *Poems* (London, 1817), 89.

9. Jonson's "Inviting a Friend to Svpper," *Epigrammes,* 799–800, is a rare if not unique early example of the expressive use of a present participle in the title of an occasional poem. It is his only omission of the traditional preposition *on* for this category of title in the volume.

10. William Wordsworth, *Lyrical Ballads with Other Poems* (London, 1800), 2: 132–35.

11. John Clare, *The Poems of John Clare*, ed. J. W. Tibble (London: J. M. Dent, 1935), 1: 540 and 2: 369, 88–89.

12. Ralph Waldo Emerson, *Poems* (London, 1847), 48.

13. Robert Frost, *Selected Letters of Robert Frost*, ed. Lawrance Thompson (New York: Holt, Rinehart and Winston, 1964), 83.

14. Robert Frost, *The Letters of Robert Frost to Louis Untermeyer* (New York: Holt, Rinehart and Winston, 1963), 163.

15. Robert Frost, *A Boy's Will* (London: David Nutt, 1913), 25.

16. Robert Frost, *North of Boston* (London: David Nutt, 1914), 11–13.

17. Frost, *Selected Letters*, 96.

18. Ibid., 344.

19. Robert Frost, *New Hampshire* (New York: Henry Holt, 1923), 87.

20. Richard Poirier, *Robert Frost: The Work of Knowing* (New York: Oxford University Press, 1977), 182.

21. Ibid.

22. Robert Frost, *A Witness Tree* (New York: Henry Holt, 1942), 23.

23. Frost's lesser self might be the poet Wade Van Dore, discussed by Poirier as the supposed model for "He" in the poem. See Poirier, *Robert Frost*, 161.

24. Philip Larkin, *The Less Deceived* (Hessle: Marvell Press, 1955), 28–29.

25. James Merrill, *The Inner Room* (New York: Alfred Knopf, 1988), 84–91. The quotation "the dying of the light" is from Dylan Thomas's "Do not go gentle into that good night."

26. Donald Sheehan, "An Interview with James Merrill," *Contemporary Literature* 9 (1968): 1–2.

27. Seamus Heaney, *Seeing Things* (New York: Farrar, Straus and Giroux, 1991), 18–20.

28. Charles Tomlinson, *American Scenes and Other Poems* (London: Oxford University Press, 1966), 13.

29. Charles Tomlinson, *Collected Poems* (Oxford: Oxford University Press, 1987).

30. A. R. Ammons, *Sumerian Vistas* (New York: W. W. Norton, 1987), 90.

31. Ibid., 113–14.

32. Anne Ferry, "Titles in George Herbert's 'little Book,'" *ELR* 23 (1993): 314–44.

33. This substitution is cited by Robert Ray, ed., "The Herbert Allusion Book," *Studies in Philology* 83 (1986): 33.

34. George Herbert, *The Temple. Sacred Poems and Private Ejaculations* (Cambridge, 1633), 87.

35. Ibid., 80.

36. Ibid., 31–32.

37. William Blake, *Songs Of Innocence and Of Experience*, Albion Facsimiles (London: Falcon Press, 1947). If the title is meant to recall Johnson's "London: A Poem," the intended effect can only be to point to the ontological distance between a satirical vision of the city in "Imitation" of Juvenal and the unmediated prophetic vision that is Blake's "London."

38. Robert Pinsky, *The Want Bone* (New York: Ecco Press, 1990), 53–54.

39. Thom Gunn, *The Man with Night Sweats* (New York: Farrar, Straus and Giroux, 1992), 65.

40. Sylvia Plath, *Ariel* (New York: Harper and Row, 1965), 49–51.

41. Herbert, *The Temple*, 147. The fullest discussions of multiple meanings in Herbert's titles are in John Mulder, *The Temple of the Mind* (New York: Pegasus, 1969), 73–77; Mary Ellen Rickey, *Utmost Art* (Lexington: University Press of Kentucky, 1966), 93–102, 116–19.

42. Blake, *Songs Of Innocence*.

43. Richard Wilbur, *The Mind-Reader* (New York: Harcourt, Brace, Jovanovich, 1976), 4–5.

44. Gwendolyn Brooks, *The Bean Eaters* (New York: Harper and Brothers, 1960), 68.

45. Adrienne Rich, *Snapshots of a Daughter-In-Law* (New York: Harper and Row, 1963), 68–69.

46. Philip Larkin, *High Windows* (New York: Farrar, Straus and Giroux, 1974), 17. For some discussion of this and other titles by Larkin, see Claude Rawson, "Larkin's Desolate Attics," *Raritan* 11 (1991): 25–47.

47. Reuben Brower, *The Fields of Light* (New York: Oxford University Press, 1951), 8.

48. Jonathan Culler, *The Pursuit of Signs* (Ithaca, N.Y.: Cornell University Press, 1981), 68–79.

49. Blake, *Songs Of Experience*.

Chapter 7

1. Philip Larkin, *The Less Deceived* (Hessle: Marvell Press, 1955), 42.

2. Thomas Hardy, *Poems of the Past and the Present* (London: Macmillan, 1912), 137–38.

3. Robert Browning, *Dramatic Romances and Lyrics* (London, 1897), 6–7.

4. William Pritchard, *Frost: A Literary Life Reconsidered* (New York: Oxford University Press, 1984), 189.

5. Frank Lentricchia, *Robert Frost: Modern Poetics and the Landscape of the Self* (Durham, N.C.: Duke University Press, 1975), 77.

6. Robert Frost, *West-Running Brook* (New York: Henry Holt, 1928), 27.

7. Elizabeth Sergeant, *Robert Frost: The Trial by Existence* (New York: Holt, Rinehart and Winston, 1960), 303.

8. William Wordsworth, *Lyrical Ballads with a Few Other Poems* (London, 1798), 110–14.

9. Samuel Taylor Coleridge, *Sibylline Leaves* (London, 1817), 89–93; John Hill, *A Coleridge Companion* (London: Macmillan, 1983), 32. The manuscript version is included in a letter to Southey of 1797, *Collected Letters of Samuel Taylor Coleridge*, ed. Earl Griggs (Oxford: Clarendon Press, 1956), 1: 334–36.

10. Reeve Parker, *Coleridge's Meditative Art* (Ithaca, N.Y.: Cornell University Press, 1975), 17–60.

11. Lamb's annoyed response to being called "gentle-hearted" suggests that he thought the evocations of him in the poem to be affectedly literary, making him

sound effete, sissyish. See his letters to Coleridge in August 1800, *The Letters of Charles and Mary Lamb*, ed. E. V. Lucas (New Haven, Conn.: Yale University Press, 1935), 1: 198, 203.

12. Robert Frost, *A Witness Tree* (New York: Henry Holt, 1942), 24.

13. Sir Walter Ralegh, "The Nimphs reply to the Sheepheard," *Englands Helicon*, ed. Hyder Rollins (Cambridge, Mass.: Harvard University Press, 1935), 1: 185; John Milton, *Poems of John Milton*, type-facsimile (Oxford: Clarendon Press, 1924), 59.

14. Frost, *A Witness Tree*, 16.

15. Reuben Brower, *The Poetry of Robert Frost* (New York: Oxford University Press, 1963), 32.

16. The suffix *-iad* in titles is discussed by Richmond Bond, "—IAD: A Progeny of the *Dunciad*," *PMLA* 44 (1929): 1099–105.

17. Edmund Spenser, *The Minor Poems*, ed. Charles Osgood and Henry Lotspeich, in *The Works of Edmund Spenser*, ed. Edwin Greenlaw et al. (Baltimore, Md.: Johns Hopkins University Press, 1943), 1: 240.

18. Neil Fraistat, *The Poem and the Book* (Chapel Hill: University of North Carolina Press, 1985), 197n3.

19. Thomas Gray, *Odes* (Dublin, 1757), 3–8.

20. Matthew Arnold, *New Poems* (London, 1867), 146.

21. These italicized lines are printed by themselves on the page preceding the table of contents, giving them the status of an epigraph.

22. Charles Tomlinson, *Notes from New York and Other Poems* (Oxford: Oxford University Press, 1984), 16; Walt Whitman, *Leaves of Grass* (Philadelphia, Pa., 1891–92), 129–33.

23. Reuben Brower, *Alexander Pope* (Oxford: Clarendon Press, 1959), 144.

24. T. S. Eliot, *Poems* (Richmond: The Hogarth Press, 1919).

25. Stevie Smith, *a good time was had by all* (London: Jonathan Cape, 1937), 30.

26. Elizabeth Bishop, "As We Like It," *Quarterly Review of Literature* 4 (1948): 129. Perhaps thinking of her own "The Fish," Bishop wonders if Moore's power of describing things with minute precision might come "simply from her gift of being able to give herself up entirely to the object under contemplation, to feel in all sincerity how it is to be *it*" (131).

27. Marianne Moore, *Poems* (London: Egoist Press, 1921), 14–15.

28. Elizabeth Bishop, *North & South* (Boston: Houghton Mifflin, 1946), 44–46.

29. Edwin Markham, *The Man with the Hoe and Other Poems* (New York: Doubleday and McClure, 1899), 15–18, prints the poem first in the volume, with the painting reproduced opposite the title page.

30. Christina Rossetti, *The Poetical Works of Christina Rossetti*, ed. William Michael Rossetti (London: Macmillan, 1906), 234–35.

31. Ibid., 156.

32. Ibid., 237.

33. Louis Martz, *Milton: Poet of Exile*, 2nd ed. (New Haven, Conn.: Yale University Press, 1980), 34–36.

34. Quoted in Carl Davison, ed., *Matthew Arnold: The Poetry, the Critical Heritage* (London: Routledge and Kegan Paul, 1973), 60.
35. Quoted in Boyd Litzinger and Donald Smalley, eds., *Browning: The Critical Heritage* (London: Routledge and Kegan Paul, 1970), 181.
36. Alfred Tennyson, *The Poems of Tennyson*, ed. Christopher Ricks (Berkeley: University of California Press, 1987), 1: 205.
37. Alfred Tennyson, *Poems, Chiefly Lyrical* (London, 1830), 14–18.
38. Christopher Ricks, *Tennyson* (New York: Collier Books, 1972), 50.
39. Quoted in Litzinger and Smalley, *Browning: The Critical Heritage*, 169.
40. Ian Jack, *Browning's Major Poetry* (Oxford: Clarendon Press, 1973), 180.
41. Hardy, *Poems of the Past and the Present*, 169–71.
42. John Hollander, *The Figure of Echo* (Berkeley: University of California Press, 1981), 90–91.
43. Robert Browning, *Dramatis Personae* (London, 1864), 239–42.
44. W. B. Yeats, *The Green Helmet and Other Poems* (Churchtown: Cuala Press, 1910), 4.
45. W. H. Auden, *The Collected Poetry of W. H. Auden* (New York: Random House, 1945), 83–85.
46. Philip Larkin, *Required Writing* (New York: Farrar, Straus and Giroux, 1984), 135.
47. Larkin, *The Less Deceived*, 20. Larkin's sister is reported as saying that the moment of responding when addressed with "Next, Please" held special dread for him because of his stutter. See Andrew Motion, *Philip Larkin: A Writer's Life* (New York: Farrar, Straus and Giroux, 1993), 208. A different emphasis still allowed by the title in its revised form is pointed to by the original title cited in *Selected Letters of Philip Larkin*, ed. Anthony Thwaite (New York: Farrar, Straus and Giroux, 1992), 234n.
48. John Ashbery, *A Wave* (New York: Penguin Books, 1985), 12.

Chapter 8

1. William Wordsworth, *The Letters of William and Dorothy Wordsworth*, ed. Ernest de Selincourt, 2nd ed., rev. Mary Moorman (Oxford: Clarendon Press, 1969), 1: 287.
2. William Carlos Williams, *The Autobiography of William Carlos Williams* (New York: Random House, 1951), 136.
3. William Carlos Williams, *The Selected Letters of William Carlos Williams*, ed. John Thirwall (New York: McDowell, Obolensky, 1957), 24.
4. Hugh Kenner, *Homemade World* (New York: Alfred Knopf, 1975), 66.
5. William Carlos Williams, *Spring and All* (n.p: Frontier Press, 1970), 2–3.
6. Ibid., 1, 3.   7. Ibid., 23.
8. Ibid., 36.   9. Ibid., 32–33.
10. Cited by Bram Dijkstra, *The Hieroglyphics of a New Speech* (Princeton, N.J.: Princeton University Press, 1969), 162.
11. John Hollander, "The Poem in the Eye," *Shenandoah* 23 (1972): 25.
12. Williams seems to have shifted ground somewhat in the poem "The Title,"

where he says about a work by Gauguin that its title (*The Loss of Virginity*) though "inessential" to its composition, "enhances the impact / and emotional dignity of the whole." William Carlos Williams, *Pictures from Brueghel and Other Poems* (Norfolk, Conn.: New Directions, 1962), 55.

13. Hazard Adams, "Titles, Titling, and Entitlement To," *Journal of Aesthetics and Art Criticism* 46 (1987): 13. For the use of "Untitled" to label photographs see Mary Price, *The Photograph* (Stanford, Calif.: Stanford University Press, 1994), 71–87.

14. W. J. T. Mitchell, "*Ut Pictura Theoria*: Abstract Painting and the Repression of Language," *Critical Inquiry* 15 (1989): 354.

15. John Ashbery, *Shadow Train* (New York: Penguin Books, 1981), 26.

16. This quotation is from Ashbery's statement on the dust jacket of John Ashbery, *The Tennis Court Oath* (Middletown, Conn.: Wesleyan University Press, 1967).

17. Frank O'Hara, *The Collected Poems of Frank O'Hara*, ed. Donald Allen (New York: Alfred Knopf, 1971), 261.

18. Gabriele Buffet, "Modern Art and the Public," *Camera Work*, special number, June 1913 (Nedeln/Liechtenstein: Kraus Reprint, 1964), 12.

19. Wallace Stevens, *Letters of Wallace Stevens*, ed. Holly Stevens (New York: Alfred Knopf, 1966), 297.

20. Buffet, "Modern Art and the Public," 12.

21. Stevens, *Letters*, 649–50.

22. Cited by John Tancock, "The Influence of Marcel Duchamp," *Marcel Duchamp*, ed. Anne d'Harnoncourt and Kynaston McShine (New York: Museum of Modern Art, 1973), 163.

23. Wallace Stevens, *Auroras of Autumn* (New York: Alfred Knopf, 1950), 192–93.

24. Wallace Stevens, *Parts of a World* (New York: Alfred Knopf, 1945), 88–89; *Letters*, 404.

25. Stevens, *Letters*, 404.

26. John Ashbery, *Reported Sightings*, ed. David Bergman (Cambridge, Mass.: Harvard University Press, 1991), 25–26. This passage was first brought to my attention by Sara Lundquist.

27. Kenner, *Homemade World*, 217.

28. Stevens, *Letters*, 753.

29. Wordsworth, *Letters*, 2: 335.

30. Derek Roper, "Notes," in William Wordsworth, *Lyrical Ballads 1805* (London: Collins, 1968), 369; Samuel Taylor Coleridge, "Marginalia II," *The Collected Works of Samuel Taylor Coleridge*, ed. George Whalley (Princeton, N.J.: Princeton University Press, 1984), 222; Samuel Taylor Coleridge, *Collected Letters of Samuel Taylor Coleridge*, ed. Earl Griggs (Oxford: Clarendon Press, 1956), 1: 632n.

31. John Donne, *The Sermons of John Donne*, ed. George Potter and Evelyn Simpson (Berkeley: University of California Press, 1959, 1955), 5: 271, 2: 72.

32. George Wither, *A Preparation to the Psalter* (London, 1619), 55.

33. William Drummond, *Conversations with William Drummond of Hawthornden, 1619* (London: Bodley Head, 1923), 5.

34. Williams, *Spring and All*, 89, 21.

35. Marianne Moore, *Tell Me, Tell Me: Granite, Steel, and Other Topics* (New York: Viking Press, 1966), 46; *The Complete Prose of Marianne Moore*, ed. Patricia Willis (New York: Viking Press, 1986), 558, 661, 452.

36. Ezra Pound, *Selected Prose* (New York: New Directions, 1973), 375; *Literary Essays of Ezra Pound* (New York: New Directions, 1968), 362.

37. Ezra Pound, *Lustra* (London: Elkin Matthews, 1916), 45.

38. Ezra Pound, *Gaudier-Brzeska* (London: John Lane, 1916), 102–3.

39. Moore, *Complete Prose*, 451.

40. Williams, *Spring and All*, 89.

41. William Carlos Williams, *An Early Martyr and Other Poems* (New York: Alcestis Press, 1935), 22.

42. William Carlos Williams, *Collected Poems 1921–1931* (New York: Objectivist Press, 1934), 50.

43. John Gerber and Emily Wallace, *Interviews with William Carlos Williams*, ed. Linda Wagner (New York: New Directions, 1976), 16.

44. John Ashbery, *As We Know* (New York: Viking Press, 1979), 95.

45. Vernon Shetley, *After the Death of Poetry* (Durham, N.C.: Duke University Press, 1993), 104.

46. John Hollander, *In Time & Place* (Baltimore, Md.: Johns Hopkins University Press, 1986), 42.

47. John Berryman, *Delusions, Etc.* (New York: Farrar, Straus and Giroux, 1972), 67.

48. Martin Dodsworth, "John Berryman: An Introduction," *The Survival of Poetry* (London: Faber and Faber, 1970), 115.

49. Alan Shapiro, *The Courtesy* (Chicago: University of Chicago Press, 1983), 35.

Index of poets cited
and poems discussed

In this index an "f" after a number indicates a separate reference on the next page, and an "ff" indicates separate references on the next two pages. A continuous discussion over two or more pages is indicated by a span of page numbers, e.g., "57–59." *Passim* is used for a cluster of references in close but not consecutive sequence.

General index

In this index an "f" after a number indicates a separate reference on the next page, and an "ff" indicates separate references on the next two pages. A continuous discussion over two or more pages is indicated by a span of page numbers, e.g., "57–59." *Passim* is used for a cluster of references in close but not consecutive sequence.

Library of Congress Cataloging-in-Publication Data
Ferry, Anne.
    The title to the poem / Anne Ferry.
        p.   cm.
    Includes bibliographical references and index.
    ISBN 0-8047-2610-8 (cl.) : ISBN 0-8047-3517-4 (pbk.)
    1. Titles of poems.   2. Rhetoric.   I. Title.
    PN1059.T5F47   1996
    821.009—dc20   95-30608
                                            CIP
                                            REV.

⊗ This book is printed on acid-free, recycled paper.

Original printing 1996
Last figure below indicates year of this printing:

05   04   03   02   01   00   99